Growth Theories in Light of the East Asian Experience

NBER–East Asia Seminar on Economics
Volume 4

National Bureau of Economic Research
Korea Development Institute
Chung-Hua Institution for Economic Research
Tokyo Center of Economic Research

Growth Theories in Light of the East Asian Experience

Edited by Takatoshi Ito and Anne O. Krueger

The University of Chicago Press

Chicago and London

Takatoshi Ito is professor of economics at Hitotsubashi University and a visiting professor at Harvard University. Anne O. Krueger is professor of economics at Stanford University. Both are research associates of the National Bureau of Economic Research.

The University of Chicago Press, Chicago 60637
The University of Chicago Press, Ltd., London

Printed in the United States of America
03 02 01 00 99 98 97 96   2 3 4 5
ISBN: 0-226-38670-8 (cloth)

Library of Congress Cataloging-in-Publication Data

Growth theories in light of the East Asian experience / Takatoshi Ito and Anne O. Krueger.
p. cm.—(NBER–East Asia seminar on economics ; v. 4)
Edited versions of papers presented and discussed at the NBER–East Asia Seminar on Economics fourth annual conference, held June 17–19, 1993, in San Francisco.
Includes bibliographical references and index.
1. Economic development—Congresses. 2. East Asia—Economic conditions—Congresses. 3. East Asia—Economic policy—Congresses. I. Itō, Takatoshi, 1950– . II. Krueger, Anne O. III. NBER–East Asia Seminar on Economics (4th : 1993 : San Francisco, Calif.) IV. Series: NBER–East Asia seminar on economics (Series) ; v. 4.
HD75.G768 1995
338.9—dc20 94-36927
CIP

⊗ The paper used in this publication meets the minimum requirements of the American National Standard for Information Sciences—Permanence of Paper for Printed Library Materials, ANSI Z39.48–1984.

National Bureau of Economic Research

Since this volume is a record of conference proceedings, it has been exempted from the rules governing critical review of manuscripts by the Board of Directors of the National Bureau (resolution adopted 8 June 1948, as revised 21 November 1949 and 20 April 1968).

Contents

Acknowledgments

This volume contains edited versions of papers presented and discussed at the NBER–East Asia Seminar in Economics Fourth Annual conference. The conference was held in San Francisco from June 17 to 19, 1993.

We are indebted to Chong-Hyun Nam and Tzong-shian Yu, who served as members of the program committee, for organizing the conference and to Martin Feldstein and Geoffrey Carliner for their support of the conference series. We also thank Kirsten Foss Davis for her tireless efforts in making conference arrangements, and Deborah Kiernan for overseeing the editorial work in preparing the volume for publication.

The National Bureau of Economic Research hosted the conference and provided logistical support, for which we are grateful. We are also indebted to the Chung-Hua Institution, the Korea Development Institute, the National Bureau of Economic Research, and the Tokyo Center of Economic Research (TCER) for their financial assistance.

Takatoshi Ito and Anne O. Krueger

Introduction

Takatoshi Ito and Anne O. Krueger

The rapid growth of the East Asian newly industrializing economies (NIEs)—Hong Kong, Korea, Singapore, and Taiwan—has astonished the entire world since the 1960s. Although the four economies share many common characteristics, there are also significant differences. The Korean and Taiwanese governments were committed to export-led growth, while Hong Kong was a prototype free-market economy. Korea grew with interlinked big corporations, while Taiwan's growth was more centered on small and medium-sized firms. All four, different as they are, achieved sustained real rates of economic growth substantially in excess both of any previously experienced and of those believed the maximum attainable, and all four achieved those rates with even more rapid growth of exports and imports.

Since that time, researchers have analyzed various aspects of that growth. Several obvious characteristics can easily be identified. All four countries relied on their comparative abundance in (and therefore comparative advantage in products using) unskilled, but highly trained, labor, and exports were a leading growth sector, growing at the unheard of rates of 30–40 percent per year for several decades. Clearly, trade policies played a major role in the success of the East Asian countries. So, too, did their focus on increasing educational opportunities for their people, as the rising average educational attainment of the labor force clearly contributed to growth. All four also achieved very high rates of savings and investment. In the case of Korea, borrowings from abroad became large, as investment exceeded saving, in the 1970s. However, Korea successfully paid back the debt by growing the economy even faster, and growth spurred saving.

Takatoshi Ito is professor of economics at Hitotsubashi University and a visiting professor at Harvard University. Anne O. Krueger is professor of economics at Stanford University. Both are research associates of the National Bureau of Economic Research.

While East Asian growth was exceeding all expectations of outside economists and observers, neoclassical economic growth theory was well developed by the 1970s, with little new research being undertaken. For many economists (and other observers), neoclassical theory seemed unsatisfactory in that it predicted a slowing down of growth rates due to diminishing returns to additional factor accumulation per person. Sustained high growth rates in Japan (in the 1950s and 1960s) and in the four NIEs seem to contradict this prediction. Robert Solow's seminal contribution shows that, within the context of a neoclassical model, a large part of growth originated in the "residual." Some economists took the residual to be technological change; others identified it with economic policies (especially after the East Asian experience). Others noted that it might be interpreted as a measure of our ignorance, containing all the elements contributing to growth other than factor accumulation per se. And, indeed, as estimates were made of the contribution of increasing human capital, improved efficiency of resource allocation, and other factors to growth, the residual did get smaller.

By the 1980s, however, the tension between neoclassical theory and growth experience was evident to many. Out of this emerged an approach to growth which has come to be characterized as "endogenous" growth theory. Starting with the observation that growth rates for individual countries are highly correlated for long periods of time and do not show the tendency to decelerate that neoclassical theory appears to predict, a number of economists developed models in which there are increasing returns to a factor or factors of production. These factors might be the accumulation of knowledge, the development of new ideas, or even experience with production techniques and processes (as, perhaps, in the infant-industry argument).

The appeal of the new approach lay in its square confrontation with the facts of development: growth rates do tend to be correlated. There has followed a host of research, which has gone in several directions. Some economists have attempted to provide direct tests of the "convergence" hypothesis that appears central to neoclassical theory. Those tests, to date, have yielded mixed results. Other economists have developed econometric estimates, based on cross-sectional data across countries and over time, of the rates of growth of output as a function of the variables identified by theory: factor accumulation (including both physical and human capital), political environment (number of assassinations), and economic policies (including export growth, government expenditures, and inflation rates).

To date, considerable progress has been made, although there is as yet no definitive consensus as to the role of increasing returns (or what those returns might emanate from) and the role for government policy in the growth process.

In these circumstances, it seemed natural to hold the fourth annual National Bureau of Economic Research–East Asia Seminar in Economics (EASE) on the East Asian experience in light of endogenous growth theory. The conference was held in San Francisco from June 16 to 19, 1993. This volume contains the results of that conference.

The first paper, by Anne O. Krueger, provides an overview of the East Asian growth experience. Krueger starts by reviewing the overall macroeconomic aggregates that show just how well East Asian NIEs did. As can be seen in table 1.1, the average annual rate of growth of real per capita income exceeded 6 percent in each of the four countries, compared to an average of 2.2 percent annually for all middle-income developing countries. She concludes that, whether there is "endogenous growth" or not, any understanding of the East Asian experience, and especially of the rapid acceleration of economic growth after policies were changed, must take into account the role of economic policy in affecting growth rates. In the East Asian case, "traditional development policies" of import substitution had earlier been followed; it was changes in these policies which immediately preceded the transition to rapid growth.

The second paper, by T. N. Srinivasan, focuses directly on endogenous growth theory and on efforts to test it empirically. Srinivasan provides an excellent comparison and evaluation of the older neoclassical growth models and the newer endogenous models and reviews a wide range of empirical research results. He, too, concludes that the role of policy is important but that, to date, efforts to understand growth have focused on the macroeconomic variables and have not, as yet, addressed the underlying microeconomic processes by which it has taken place.

After the overview of the growth experience of the East Asian countries and of endogenous growth theory provided by the first two papers, attention in the next section turns to experience in individual countries. An overarching question posed in many of the papers focuses on the role of trade and an "outward orientation" in accounting for the stellar performance of the East Asian countries.

The first paper in the second section, by Shang-Jin Wei, focuses on one of the potentially important reasons for China's rapid growth. Wei uses city-level data on exports, foreign investment, and growth of individual Chinese cities to analyze the association between more rapid growth rates and more exports or foreign direct investment. During the 1980s, Chinese cities with higher growth rates were indeed those with more exports. Wei finds that by the late 1980s, foreign investment contributed significantly to differentials in growth rates, and did so through technological or managerial spillovers, rather than because of the magnitude of physical investment. Perhaps even more surprising, Wei's cross-sectional data suggest that the very high growth rates of the coastal cities in China can be explained entirely by their export performance and their attraction of direct foreign investment.

The next pair of papers deal with Taiwan's growth. Ji Chou estimates a modified neoclassical production function with human capital and endogenous factor accumulation and considers the role of exports in permitting realization of scale economies. He finds that a neoclassical specification of the production function which includes human capital fits the Taiwanese experience well after account is taken of the role of trade in permitting exploitation of economies of scale.

Chen-Min Hsu considers the role of public finance in permitting rapid growth in Taiwan, with the assistance of a simulation model. He estimates the effects of financing public investment in Taiwan through fiscal deficits and finds that crowding out of private investment would significantly reduce the rate of economic growth.

The next two papers analyze aspects of Korea's rapid economic growth. First, Chong-Hyun Nam examines the role of trade and exchange rate policies. He first traces the trade and exchange rate policies that were followed starting in the 1960s. He concludes that Korea's initial effort to encourage exports through (uniform) export subsidies was possible in part because the level of antiexport bias was low. He notes, however, that costs were paid in the form of retarded financial market development; moreover, the export subsidy strategy ran risks of provoking retaliation from foreign countries. He also concludes that maintenance of a realistic real exchange rate for exports was essential for rapid export growth, along with a high rate of investment, including adequate investment in infrastructure.

In their paper, Joon-Kyung Kim, Sang Dal Shim, and Jun-Il Kim assess the role of government in Korea's economic development. They analyze the role of government in supporting firms' export efforts, the export incentives, and aspects of risk sharing. They also briefly consider the controversial heavy and chemical industry drive, noting that it may have enabled producers to learn to cope with economies of scale but that criticisms center upon a number of aspects of those policies. They conclude that the support of education and training was highly important in Korea's growth and that the fact that there was an "international market" test permitted the government to support exporters and yet maintain incentives for economically efficient production.

The final paper in this section is by Hirohisa Kohama, who analyzes the characteristics of Japan's Official Development Assistance (ODA). Kohama shows that Japan's ODA has been allocated largely to countries with strong trading (primarily exporting) links with Japan and other Asian countries. In contrast with the aid programs of other industrialized countries, Japan's ODA is concentrated much more heavily on loans to social infrastructure projects. He suggests that an emphasis on aid to infrastructure is consistent with Japan's own experience and belief that infrastructure is important in initiating, supporting, and sustaining economic growth. He infers that Japan's ODA contributed to the economic growth of the NIEs.

Whereas the papers in the second section describe individual aspects of the growth experience in individual Asian countries, the three papers in the final section of the volume address the broader question of the relevance of endogenous growth theory for understanding the region's growth experience.

In the first paper, Hak K. Pyo estimates aggregate production functions for the United States and South Korea, using direct estimates of human capital, rather than proxy variables as had earlier been done. For both countries, the inclusion of human capital is, as expected, very important. Once he takes human capital accumulation and stock into account, he finds South Korea converging toward the levels in the developed countries, while he estimates constant returns to capital from U.S. data. His provocative interpretation of his findings is that developing countries which use their human capital well are enabled to converge with developed countries, whereas other developing countries which do not effectively employ their human capital are unable to do so. He concludes that this raises a key question requiring more research: Why are some developing countries unable to begin to accumulate and utilize effectively human capital?

Shin-ichi Fukuda and Hideki Toya also attempt to test the convergence hypothesis on East Asian data, examining the role of exports in economic growth. They start by demonstrating that the straightforward convergence hypothesis, that the rate of growth is negatively related to the initial level of per capita income, is rejected for East Asian data when account is taken of physical and human capital accumulation. However, they then include the share of exports in GDP in the regression estimates; while coefficients of other estimated variables are unaffected, the coefficient testing convergence changes significantly. They conclude that, given export-GDP ratios, East Asian countries do show conditional convergence, so that initially poorer countries tended to grow more rapidly than richer ones. In addition, they note that a higher export share also tends to lead to a higher growth rate, and they believe that this characteristic is part of what differentiated East Asia from Latin America. Finally, they examine the role of government consumption and find that it positively affected growth only when considered in conjunction with exports: they interpret this finding to mean that government consumption consisted of the provision of services which supported the growth of exports.

In the final paper, William Easterly presents a thorough cross-country convergence regression. According to his results, the rapid growth of the Asian "tigers" is not explained even after controlling for educational attainment and capital stock: residuals are still very large. He takes the view that this is not surprising since successful economies must have received large favorable shocks and that any ranking of countries by growth rates tends to have economies with prior favorable shocks at the top. Under his interpretation, those economies with high total factor productivity growth rates are the ones that are catching up with developed countries by adopting technology successfully, and total factor productivity growth is represented in large residuals.

As the reader will see, the papers included in this volume do not provide a clear-cut conclusion as to the relevance of endogenous growth theory in explaining the East Asian experience. Clearly a great deal more research, especially on the microeconomic aspects of growth, will be required before the avenues by which rapid growth occurs are reasonably well understood. Nonetheless, there is agreement that accumulation of physical and human capital was important, that outward-oriented trade strategies played a crucial role, and that government policies were supportive of export growth and factor accumulation. How these important observations link to theory is left for future research. The reader will find much that sheds light on the growth experience of East Asia, as well as much that is provocative for further research, in these papers.

I An Overview of East Asian Growth Experience

1 East Asian Experience and Endogenous Growth Theory

Anne O. Krueger

The spectacularly rapid growth of the East Asian countries has focused the attention of all analysts of growth and development on the lessons that may be learned of relevance for other countries. On some issues, there is by now fairly widespread agreement. On others, those concerned with development remain divided. No part of the literature, however, confronts endogenous growth theory with the analysis of the East Asian experience.

In this paper, the East Asian experience is reviewed with respect to the salient characteristics of growth and to the current state of understanding of that experience, drawing largely on accumulated research and analysis. Then, in that light, the experience is examined in terms of its relevance for endogenous growth theory.

To set the stage, an initial section briefly reviews the salient characteristics of East Asian growth. A second then examines the policy regimes under which growth occurred. The third section provides an assessment of the current state of knowledge with regard to understanding the East Asian experience. In light of that analysis, a final section considers the relevance of endogenous growth theory.

1.1 East Asian Growth[1]

By now, the salient characteristics of East Asian growth have received so much attention that a very brief review will suffice. In broad terms, Japan,

Anne O. Krueger is professor of economics at Stanford University and a research associate of the National Bureau of Economic Research.

The author is indebted to Leonardo Giacchino for valuable research assistance in the preparation of this paper.

1. All data in this section for which a source is not otherwise indicated are taken from World Bank (1992, various indicators tables).

Korea, Singapore, Taiwan, and Hong Kong have all experienced sustained rates of economic growth well in excess of those earlier thought attainable.[2] Each started from a relatively low per capita income;[3] each adopted policies which resulted in rapid growth of exports; each had fairly conservative monetary and fiscal policies; each government provided infrastructure consistent with rapid growth; the educational attainments of the labor force rose rapidly—there was a rapid shift of the labor force from agricultural to industrial employment; and once rapid growth began, savings and investment rates rose. All were and are regarded as resource-poor economies, although Taiwan and Korea were net exporters of primary commodities in the 1950s.

Table 1.1 provides data on their comparative growth rates and per capita GDPs over the 1965–90 period. As can be seen, all five East Asian economies have grown exceptionally rapidly by world standards. Middle-income countries as a group are estimated by the World Bank to have experienced per capita income growth of 2.2 percent over that same period, while other OECD countries grew at 2.4 percent, compared with Japan's 4.1 percent.

Table 1.2 provides data on the rate of growth of GDP and of exports in each country. As can be seen, in each country in each time period covered, the rate of growth of exports exceeded that of GDP, except for Hong Kong in the period right after the oil price increase of 1973 and Singapore in the 1963–70 period.[4] Table 1.4, which gives the share of exports in each country's GDP for selected years over the period, again reflects the growing importance of trade as growth took place.

Since rapid growth of exports (and the policies under which it took place) is a central feature of the East Asian economies, it is worthwhile to examine this aspect somewhat more closely. Inspection of data on growth of Korean exports will suffice. Table 1.3 gives data on Korea's exports.

The dramatic increase in exports shows up even more clearly from the very small base. From $33 million in 1960, exports grew almost 20-fold to $882 million in 1970, and then grew almost 10-fold over the following decade, reaching $17 billion in 1980; growth tapered off still more over the 1980s, with

2. In the 1960s, Chenery and others developed the "two-gap" model of developing countries' growth, in which either the rate of savings or the availability of foreign exchange was thought to be the binding constraint on overall growth. As they developed that model, Chenery and Strout (1966) assumed there was a third constraint, which they described as the maximum attainable rate of growth, and suggested that the number was between 6 and 8 percent. All East Asian countries exceeded that rate for extended periods of time, with Taiwan and Korea each achieving periods of a decade or longer with rates in excess of 10 percent.

3. In the Japanese case, there was debate in the 1950s as to whether Japan was a developed or a developing country (see Higgins 1959, the classic text of that period, for the argument).

4. Exports can exceed 100 percent of GDP because GDP is a value-added concept and exports are measured in value of output. In Singapore's case, there is a very large entrepot trade and, in addition, oil refining is a large industry as petroleum is imported and reexported in various refined forms. In Hong Kong's case, the rapid growth in exports in the 1980s reflects the rapid increase in imports from the People's Republic of China for reexport. Singapore did not separate from Malaysia until 1965, which biases Singaporean statistics for the 1963–72 period.

Table 1.1 **Economic Growth of East Asian NICs**

Country	GDP per Capita (1990 U.S. $) 1965	1991	Average Annual Rate of Growth of Per Capita Income 1965–90
Hong Kong	2,544	13,430	6.2
Japan	9,828	26,930	4.1
Korea	970	6,330	7.1
Singapore	2,312	14,210	6.5
Taiwan	995[a]	8,800[b]	8.1
All middle-income countries	1,353	2,220	2.2

Sources: For Hong Kong, Japan, Korea, and Singapore: World Bank (1992, world development indicators, table 1); World Bank, *World Bank News,* April 29, 1993, for 1991 data.

[a]1965 per capita income for Taiwan derived from International Monetary Fund (IMF), *International Financial Statistics* (Washington, D.C., May 1976), China page. Converted to 1990 prices by using the IMF index of dollar export unit values.

[b]Per capita income for Taiwan is in current dollars for 1991 from the *Economist* survey, October 19, 1992, 5.

Table 1.2 **Growth of Real GDP and Exports by Country, 1953–91**

Countries	1953–62	1963–72	1973–80	1981–91
Hong Kong				
GDP	12.84[a]	11.74	10.13	6.68
Exports	6.91[a]	14.04	9.79	13.62
Japan				
GDP	8.31	9.39	4.08	4.25
Exports	16.27	15.84	6.16	4.34
Korea				
GDP	3.85[a]	9.14	8.34	9.31
Exports	16.14	30.32	17.57	11.60
Singapore				
GDP	n.a.	10.30	8.08	7.07
Exports	0.27	6.05	29.13	9.47
Taiwan				
GDP	7.32	10.95	8.38	7.83
Exports	17.90	27.65	22.64	9.42

Sources: For Hong Kong: United Nations (various years, b). For Japan, Korea, and Singapore: IMF, *IFS* CD-ROM (Washington, D.C.). For Taiwan: data kindly provided by J. Chou and T.-S. Yu of Chung-Hua Institution for Economic Research.

Note: n.a. = not available.

[a]Average nominal change without 1952–53.

exports "only" increasing by a factor of 3.78. It should be noted that imports also rose dramatically, although the proportionate size of Korea's trade deficit fell sharply over time. Nonetheless, imports as a percentage of GDP rose from around 10 percent in the mid-1950s to over 30 percent by the late 1980s (see table 1.4).

Table 1.3 Evolution of Korean Exports and Imports, 1960–90

	Level (million U.S. $)		Share of GNP (%)	
Year	Exports	Imports	Exports	Imports
1960	33	306	3.3	13.3
1965	175	416	8.5	15.8
1970	882	1,804	13.9	23.5
1975	5,003	6,674	28.3	37.0
1980	17,214	21,598	35.2	42.9
1985	26,442	26,461	35.8	34.5
1990	63,123	65,127	31.8	32.3

Source: IMF (1990, 1991, Korea pages).

Note: Both exports and imports are reported f.o.b. and are from balance-of-payments data. Exports and imports cover both goods and nonfactor services. Shares of GNP were calculated from the national income accounts.

Table 1.4 Share of Exports and Imports in GDP, Various Years (%)

Country	1953	1963	1973	1980	1990
Hong Kong					
Exports	109.13	67.14	89.26	95.71	135.15
Imports	154.61	99.74	85.53	100.61	129.72
Japan					
Exports	6.54	7.82	8.92	12.23	9.77
Imports	12.36	9.66	9.25	13.32	7.97
Korea					
Exports	2.11	4.76	29.13	34.03	30.96
Imports	9.92	15.91	32.12	41.47	31.52
Singapore					
Exports	n.a.	124.55	87.28	165.21	149.52
Imports	n.a.	153.41	122.62	204.67	172.81
Taiwan					
Exports	8.64	15.22	41.60	47.76	42.70
Imports	12.00	16.60	35.35	47.71	34.86

Sources: For Hong Kong: United Nations (various years, b); United Nations (1954a) for 1953; United Nations (1964a) for 1963. For Japan, Korea, and Singapore: IMF, *IFS* CD-ROM (Washington, D.C.). For Taiwan: data kindly provided by J. Chou and T.-S. Yu of Chung-Hua Institution for Economic Research.

Phenomenal growth was, of course, accompanied by a major change in the economic structure of each country. Not only did the importance of trade increase markedly as a share of GDP, as reflected in table 1.4, but the relative importance of urban activities increased greatly in Korea, Taiwan, and Japan, while that of the rural areas diminished. Over the 1965–90 period, agriculture's share of GDP fell from 38 to 9 percent in Korea, from 10 to 3 percent in

Japan,[5] and from 24 to 4 percent in Taiwan. Since Hong Kong and Singapore were city-states, there was little agriculture at the beginning of the period.[6] Over that same period, manufacturing as a percentage of GDP rose from 25 to 45 percent in Korea, from 22 to 24 percent in Taiwan, from 24 to 37 percent in Singapore, and fell from 44 to 42 percent in Japan and from 40 to 26 percent in Hong Kong.

In all countries, savings and investment rose as a percentage of GDP, at least until the 1980s, as indicated in table 1.5. The most dramatic increases were in the poorest countries, although even Japan's investment rate rose from an already highly respectable 24 percent of GDP in 1953 to a peak of 38 percent in 1973, before falling back to 32 percent at the beginning and end of the 1980s. Korea, Taiwan, and Singapore experienced fairly sizable capital inflows to sustain rates of investment above those of savings, whereas Japan's current account was very close to balanced until the 1980s, when sizable capital outflows were experienced.

Table 1.6 provides cursory data on the size of the government sector, as reflected by the share of government expenditures in GDP and by the magnitude of the fiscal deficit. As can be seen, the share of government expenditures was fairly small relative to most other countries, and where there were fiscal deficits, they tended to be comparatively small.

All five economies are regarded as having had fairly egalitarian distributions of income over the years of rapid growth. Except for Korea in the 1970s (see sec. 1.2 below for further discussion) there is no evidence of increasingly unequal distribution of income and, indeed, real wages rose rapidly in all five. Over the two decades following 1970, real earnings per employee rose at average annual rates of over 8 percent in Korea, 2.5 percent in Japan, 7.4 percent in Taiwan, 4 percent in Singapore, and 5.5 percent in Hong Kong.

Despite all these similarities, there are a number of significant differences among the East Asian countries. Japan's economy, of course, is much larger than any of the others, both because Japan's population of 124 million greatly exceeds that of any of the others, and because of Japan's much higher per capita income (see table 1.1). At the opposite end are the city-states of Hong Kong and Singapore, with populations of 5.8 million and 3.0 million, respectively. Although their per capita incomes are relatively high, their small size and absence of significant agriculture differentiates them not only from other East

5. As late as 1960, agriculture's share of GDP in Japan still stood at 13 percent. The percentage of the population still engaged in agriculture at that time was even greater; even in 1965, 27 percent of the labor force was employed in agriculture. Until the 1960s, Japanese economic growth was enhanced by Japan's ability to attract farm workers to off-farm employment. See Anderson and Hayami (1986, chap. 1) for details.

6. Some analysts have contended that the absence of a rural sector provided a major advantage for Hong Kong and Singapore. It is true that growth of agricultural output was slower than that of industrial output in the other three East Asian economies (in Korea, agricultural output grew at an average annual rate of just under 3 percent over the 1965–90 period, while industrial production grew at an average annual rate in excess of 14 percent).

Table 1.5 **Savings, Investment, and the Foreign Balance in GDP, 1953–90 (%)**

Country	1953	1963	1973	1980	1990
Hong Kong					
Savings	n.a.	n.a.	n.a.	n.a.	n.a.
Investment	n.a.	n.a.	20.61	30.61	28.53
Current account balance	n.a.	n.a.	n.a.	n.a.	n.a.
Japan					
Savings	20.18	21.62	25.46	18.13	n.a.
Investment	24.26	33.75	38.07	32.24	32.75
Current account balance	−0.11	−1.11	−0.03	−1.01	−1.22
Korea					
Savings	n.a.	n.a.	16.44	15.08	n.a.
Investment	15.61	18.23	25.50	31.73	36.95
Current account balance	−3.23	−3.72	−2.25	−9.23	−0.90
Singapore					
Savings	n.a.	n.a.	27.11	30.46	n.a.
Investment	n.a.	17.46	39.20	46.34	39.14
Current account balance	n.a.	−11.85	−15.25	−16.63	8.46
Taiwan					
Savings	14.46	19.06	34.36	32.23	29.88
Investment	14.04	18.28	29.09	33.80	22.40
Current account balance	0.40	0.78	5.28	−1.56	7.47

Sources: For Hong Kong: United Nations (various years, b); United Nations (1954a) for 1953; United Nations (1964a) for 1963. For Japan: 1953 investment from United Nations (1958b); other data from IMF, *IFS* CD-ROM (Washington, D.C.). For Korea: 1973 savings from United Nations (1974b, vol. 3); 1980 from *1986 Korea Statistical Yearbook;* others from IMF, *IFS* CD-ROM (Washington, D.C.). For Singapore: savings from United Nations (various years, b); others from IMF, *IFS* CD-ROM (Washington, D.C.). For Taiwan: data kindly provided by J. Chou and T.-S. Yu of Chung-Hua Institution for Economic Research.

Note: n.a. = not available.

Asian countries but from most of the developing world. In between the giant and the small city-states are Korea, population 43 million, and Taiwan, population 22 million.

Hong Kong experienced substantial inmigration throughout the period, with an average annual rate of growth of total population of 2 percent over the 1965–80 period, and 1.4 percent thereafter, despite the much lower natural rate of population growth.[7] Singapore also experienced inmigration, although the authorities appear to have been able to regulate the flow of migrants and to decide on the numbers to be admitted. Hence, population growth was 1.6 percent annually from 1965 to 1980, and 2.1 percent annually during the 1980s, when more inmigration was permitted. Korea, by contrast, started with the demographic characteristics of a poor country. The average annual rate of population growth fell to 2.0 percent in the late 1960s and 1970s, and to 1.1 percent during

7. Gross migration into Hong Kong exceeded net migration because a considerable number of Hong Kong residents moved on to other destinations. See Krause (1988) for particulars.

Table 1.6 **Government Expenditures and Fiscal Balance as a Percentage of GDP**

Country	1953	1963	1973	1980	1990
Hong Kong					
Government expenditure	11.93	n.a.	5.63	6.56	7.90
Fiscal surplus	2.87	n.a.	1.51	3.82	n.a.
Japan					
Government expenditure	16.03	14.81	10.39	18.38	15.91
Fiscal surplus	5.62	−0.79	−1.62	−7.02	−1.60
Korea					
Government expenditure	11.98	11.95	13.06	17.25	16.79
Fiscal surplus	−6.40	0.02	−0.49	−2.23	−0.70
Singapore					
Government expenditure	n.a.	16.59	15.56	20.04	22.34
Fiscal surplus	n.a.	−0.39	−0.12	2.14	11.30
Taiwan[a]					
Government expenditure	16.32	18.86	19.46	23.16	27.37
Fiscal surplus	0.57	−0.71	2.38	1.58	1.02

Sources: For Hong Kong: United Nations (various years, b); United Nations (1954a) for 1953; United Nations (1964a) for 1963. For Japan: 1953 fiscal surplus from United Nations (1958a); others from IMF, *IFS* CD-ROM (Washington, D.C.). For Korea: 1953 data from United Nations (1959b); others from IMF, *IFS* CD-ROM (Washington, D.C.). For Singapore: IMF, *IFS* CD-ROM (Washington, D.C.). For Taiwan: data kindly provided by J. Chou and T.-S. Yu of Chung-Hua Institution for Economic Research.

Note: n.a. = not available.

[a]All data are fiscal-year based except for 1953 which is calendar-year based.

the 1980–89 period. Taiwan as well experienced a demographic transition, although continuing immigration was also a factor, especially in the 1950s. Japan's demographic characteristics are typical of those of developed countries, with an annual population growth rate of less than 1 percent throughout the period since 1960.

Thus, the similarities among the East Asian economies center on their growth performance and on their emergence as major exporters in the world economy. Size, economic structure, demographic status, developmental status, and, as will be seen below, many aspects of economic policy differentiate them.

1.2 Economic Policies in the East Asian Countries

As with any description of the overall features and growth experience of East Asian countries, any account of economic policies encounters both similarities and key differences. The histories of the different economies are significantly different and provide important clues as to interpretation of growth experiences. I therefore start with a brief account of the key features for each country. Thereafter, attention turns to a comparative analysis of the trade and payments regime, regulation of labor and capital markets, monetary and fiscal policies, and the role of government in each economy, since those are the variables on which most analysts attempting to explain East Asian success focus.

1.2.1 Japan

Japan's economic history needs little comment. In many regards, the most salient characteristic of Japan's economic history since the end of World War II has been its continuity. Although much of the Japanese economy had been heavily damaged by World War II, economic recovery began rapidly.

For present purposes, the key questions concern the trade and payments regime and the role of government in the export drive. Turning first to the trade and payments regime, Japanese productive capacity was seriously impaired by the end of World War II. With excess demand for imports and little productive capacity for exporting, Japan (like the European countries) imposed quantitative restrictions on imports, allocating scarce foreign exchange through administrative measures. Starting in the 1950s, Japan began liberalizing its trade and payments regime, albeit at a slower pace than did the European countries.

By the 1980s, there were no remaining formal restrictions on imports. However, arguments had risen among economists as to the extent to which "informal" arrangements restricted imports. As analyzed by Lawrence (1991) and others, there is little question that the import regime itself is open and that restrictions, if there are any, take the form of industrial organization arrangements in production (among *keiretsu*) or distribution. For present purposes, the arrangements guiding exports are of even greater concern. Here, too, the evidence is mixed. On one hand, there was a uniform exchange rate applicable to all export transactions.[8] On the other hand, there seems to have been credit rationing at least until the 1980s, and exporters apparently had preferential access to credit. Perhaps even more significant but difficult to document is the extent of bureaucratic support of exporters: the role of the Ministry of Industry and Trade in support of individual industries or groups of industries remains subject to contention. Discussion of this issue is deferred to section 1.3 below. At this stage, all that needs to be noted is that Japanese tariffs on nonagricultural imports fell and reached low levels approximately equal to those of Europe and the United States by the 1980s. That phenomenon, combined with a uniform exchange rate, restricted considerably the scope of bureaucratic "intervention" in support of particular industries.

1.2.2 Korea

The Korean experience is the best documented among the East Asian developing countries (see Mason et al. 1980; Kim 1991; Krueger 1980; Frank, Kim,

8. The yen-dollar exchange rate remained constant from the late 1940s to 1971. Given Japan's low rate of inflation, this implied a slow real appreciation of the purchasing power parity (PPP) yen-dollar exchange rate. In more recent years, of course, the yen has appreciated relative to the dollar in nominal terms.

and Westphal 1975; Cole and Lyman 1971). After a hyperinflation associated with the end of World War II and the departure of the Japanese after 45 years of colonization, the Korean economy was devastated by still further disruptions. The first came in the form of partition from North Korea, which had most of the manufacturing and generated much of the power supply for the entire peninsula. Distribution of formerly Japanese-owned assets and initial reconstruction and recovery from partition had not yet been completed when the Korean War broke out.

When hostilities ended in 1953, South Korea was among the poorest countries in Asia. With few natural resources and the highest ratio of people to arable land of any country in the world, there seemed little prospect for economic growth. Indeed, the domestic savings rate was close to zero, and only U.S. foreign aid permitted some investment. The current account deficit, financed by foreign aid, equaled around 10 percent of GDP in each year from 1954 to 1959, with exports fluctuating at around 3 percent annually.

Although growth averaged between 3 and 4 percent during that period, what is notable is how slow it was given the opportunities that reconstruction creates. For present purposes, however, it is noteworthy that Korean economic policies were typical of many developing countries at that time; if anything, they were slightly worse than most. There were multiple exchange rates, with the official rate set far below any realistic level (in order to argue for larger inflows of foreign aid) and consequently a flourishing black market; quantitative restrictions on imports were severe. Inflation was at that time at a rate among the highest in the world; the public-sector deficit was large, in part again in order to provide a case for more foreign aid; the labor market was regulated, with a high minimum wage relative to agricultural workers and a recorded unemployment rate of around 25 percent in urban areas.

Between 1958 and 1963, policies changed markedly. From an inner-oriented economy, incentives for exporting were greatly increased both through a change in the nominal exchange rate greater than that in prices and through the addition of export subsidies and incentives (which applied to all commodities which were exported) to offset the bias toward import-competing industries inherent in the trade regime.[9] Quantitative controls on imports were significantly relaxed (and then dismantled further in discrete steps over the next 30 years), with exporters able to import needed inputs without significant restriction.[10]

Budgetary reforms resulted in much smaller fiscal deficits starting in the

9. For an analysis of the impact of all interventions on the rates of effective protection received by various Korean industries in the late 1970s, see Nam (1980). See also the comments by Corden on that paper, in which he puzzles over the apparently "low" rates of protection reported by Nam.

10. Starting in the early 1970s, the Korean authorities began protecting domestic agriculture. The rate of protection rose and, by the 1980s, was high by any standard. That set of policies was not adopted in order to promote economic growth and was probably detrimental to it. For purposes of the present paper, however, policies toward the agricultural sector have little relevance and are not further discussed here.

mid-1960s, and inflation fell from its earlier levels to an average of around 10 percent in the late 1960s.

These, and other reforms, have been thoroughly analyzed elsewhere, as have their consequences.[11] Savings and investment rates rose markedly, the rate of inflation fell, the current account even became positive for a period in the late 1980s, and rapid growth continued. For present purposes, there are two key points. First, all analysts agree that the change in policies was a key variable in permitting the rapid rate of growth that Korea experienced over the next three decades. Second, and equally important, opening up the trade regime played a key role in that transformation.

1.2.3 Taiwan

In most regards, Taiwan's economic growth has been similar to Korea's. Taiwan's growth rate, averaging 8.1 percent annually over the entire 1965–90 period, was even more spectacular than Korea's. Taiwan's economic circumstances in the late 1940s were as unpromising as Korea's appeared to be a decade later, although Taiwan's endowment of agricultural resources per man was significantly greater than Korea's. Both governments had significant national security concerns, receiving sizable American support but also devoting considerable national resources to defense expenditures.

Policy reforms in Taiwan, however, began in the early 1950s, and rapid growth started a half a decade earlier than in Korea. Again, a realistic exchange rate and an outer-oriented trade regime were hallmarks of economic policy, and rapid export growth as seen in section 1.1 was a key characteristic.

There were a few significant differences between Taiwan and Korea that deserve mention. First, much has been made of Korea's economic structure, in which large *chaebol* (industrial conglomerates) were key factors in growth. By contrast, most Taiwanese exporting companies were small by most international standards. Second, Korea (like Japan) did not encourage or experience very much direct foreign investment, at least through the 1970s.[12] Taiwan, on the other hand, was highly receptive to direct foreign investment.

1.2.4 Hong Kong

Hong Kong represents a quintessential case of laissez faire. The British authorities in effect did not undertake interventionist economic policies, but rather permitted free trade and exercised virtually no exchange control over the Hong Kong dollar. Except for investments in infrastructure and education, it is generally agreed that the Hong Kong authorities did not intervene in domestic economic activity.

11. See especially Mason et al. (1980).

12. There was a large capital inflow financed by borrowing from private commercial banks. That borrowing was regulated by the Korean authorities, both in order to achieve macroeconomic balance and to prevent arbitrage between the foreign interest rate and domestic rates translated at the official exchange rate. See Krueger (1980) for an analysis.

1.2.5 Singapore

Singapore, like Hong Kong, is a city-state, and as such has virtually no agricultural economic activity. It had adopted policies of import substitution in the 1950s, and then continued those policies when it became part of the Federation of Malaysia in 1963. The merger lasted only until 1965. Thereafter, policy was shifted from import substitution to an outward orientation.[13]

Singapore's growth since 1965, like that of the other East Asian NICs, has been export led; there has been virtually free trade. To the extent that Singaporean policy was interventionist, it was so largely with respect to land rights and utilization. Given Singapore's geography, the government exercised considerable control over allocation of land and as such did affect economic activity.

The government has also directly controlled immigration policy, and has maintained a compulsory savings scheme. With respect to the former, it has restricted immigration, estimating the number of additional workers for which there is demand and issuing immigration permits accordingly. In the mid-1980s, there was a significant, but short-lived, change in the way this was done, as the government believed it could accelerate the rate of increase in the real wage by restricting immigration, and thus encourage the shift of Singaporean industry to higher value-adding activities. Instead, the result was the virtual stagnation of economic activity and the rapid (within a year) reversal of policy once the effects became evident.

Singapore has encouraged a high savings rate through its Workers Provident Fund, which imposes a very high rate (50 percent) of compulsory savings on earnings in Singapore. These are then deposited in individual accounts and may be withdrawn only under very restricted circumstances.

1.2.6 Trade and Payments Regime[14]

Common to all East Asian policy regimes was the commitment to integration with the world economy and, subsequently, to facilitating exports. Although a variety of policy measures—preferential access to rationed credit, tax breaks, etc.—were designed to stimulate export growth, those measures were almost entirely uniform and across the board, applying to any would-be exporter. The hallmark of trade policy, therefore, was a lack of discrimination among export activities.[15] Policymakers in each country seem to have been

13. See Aw (1991) for an account.

14. There have been several terms used to describe East Asian trade policies. These include "outer oriented" (as contrasted with "inner-oriented" import substitution) and "export promotion." In most empirical analyses of East Asian trade and payments regimes, researchers have found very little bias of the trade regime toward exports: what has been different in East Asia is that exports were not discriminated against, and policies have been relatively uniform across exportables. Hence, the terms "outer oriented" and "export oriented" will be used synonymously here to denote the absence of discrimination in favor of import substitution.

15. It should be recalled that even Japan was perceived as a poor country in the large international economy in the 1950s and 1960s. It is often forgotten that Japanese exports were not always

committed to increasing exports, with little regard for the nature of the commodity or service to be exported.

Moreover, as exports grew in importance in each of the East Asian countries, policymakers increasingly found that it was costly to rely on tax credits, credit rationing, or export subsidies, and there was a tendency to rely increasingly on a uniform exchange rate as the principal means of encouraging exports. Indeed, the Japanese economic growth strategy was once described (Corden 1985) as being one of "export promotion" through "exchange rate protection," by which was meant the maintenance of an "undervalued" exchange rate.

The outer-oriented trade policies were, in turn, accompanied by exchange rate regimes which provided exporters reasonable assurance that the real value of their export earnings, relative to domestic costs, would not be affected by vagaries of exchange rate policy. In Korea, as already seen, this policy was effected in early years by adjusting tax credits, interest subsidies, and export subsidies, but the exchange rate came increasingly to be used for the purpose. In Singapore and Hong Kong, a unified exchange rate was used throughout. Taiwan by the early 1960s had achieved a unified and realistic exchange rate (see Kuo 1983).

On the import side, there was more variability. Hong Kong, of course, had free trade throughout. Singapore, too, rapidly achieved very low tariffs on all imports. At the opposite end of the spectrum was Korea, which began the export-oriented drive with a highly restrictive import regime. However, starting as early as 1960, mechanisms were established so that exporters could import duty-free intermediate goods and other commodities and services used in the production of exportables.[16] Thereafter, the import regime was liberalized: quantitative restrictions were liberalized and then abandoned, except on luxury good imports where there was no competing domestic industry, and tariff rates fell over time.[17] Japan, too, liberalized imports: quantitative restrictions were abandoned by the late 1960s—about 10 years after Europe. To what extent Japan has protected imports through nontariff and nonborder measures is a subject that is still the subject of dispute, although the consensus appears to be that such constraints as exist are largely nonborder and nongovernmental.[18] Certainly, Japanese import restrictions have diminished greatly over the past several decades, and exporters have been able to import inputs into export without cost or bureaucratic delays.

Liberalization of capital account transactions has also taken place in all the East Asian countries except Hong Kong (which never had any), although at varying paces. In general, inward capital flows were liberalized earlier and

as important on the world stage as they are now: indeed, as late as 1952, the value of Japan's exports was less than that of India's.

16. See Krueger (1980) for a description.

17. See Kim (1991) for a full account.

18. See the collection of papers in Krugman (1991).

more completely than outward flows. Japan and Korea tended to discourage direct foreign investment (DFI), while Singapore explicitly encouraged DFI as a key component of its development strategy (see Aw 1991 for an account).

The broad picture, then, is that all East Asian exporters had fairly uniform incentives for exporting across virtually all industries and activities. Although occasional episodes of intervention can be found, some of them proved to be major policy mistakes, and in any event the degree of intervention was small contrasted with that in inner-oriented developing countries.

As noteworthy as the uniformity of incentives for exporting is the trend toward greater liberalization over time of both imports and capital flows. All were liberalizing imports over time, although the pace and extent of liberalization varied among them. Capital controls were gradually relaxed on capital inflows, with positive inducements for those flows in some instances. In more recent years, those controls, too, have been liberalized. In Japan, the entire capital account is now largely free of control; in the other NICs (except Hong Kong), the process of liberalization continues but is not yet complete. In section 1.3, the role of governmental industry-specific intervention is further analyzed.

1.2.7 Monetary and Fiscal Policies

Relative to most developing countries, the share of government expenditures in GDP of the East Asian NICs and of Japan was relatively small.[19] Moreover, all of them have undertaken tax reform and other measures to insure that their fiscal deficits will be relatively small.

Of the NICs covered here, the largest fiscal deficit in any country in the 1980s was 3.34 percent of GDP in Korea in 1983. However, Korea's fiscal balance turned positive in the mid-1980s. Singapore averaged a fiscal surplus, Hong Kong did not have its own budget, and Taiwan has generally had a fiscal surplus (see table 1.6). Japan, along with Germany, has run the smallest fiscal deficits among OECD countries.

This has been reflected in relatively stable price levels. During the 1980s, the GDP deflator rose at an annual average rate of less than 4 percent in Japan, 8 percent in Korea, and 7 percent in Singapore.[20]

In all countries, fiscal reforms were undertaken almost continuously. Korea had been a high-inflation country in the 1950s; a major fiscal reform in 1964 was an important component of the overall policy reform in that country. The tax system has been almost continuously reformed since that time, as the Korean tax system seems to have been unusually inelastic with respect to income (see Tanzi and Shome 1992). Taiwan also managed reforms, although they

19. See Kuznets (1988, S24–S27) and Tanzi and Shome (1992) for an analysis and comparative figures.

20. Data are from IMF (1991, GDP deflators table, 164–65, and fiscal deficits, 154–55).

appear to have been as much on the side of restricting government consumption as on tax reform (see Kuo 1983, 17–19).

1.2.8 Regulation of Labor and Capital Markets

Although less attention has been devoted to analyses of the labor and capital markets than to the trade regime, many observers have at least noted that there was little intervention in the labor market in most of the East Asian countries. It is almost tautological that, given the reliance on an outward orientation and the growth of labor-intensive manufactured exports, growth rates could have been severely reduced had artificially high real wages or regulations driving up labor costs been enforced.

One of the striking characteristics of the early Korean policy reforms was the freeing of the labor market and the subsequent increase in urban employment and emergence of labor-intensive manufactured exports (see Frank et al. 1975 and Krueger 1987 for an account). Taiwan, also, has had a relatively free and flexible labor market (see Kuznets 1988, S27ff). Hong Kong's rapid immigration supported a very flexible labor market there. Singapore's policy of permitting immigration has already been cited, although there were labor market (and wage) regulations. And Japan, as well, has had a relatively competitive labor market.

In addition, most East Asian countries have focused heavily on education and improving the quality of the labor force. In 1982, for example, Taiwan had 85 percent of the relevant age group enrolled in secondary school, South Korea had 89 percent, and Japan had 92 percent. The average for all industrial market economies was 87 percent, and for middle-income developing countries, 51 percent.[21]

The picture is considerably less clear when it comes to capital markets, especially in the early years of rapid growth. There was extensive credit rationing in both Japan and Korea, although real interest rates were always positive in Japan, and positive after 1964 in Korea.[22] As already mentioned, the Korean authorities regulated the total net inflow of private foreign commercial bank financing and allocated the (relatively low interest) credit among domestic producers, favoring exporters.

Savings rates rose dramatically in all East Asian countries. Taiwan's average saving as a percentage of income was less than 5 percent in the 1950s, as was Korea's. Each had savings rates in excess of 30 percent by the 1980s. Japan started from a somewhat higher base but also realized savings rates of the same order of magnitude. Data are not available for Hong Kong, and Singapore's

21. See Kuznets (1988, S21).

22. On Taiwan, see Kuo (1983, 17). On Korea, see Frank et al. (1975). In Korea, there also seems to have been a policy under which borrowers received only a part of their financing from banks at regulated interest rates, and had to resort to curb market financing at truly free rates for the remainder. This may have confronted borrowers with a "true" social marginal cost of funds at the margin. See Hong (1981).

savings performance was conditioned by the compulsory savings scheme mentioned above. Whether the East Asian countries simply have high marginal propensities to save, or whether positive real interest rates and other institutions surrounding savings behavior were responsible, is not definitively established.[23]

1.2.9 Role of Government

Some characteristics of government policies have already been mentioned: the relatively small share of the government in total expenditures, relatively small fiscal deficits, policy reforms achieving realistic real exchange rates and relatively and increasingly open trade and payments regimes, the move toward positive real interest rates and reduced reliance on quantitative allocation of credit, and the failure to restrict the flexibility of the labor market.

Another key characteristic has been noted by virtually all analysts: all East Asian governments have attempted, for the most part successfully, to provide infrastructure in support of production activities. The high educational attainments of the populations, and the importance of the resulting quality of the labor force as an enabling factor in rapid growth, have already been mentioned. In addition, governments in all East Asian countries devoted much of their efforts to provision of adequate infrastructure—telephone, mail service, port capacity, electricity and power, railroads and roads—to support rapid increases in manufactured output and exports. Relative to other developing countries, Korean, Taiwanese, and Singaporean infrastructure were impressive to all who visited in the 1960s and 1970s.

The authorities also seem to have paid considerably more attention to equity issues than have those in some other developing countries. Income distribution was, and remained during rapid growth, relatively more equal in Taiwan, Korea, and Japan, than in other countries at comparable stages of development.[24]

1.3 Determinants of Growth Rates in the Development Literature

In the development literature, most analysts have noted the points mentioned above. All would agree that growth in the East Asian countries was export oriented and that the outer orientation was a necessary condition for the very rapid and successful growth performance of East Asian countries.[25] Controversy over outward orientation does not focus on its importance, but rather on the extent to which that orientation was the consequence of uniform incentives, thus approximating the textbook "free trade" case, or whether instead "picking the winners" on a selective basis was an important component of policy. Attention returns to that issue below.

23. See Deaton (forthcoming).
24. See Kuznets (1988, S14–S17).
25. See, e.g., World Bank (1991) for a summary of the consensus argument.

When countries shifted their policies toward an outer orientation, attention was paid to maintaining a realistic real exchange rate for exports. The importance of the real exchange rate as a necessary condition for successful growth is again unchallenged.

Having agreed that outward orientation was a necessary condition for rapid economic growth, analysts have then considered the extent to which it was sufficient. Clearly, it was not. High rates of investment, provision of infrastructure, a well-functioning labor market, and the overall policy framework conducive to efficient production were clearly major contributing factors.

For present purposes, what is important is that the focus of discussion in the development literature is on the differences in policy between outer-oriented and other developing countries as a key factor in differential growth performance. All observers would agree that a very large, if not necessarily quantifiable, percentage of East Asia's above-average growth performance is attributable to policies adopted in those countries, in contrast to the inner-oriented, selective interventions in many other developing countries.[26]

While there are differences over whether, e.g., the Japanese or Korean governments intervened to assist exporters,[27] the change in fortunes in Korea, Taiwan, and Singapore after policies were changed, and their dramatic growth rates and performance was too pronounced not to be associated with a shift in policies.

Recent studies have tended to support the view that, where there was intervention in Korea and Taiwan, it was harmful rather than helpful. Yang (1993), for example, attempted to link total factor productivity growth rates by industry to the amount of support they received (through credit rationing, etc.) from the government. He found a strong negative correlation. He also analyzed the support of the Taiwanese government for firms in the 1980s and found that they had little influence on firms' behavior. Yoo (1990) undertook a detailed analysis of the Korean government's efforts to promote heavy and chemical industries in the 1970s and concluded that those efforts retarded growth significantly. To the extent that these findings are robust, they support the view that growth would have been even faster in the absence of these interventions.

26. Import substitution accomplished through automatic prohibition of imports once domestic production has begun or through very high tariffs at made-to-measure rates for different industries inherently differentiates strongly among activities. Discrimination among activities also occurs as authorities are involved in deciding which industries are next to be developed, especially in public-sector enterprises.

27. Amsden (1989) is perhaps the foremost proponent of the "interventionist" interpretation of Korean growth. See also Wade (1990). The catchphrase for East Asian policies as interpreted by these analysts has been "picking the winners." The argument is that other countries' policies are basically defensive (supporting existing industries) whereas East Asian countries' policies supported the development of new industries. For a bibliography of much of this literature, see Hicks (1989).

1.4 Determinants of Growth: Endogenous or Policy?

The split between neoclassical growth theory and development theory was in large part a consequence of the neoclassical conclusion that growth was necessarily subject to diminishing returns and that, save for (presumably exogenous) technical change, there was a tendency for convergence to a steady state in which per capita income would be constant. On that interpretation, "catch-up" could result in rapid growth for developing countries for a period of time, but would inevitably decelerate as the gap diminished.

Development economists noted that middle-income countries tended to grow more rapidly than low-income countries, an empirical regularity that sits uncomfortably with the catch-up, or convergence, hypothesis. Moreover, economies such as the Korean one showed no tendency for growth to decelerate: indeed, growth rates in the late 1980s exceeded those of a decade earlier.

To be sure, one might have argued that the per capita incomes of the East Asian NICs were so far below those of the developed countries that catch-up might be a process of many decades. If so, then neoclassical growth theory was in any event useless for understanding development if development was understood as a several-decade process of rapid growth. For purposes of understanding the development process, central questions focused on why growth rates differed among poor countries and on the factors discussed in section 1.3.

The hypothesis of endogenous growth theory—that the accumulation of knowledge or the presence of some other factor whose accumulation is not subject to diminishing returns or depreciation—changed that perspective. Under that hypothesis, once growth starts, there are factors that will contribute to the perpetuation of growth. Stated another way, growth rates are likely to be highly correlated over time.[28]

Efforts to test endogenous growth theory and the importance of economic policy have been made using a variety of cross-country regressions. Even on a priori grounds, it might be expected that such efforts would provide at best only ambiguous results: (1) quantification of policy variables comparably across countries is difficult and inevitably contains arbitrary elements; (2) external events may have significantly different impacts on different countries and their growth rates (e.g., oil exporters and oil importers); (3) clearly, a number of factors such as rising savings rates do accompany growth; (4) there are relatively few observations of countries' growth over long time periods when policy consistency is required for the period of observation; (5) when growth rates are the variable to be explained, small errors in measurement of underlying aggregates such as GDP, not to mention comparability of measures across countries, may significantly affect the results; and (6) countries' initial economic structures are significantly different.

28. Romer (1986) was the first expositor of this view in its modern form. Earlier analysts had, of course, noted the nondepreciability of knowledge and the importance of technical change.

Nonetheless, a number of researchers have found significant relationships between a variety of variables and growth rates. Recently, Levine and Renelt (1992) evaluated much of this work, and demonstrated that few of the results were robust and that some could be altered by the addition of other explanatory variables. They then attempted to enter additional variables and examine which explanatory variables had consistently significant partial correlation coefficients with growth rates.

They summarized their findings, which are worth repeating here. First, they found a "positive and robust correlation" between average growth rates and the average share of investment in GDP. Second, there was a similar positive and robust correlation between the share of investment in GDP and the average share of trade in GDP. Third, they found that any growth rate regression that had been attempted using the share of exports in GDP as an explanatory variable could yield almost identical results if the share of imports, or the share of trade (exports plus imports), were used as the explanatory variable. Fourth, they found measures of trade policy (such as a measure of distortion in the real exchange rate) not to be robust once the share of investment in GDP was included in the regression.[29]

They concluded that: "National policies appear to be a complex package, and future researchers may wish to focus on macroeconomic policy regimes and interactions among policies as opposed to the independent influence of any particular policy" (Levine and Renelt 1992, 960).

Without questioning this conclusion, two phenomena are evident: (1) the investment share and trade/export/import share of GDP are not policy variables, but rather the outcome of the interaction of policy with underlying behavioral relationships and (2) one can question whether one might not better attempt to undertake analyses of growth rates in individual countries.

For purposes of this analysis, therefore, time series of the major policy variables, used by Levine and Renelt, were gathered for Korea and Japan. The intent was to test whether, on an individual country basis, relationships might appear robust that do not do so in cross-country regressions.

Statistics were gathered first for Korea for the period 1953–90, with an exhaustive test of their relationship. Key variables that met the Schwarz criterion for selection of significantly related variables were the inflation rate, the investment share of GDP, exports as a percentage of GDP, the government fiscal surplus as a percentage of GDP, growth rate of population, and the real exchange rate.[30]

The simple correlation matrix between these variables is given in table 1.7. As can be seen, the signs are all as might be expected, although only the invest-

29. They also found some support for the convergence hypothesis, were unable to correlate measures of fiscal policy with growth or the investment share, and failed to find robust relationships for other variables examined. (see Levine and Renelt 1992, 959).

30. In earlier regressions, Giacchino had included the growth rate of nominal domestic credit. It turned out to be positive and significantly correlated with growth, but was dropped because of the difficulty of interpretation of results when it was included.

Table 1.7 **Simple Correlation Matrix between Korean Variables Meeting Schwarz Criterion**

	GY	INF	INVTM	X	SUR	GOP	RER
GY	1.00						
INF	−0.24	1.00					
INVTM	0.36*	−0.29*	1.00				
X	0.30	−0.32*	0.86*	1.00			
SUR	0.04	−0.45*	0.27*	0.29*	1.00		
GOP	−0.53*	0.06	−0.65*	−0.72*	0.09	1.00	
RER	−0.46	−0.17	−0.12	−0.11	0.60*	0.54*	1.00

Notes: GY = rate of growth of real GDP. INF = annual rate of inflation. INVTM = share of investment in GDP. X = share of exports in GDP. SUR = fiscal surplus as a percentage of GDP. GOP = growth of population. RER = an index of the real exchange rate, calculated as in Frank et al. (1975) (base 1953).
*Significant at the 5 percent level.

ment share and the population growth rate were significant at the 5 percent level. When alternative combinations of variables were included in multiple regressions, the best results, according to the Schwarz criterion, came when current-period and lagged inflation and investment were included.[31]

However, much as in the cross-country findings, a number of equations (with different combinations of explanatory variables) appeared to perform at about the same confidence level. There was little difference in the criterion values. Interestingly, when a Chow test was used to test the hypothesis that the structure had changed over time, the hypothesis of structural change before 1980 could not be rejected. If the 1953–55 period was eliminated, the Chow test confirmed a structural break in 1980.

Thus, for Korea, econometric tests showed much the same variables as Levine-Renelt, despite the apparent appropriateness of all the simple correlations. Similar procedures were followed for Japan (1951–90) with no structural change after 1971, Singapore (1961–90) with the possibility of structural change throughout, and Thailand (1951–90) with no structural change.[32] How-

31. The estimated regression was

$$\underset{}{GY} = \underset{(4.677)}{-13.548} - \underset{(0.048)}{0.133 \cdot INF} + \underset{(0.031)}{0.095 \cdot INF_{-1}} + \underset{(0.120)}{0.873 \cdot INVTM}$$

$$- \underset{(0.084)}{0.471 \cdot INVTM_{-1}} + \underset{(0.305)}{0.620 \cdot SUR} + \underset{(0.006)}{0.018 \cdot RER}, \quad R^2 = 0.532$$

When growth of population was dropped as a variable from the regression, the estimated relation was

$$GY = \underset{(3.722)}{-15.000} - \underset{(0.029)}{0.137 \cdot INF} + \underset{(0.023)}{0.104 \cdot INF_{-1}} + \underset{(0.108)}{0.792 \cdot INVTM} - \underset{(0.082)}{0.549 \cdot INVTM_{-1}}$$

$$+ \underset{(0.042)}{0.115 \cdot EXPORTS} + \underset{(0.005)}{0.024 \cdot RER} + \underset{(0.229)}{0.666 \cdot SUR}, \quad R^2 = 0.589.$$

32. A printout of the data, obtained from the IMF, *IFS* tapes, and of the regression results, is available on request.

ever, in those cases, there were no consistent robust relationships, and those that appeared in one form or another had no economic meaning.

1.5 Conclusions

Anyone acquainted with the performance of the East Asian countries, and especially the NICs which earlier followed policies of import substitution, is convinced of the importance of policy reform and of outward orientation in the spectacular growth performance of those countries.

While interpretations differ, especially with regard to the nature of government intervention, there is virtual unanimity as to the importance of policy in the development process. The linkages between policy changes and growth, however, have not yet been modeled in satisfactory ways. Clearly, the hypothesis that appropriate policies are necessary for growth is consistent with a growth story which starts with appropriate policies (perhaps as a necessary condition), then focuses on rising savings and investment rates, other policy reforms,[33] increased technical efficiency, and other variables and behavioral relations.

The Levine-Renelt conclusion, that confrontation of theories with the data must be undertaken in the context of a multivariable explanatory model, however, appears to be confirmed when time-series data for individual countries are used. Results for the East Asian countries, although preliminary, are so negative that it is difficult to believe that further work will reveal strong robust relationships.

References

Amsden, Alice. 1989. *Asia's next giant: South Korea and the late industrialization.* Oxford: Oxford University Press.

Anderson, Kym, and Hayami, Yujiro. 1986. *The political economy of agricultural protection.* Australia: Allen and Unwin.

Aw, Bee-Yan. 1991. Singapore. In *Liberalizing foreign trade: Korea, the Philippines, and Singapore,* ed. D. Papageorgiou, M. Michaely, and A. Choksi, 309–428. Cambridge, Mass.: Blackwell.

Chenery, Hollis B., and Alan Strout. 1966. Foreign assistance and economic development. *American Economic Review* 56, no. 4 (September): 679–733.

Cole, David, and Princeton Lyman. 1971. *Korean development: The interplay of politics and economics.* Cambridge: Harvard University Press.

Corden, W. M. 1985. Exchange rate protection. In *Protection, growth and trade,* ed. W. M. Corden, 271–87. Oxford: Blackwell.

Deaton, Angus. Forthcoming. Data and Econometric Tools for Development Econom-

33. It is possible to argue that there are virtuous and vicious circles of policy formulation, just as there may be of economic growth. See Krueger (1993) for the argument.

ics. In *Handbook of development economics,* vol. 3, ed. Jere Behrman and T. N. Srinivasan. Amsterdam: North-Holland.

Frank, Charles R., Jr., Kwang Suk Kim, and Larry E. Westphal. 1975. *Foreign trade regimes and economic development.* Vol. 7: *South Korea.* New York: Columbia University Press.

Hicks, George. 1989. The four Little Dragons: An enthusiast's reading guide. *Asian-Pacific Economic Literature* 3, no. 2 (September): 35–49.

Higgins, Benjamin. 1959. *Economic development: Principles, problems and politics.* New York: Norton.

Hong, Wontack. 1981. Export growth and employment promotion in South Korea. In *Trade and employment in developing countries,* vol. 1, ed. Anne O. Krueger, Hal B. Lary, Terry Monson, and Narongchai Akrasanee, 341–92. Chicago: University of Chicago Press.

International Monetary Fund (IMF). Various years. *International financial statistics (IFS)* (Yearbook). Washington, D.C.: IMF.

Kim, Kwang Suk. 1991. Korea. In *Liberalizing foreign trade: Korea, the Philippines, and Singapore,* ed. Demetris Papageorgiou, Michael Michaely, and Armeane M. Choksi, 1–131. Cambridge, Mass.: Blackwell.

Krause, Lawrence B. 1988. Hong Kong and Singapore: Twins or kissing cousins? *Economic Development and Cultural Change* 36, no. 3 (April): 545–66.

Krueger, Anne O. 1980. *The foreign sector and aid.* Cambridge: Harvard University Press.

———. 1987. The importance of economic policy in development: Contrasts between Korea and Turkey. In *Protection and competition in international trade: Essays in honor of W. M. Corden,* ed. Henryk Kierzkowski. Oxford: Blackwell.

———. 1993. *The political economy of policy reform in developing countries.* Cambridge: MIT Press.

Krugman, Paul, ed. 1991. *Trade with Japan: Has the door opened wider?* Chicago: University of Chicago Press.

Kuznets, Paul. 1988. An East Asian model of economic development: Japan, Taiwan and South Korea. *Economic Development and Cultural Change* 36, no. 3 (April): S11–S43.

Kuo, Shirley W. Y. 1983. *The Taiwan economy in transition.* Boulder, Colo.: Westview.

Lawrence, Robert Z. 1991. How open is Japan? In *Trade with Japan: Has the door opened wider?* ed. P. Krugman, 9–51. Chicago: University of Chicago Press.

Levine, Ross, and Renelt, David. 1992. A sensitivity analysis of cross-country growth regressions. *American Economic Review* 82, no. 4 (September): 942–63.

Liang, K., and C. Liang. 1988. Development policy formation and future priorities in the Republic of China. *Economic Development and Cultural Change* 36 (3): S67–S101.

Lim, Chong-Yah, and Peter J. Lloyd, eds. 1986. *Singapore: resources and growth.* Oxford: Oxford University Press.

Mason, Edward S., Dwight H. Perkins, Kwang Suk Kim, and David C. Cole. 1980. *The economic and social modernization of the Republic of Korea.* Cambridge: Harvard University Press.

Nam, Chong Hyun. 1980. Trade and industrial policies, and the structure of protection in Korea. In *Trade and growth of the advanced developing countries in the Pacific Basin,* ed. Wontack Hong and Lawrence B. Krause, 187–211. Seoul: Korea Development Institute.

Ranis, Gustav. 1992. From developing to mature economy: An overview. In *Taiwan: From developing to mature economy,* ed. G. Ranis. Boulder, Colo.: Westview.

Romer, Paul. 1986. Increasing returns and long-run growth. *Journal of Political Economy* 94, no. 5 (October): 1002–37.

Tanzi, Vito, and Parthasarathi Shome. 1992. The role of taxation in the development of East Asian economies. In *The political economy of tax reform*, ed. Takatoshi Ito and Anne O. Krueger, 31–61. Chicago: University of Chicago Press.

Wade, Robert. 1990. *Governing the market: Economic theory and the role of government in East Asian industrialization.* Princeton, N.J.: Princeton University Press.

United Nations. Various years, a. *Economic survey of Asia and the Far East.* New York: United Nations.

———. Various years, b. *Yearbook of national accounts statistics.* New York: United Nations.

World Bank. Various years. *World development report.* Washington, D.C.: World Bank.

Yang, Ya-Hwei. 1993. Government policy and strategic industries in Taiwan. In *Trade and Protectionism,* ed. Takatoshi Ito and Anne O. Krueger, 387–408. Chicago: University of Chicago Press.

Yoo, Jung-Ho. 1990. The industrial policy of the 1970s and the evolution of the manufacturing sector in Korea. KDI Working Paper no. 9017. Seoul: Korea Development Institute, October.

Comment Geoffrey Carliner

Anne Krueger's paper presents a very useful review of the economic success of East Asia over the past four decades. The lessons which she draws from this outstanding performance reflects an emerging consensus among economists and others on five key aspects of economic growth. My comments briefly summarize these aspects and then discuss four other issues on which there is no consensus.

First, developing countries with an outward orientation, in which exports lead growth, grow considerably faster than countries that try to grow by import substitution. Competition in international markets seems to force domestic producers to become more efficient, to learn new technologies, to improve the skills of their employees. By contrast, firms that operate only in protected domestic markets can remain inefficient. With little competition from the rest of the world, they feel less pressure constantly to improve. Producing for world markets may also allow domestic firms to benefit more from economies of scale. Papers in this volume by Ji Chou, Chong-Hyun Nam, and Shin-ichi Fukuda present evidence on this point for the Asian NICs, and Shang-Jin Wei's paper shows that similar forces are at work in China.

Some governments have promoted an outward orientation by keeping import barriers low, especially on industrial inputs. Others have used export incentives to encourage domestic firms to compete abroad. More important to achieving an outward orientation is preventing the real exchange rate from becoming overvalued. Once the exchange rate becomes overvalued, exports will no longer be able to compete in foreign markets and imports will surge domesti-

Geoffrey Carliner is executive director of the National Bureau of Economic Research.

cally. Even if the country avoids a balance of payments crisis, its outward orientation will be destroyed. The key to successful export-led growth is thus to keep the real exchange rate low, so that exports will stay highly competitive in foreign markets.

A second point of consensus is that having governments squander resources slows growth. In any case, wasteful government spending is likely to crowd out investment, but when such spending is financed by deficits or inflation, it is especially harmful to growth. When governments spend considerably more than they raise in taxes, printing money to finance the deficit often leads to high inflation and an overvalued exchange rate. Alternatively, if governments finance deficits with foreign borrowing, they risk a debt crisis down the road.

A third point of consensus is that a high rate of investment in physical and human capital, including infrastructure, stimulates growth. Whether or not capital shows dramatically increasing returns to scale, has large externalities, embodies new technology, or is complementary to inputs of other factors, having a lot of it increases labor productivity and raises growth.

This of course does not mean that any government investment scheme however misguided will raise living standards. Inefficient steel mills, oil refineries, and hydroelectric projects around the world provide strong evidence to the contrary. It does mean that government policies which raise the domestic saving rate and encourage investments that reflect market forces seem to be important ingredients to the East Asian miracle.

Raising domestic saving rates is important because most of the money for increasing the capital stock must come from home. Obtaining some money for investment from abroad is common among high-growth developing economies. However, borrowing to finance consumption is dangerous because once the money is spent there is no increase in output to help pay back the loan. The end result is all too often a debt crisis.

Fourth, the relatively equal distribution of income which existed in East Asian countries probably contributed to their impressive performance. Unequal income distributions probably hurt growth in other regions, for instance, Latin America. When the pie is divided equally, there seems to be less fighting about keeping large slices or cutting the slices differently. With less social and political conflict about the distribution of income, the country can devote its energy and design its government policies to promote growth. Fukuda's paper suggests that East Asia's political stability was an important source of rapid economic growth, compared, for instance, to Latin America.

The policy implications of this are not clear, however. Many countries are not lucky enough to have departing colonial landlords whose land can be confiscated and then redistributed (Korea and Taiwan) or a foreign occupation that forces massive redistribution on it (MacArthur in Japan). For countries which inherit very unequal distributions of income and wealth, it is not clear how much redistribution is possible without increasing social frictions to the point that growth declines.

Finally, there is a fifth point about which there is probably too little consensus: economists should maintain a strong sense of humility when offering recipes to promote growth. Although we may think we know some of the key ingredients, we may turn out to be wrong. For instance, many countries which adopted import substitution strategies during the 1950s and 1960s were simply following the advice of economists of the day. Moreover, as Easterly's paper emphasizes, we remain unable to explain a large fraction of the variation in growth rates among developing countries. Perhaps, as Easterly suggests, much of East Asia's success is due to luck rather than to good policies.

With the importance of humility in mind, let me now turn to four key issues about which economists do not agree. First is the role of government intervention. Hong Kong is well known for its almost complete lack of intervention, but as Nam and Kim, Shim, and Kim document, the Korean government intervened heavily in the allocation of credit and foreign exchange. Hirohisa Kohama's stories about the victories which private firms occasionally won over MITI only serve to emphasize how powerful MITI was in guiding resources, especially during Japan's high-growth period before 1973. Young and others have described the role of Singapore's government in raising the saving rate and attracting foreign direct investment that it thought was desirable.

Since Hong Kong grew rapidly with minimal government intervention, it is clear that at least in certain circumstances, the government's role in promoting growth need not be large. In fact, Nam, Young, and many others argue that interference with market forces by the government in Korea and elsewhere in East Asia actually retarded growth. However, Kohama and other observers have concluded that various market failures, especially in developing countries, justify a role for government. As Sebastian Edwards observed during a discussion at the conference, the question is not *whether* governments should intervene, but *how* they should intervene to raise growth.

Even if economists knew which specific policies promote growth, political forces may prevent governments from adopting such policies. Why did government intervention raise growth in Japan, Korea, and Singapore, or at least not lower it drastically, while governments in Africa, India, and the Philippines managed to strangle it? Does successful intervention require the right political institutions, such as an elite bureaucracy (which India had)? Or did East Asia's outward orientation impose a limit on government policy that kept it from inflicting too many distortions and lowering growth rates sharply?

A second issue about which there is no consensus is the role of foreign direct investment (FDI). Although it is now highly recommended as the best if not only way of importing modern technology and management practices, East Asia's experience does not support this view. Japan virtually prohibited FDI, Korea managed it very carefully, Hong Kong of course adopted a laissez-faire policy, and Singapore actively encouraged it, at least in certain industries. It is thus clear that FDI is not the only way to transfer technology. East Asia offers no lessons about whether it is the best way.

A third unresolved question is the effect of inflation on growth. Many economists recommend that inflation in developing countries should be no greater than the rate in the OECD. However, Japan and Korea both had annual inflation well above 10 percent during their high-growth years. And India, as T. N. Srinivasan observed at the conference, had the low inflation of the graveyard. The lessons seem to be that low inflation alone is of course not enough to achieve high growth, while extremely high inflation, for instance 500 percent annually, is so distorting that it severely inhibits growth. However, there is no consensus on the consequences of 10–30 percent inflation rates in developing countries.

A final area of uncertainty concerns the issues raised by the new growth economics. Srinivasan's theoretical paper shows that these issues were also raised by previous generations of growth economists. He also shows that models with increasing or decreasing returns to scale in production, externalities, and multiple equilibria are all plausible. Empirical papers in this volume by Chou, Fukuda and Toya, Nam, and Hak Pyo, as well as a large number of other recent studies, have not reached a consensus on these questions.

The only consensus on the new growth theory that does seem to be emerging, voiced by Paul Romer, Edwards, and others at the conference, is the diminishing return to further cross-sectional regressions for a large number of countries with growth rates as the dependent variable. As Krueger concluded, to understand the process of economic growth, we need to perform detailed studies of the economic history of a country, within a solid theoretical framework.

Comment Koichi Hamada

Like much of Krueger's work, this paper provides a clear overview of the central issues, in this case the economic development of varied East Asian economies. It also presents a basic framework for the discussions of this conference, even though many puzzles still remain, as I will discuss below.

I more than agree with Krueger's statement that, "the histories of the different economies are significantly different and provide important clues as to interpretation of growth experiences." Recent quantitative cross-country studies, many of which depend on the Summers-Heston data set, are very welcome but should be supplemented by careful country-by-country studies with, I would like to stress, more theoretical and structural thinking on the economy as well as on the political economy of the development process.

My impression is that the initial sections are very well written, while the latter sections could be substantiated by more structured arguments. Let me start with the relatively technical points.

1. The years of comparison should be chosen more carefully. For example,

Koichi Hamada is professor of economics at the Economic Growth Center, Yale University.

in table 1.4 the year 1973 was the pre–oil crisis year when most of the NIEs were adversely affected. In table 1.5, the year 1980 was during the second oil crisis; in 1990 Japan's stock market crashed precipitously. Therefore, the balance of payments in the current account as well as the saving-investment balance may not reflect regular patterns. In particular, even before 1980, Japan had accumulated a large trade surplus.

2. We may divide these five countries into two groups. Japan, Korea, and Taiwan are countries that possess sufficient land area. Hong Kong and Singapore are spatially small countries—like points. They may not be "small countries" in the sense of trade theory, because the terms of trade are not conceivably special to those countries with substantial mass in production, but the trading patterns and macroeconomic features of these spatially small countries have much in common. These economies follow open trade policies almost by necessity because autarky is difficult with such small area. The monetary policy of these countries tends to be passive. We may add other city-states, for example, Monaco and Luxembourg, which can be regarded as "small countries" in the trade theory sense, to the list of countries for such a study.

3. The attempt to go back to time-series analysis of the development process is welcome. However, time-series analysis presents another problem, the problem of timing and causality. Regressions like those in footnote 31, though the results look quite reasonable, open up all the problems associated with lead-lag or contemporaneous relations between macroeconomic variables.

My major comments are related to the later sections of the paper. One of the central questions in the paper is how development policies affect growth performance. The following comments are not so much criticism of the approaches taken as speculation on how we can deepen our understanding of structural development.

In short, growth theory—old or new—leaves so many black boxes. This paper suggests how we might open these black boxes, but leaves the actual task of opening them to further research. After all, the growth theory used here is primarily single-sector analysis and cannot handle intersectoral movement of factors. The following are several links under investigation in the empirical analysis of endogenous growth, the links that connect possible exogenous determinants to economic development. The exact process by which these factors influence technical progress and the growth rate have not been explored enough.

1. Physical investment in equipment and machinery may lead to the acceleration of growth, presumably through the creation of technical and managerial skills, human capital, and their externalities. This link was relatively well explored by the empirical analysis of new growth theory.

2. At the conference, the link between export-oriented policy and Asian growth was emphasized. Liberalization of trade will be accompanied by less government regulation and intervention, and accordingly with less rent seeking, all of which are congenial to the functioning of a market economy.

3. Real exchange rate policy may change the relative price between traded and nontraded goods and accordingly affect the production mix between the traded and nontraded sectors as well as the production mix between the manufacturing and nonmanufacturing sectors. Those changes may well trigger the above two links, 1 and 2.

4. Education and investment in human capital is important. In this link, the capability of human capital to adapt foreign technology assumes a crucial importance. (For a study of the adaptation process of the postwar Japanese economy see Hamada and Honda 1992.) In East Asia, Confucian ethics may have played some role (Morishima 1982). Ethnic factors, legal systems, and the legacy of British and Japanese colonial policies, including their atrocities as well as their educational functions, should be objectively evaluated.

5. In this paper, the link between financial policy and development is largely neglected. The link between financial policy and financial repression will affect the amount of financial intermediation (McKinnon 1973, 1991).

6. Inflation, particularly its variability, is an important factor that affects economic growth.

In my opinion, there is a rich potential field of research that connects the information-oriented literature on screening, monitoring, verification, and bankruptcies to institutional development. Such research would give a clue to analyzing the questions arising from items 5 and 6 above. One can analyze the relationship between a monitoring technology such as the property right system and an enforcement mechanism on the one hand, and some degree of financial maturity on the other. Contracting debt always involves some agency costs or monitoring costs. The state of monitoring technology, with interaction between poolable and unpoolable risks, will determine the degree of financial intermediation, the incidence of bankruptcy, and capital movements. Financial repression is brought about by government interest ceilings but also by incompleteness of information and lack of proper monitoring schemes.

If it is more costly to write a real contract than to write a nominal contract, then more volatile inflation should lead to a deterioration in economic performance. Thus, by the analysis of asymmetric information, financial aspects and real aspects could be integrated; historical description would be combined with structural insight.

Studies of economic development started from descriptive, historical approaches, shifted then to more quantitative cliometrics and now to cross-country analysis. Needless to say, this trend is basically welcome. However, we know very little about the structural and incentive mechanisms linking possibly important factors to the process of development. Now may be the time to combine quantitative cross-country studies with the historical, institutional, country-specific study of the actual process of development. This does not mean that we should return to the mere description of history. Modern economic analysis, including, for example, the microeconomics of incomplete information, the macroeconomics seigniorage gain, and the political economy of rent seeking, could make historical study more theoretical and operationally meaningful.

References

Hamada, Koichi, and Tetsushi Honda. 1992. Engine of the rising Sun: Productivity growth in postwar Japan. *Rivista di Politica Economica,* Ser. 3, no. 12: 397–438.

McKinnon, R. I. 1973. *Money and capital in economic development.* Washington, D.C.: Brookings Institution.

———. 1991. *The order of economic liberalization: Financial control in the transition to a market economy.* Baltimore: Johns Hopkins University Press.

Morishima, M. 1982. *Why has Japan succeeded?* Cambridge: Cambridge University Press.

2 Long-Run Growth Theories and Empirics: Anything New?

T. N. Srinivasan

2.1 Introduction

After a hiatus of over two decades, scholarly attention has returned to theoretical and empirical analyses of economic growth and development. Recent contributions, variously described as "endogenous" growth theory and "new" growth theory, have included many of the factors that have long been viewed as contributing to growth and development in an analytically coherent framework. Such features as significant scale economies, pervasive externalities (particularly in the generation and diffusion of technological knowledge), and the accumulation of human capital have been incorporated, not as some exogenous deus ex machina for generating growth, but as processes interacting with, if not also generated by, the behavior of producers, consumers, and the government. Renewed interest in empirically testing some of the implications of theories and estimating the contributions to growth of various factors has also been stimulated by these contributions. Interestingly, the revival of interest in growth theory came soon after developments in the theory of international trade, which also grounded scale economies and the generation of technological knowledge in the rational behavior of agents operating in necessarily imperfectly competitive markets. For this reason, recent models of growth and trade not only have recognizable analytical similarities, but also more importantly, shed light on related issues in theory, empirics, and policy. Let me illustrate with just one among many possible examples.

In the context of the long-run effects of variations in saving and investment

T. N. Srinivasan is the Samuel C. Park, Jr., Professor of Economics, Economic Growth Center, Yale University.

The author thanks Sebastian Edwards, Paul Romer, participants of the Fourth Annual East Asian Seminar on Economics of the National Bureau of Economic Research, and the staff reviewer of the National Bureau of Economic Research for their comments on an earlier version of this paper.

rates, an important theoretical question is, Does an increase in the rate of investment (leaving aside for the moment the question of whether the rate is exogenous or endogenous) have only a *level* effect, i.e., it changes only the long-run *level of output per worker,* or does it also have a *growth* effect, i.e., it changes the long-run *rate of growth of output per worker?* An analogous theoretical question in the context of international trade is, Does opening up a closed economy to foreign trade have only a level effect (i.e., yield only *static and once and for all* gains from trade) or does it also have a growth effect (i.e., yield *dynamic* gains from trade as well)? In the context of finance, the issue is, Does the relaxation of financial repression generate largely static gains or does the functioning of financial institutions have a key role in the growth process?

A related empirical question is the following: Does the evidence—either from a long time series for individual entities such as regions, countries, or subregions within countries or from a cross section of entities at different points of time—confirm, for example, that variations in factor accumulation have, in effect, only level effects? This is the implication of a neoclassical model in which all entities have access to the same constant-returns-to-scale production function with the marginal product of any factor diminishing to zero as its use is increased indefinitely relative to other factors. That is, loosely speaking, regardless of their differences with respect to accumulation, do all entities grow in the long run at a rate determined by the rate of growth of exogenous factors such as its labor force and technical progress? An interesting empirical-cum-policy issue is whether orientation toward foreign trade is at the heart of the spectacular growth performance of East Asian economies and their Southeast Asian followers, and, by the same token, whether the poor performance of some of their South Asian neighbors is explained by excessive inward orientation? Put another way, does openness to trade generate dynamic gains?

The theoretical, empirical, and policy-oriented literature on long-run growth and trade has grown by leaps and bounds since its revival by Lucas (1988) and Romer (1986). The recent literature on international trade, innovations, and growth, initiated by Grossman and Helpman (1990), is well covered in their later monograph (Grossman and Helpman 1991). I do not propose to survey these literatures. Instead, in section 2.2, by placing some of the recent theoretical models in juxtaposition with the earlier growth models, I argue that it is misleading to characterize the earlier models as necessarily implying that sustained growth in per capita income is impossible in the absence of exogenous technical progress and to suggest that, in contrast, recent models generate such growth by endogenizing the growth process including that of technical change. On the contrary, sustained growth is possible in the former even in the absence of technical progress as long as the marginal product of an accumulable factor of production (such as capital) has a positive lower bound, regardless of how much it is accumulated relative to other factors. While it is true that in recent growth models the process of growth and technical progress is *endogenous* and that, in some, multiple steady states are possible, these features were also present in some of the earlier models. Also, increasing, rather than constant, returns to scale, which are characteristic of some of the recent models, are neither necessary nor sufficient to generate sustained growth. Section 2.2 also briefly describes a growth model due to Raut and Srinivasan (1991) with endogenous fertility and externalities to population density, where nonlinear dynamics generates a plethora of outcomes (depending on the functional forms, parameters, and initial conditions) that include not only the neoclassical steady state with exponential growth of population with constant per capita income and consumption, but also growth paths which do not converge to a steady state and are even chaotic. Per capita output grows exponentially (and superexponentially) in some of the examples.

In section 2.3 I briefly and selectively review the recent empirical literature on growth, focusing attention in particular on the serious inadequacies of cross-country studies from the perspective of the specification of the model to be estimated, the techniques of estimation, and above all the database used for estimation. Section 2.4 concludes the paper with a few remarks on the findings from the recent growth literature and their policy implications, if any.[1]

2.2 Growth Theories: Past and Present

Theorizing about long-run growth revived after a hiatus of over two decades since the last spurt in the 1950s and 1960s. The latter was itself inspired by much earlier and pioneering works of Frank Ramsey (1928) on optimal saving and of von Neumann (1945) on balanced growth at a maximal rate, and also by dynamic extensions of the Keynesian model by Harrod (1939) and later by Domar (1947). In the largely neoclassical growth-theoretic literature of the 1960s and earlier, one could distinguish three strands.

The first strand is *positive* or, better still, *descriptive* theory aimed at explaining the stylized facts of long-run growth in industrialized countries (particularly in the United States), such as the steady secular growth of aggregate output and the relative constancy of the share of savings, investment, labor, and capital income in aggregate output. These stylized facts themselves had been established by the works of empirically oriented economists, such as Abramovitz (1956), Denison (1962), and Kuznets (1966), who were mainly interested in accounting for observed growth. Solow's (1956, 1957) celebrated articles and later work by Jorgenson and Griliches (1966) and others are examples of descriptive growth theory and related empirical analysis. Uzawa (1961, 1963) extended Solow's descriptive one-sector model into a two-sector model. As Stiglitz (1990) remarked, by showing that the long-run steady state growth rate could be unaffected by the rate of savings (and investment) and that, even in the short run, the rate of growth was mostly accounted for by

1. I have drawn extensively from Raut and Srinivasan (1993) in writing this paper.

the rate of labor-augmenting technical progress, Solow challenged the then-conventional wisdom.

The second strand is *normative* theory, which drew its inspiration from Ramsey's (1928) classic paper on optimal saving. In contrast to the descriptive models in which the aggregate savings rate was exogenously specified (usually as a constant over time), the normative models derived time-varying savings rates from the optimization of an intertemporal social welfare function. There were mainly two variants of such normative models: one-sector models (e.g., Koopmans 1965; Cass 1965) and two-sector models (Srinivasan 1962, 1964; Uzawa 1964). The contribution of Phelps (1961) is also normative, but it focused only on the steady state level of consumption per worker, rather than on the entire transitional time path to the steady state, and solved for that savings rate which maximized the steady state level of consumption per worker.

The third strand of theory is neither primarily descriptive nor primarily normative, though it is related to both. Harrod's dynamic extension of the Keynesian model (with its constant marginal propensity to save) raised the issue of stability of the growth path by contrasting two growth rates: the *warranted* rate of growth that would be consistent with maintaining the savings-investment equilibrium and the *natural* growth rate as determined by the growth of the labor force and technical change. In this model, unless the economy's behavioral and technical parameters keep it on the knife edge of equality between warranted and natural growth rates, there would be either growing underutilization of capacity if the warranted rate exceeds the natural rate or growing unemployment if the natural rate exceeds the warranted rate. Indeed this knife-edge property resulting from Harrod's assumption that capital and labor are used in fixed proportions led Solow to look for growth paths converging to a steady state by replacing Harrod's technology with a neoclassical technology of positive elasticity of substitution between labor and capital.

Von Neumann's (1945) model is also part of the third strand. In this model production technology is characterized by a finite set of constant-returns-to-scale activities with inputs being committed at the beginning of each discrete production period and outputs emerging at the end. There are no nonproduced factors of production such as labor or exhaustible natural resources. In the "primal" version, von Neumann characterized the vector of activity levels that permitted the maximal rate of *balanced growth* (i.e., growth in which outputs of all commodities grew at the same rate) given that the outputs of each period were to be ploughed back as inputs in the next period. In the "dual" version, a vector of commodity prices and an interest rate were derived which had the properties that the value of output of each activity was no higher than the value of inputs inclusive of interest and that the interest rate was the lowest possible. Under certain assumptions about the technology, von Neumann showed, first, that the maximal growth rate of output of the primal version was equal to the (minimal) interest rate of the dual and, second, that the usual complementary slackness relations obtained between the vector of activity levels, prices, growth, and interest rates.

Although prima facie there is no normative rationale for balanced growth and the maximization of the growth rate, particularly in a setup with no final consumption of any good, it turned out that the von Neumann path of balanced growth at the maximal rate has a "normative" property. As Dorfman, Samuelson, and Solow (1958) conjectured and Radner (1961) later rigorously proved, given an objective that is a function only of the terminal stocks of commodities, the path starting from a given initial vector of stocks that maximizes this objective will be "close" to the von Neumann path "most" of the time, as long as the terminal date is sufficiently distant from the initial date, regardless of the initial stocks and of the form of the objective function. This "turnpike" feature was later seen in other growth models in which final consumption is allowed and production involves the use of nonproduced factors. For example, in the Koopmans-Cass model, in which the objective is to maximize the discounted sum of the stream of utility of per capita consumption over time, a unique steady state exists which is defined by the discount rate, the rate of growth of the labor force, and the technology of production. *All* optimal paths, i.e., paths that maximize the objective function and start from different initial conditions, converge to this steady state regardless of the functional form of the utility function. As such, all optimal paths stay "close" to the steady state path "most" of the time.

Barring a few exceptions to be noted below, in the neoclassical growth models production technology was assumed to exhibit constant returns to scale and in many, though not all models, smooth substitution among inputs with strictly diminishing marginal rates of substitution between any two inputs along an isoquant was also posited. Analytical attention was focused on conditions ensuring the existence and uniqueness of steady state growth paths along which all inputs and outputs grew at the same rate—the steady state being the path to which all transitional paths starting from any given initial conditions and satisfying the requirements of specified descriptive rates of accumulation or of intertemporal welfare optimality converged. The steady state growth rate was the *exogenous* rate of growth of the labor force in efficiency units, so that in the absence of (exogenous) labor-augmenting technical progress, output per worker was constant along the steady state.

Turning to the exceptions, Solow (1956) himself drew attention to the possibility that a steady state need not even exist and that even if one existed it need not be unique. Indeed output per worker could grow indefinitely, even in the absence of labor-augmenting technical progress, if the marginal product of capital were bounded below by a sufficiently high positive number. Helpman (1992) also draws attention to this. Also, there could be multiple steady states, some of which are unstable, if the production technology exhibits nonconvexities. We return to these issues below.

There were also exceptions to the exogeneity of technical progress and of the rate of growth of output along a steady state. In the one-sector, one-factor models of Harrod and Domar and the two-sector models of Fel'dman (1928, as described in Domar 1957) and Mahalanobis (1955), marginal capital-output ratios were assumed to be constant so that by definition the marginal product of capital did not decline. The growth rate was *endogenous* and depended on the rate of savings (investment) in such one-sector models and on the aggregate rate of investment and its allocation between sectors producing capital and consumer goods in the two-sector models. Kaldor and Mirrlees (1962) endogenized technical progress (and hence the rate of growth of output) by relating productivity of workers operating newly produced equipment to the rate of growth of investment per worker. And there was the celebrated model of Arrow (1962) of "learning by doing," in which factor productivity was an increasing function of cumulated output or investment. Uzawa (1965) also endogenized technical progress by postulating that the rate of growth of labor-augmenting technical progress was a concave function of the ratio of labor employed in the education sector to total employment. The education sector was assumed to use labor as the only input. Uzawa's model has influenced recent contributions to growth theory. In addition, in the literature on induced innovation (Ahmad 1966; Boserup 1965; Kennedy 1964) technical change was, by definition, endogenous.

The recent revival of growth theory started with the influential papers of Lucas (1988) and Romer (1986). Lucas motivated his approach by arguing that neoclassical growth theory cannot account for observed differences in growth across countries and over time and for its evidently counterfactual prediction that international trade should induce rapid movements toward equality in capital-labor ratios and factor prices.[2] He argued that, "In the absence of differences in pure technology then, and under the assumption of no factor mobility, the neoclassical model predicts a strong tendency to income equality and equality in growth rates, tendencies we can observe within countries and, perhaps, within the wealthiest countries taken as a group, but which simply cannot be seen in the world at large. When factor mobility is permitted, this prediction is powerfully reinforced" (Lucas 1988, 15–16). He then goes on to suggest that the one factor isolated by the neoclassical model, namely, variation across countries in technology, "has the potential to account for wide differences in income levels and growth rates. . . . When we talk about differences in 'technology' across countries we are not talking about knowledge in general, but about the knowledge of particular people, or particular subcultures of people. If so, then while it is not exactly wrong to describe these differences [as] exogenous . . . neither is it useful to do so. We want a formalism that leads us to think about individual decisions to acquire knowledge, and about the conse-

2. In fact, besides introducing the constant elasticity of substitution production function, Arrow et al. (1961) and, in his dissertation, Minhas (1963) were concerned precisely with this issue.

quences of these decisions for productivity." He draws on the theory of "human capital" to provide such a formalism: each individual acquires productivity-enhancing skills by devoting time to such acquisition and away from paying work. The acquisition of skills by a worker not only increases her productivity but, by increasing the average level of skills in the economy as a whole, has a spillover effect on the productivity of all workers by increasing the average level of skills in the economy as a whole.

Romer also looked for an alternative to the neoclassical model of long-run growth to escape from its implications that "initial conditions or current disturbances have no long-run effect on the level of output and consumption. . . . In the absence of technical change, per capita output should converge to a steady-state value with no per capita growth" (Romer 1986, 1002–3). His is "an equilibrium model of endogenous technological change in which long-run growth is driven primarily by the accumulation of knowledge by forward-looking, profit-maximizing agents" (1003). While the production of new knowledge is through a technology that exhibits diminishing returns, "the creation of new knowledge by one firm is assumed to have a positive external effect on the production possibilities of other firms . . . [so that] production of consumption goods as a function of stock of knowledge exhibits increasing returns; more precisely, knowledge may have an increasing marginal product" (1003).

It should be noted that the spillover effect of the average stock of human capital per worker in the Lucas model and of knowledge in the Romer model are externalities unperceived (and hence not internalized) by individual agents. However, for the economy *as a whole* they generate increasing scale economies even though the perceived production function of each agent exhibits constant returns to scale. Thus by introducing nonconvexities through the device of a Marshallian externality Lucas and Romer were able to work with an intertemporal competitive (albeit a socially nonoptimal) equilibrium. Thus both avoid facing the problem[3] that research and development (R&D) efforts that lead to technical progress are "naturally associated with imperfectly competitive markets, as Schumpeter (1942) had forcefully argued" (Stiglitz 1990, 25). Later work by others (e.g., Grossman and Helpman 1991) formulated models in which firms operating in imperfectly competitive markets undertook R&D.

In sorting out the differences between neoclassical and recent growth models it is useful to start with Solow's growth model. Solow assumes an aggregate production function,

$$Y_t = A_t F(K_t, b_t L_t), \tag{1}$$

where Y_t is aggregate output at time t, K_t is the stock of capital, L_t is labor hours at time t, and A_t ($A_0 \equiv 1$) is the disembodied technology factor (i.e., index of total factor productivity), so that output at time t associated with any combina-

3. However, in Romer (1990) innovation is driven by profit-maximizing entrepreneurs.

tion of capital stock and labor input in efficiency units is A_t times the output at time zero associated with the same combination. Analogously, b_t (with $b_0 \equiv 1$) is the efficiency level of a unit of labor in period t, so that a unit of labor at time t is equivalent to b_t units of labor at time zero. Thus the technical progress induced by increases in b_t is *labor augmenting*. It is easily seen that technical progress through A_t is Hicks neutral, and that through b_t is Harrod neutral.

Let $\tilde{k}_t \equiv K_t/b_tL_t$, the ratio of capital to labor in efficiency units in period t, let $k_t \equiv K_t/L_t$, the ratio of capital to labor in natural units, and let $y_t \equiv Y_t/b_tL_t$, the level of output or income per unit of labor in efficiency units. Solow made the following crucial assumptions:

ASSUMPTION 1 (Neoclassical). F is homogeneous of degree one in its arguments and concave.

Given assumption 1, the average product of an efficiency unit of labor, i.e., $(1/b_tL_t)F(k_t, b_tL_t)$, equals $F(\tilde{k}_t, 1)$. Let $f(\tilde{k}_t) = F(\tilde{k}_t, 1)$. Clearly, concavity of F implies concavity of f as a function of $\tilde{k}_t$. In fact, f is assumed to be strictly concave with $f(0) = 0$.

ASSUMPTION 2 (Inada).

$$\lim_{\tilde{k}\to 0} f'(\tilde{k}) = \infty \quad \text{and} \quad \lim_{\tilde{k}\to\infty} f'(\tilde{k}) = 0.$$

In a closed economy, assuming that labor is growing exogenously as $L_t = (1 + n)^t L_0$, human capital or skill level is growing exogenously as $b_t = (1 + b)^t$, capital is depreciating at the rate δ per period, and denoting by c_t the level of consumption per efficiency unit of labor, we have

$$\tilde{k}_{t+1} = \frac{A_t f(\tilde{k}_t) + (1 - \delta)\tilde{k}_t - c_t}{(1 + n)(1 + b)}. \tag{2}$$

Solow further assumed that the savings rate is constant, i.e., $c_t = (1 - s)y_t$. Then equation (2) becomes

$$\tilde{k}_{t+1} = \frac{sA_t f(\tilde{k}_t) + (1 - \delta)\tilde{k}_t}{(1 + n)(1 + b)} \equiv g(\tilde{k}_t). \tag{3}$$

Equation (3) is the fundamental difference equation of the Solow model. If there is no disembodied technical progress, so that $A_t = 1$ for all t, then the phase diagram of the dynamic system can be represented as in figure 2.1. It is clear from figure 2.1 that, starting from any arbitrary initial capital-labor ratio $\tilde{k}_0$, the economy will converge (ignoring the inessential problem due to discreteness of time) to the steady state $\tilde{k}^*$, defined by $g(\tilde{k}^*) = \tilde{k}^*$, in which all the per capita variables, including per capita income, will grow at the rate b. Thus if $b = 0$, per capita income, consumption, and savings do not grow along the steady state. Further, policies that permanently affect the savings rate, or fertility rate, will have no long-run growth effects.

It is clear from figure 2.1, however, that out of the steady state (i.e., in the short run) economies will exhibit growth in per capita income even without

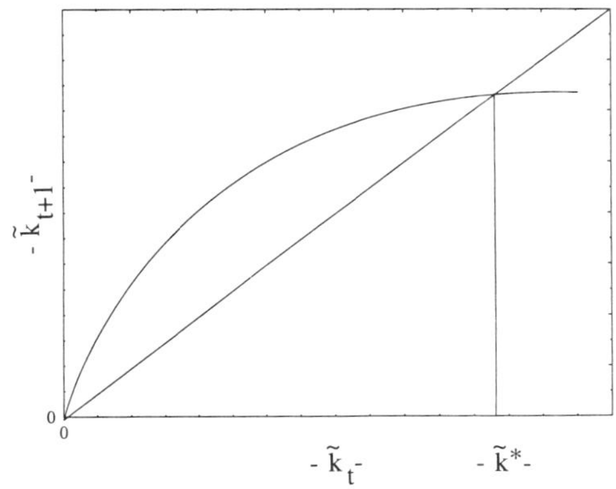

Fig. 2.1 Phase diagram of Solow model $g(\tilde{k}_t)$

technological change. The rate of growth will depend on the initial capital-labor ratio and the time period over which the average growth rate is calculated. It can be shown that the average growth rate *decreases* as the initial capital-labor ratio $\tilde{k}_0$ (and hence initial income per head) *increases.* As the initial capital-labor ratio tends to $\tilde{k}^*$, the average growth rate of per capita income converges to b, the exogenously given rate of labor-augmenting technical progress. This is indeed one of the convergence hypotheses that are tested in the recent empirical literature on growth. Policies that affect s and n clearly affect growth rates out of the steady state. However, the effects of changes in s and n on the growth rate of per capita income are only temporary, and the marginal product of capital will be declining over time. It should be noted, however, that this predicted fall in the marginal product of capital is not observed, for example, in U.S. historical data.

It is also clear that per capita output can grow indefinitely even in traditional growth models if the marginal product of capital is bounded away from zero as the capital-labor ratio grows indefinitely. Thus the standard neoclassical assumption that the marginal product of capital is a strictly decreasing function of the capital-labor ratio is not inconsistent with indefinite growth of per capita output. It has to diminish to zero as the capital-labor ratio increases indefinitely to preclude such growth. This is easily seen from equation (3).

Consider the simplest version of the neoclassical growth model with $b_t = 1$ and $A_t = 1$ for all t, so that $\tilde{k}_t = k_t$. Let $f(0) = 0$ and let the marginal product of capital, i.e., $f'(k)$, be bounded away from $(n + \delta)/s$ (i.e., $f'(k) > (n + \delta)/s$ for all k). Strict concavity of $f(k)$, together with $f(0) = 0$, implies $f(k) > kf'(k) > k(n + \delta)/s$, so that from equation (3) it follows that $k_{t+1} > k_t$. This in turn implies that output per worker, $f(k_t)$, grows at a positive rate at all t. Moreover, given strict concavity of $f(k)$, it follows that $f'(k)$ is monotonically decreasing and, hence, has a limiting value as $k \to \infty$, say, γ_y, that is at least as large as $(n + \delta)/s$. As such it can be verified that the asymptotic growth rate of output and consumption will be at least as large as $[s\gamma_y - (n + \delta)](1 + n) \geq 0$. The savings rate, s, can be made endogenous, thus leading to a theory of endogenous and sustained long-run growth in per capita income. Thus the neoclassical framework can endogenously generate long-run growth in per capita income. However, the assumption that the marginal product has a positive lower bound is not particularly attractive since it implies that labor is not essential for production.[4]

A primary goal of the recently revived growth theory is to build models that can generate sustained long-run growth in per capita income. A related objective is to ensure that the long-run growth rate of income (and, in fact, the entire time path of income) not only depends on the parameters of the production and utility functions, but also on fiscal policies, foreign trade policies, and population policies. In most models of "new" theory, the primary goal is accomplished through increasing scale economies in aggregate production. The resulting nonconvexities lead to multiple equilibria and hysteresis in some models so that history (i.e., initial conditions as well as any past shocks experienced by the economy) and policies have long-term effects.

In assessing the role of increasing scale economies in growth, it is useful to distinguish between generating *sustained growth* in output per head and *endogenizing* the rate of growth. For example, with the production function $Y = K^a L^b$, where $0 < a, b < 1$ and $a + b > 1$, and the labor force growing *exogenously* at the rate n there exists a unique steady state (regardless of the savings rate) in which output grows at the exogenous rate of $n(a + b - 1)/1 - a > 0$. Thus *increasing scale economies together with a marginal product of capital strictly diminishing to zero* (i.e., $0 < a < 1$) leads to *sustained* but *exogenous* growth. On the other hand, *constant returns to scale with a marginal product of capital bounded away from zero* at a sufficiently high positive number leads to *endogenous* and *sustained* growth. Thus increasing scale economies by themselves need not generate endogenous growth. It is also important to distinguish how different types of increasing returns to scale in aggregate production arise in various growth models. I consider here only two types: locally increasing marginal product of capital and scale economies due to spillover effects. For simplicity assume that in equation (1) $L_t \equiv 1$, $A_t = 1$, and $b_t = 1$, for all $t \geq 0$. The first type arises when the marginal product of capital, $f'(k)$, first increases with k and then decreases, or more generally when $f''(k) = 0$ has more than one but a finite number of solutions.

The second type arises in the models of Lucas and Romer. Building on the works of Arrow (1962) and Sheshinski (1967), Romer (1986) considers an economy in which there are n identical firms; each has a production function

4. One can easily prove this as follows: Suppose $\underset{(K,L)>0}{\operatorname{Inf}} \frac{\partial F}{\partial K} \equiv \gamma > 0$. Since F is homogeneous of degree one, $F(1, L/K) = \partial F/\partial K + (L/K)(\partial F/\partial L) \geq \partial F/\partial K > \gamma > 0$. Now suppose $L \rightarrow 0$, then it follows that $F(1, 0) > 0$.

of the form $Y_i = G(K_i, L_i, K)$, where K_i is the stock of knowledge capital or R&D capital employed by firm i, $K = \sum_{i=1}^{n} K_i$ is the industry level aggregate stock of knowledge, and L_i is labor or any other inputs. K is assumed to have a positive spillover effect on the output of each firm, although the choice of K is external to the firm. Romer assumes that, for fixed K, G is homogeneous of degree one in other inputs. Supposing that all identical firms choose identical inputs, we can write $Y_i = G(K_i, L_i, nK_i)$. Define $F(K_i, L_i) \equiv G(K_i, L_i, nK_i)$. It is obvious that F exhibits increasing returns to scale in the inputs K_i and L_i. Again, in addition to these scale economies one needs to assume that the asymptotic marginal product of aggregate capital is positive in order to generate endogenous growth. Empirical support for the spillover effect of R&D capital is found in several empirical investigations (see Bernstein and Nadiri 1989 on Canadian industry data; Jaffe 1986 on the U.S. manufacturing firm–level data; Raut 1991b on Indian manufacturing firm–level data).[5]

Following Uzawa (1965), Lucas (1988) endogenizes Harrod-neutral (i.e., labor-augmenting) technological change through a mechanism of human capital accumulation. Suppose a worker of period t is endowed with b_t of human capital, or skill, and one unit of labor. He has to allocate his labor endowment between accumulating skills and earning wage income. If he devotes the fraction ϕ_t of his time in the current production sector and $1 - \phi_t$ (where $0 \leq \phi_t \leq 1$) in the learning sector (such as school or some vocational training program), he can increase his human capital in the next period by

$$\dot{b}_t = b_t\delta(1 - \phi_t). \tag{4}$$

The budget constraint for the representative agent is given by

$$c_t + \dot{k}_t = F(k_t, \phi_t b_t) - (n + \delta)k_t. \tag{5}$$

From equation (5) it is clear that for given c_t and k_t, the agent faces a trade-off. He can spend more time currently (i.e., choose a larger ϕ_t) in the production sector and thus have a larger *current consumption* or *future physical capital,* or choose a lower ϕ_t and thus have *larger future human capital* (i.e., higher $\dot{b}_t$) and hence a *larger future stream of output.* It is clear that he would divide his savings between human capital and physical capital in a balanced way so that the marginal product of capital does not fall to zero. Under the further assumption that the production function is of the Cobb-Douglas form

$$F(K, L) = A(b_t)K_t^{\alpha}(b_t L_t)^{\beta}, \quad \alpha + \beta = 1, \quad \alpha, \beta > 0, \tag{6}$$

where the spillover effect is given by $A(b_t) = Ab_t^{\mu}$, $0 < \mu$, it can be shown that, along the balanced growth path, the capital-labor ratio and hence per capita income and consumption will be growing at the rate

5. However, Benhabib and Jovanovic (1991) do not find any evidence for spillover using the U.S. macrodata.

$$\gamma_y = \left(\frac{1 - \beta + \mu}{1 - \beta}\right)(1 - \phi)\delta, \tag{7}$$

where ϕ_t is a constant equal to ϕ. Since γ_y is a function of ϕ, which is endogenously determined, the growth rate of per capita income is endogenously determined.

It should be noted that even if there is no spillover effect, i.e., $\mu = 0$, γ_y is positive, and this of course is the consequence of the assumption that the marginal return to time devoted to skill accumulation is constant and not diminishing. As Lucas himself points out, this is crucial for generating sustained growth per capita consumption in the long run. Since the opportunity cost of time spent on skill acquisition is foregone income that could have been used for consumption or accumulation of physical capital, this crucial assumption should be viewed as the equivalent of assuming that the marginal product of physical capital is constant as in the Harrod-Domar model.

The Lucas model is essentially a two-sector growth model. Human capital and the process of its accumulation play essentially the same role as the capital goods sector in the two-sector model of Mahalanobis (1955). In this model, marginal product of capital in the capital goods sector is constant—an assumption that is the equivalent of Lucas's crucial assumption about the process of human capital accumulation (Srinivasan 1993a).[6] The rate of growth of income and consumption was endogenously determined in the Mahalanobis model by the share of investment devoted to the accumulation of capacity to produce capital goods. The share $(1 - \phi_t)$ of time devoted to skill acquisition plays an analogous role in the Lucas model.

Linearity of the technology of skill acquisition in the Lucas model is restrictive. It leads to a unique balanced growth solution. However, if a nonlinear (convex) technology is assumed, there could be multiple optimal balanced growth paths that are locally stable, as has been shown by Azariadis and Drazen (1990).

Raut and Srinivasan (1991) present a model that not only endogenizes growth and the process of shifts in production possibilities over time (i.e., technical change) but also generates richer dynamics than the models of recent growth theory. First, by assuming fertility to be endogenous,[7] they preclude the possibility of aggregate growth being driven solely by exogenous labor force growth in the absence of technical change. Second, by assuming that population density has an external effect (not perceived by individual agents) on the

6. It is also evident that the absence of long-run growth effects of trade in dynamic versions of Heckscher-Ohlin-Samuelson–type models of international trade is again due to their implicitly or explicitly precluding the marginal product of capital being bounded away from zero.

7. There are a number of models in the literature in which the interaction of endogenous fertility and productive investment in human capital are analyzed in a growth context. My purpose here is not to survey this literature. I refer the interested reader to one of the very interesting such models by Becker et al. (1990).

production process either through its negative congestion effect or through its positive effect in stimulating innovation and technical change, they make the change in production possibilities endogenously determined by fertility decisions of individual agents. However, unlike the new growth literature, their model, which is an extension of Raut (1985, 1991a), is not necessarily geared to generating steady states. In fact, the nonlinear dynamics of the model generates a plethora of outcomes (depending on the functional forms, parameters, and initial conditions) that include not only the neoclassical steady state with exponential growth of population with constant per capita income and consumption, but also growth paths which do not converge to a steady state and are even chaotic. Per capita output grows exponentially (and superexponentially) in some of the examples.

The model draws on the insights of E. Boserup (1981) and J. Simon (1981) who, among others, have argued that the growth of population could itself induce technical change. In the Boserup model, increasing population pressure on a fixed or very slowly growing supply of arable land induces changes in methods of cultivation, not simply through substitution of labor for land by choice of techniques within a known set but, more importantly, through the invention of new techniques. Simon also attributes a positive role for increases in population density in inducing technical progress. Since having a large population is not sufficient to generate growth (Romer 1990), it is important to examine the mechanism by which population density influences innovation. However, neither of the two authors provides a complete theory of induced innovation. Raut and Srinivasan do not provide one either; they point out that the inducement to innovate will depend largely on the returns and risks to resources devoted to innovative activity and that there is no particular reason to suggest that preexisting relative factor prices or endowments will necessarily tilt these returns toward search for technologies that save particular factors. They simply analyze the implications of assuming that technical change is influenced by population density (strictly speaking, population size) in a world where fertility is endogenous.

More precisely, they assume that technical change in our model economy is Hicks neutral and that its rate is determined by the change in the size of the working population. Thus, instead of the aggregate production function in equation (1), they use the following:

$$Y_t = A(L_t)F(K_t, L_t). \tag{8}$$

However, for both consumers and firms in this economy, $A(L_t)$ is an externality. This externality is introduced in a model of overlapping generations in which a member of each generation lives for three periods, the first of which is spent as a child in the parent's household. The second period is spent as a young person working, having and raising children, and accumulating capital. The third and last period of life is spent as an old person in retirement, living off support received from each of one's offspring and from the sale of accumulated capital. All members of each generation are identical in their preferences defined over their consumption in their working and retired periods. Thus, in this model the only reason that an individual would want to have a child is the support the child will provide during the individual's retired life. Production (of a single commodity which can be consumed or accumulated) is organized in firms which buy capital from the retired and hire the young as workers. Markets for product, labor, and capital are assumed to be competitive.

Formally, a typical individual of the generation which is young in period t has n_t children (reproduction is by parthenogenesis!), consumes c_t^t and c_{t+1}^t in periods t and $t + 1$, and saves s_t in period t. She supplies one unit of labor for wage employment. Her income from wage labor while young in period t is w_t, and that is her only income in that period. A proportion α of this wage income is given to her parents as old age support. While old in period $t + 1$, she sells her accumulated saving to firms and receives from each of her offspring the proportion α of his or her wage income. She enjoys a utility $U(c_t^t, c_{t+1}^t)$ from consumption. Thus her choice problem can be stated as

$$\max_{st,nt>0} U(c_t^t, c_{t+1}^t), \tag{9}$$

$$c_t^t + \theta_t n_t + s_t = (1 - \alpha)w_t, \tag{10}$$

$$c_{t+1}^t = (1 + r_{t+1})s_t + \alpha w_{t+1} n_t, \tag{11}$$

where θ_t is the output cost of rearing a child until young.

Profit maximization of the producer yields

$$w_{t+1} = A(L_{t+1})[f(k_{t+1}) - K_{t+1} f'(k_{t+1})], \tag{12}$$

$$1 + r_{t+1} = A(L_{t+1}) f'(k_{t+1}), \tag{13}$$

where $f(k) = F(k, 1)$ (since $F(K, L)$ is assumed to be homogeneous of degree one) and $1 + r_t$ is the price of capital in period t. In equilibrium, the private rates of return from investing in children and physical capital are equal so that arbitrage opportunities are ruled out. This implies that

$$\frac{\alpha w_{t+1}}{\theta_t} = 1 + r_{t+1}. \tag{14}$$

Plugging equations (12) and (13) in equation (14), we get an implicit equation linking k_{t+1}, θ_t, and α. It can be shown that, under standard neoclassical assumptions on the production function, we can solve for k_{t+1} as a function $\Psi(\theta_t/\alpha)$. Since $k_{t+1} = s_t/n_t$ (given the assumption that capital depreciates fully in one generation), the budget constraints (10) and (11) become, respectively,

$c_t^t = (1 - \alpha)w_t - S_t$ and $c_{t+1}^t = (1 + r_{t+1})S_t$, where $S_t = [\theta_t + \Psi(\theta_t/\alpha)]n_t$. S_t can be thought of as total savings.

Denote the solution of the above utility maximization problem by $S_t = H(w_t, 1 + r_{t+1})$. The solutions for n_t and s_t can be expressed as

$$(15) \qquad n_t = \frac{H(w_t, 1 + r_{t+1})}{\theta_t + \Psi(\theta_t/\alpha)}, \quad s_t = \frac{H(w_t, 1 + r_{t+1})}{\Psi(\theta_t/\alpha)[\theta_t + \psi(\theta_t/\alpha)]}.$$

Equation (15) determines the dynamics of the system. First consider the simplest case in which the child-rearing cost $\theta_t = \theta$, for all $t \geq 0$. It is clear that $k_{t+1} = k^*$, defined by $k^* = \psi(\theta/\alpha)$, for all $t \geq 1$ in this case. Assuming further that the utility function is Cobb-Douglas, i.e., $U = a \log c_t^t + (1 - a) \log c_{t+1}^t$, we have $H(w_t, 1 + r_{t+1}) = (1 - a)w_t$. Equation (15) now yields

$$n_t = \frac{L_{t+1}}{L_t} = \frac{(1 - \alpha)(1 - a)}{(\theta + K^*)} w^* A(L_t),$$

or

$$(16) \qquad L_{t+1} = \lambda L_t A(L_t) \equiv G(L_t),$$

where $\lambda = [(1 - \alpha)(1 - a)w^*]/(\theta + k^*)$. From equation (8), one notes that per capita income is given by $y_t = A(L_t)f(k^*)$. Thus, the dynamics of population long-run behavior of per capita income hinge on the function $A(L_t)$. It should be recalled that, although the fertility decisions of individuals determine L_t and hence $A(L_t)$, this is an unperceived externality. A few possibilities are depicted in figures 2.2*A*–2.2*C*.

Suppose $A(L_t)$ is such that $G(L_t)$ is a concave function which is zero at $L_t = 0$ and satisfies the Inada condition. Then, in the long run, the population will be stationary and per capita income will be constant as in the standard neoclassical growth model. This is shown in figure 2.2*A*. Now suppose that $G(L_t)$ is concave but $G'(L_t)$ is bounded away from one. In this case, we have long-run growth in L_t and hence in per capita income. This is shown in figure 2.2*B*.

Suppose now that $A(L_t)$ is a logistic function with a positive asymptote, such as $A(L) = \gamma e^{-(L-\hat{L})2}$, for $L \geq 0$. It can be shown (Raut and Srinivasan 1991) that there are multiple steady states. Figure 2.2*C* shows a case of two steady states L^* and L^{**}. $G(L)$ reaches its maximum at $\bar{L}$. The properties of these steady states depend on the parameter values. If the maximum $\bar{L}$ is to the right of L^{**}, then L^{**} is locally stable and there exists a neighborhood around L^{**} within which the system is monotonic. On the other hand, if $\bar{L}$ is to the left of L^{**}, as in figure 2.2*C*, there can be a nongeneric set of parameter values for which the system will exhibit endogenous fluctuations that can be damped, exploding, or even chaotic. However, since α can affect λ, if α is partly influenced by the government through social security schemes, the government can shift $\bar{L}$ to the right of L^{**} and thus, locally at least, a social security program can stabilize fluctuations.

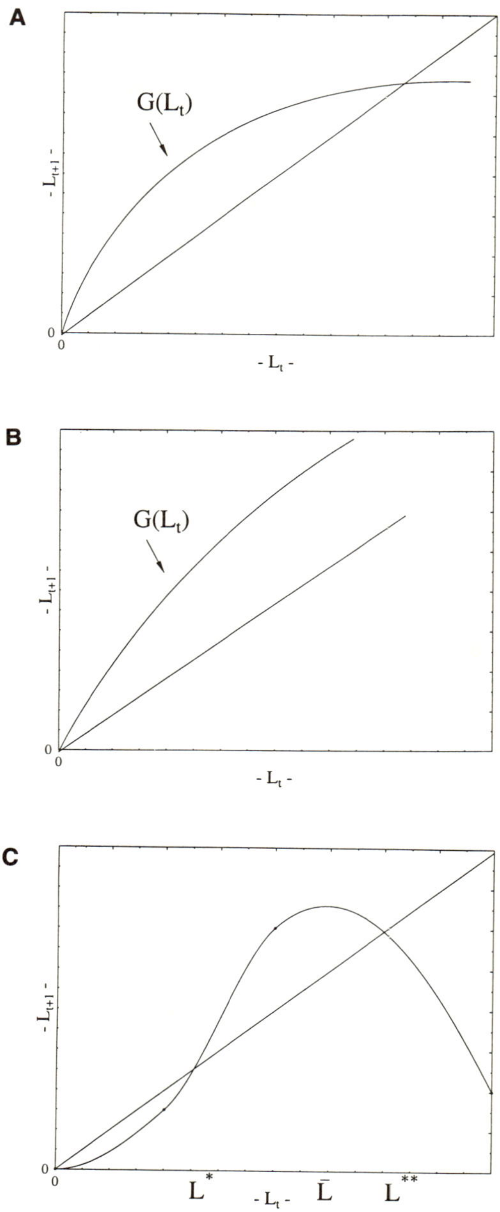

Fig. 2.2 ***A:*** **Stationary population and income.** ***B:*** **Sustained growth in population and income.** ***C:*** **Phase diagram of** $G(L_t)$**.**

More general childbearing costs are considered by Raut and Srinivasan (1991, sec. 4a), involving parent's time and depending on the rate of technological change. Naturally these lead to more complicated dynamical problems. They show that there can be superexponential growth in per capita income in the long run in the case of some specific functional forms for general costs of childbearing.

To sum up this section, the starting point of some, though not all, of the recent contributions to growth theory is a misleading characterization of neoclassical growth theory of the 1960s and earlier as implying that a steady state growth path always exists along which output grows at a rate equal to the exogenously specified rate of growth of the labor force in efficiency units. Thus, in the absence of labor-augmenting technical progress, per capita income does not grow along the steady state path. Policies that affect savings (investment) rates have only transient effects on the growth rate of per capita output, though its steady state *level* is affected. Even a cursory reading of the literature is enough to convince a reader that neoclassical growth theorists were fully aware that a steady state need not exist and that per capita output can grow indefinitely even in the absence of technical progress, provided the marginal product of capital is bounded away from zero by a sufficiently high positive number. Moreover, they showed that, once one departs from the assumption that the marginal product of capital *monotonically* declines to zero as the capital-labor ratio increases indefinitely, multiple steady state growth paths (only some of which are stable) are likely and that the steady state to which a transition path converges will depend on initial conditions. Attempts at endogenizing technical progress were also made by theorists of the era.

It was argued above that the perceived problems of neoclassical growth theory are not inherent features of all the growth models of the era but only of those which assumed the marginal product of capital (or more generally of any reproducible factor) diminishes to *zero* as the input of capital (or that factor) is increased indefinitely relative to other inputs. Instead of directly relaxing this assumption about production technology, the "new" growth theorists in effect make assumptions that are analogous to assuming that the marginal product of capital is bounded away from zero. In some of the models this is achieved by introducing a factor other than physical capital (e.g., human capital, or stock of knowledge) which is not subject to inexorable returns. In doing so, some authors end up with an aggregate production function that exhibits increasing scale economies. Unsurprisingly, in such models multiple equilibria are possible.

The Raut-Srinivasan (1991) model takes a different approach to endogenizing technical progress and growth by assuming fertility and savings to be *endogenous* and the size of the total population to have an external effect (of a Hicks-neutral type) either through the negative influence of congestion or the positive stimulation of faster innovation. This model generates a rich set of growth paths for per capita income and consumption, some of which do not converge to a steady state and are even chaotic.

2.3 Empirics of Growth

The recent revival in theories of long-run growth has also revived its empirical analysis. Of course, such analysis has a long history going back to the pioneering works of Simon Kuznets (1966), Abramowitz (1956), and Denison (1962). Solow himself followed his justly celebrated article (Solow 1956) on the theory of growth with an almost equally celebrated empirical analysis (Solow 1957) of long-run growth in the United States. The early pioneers and Solow were interested in growth accounting, i.e., apportioning the observed long-run growth in real output between the growth of factor inputs on the one hand and the growth of total factor productivity on the other. Some recent studies (Benhabib and Jovanovic 1991; Boskin and Lau 1992a, 1992b; Jorgenson 1990; Kim and Lau 1992a, 1992b, 1992c) are in the growth accounting tradition. Many of the other recent empirical studies (Baumol 1986; Barro 1989; Barro and Sala-i-Martin 1992; DeLong 1988; Dowrick and Nguyen 1989; Jorgenson 1990; Mankiw, Romer, and Weil 1992) attempt to test an aspect of neoclassical growth theory, namely, convergence of the economy to the steady state.

The strong version of the convergence hypothesis asserts that, if all economies had access to the *same aggregate production function* exhibiting constant returns to scale in capital and effective labor inputs, experienced the *same rate of growth of labor force* and labor-augmenting technical progress, and saved and invested the *same share of output,* they would all converge to the *same steady state* at which output and capital would grow at the same rate as effective labor, i.e., the sum of the rates of growth of labor force and labor-augmenting technical progress. The weak version, known as "conditional" convergence, allows for possible differences in steady state levels of output across economies due to differences in savings rates and initial level of labor-augmenting technical progress functions. The publication by Summers and Heston (1988, 1991) of purchasing power parity (PPP) adjusted data for a large number of countries for the period since 1960 enabled tests of a variety of convergence hypotheses.

Jorgenson (1990) commemorated 50 years of research on economic measurement by contributing to the theme of economic growth and its sources. He points out that until recently "the study of sources of economic growth has been based on the notion of an aggregate production function [which makes] it possible to summarize a welter of detailed information within a single overarching framework. . . . At the same time the concept of an aggregate production function is highly problematical, requiring very stringent assumptions on production patterns at the level of individual sectors of the economy" (1990, 19). In contrast to Solow (1957), Jorgenson finds that growth of inputs, rather than growth in total factor productivity, was the driving force behind the expansion of the U.S. economy between 1947 and 1985. In the growth of value added at 3.28 percent per year on the average during this period, growth of capital inputs accounted for 44 percent, labor inputs 34 percent, and productivity accounted for the least, namely, 22 percent. The difference between followers of Solow (1957) and of Jorgenson arises from the fact that Jorgenson carefully distinguishes the separate contributions of capital and labor quality from the contributions of capital stock and hours worked. This distinction is extremely important since both capital and labor inputs are very heterogeneous. Solow (1957) and others following him do not allow for quality differences in their measurement of quantity of inputs. Since Jorgenson's assumptions about the aggregate production function are strictly neoclassical (in particular, returns to scale are assumed to be constant and externalities are virtually absent), the fact that he is able to explain most of the observed growth in the United States by growth of inputs appropriately measured suggests that, if his framework is accepted, the analytical innovations of recent growth theory need not be invoked to explain growth performance!

Unfortunately, it is not simple to decide whether Jorgenson's framework or other frameworks that maintain neoclassical assumptions are indeed the appropriate ones. After reviewing the conventional methodology of the measurement of technical progress and growth accounting and the results of the growth-accounting exercises of various authors, Boskin and Lau point to two major

> pitfalls of maintaining the traditional assumptions of constant returns to scale, neutrality of technical progress and profit maximization with competitive output and input markets in the measurement of technical progress and growth accounting. First, . . . for an economy in which aggregate real output and inputs are all growing over time, it is in general difficult to identify separately the effects of returns to scale and technical progress—either one can be used as a substitute explanation for the other. Thus, to the extent that there are increasing returns to scale, maintaining the hypothesis of constant returns to scale results in an over estimate of technical progress; and to the extent there are decreasing returns to scale, maintaining the hypothesis results in an underestimate. . . . A further implication (of maintaining constant returns to scale when there are increasing returns to scale) is that the contributions of the capital and labor inputs to economic growth will also be underestimated. The reverse is true if there are decreasing returns to scale.
>
> Second, . . . if technical progress is non-neutral, then the rate of technical progress at time *t* will vary depending on the quantities of capital and labor inputs at time *t*. Moreover, technical progress by many periods cannot be expressed simply as a cumulative sum of the technical progress that has occurred over the individual periods, nor can it be expressed simply as an average (Boskin and Lau 1992a, 24).

In a series of papers, Boskin and Lau (1992a, 1992b) and Kim and Lau (1992a, 1992b, 1992c) apply "a new framework for analysis of productivity and technical progress, based on the direct econometric estimation of an aggregate meta–production function, that does not require the traditionally maintained assumption. . . . This new approach enables the separate identification of not only the degree of returns to scale and the rate of technical progress . . . but also their biases, if any" (Boskin and Lau 1992a, 33).

Their application (Boskin and Lau 1992b) to the Group of Five countries (France, West Germany, Japan, the United Kingdom, and the United States) shows that, while the assumption that all countries have the same underlying meta–production function of the transcendental logarithmic form cannot be rejected, traditional growth-accounting assumptions are all rejected. Returns to scale are found to be sharply diminishing, and technical progress may be represented as purely capital augmenting and capital saving rather than labor saving. Their growth-accounting exercise leads them to conclude that technical progress is found to be the most important source of growth, accounting for more than 45 percent, followed by growth of capital input. Kim and Lau (1992c) apply the same approach to nine countries including the Group of Five and the four East Asian newly industrialized countries (NICs)—Hong Kong, Singapore, South Korea, and Taiwan. Interestingly, they find that the hypothesis of a single meta–production function applying to all nine countries cannot be rejected. While they reaffirm the findings of Boskin and Lau that technical progress can be represented as purely capital augmenting, they cannot reject the hypothesis that there has been no technical progress in the NICs, with more than 80 percent of their economic growth being explained by capital accumulation.

It has long been argued (Mahalanobis 1955; Rosenberg 1963) that the cost of equipment (and alternatively investment in equipment) might have an important role to play in the growth process. Indeed, in arguing for the establishment of a domestic heavy machinery industry, Mahalanobis insisted that "for rapid industrialization of an under-developed country it would be desirable to keep the cost of capital goods as low as possible. The further removed the type of capital goods under consideration is from the production of final consumer goods the greater is the need of keeping the price low. Heavy machinery which would manufacture machinery to produce investment goods is the furthest removed from the consumption end" (Mahalanobis 1955, 51).

Interestingly enough, some economic historians have attributed the Western success in industrialization to the development of heavy industries, particularly those producing machine tools and capital goods. In words that echo Mahalanobis's, quoted above, Nathan Rosenberg asserts that "a major handicap of underdeveloped countries, then, is located in their inability to produce investment goods at prices sufficiently low to assure a reasonable rate of return on prospective investments. Reasoning symmetrically, of the most significant propelling forces in the growth of currently high-income countries has been the technological dynamism of their capital goods industries which has maintained the marginal efficiency of capital at a high level" (Rosenberg 1963, 226).

More recently DeLong and Summers (1991) found that variations in investment in equipment explained a significant part of the variations in economic growth in countries. Kim and Lau (1992b) test a version of a related hypothesis, namely, that technical progress is embodied in new investments so that it can affect the output of an economy only through the form of new capital goods. They found, using an aggregate meta–production model incorporating vintage effects, that the hypothesis of no embodied technical progress can be rejected for the Group of Five countries, with the vintage effect; namely, the productivity of new equipment relative to that in the preceding period is higher by 4 to 5 percent. The contribution of embodied technical progress to growth was found to range from 55 percent for Japan to 70 percent for the other four countries.

The studies by Lau and his coauthors, on the one hand, restore a significant role for productivity growth in explaining aggregate growth, but on the other, they find little productivity growth in NICs. This creates a problem for those who attribute the spectacular growth of NICs to the dynamic productivity gains arising from their outward orientation!

The time-series–cum–cross-section analyses of growth by Jorgenson and by Lau and his coauthors have the virtue that the econometric model they estimate is derived from a well-specified theory and, further, that the possibility of testing the specification is also present. Unfortunately, many recent cross-sectional analyses of growth using "data" from literally a hundred or more countries (e.g., Barro and Lee 1994 include 133 countries in growth-rate regressions) are rarely based on a well-specified theoretical model. For example, inclusion of variables such as school attainment of the population or some measure of educational stock is motivated merely by appeals to the role of human capital in growth. However, without an analytical framework that formalizes the process of human capital accumulation (e.g., learning by doing) and how it relates to *aggregate* growth in different economies, it is impossible to infer anything meaningful from the significant statistical significance (or lack thereof) of the estimated parameter associated with the human capital variable.

Indeed, as Lucas (1993) points out in his extremely stimulating paper, "establishing the importance of learning by doing for productivity growth on a specific production process is very different from establishing its importance for an entire economy as a whole, or even an entire sector" (252–53). In attempting to explain episodes of sustained and rapid growth over nearly three decades, as in East Asian economies, Lucas correctly suggests that one needs a theory that incorporates the *possibility* of rapid growth episodes, but that at the same time does not imply their occurrence as a simple consequence of the relative backwardness of the countries experiencing them. In his view, a successful theory should be as consistent with the experience of Korea, with its rapid growth since the mid-1960s, as with that of the Philippines, which experienced no such growth, although both economies started from roughly similar situations. Lucas finds that models of technical learning with spillover such as those of Stokey (1988), Young (1991), and Grossman and Helpman

(1991) constitute such a theory. Whether or not this is the case, the cross-sectional growth analysts, by the very fact of their estimating the same model using data from many countries, *assume* that the theory, if any, that is implicit in the estimated model is applicable to all of them! For example, Mankiw et al. (1992) go as far as to *assume* that the *sum* of the rates of labor-augmenting technical progress and depreciation of capital are the *same* (i.e., 5 percent per year) *across* 98 *countries* ranging from Angola to Zimbabwe and *over time,* between 1960 and 1985!

In a series of papers Levine and Renelt (1991, 1992) and Levine and Zervos (1993a, 1993b) have thoroughly reviewed the methodological, conceptual, and statistical problems of, as well as isolated what they deem "robust" findings from, cross-country studies. The data and measurement problems are far more serious than they realize. For example, in the cross-country study of growth by Barro and Lee (1994) the variables considered include school attainment, life expectancy at birth, and infant mortality in 1965, 1975, and 1985. In Sen's (1993) study of "regress," the change in the rate of mortality of children under five years during 1965–91 is an important indicator. Unfortunately, the authors do not recognize that the data they use for many developing countries are at best projections and certainly not actual observations. According to the United Nations (1991), relatively reliable and recent (i.e., a reference period of 1980 or later) data for estimating life expectancy at birth (respectively, infant mortality) are not available for as many as 87 (respectively, 65) out of 177 less-developed countries, many of which are included in the Barro and Lee (1994) study! The same source points out that reliable data on levels of mortality under age five are not available for 29 countries, and available data related to a period prior to 1980 for as many as 54 out of the same 117 countries. UNESCO (1991) finds that, out of a total of 145 countries (including developed countries), for 19 no data exist on adult literacy since 1970 and for 41 the latest data relate to a year in the decade 1970–79!

Many of the cross-country studies use GDP data based on the PPP exchange rate, put together by Summers and Heston (1988, 1991). Although Summers and Heston are careful to list the problems with their data, including in particular identifying commodities that are close to being identical in different countries so that they can be priced out using a common set of prices, users pay scant attention to their warnings (see the appendix). It is one thing to adjust for international differences in *price* structures as Summers and Heston do. But what they do not adjust for, and what in many cases is more serious, are *biases* in measurement of quantities (Srinivasan 1993b). Indeed Summers and Heston (1991) themselves assign a quality rating of D+ or D to the data of 66 out of their 138 countries, most of which are less-developed countries, 37 of them African countries. Data on investment are particularly unreliable. Biases, as well as measurement errors, might vary in an unknown fashion over time and across countries, and obviously such variations have implications for growth regressions.

Levine and Renelt (1992) and Levine and Zervos (1993b) use the methodology of extreme-bound analysis pioneered by Edward Leamer for distinguishing "robust" from "fragile" relationships between policy and outcome indicators. In this methodology, in a cross-country regression, a set of basic explanatory variables, *I,* is always included and *Z* is a set of up to three explanatory variables chosen from a pool of policy indicators. *M* is the policy indicator of particular interest. If the coefficient of *M* in the regression is consistently significant and of the same sign as the set of *Z* variables is varied over the pool of policy indicators, then the relationship between the dependent variable and policy indicator *M* is deemed "robust," otherwise it is "fragile." The motivation for this is the finding in Levine and Renelt (1992) that small changes in the explanatory variables produce different conclusions about the relationship between individual policies and growth outcomes in cross-country studies. While the motivation is admirable and the procedure certainly interesting, there are conceptual problems with the procedure. In principle, the use of different sets of variables to explain the *same* dependent variable imply different "models" of growth. As such, the sign, as well as the statistical significance, of the coefficient of a given variable *M* is thus model specific. Should the sign or significance change as "models" are changed, does it imply that the relationship between *M* and the dependent variable should be viewed as fragile? I think not: The reason is that the sign itself may be specific to the model, and certainly the test of significance is model specific. For example, the same policy variable *M* may be positively related to growth in one model or theory of growth as represented by the other variables included, and negatively related in another. This problem does not disappear, even if the policy variables included in the pool are of the same "genre" (i.e., trade policy, financial policy, etc.) as *M.*

It is worth recognizing that policy indicators as well as some of the other variables often included in cross-country regressions are *endogenous.* In studies involving cross sections repeated over time, country-specific effects (fixed or random) are sometimes included. Since the other explanatory variables (particularly policy variables) might plausibly correlate with country-specific effects as Deaton (1995) points out, the random effects estimator will be inconsistent. On the other hand, if these effects are treated as *fixed,* removing fixed effects by differencing introduces a correlation between the disturbance term in the differenced regression and its explanatory variables, if the latter include lagged values of the dependent variable. If the number of time periods over which the cross sections are repeated is small relative to the number of countries included in each cross section, the fixed effect estimate will also be inconsistent. Not all analysts address such problems by the use of appropriate econometric techniques, such as the use of instrumental variables. Even those who do rarely report how good the instruments actually used were and how robust the results were to changes in the instruments.

2.4 Conclusions and Policy Implications

The purpose of the cross-country regression analysis is not only to "explain" the growth process and its determinants but also presumably to derive policy lessons. In an earlier set of studies, Chenery (1960) and Chenery and Syrquin (1975, 1989) suggested that their cross-country regression "can be thought of as reduced forms of a more detailed general equilibrium system" (Chenery and Syrquin 1975, 10) and viewed their analysis as leading "to the identification of three main patterns of resource allocation identified . . . as: *large country, balanced allocation; small country, primary specialization; small country, industry specialization*" (1975, 4). In inferring a typology of development patterns from a policy perspective, these authors were eclectic since they were aware that causal interpretation of reduced-form relationships is hazardous. Their inferences were based on comparing countries that are following similar development patterns and the policies chosen by countries under similar conditions.

There can be no doubt that the recent contributions to the theory and empirical analysis of the process of growth have substantially increased our knowledge about the analytics of growth and the potential role of human capital accumulation, investment in research and development, international trade, and externalities and scale economies (arising in part from nonrivalry and nonexcludability in use of knowledge) in the growth process. Whether public policy intervention in the economy is called for from the perspective of influencing the growth process and, if so, what the character of such intervention should be are issues on which recent work has provided some valuable insights; but understandably, no conclusive answers have yet emerged. For example, if the contribution of *endogenous* factor accumulation is *small* and an overwhelming share of observed growth is due to *exogenous* technical progress, as in the Solow (1957) story of U.S. growth, there is little that public policy could do to affect the growth process significantly. In contrast, if most of growth could be attributed to factor accumulation (physical and human), as in Jorgenson (1990), then public policy intervention could influence growth. This is not to say either that the U.S. experience is likely to be repeated in the developing world or that public policy intervention is desirable from a welfare perspective.

To take another example, it is undeniable that the East Asian economies of Hong Kong, Korea, Singapore, and Taiwan have not only grown substantially faster than almost all other developing countries over the three decades since 1960, but also shown rapid and sustained growth that is historically unprecedented. Whether it is a miracle, as a recent study (World Bank 1993) and Lucas (1993) deem it, is arguable. All four countries had two things in common in their policy, namely, their emphasis on human capital and on outward orientation, while they differed in the extent of government intervention in markets, ranging from no intervention in Hong Kong to extensive intervention in Korea.

The nature of their regimes differed as well, although all were authoritarian to a considerable extent. Analogous to the Solow-Jorgenson differences in accounting for U.S. growth, in the case of East Asia some find substantial contribution of total factor productivity growth to total growth, whereas Kim and Lau (1992c) and Young (1993) find factor accumulation (human and physical capital) accounting for most of their growth. To what extent their outward orientation and public policy interventions contributed to their unprecedented growth is a matter of intensive debate as well, with some (e.g., Anderson 1989) emphasizing that interventions in the economy succeeded only where they met the test of competitiveness in world markets and the World Bank (1993) being in the middle!

Cross-country regressions testing some version or the other of the convergence hypothesis relating to *aggregate* growth, whatever other insights they have yielded about the growth process, by their very nature have little to say about the microeconomic forces that together generate the aggregate outcome. Here again the observations of Lucas are pertinent:

> I do not intend these conjectures about the implications of a learning spillover technology for small countries facing given world prices to be a substitute for the actual construction of such a theory. . . . What is the nature of human capital accumulation decision problems faced by workers, capitalists and managers? What are the external consequences of the decisions they take? The purpose cited here considers a variety of possible assumptions on these economic issues, but it must be said that little is known, and without such knowledge there is little we can say about the way policies that affect incentives can be expected to influence economic growth (Lucas 1993, 270).

Appendix
The Summers-Heston Data

There are two extrapolations involved in the Summers-Heston data: the first from *benchmark countries* (which varied from 16 in 1970 to 56 in 1985) to *other countries* for the benchmark year, and the second, from *benchmark years* (1970, 1975, 1980, and 1985) to *other years* in the period 1960–85 (Summers and Heston 1991, app. A-2).

For the first, they use "capital city price surveys conducted around the world by the United Nations International Civil Service Commission, a British firm serving an association of international businesses, and the U.S. State Department" (1991, 341). While recognizing that "the price indexes appropriate for this very special population—high-income non-nationals, living usually in capital cities—does not properly reflect all the prices in the country, of course, nor do the individual price weights reflect the relative importance of the individual goods in the countries for the nationals" (341), they nonetheless found a structural relationship "in the benchmark country's PPP and its postallowance PPP" and exploited it "to estimate for the non-benchmark countries missing PPP's from their post allowance PPP's" (342).

For the second, they go from a benchmark year, say 1985, to other years "by applying the relevant growth rates from the constant-price national accounts series—the values for the year of interest divided by the corresponding 1985 ones—to the 1985 number" (343). As is well known, using one set of prices as opposed to another in appraising growth performance can lead to biases. For example, if the domestic price structure deviates significantly from world prices (assumed to be constant over time for simplicity) because of distortionary nonoptimal tariff policies, the production possibility frontier could unambiguously shift outward and real GDP at domestic prices could show *growth* from one period to the next, while the same outputs evaluated at world prices, show a *decline* (Bhagwati and Hansen 1973). In any case, Summers and Heston correctly caution that "growth rates based on international prices can differ significantly from those based on national prices, but when they do, it is nearly always the case that relative prices within the countries have changed substantially over the period" (1991, 361). I might add that rapid development over an extended period will almost always involve substantial changes in relative prices, particularly of the basket of internationally traded goods relative to nontraded goods.

References

Abramovitz, M. 1956. Resource and output trends in the United States since 1870. *American Economic Review* 46: 5–23.

Ahmad, Syed. 1966. On the theory of induced innovation. *Economic Journal* 76: 344–57.

Anderson, A. 1989. *Asia's next giant: South Korea and late industrialization.* New York: Oxford University Press.

Arrow, K. J. 1962. The economic implications of learning by doing. *Review of Economic Studies* 29: 155–73.

Arrow, K. J., H. B. Chenery, B. S. Minhas, and R. M. Solow. 1961. Capital labor substitution and economic efficiency. *Review of Economics and Statistics* 63: 225–47.

Azariadis, C., and A. Drazen. 1990. Threshold externalities in economic development. *Quarterly Journal of Economics* 105: 501–26.

Barro, R. J. 1989. Economic growth in a cross section of countries. NBER Working Paper no. 3120. Cambridge, Mass.: National Bureau of Economic Research.

Barro, R. J., and J. Lee. 1994. Losers and winners in economic growth. In *Proceedings of the World Bank Annual Conference on Development Economics, 1993. World Bank Economic Review,* Supplement: 267–97.

Barro, R. J., and X. Sala-i-Martin. 1992. Convergence. *Journal of Political Economy* 100 (2): 223–51.

Baumol, W. J. 1986. Productivity growth, convergence and welfare: What the long run data show? *American Economic Review* 76 (December): 1072–85.
Becker, G. S., Kevin M. Murphy, and Robert Tamura. 1990. Human capital, fertility, and economic growth. *Journal of Political Economy* 98, no. 5 (October): S12–S37.
Benhabib, J., and B. Jovanovic. 1991. Externalities and growth accounting. *American Economic Review* 81 (1): 82–113.
Bernstein, J., and M. Nadiri. 1989. Research and development and intraindustry spillovers: An empirical implication of dynamic duality. *Review of Economic Studies* 56: 249–68.
Bhagwati, J., and B. Hansen. 1973. Should growth rates be evaluated at world prices? In *Development and planning,* ed. J. N. Bhagwati and R. S. Eckaus, 53–68. Cambridge: MIT Press.
Boserup, E. 1965. *The conditions of agricultural growth.* Chicago: Aldine.
———. 1981. *Population and technical change: A study of long-term trends.* Chicago: University of Chicago Press.
Boskin, M. J., and L. J. Lau. 1992a. Capital, technology, and economic growth. In *Technology and wealth of nations,* ed. N. Rosenberg, R. Landau, and D. Mowery, 17–55. Stanford, Calif.: Stanford University Press.
———. 1992b. Post-war economic growth in the Group-of-Five countries: A new analysis. Department of Economics, Stanford University. Processed.
Cass, D. 1965. Optimum growth in an aggregative model of capital accumulation. *Review of Economic Studies* 32: 233–40.
Chenery, H. 1960. Patterns of industrial growth. *American Economic Review* 50 (September): 624–54.
Chenery, H., and M. Syrquin. 1975. *Patterns of development 1950–1970.* London: Oxford University Press.
———. 1989. *Patterns of development: 1950 to 1983.* Washington, D.C.: World Bank.
Deaton, A. 1995. Data and econometric tools for development analysis. In *Handbook of Development Economics,* vol. 3, ed. T. N. Srinivasan and J. Behrman. Amsterdam: North-Holland. In press.
DeLong, B. J. 1988. Productivity growth, convergence, and welfare. *American Economic Review* 78: 1138–54.
DeLong, B. J., and L. Summers. 1991. Equipment investment and economic growth. *Quarterly Journal of Economics* 106 (May): 445–502.
Denison, E. F. 1962. Sources of economic growth in the United States and the alternatives before us. New York: Committee for Economic Development.
Domar, E. 1947. Expansion and employment. *American Economic Review* 37: 34–55.
———. 1957. *Essays in the theory of economic growth.* London: Oxford University Press.
Dorfman, R., P. Samuelson, and R. Solow. 1958. *Linear programming and economic analysis.* New York: McGraw-Hill.
Dowrick, S., and D. Nguyen. 1989. OECD comparative economic growth 1950–85: Catch-up and convergence. *American Economic Review* 79 (December): 1010–30.
Fel'dman, G. A. 1928. K teorii tempov narodnogo dokhoda. *Planovoe Khoziaistvo* 11: 146–70; 12: 152–78. (Discussed in Domar 1957, chap. 9).
Grossman, G., and E. Helpman. 1990. Comparative advantage and long-run growth. *American Economic Review* 80: 796–815.
———. 1991. *Innovation and growth in the global economy.* Cambridge: MIT Press.
Harrod, R. F. 1939. An essay in dynamic theory. *Economic Journal* 49: 14–33.
Helpman, E. 1992. Endogenous macroeconomic growth theory. *European Economic Review* 36: 237–67.
Jaffe, A. B. 1986. Technological opportunity and spillovers of R&D: Evidence from firms' patents, profits, and market value. *American Economic Review* 76: 984–1001.

Jorgenson, D. 1990. Productivity and economic growth. In *Fifty years of economic measurement: The jubilee of the Conference on Research in Income and Wealth,* ed. E. R. Berndt and J. E. Triplett, chap. 3. Chicago: University of Chicago Press.

Jorgenson, D. W., and Z. Griliches. 1966. Sources of measured productivity change. *American Economic Review* 56: 50–61.

Kaldor, N., and J. Mirrlees. 1962. A new model of economic growth. *Review of Economic Studies* 29 (3): 174–92.

Kennedy, C. 1964. Induced bias in innovation and the theory of distribution. *Economic Journal* 74: 541–47.

Kim, J., and L. J. Lau. 1992a. Human capital and aggregate productivity: Some empirical evidence from the Group of Five countries. Department of Economics, Stanford University. Processed.

———. 1992b. The importance of embodied technical progress: Some empirical evidence from the Group of Five countries. Department of Economics, Stanford University. Processed.

———. 1992c. The sources of economic growth of the newly industrialized countries on the Pacific Rim. Department of Economics, Stanford University. Processed.

Koopmans, T. C. 1965. On the concept of optimal economic growth. In *The econometric approach to development planning,* 225–87. Amsterdam: North-Holland.

Kuznets, S. 1966. *Modern economic growth: Rate, structure and spread.* New Haven, Conn.: Yale University Press.

Levine, R., and D. Renelt. 1991. Cross-country studies of growth and policy: Methodological, conceptual and statistical problems. Working Paper WPS 608. Washington, D.C.: World Bank. Processed.

———. 1992. A sensitivity analysis of cross-country growth regression. *American Economic Review* 82: 942–63.

Levine, R., and S. Zervos. 1993a. Looking at the facts: What we know about policy and growth from cross-country regressions. Working Paper WPS 1115. Washington, D.C.: World Bank. Processed.

———. 1993b. What we have learned about policy and growth from cross-country regressions! *American Economic Review* 84: 426–30.

Lucas, R. E. 1988. On the mechanics of economic development. *Journal of Monetary Economics* 22: 3–42.

———. 1993. Making a miracle. *Econometrica* 61 (2): 251–72.

Mahalanobis, P. C. 1955. The approach of operational research to planning in India. *Sankhya: Indian Journal of Statistics* 16: 3–62.

Mankiw, N. G., D. Romer, and D. Weil. 1992. A contribution to the empirics of economic growth. *Quarterly Journal of Economics* 107 (2): 407–37.

Minhas, B. S. 1963. *An international comparison of factor cost and factor use.* Amsterdam: North-Holland.

Phelps, E. S. 1961. The golden rule of accumulation: A fable for growthmen. *American Economic Review* 51: 638–43.

Radner, R. 1961. Paths of economic growth that are optimal with regard only to final states: A turnpike theorem. *Review of Economic Studies* 28: 98–104.

Ramsey, F. P. 1928. A mathematical theory of saving. *Economic Journal* 38: 543–59.

Raut, L. 1985. Three essays on inter-temporal economic development. Doctoral dissertation. Graduate School, Yale University.

———. 1991a. Capital accumulation, income distribution, and endogenous fertility in an overlapping generations general equilibrium model. *Journal of Development Economics* 34: 123–50.

———. 1991b. R&D spillover and productivity growth: Evidence from Indian private firms. Department of Economics, University of California, San Diego. Processed.

Raut, L., and Srinivasan, T. N. 1991. Endogenous fertility, technical change and growth in a model of overlapping generations. Economic Growth Center Discussion Paper no. 628. Yale University.

———. 1993. Long run theories of growth: Old and new. In *Capital investment and development: Essays in memory of Sukhamoy Chakravarty,* ed. K. Basu, M. Majumdar, and T. Mitra, 3–32. London: Basil Blackwell.

Romer, P. M. 1986. Increasing returns and long-run growth. *Journal of Political Economy* 94 (5): 1002–37.

———. 1990. Endogenous technological change. *Journal of Political Economy* 98, no. 5 (October): S71–S102.

Rosenberg, N. 1963. Capital goods, technology, and economic growth. *Oxford Economic Papers* 15: 217–27.

Schumpeter, J. 1942. *Capitalism, socialism and democracy.* New York: Harper.

Sen, A. K. 1993. Economic regress: Concepts and features. Paper presented at the annual World Bank Conference on Development Economics. Washington, D.C.: World Bank. Processed.

Sheshinski, E. 1967. Optimal accumulation with learning by doing. In *Essays on the theory of optimal growth,* ed. K. Shell. Cambridge: MIT Press.

Simon, J. L. 1981. *The ultimate resource.* Princeton, N.J.: Princeton University Press.

Solow, R. M. 1956. A contribution to the theory of economic growth. *Quarterly Journal of Economics* 70: 65–94.

———. 1957. Technical change and the aggregate production function. *Review of Economics and Statistics* 39: 312–20.

Srinivasan, T. N. 1962. Investment criteria and choice of techniques of production. *Yale Economic Essays* 32: 59–115.

———. 1964. Optimal savings in a two-sector model of growth. *Econometrica* 2: 358–73.

———. 1993a. Comments on Paul Romer, "Two strategies for economic development: Using ideas vs. producing ideas." In *Proceedings of the World Bank Conference on Development Economics, 1992. World Bank Economic Review,* Supplement: 103–9.

———. 1993b. Data base for development analysis: An overview. Paper presented at the Conference on Data Base for Developed Analysis. Economic Growth Center, Yale University. Processed.

Stiglitz, J. 1990. Comments: Some retrospective views on growth theory. In *Growth/productivity/unemployment,* ed. P. Diamond. Cambridge: MIT Press.

Stokey, N. 1988. Learning by doing and the introduction of new goods. *Journal of Political Economy* 96: 701–17.

Summers, R., and Heston, A. 1988. A new set of international comparisons of real product and price levels: Estimates for 130 countries. *Review of Income and Wealth* 34: 1–25.

———. 1991. The Penn World Table (Mark 5): An expanded set of international comparisons, 1950–1988. *Quarterly Journal of Economics* 106: 327–68.

UNESCO. 1991. *Statistical year book, 1991.* Paris: UNESCO.

United Nations. 1991. *World population monitoring 1990.* New York: United Nations.

Uzawa, H. 1961. On a two-sector model of economic growth. Part I. *Review of Economic Studies* 29: 40–47.

———. 1963. On a two-sector model of economic growth. Part II. *Review of Economic Studies* 30: 105–18.

———. 1964. Optimum growth in a two-sector model of capital accumulation. *Review of Economic Studies* 31: 1–24.

———. 1965. Optimum technical change in an aggregative model of economic growth. *International Economic Review* 6: 18–31.

von Neumann, J. 1945. A model of general equilibrium. *Review of Economic Studies* 13: 1–9.
World Bank. 1993. *The East Asian miracle.* Washington, D.C.: World Bank.
Young, A. 1991. Learning by doing and the dynamic effects of international trade. *Quarterly Journal of Economics* 106: 369–406.
———. 1993. Lessons from the East Asian NIC's: A contrarian view. NBER Working Paper no. 4482. Cambridge, Mass.: National Bureau of Economic Research.

Comment Paul M. Romer

Research on economic growth alternates between periods of boom and bust. These fluctuations disrupt the cumulative nature of scientific inquiry. When a topic like growth goes out of fashion, much of what is known in the area is not transmitted to students. Then when activity picks up, a new generation of researchers wastes time rediscovering results that have previously been established.

This inefficiency can be reduced if there are economists who can span more than one boom in research on growth. The profession is fortunate to have such a scholar in T. N. Srinivasan. He made important contributions to the theory of growth during the 1960s. The work with Lakshmi Raut described here shows that he is doing so once again in the 1990s. This particular paper uses the experience acquired in the first round to comment on recent developments in growth theory. Any economist who was not active in growth theory during the 1950s and 1960s can learn from what he has to say.

Srinivasan makes two general points. As the title suggests, one is about theory and the other is about empirics. The warning about the empirical work is easy to state and hard to dispute: The cross-country data on aggregate measures such as growth rates, literacy rates, and life expectancy suffer from many deficiencies.

Srinivasan would no doubt agree that there is something to be learned from cross-country data. For example, when I was a graduate student, I was taught that there was no correlation in the data between aggregate rates of investment and the rate of growth of income per capita. Now we know that this correlation is quite strong and survives all attempts to hold constant the effects of other variables. Of course, correlation does not resolve questions about causality. Many different theories of growth are consistent with this new addition to our list of stylized facts about growth. But if one is going to use stylized facts, it is surely better to rely on ones that are true instead of ones that are false.

That being said, Srinivasan is correct in arguing that some of the claims

Paul M. Romer is professor of economics at the University of California, Berkeley, and a research associate of the National Bureau of Economic Research.

derived from an analysis of the cross-country data are too strong. There is important measurement error in the underlying data. Empirical analyses would be more useful if they took explicit account of this fact.

I will direct the balance of my comments to the theoretical point in this paper. It can be summarized as follows. All models that exhibit growth at a constant exponential rate contain an equation of the form

$$\frac{dX}{dt} = \_\_X(t). \tag{1}$$

All the disagreement is about the expression that fills in the blank and the name that is attached to the variable X. This equation, or the variable X itself, is often given the colorful label "the engine of growth." When the theory fills in the blank with an expression that remains constant over time, $X(t)$ grows at a constant exponential rate. True to its name as an engine, $X(t)$ pulls the rest of the economy along with it.

In a model with exogenous technological change, $X(t)$ is the level of the technology at date t and a constant—the rate of exogenous technological change—fills in the blank. Linear growth models treat X as a capital good (or a vector of capital goods) and fill in the blank with an expression that depends on the savings or investment rate. Models based on human capital accumulation give a corresponding label to X and fill in the blank with an expression that depends on investment in schooling or on-the-job training. Models of intentional research and development interpret X as a measure of technology and fill in the blank with an expression that depends on research effort.

In this context, the difference between endogenous and exogenous growth models is easy to describe. Exogenous growth models fill in the blank with a constant that is a fundamental parameter of the economy. Endogenous growth models fill it in with an expression that is a function of other basic parameters of the model, including parameters that can be changed by policymakers.

Srinivasan's theoretical point is that there is nothing new about endogenous growth models per se. For decades, there have been models that fill in the blank with an expression that depends on preferences and policy variables. If the construction of an endogenous growth model were the only goal of growth theory, then we could have stopped after John von Neumann presented his linear growth model at a seminar in Princeton in 1932.[1]

Srinivasan reproaches recent growth theorists for claiming that the construction of an endogenous growth rate is an important research achievement. If there are any growth theorists still making this claim, they deserve the rebuke.

1. The paper was not published in German until 1938, when Karl Menger invited von Neumann to submit it to a collection of papers. It was not published in English until 1945 (von Neumann 1945). One suspects that von Neumann felt that a problem that, from a mathematical point of view, could be reduced to eq. (1) was too trivial to bother submitting for publication.

Doing so suggests that our methodological preferences should be lexicographic; any endogenous growth model should dominate an exogenous growth model. In fact, the challenge for growth theory is not to produce a model with this particular property—that policy can influence the growth rate. The fundamental goal must be to formulate new models that are right, or at least closer to being right, than existing models.

I can clearly remember the classroom interaction that first pushed me in the direction of work on economic growth. It was not an *exogenous* growth model that I objected to, but an *endogenous* growth model. The professor had just finished presenting the von Neumann model. I interjected that it was obviously a stupid model of growth. Pressed to give a somewhat more articulate description of the model's failings, I set to work on a project that has kept me busy for 15 years.

In retrospect, it is clear that I did not appreciate the subtlety of von Neumann's early contribution to general equilibrium theory. (It is also clear that I was not very tactful.) But all my subsequent work persuades me that my harsh judgment of the model as a model of growth was correct. In the von Neumann model, a vector of goods X can produce a new vector of goods $X' = aX$ for some number $a > 1$. In place of a discussion of new products, new processes, universities, private research labs, patent law, scientific inquiry—all the things that seemed to me then and still seem to me now to be at the heart of economic growth—the model blithely offers up an attractive mathematical assumption that cannot be given any meaningful interpretation.

It is this kind of assumption, one that violates the most obvious facts about the world, that leaves economists open to ridicule. If economists start from assumptions about production that violate physical laws about the conservation of mass—that let goods reproduce like rabbits with an infinite food supply—why should anyone take what we say seriously? It was this kind of analysis by mainstream economists that provoked the equally misleading analysis of the environmental alarmists of the 1970s. They predicted that we were on the verge of economic catastrophe because our food supply (i.e., our natural resources) was running out.

By now it should be beyond dispute that economic growth takes place because people find more valuable ways to make use of the raw materials that have always been available to us in the crust of the earth and in the atmosphere. We have a standard of living that is higher than that of our grandparents, not because we have more stuff—more mass—but because we have learned to do interesting things like make memory chips from existing stuff like silicon. When we rearrange the silicon by growing it in a crystal and mixing it with a few other elements, we make it much more valuable.

Once one starts to think this way, it is clear that a neoclassical model that allows for technological progress is a significant improvement over a linear model like von Neumann's, in which a fixed set of goods breeds ever larger quantities of these same goods. In the long run, the fundamental driving force in our economy is change in what we know, and the neoclassical model highlights a crucial mathematical implication of treating knowledge as an economic good. When we use an expression of the form $Y = AF(K, L)$ or $Y = F(K, BL)$ and admit that F is a constant-returns-to-scale production function, we implicitly acknowledge that aggregate output is not a concave function of *K, L, and A* or *B*.

So if one takes the economics of discovery, innovation, and invention seriously, a neoclassical model with technological change is clearly to be preferred to a model with a fixed set of goods that replicate like rabbits. This is true despite the fact that the neoclassical model makes the rate of growth exogenous and the linear model makes it endogenous. The neoclassical model gets important parts of the economics of growth right in a way that the linear model does not.

But as anyone with any sense will admit, the neoclassical model with exogenous technological change is not the end of the story. The next step is to construct models that can explain where technological change comes from and explore the economic implications of the nonconvexity that the neoclassical model exhibits and then ignores.

It is true that some recent models of growth do little more than revive the von Neumann model and label one of the capital stocks human capital. This is not very helpful. It is these models that Srinivasan justifiably criticizes. But much of the recent work has been concerned with a serious attempt to characterize the economics of processes like learning, discovery, and the diffusion of knowledge.

The goods in the von Neumann model are entirely conventional. Recent models recognize that knowledge or discoveries or ideas are goods that differ from conventional goods in two very important ways. First, it is difficult to establish property rights over these goods—hence the emphasis on spillovers and external effects. Second, in the language of public finance, these goods are also nonrival goods, so they are intrinsically associated with nonconvexities.

We have not yet reached consensus about how to write down a model that blends elements like learning by doing, knowledge spillovers, patents, explicit research and development, and government support for science. But we are once again making a serious effort toward reaching this goal.

So the answer to the question posed in the title of Srinivasan's paper is unambiguously yes. There is something new in long-run growth theory. As he suggests, it does not lie merely in the construction of endogenous growth models. Instead, it comes from efforts to understand ideas and knowledge. Microeconomists have known for some time that the economics of ideas and knowledge differs in important ways from the familiar economics of objects. What growth theory has established is that these differences can be of decisive importance for an analysis of the economy as a whole. We now know that we cannot keep relegating the issues they raise to the footnotes. We cannot content ourselves with bland calls for additional research that we never get around to doing. The economics of ideas can change how we think about fundamental policy issues in growth and development. A great deal is at stake if we get the basic policy answers wrong.

Reference

von Neumann, J. 1945. A model of general equilibrium. *Review of Economic Studies* 13: 1–9.

II Understanding Growth in Individual Countries

3 The Open Door Policy and China's Rapid Growth: Evidence from City-Level Data

Shang-Jin Wei

China was one of the fastest growing economies in the 1980s. The average annual growth rate of (inflation-adjusted) GDP for China from 1980–90 was 9.5 percent. The corresponding growth rate for the world as a whole was 3.1 percent (World Bank 1992, 221, table 2). The growth rate for China in 1992 was 12.6 percent.

The rapid growth in China is obviously related to its relentless (but not necessarily consistent) pursuit of economic reform, which has unleashed productive forces previously suppressed by rigid central planning. One particularly important component of the reform program is China's open door policy. Indeed, China is literally a textbook example of export-led growth.[1]

The modest objective of this paper is to ascertain answers to two questions. First, what is the contribution of exports and foreign investment to rapid industrial growth in China? Second, is there any spillover effect from exports or foreign investment? Because the 12-year reform period is relatively short, it is difficult to do statistical analysis based on the limited number of aggre-

Shang-Jin Wei is assistant professor of public policy at the John F. Kennedy School of Government, Harvard University, and faculty research fellow of the National Bureau of Economic Research.

The author thanks John Page, Takatoshi Ito, Anne Krueger, and other participants at the Fourth Annual East Asian Seminar on Economics, in San Francisco, for helpful comments, Sarah Cook for constructive comments and proofreading, and Xiongbai Fan for efficient research assistance. Part of the research was conducted during a visit to the Research Department of the Federal Reserve Bank of San Francisco. The author gratefully acknowledges support from the Center for Pacific Basin Monetary and Economic Studies, the Federal Reserve Bank of San Francisco, and Harvard University's William F. Milton Fund. None of the above named individuals or institutions is responsible for the views, and in particular the errors, in this paper.

1. In a widely used textbook on international economics (Krugman and Obstfeld 1991, 247), the authors wrote that Chinese economic growth in the 1980s "amounted to a virtual economic miracle—and a classical demonstration of the potential of export-oriented industrialization."

gate observations. One small innovation of this paper is to employ city-level data.[2]

To preview the conclusions of the paper, I have found some clear evidence that during 1980–90 more exports are positively associated with higher growth rates across Chinese cities. In the late 1980s, the contribution to growth comes mainly from foreign investment. Furthermore, the contribution of foreign investment comes in the form of technological or managerial spillovers across firms as opposed to an infusion of new capital. Finally, the superb growth rates of coastal areas relative to the national average can be entirely explained by their effective use of exports and foreign investment.

The rest of the paper is organized as follows. In section 3.1, the process of opening to the outside world is briefly reviewed. Section 3.2 discusses a minimalist conceptual framework that will be used to assess statistically the contribution of the open door policy to rapid Chinese growth. In section 3.3, the two data sets are described. Sections 3.4 and 3.5 present and interpret the statistical results from the two samples. Section 3.6 concludes the paper.

3.1 Opening Up the Chinese Economy in the 1980s

To assess the contribution of the Chinese open door policy, it is useful to review briefly the path China has taken in this direction.[3] In 1978, China was ranked thirty-second in the world in export volume. In 1989, it became the world's thirteenth largest exporter. Its share of world trade almost doubled during this period. Between 1978 and 1990, the average annual rate of trade expansion was above 15 percent, more than three times higher than that of total world trade (Lardy 1992).

This change in the degree of outward orientation is truly remarkable, particularly when one considers China's strong aversion to trade and foreign investment before the reform.[4] China's trade regime before 1978 was an extreme version of import substitution. Many official statements made this very explicit. One official in 1955 said that "the purpose of importing . . . is to lay the foundation of China's industrial independence, so that in the future China can produce all of the producer goods it needs and will not have to rely on imports from the outside" (Lardy 1992).

A few characteristics highlight the nature of the prereform trade regime:

2. There are 434 and 74 cities in the two data sets. After a draft of this paper was completed, I learned that Wang (1993) was using data on 231 cities and Wang and Mody (1993) have used data on seven coastal provinces to assess Chinese growth.

3. For an excellent discussion of the prereform trade system during 1950–78 and the evolution of trade reform in the 1980s, see Sung (1991), Lardy (1992), and Cheng (1992). The first book has also expertly delineated the important role of Hong Kong in China's drive to open up to the outside world. The following discussion of the evolution of China's trade regime is based mainly on Lardy (1992).

4. Kamm (1989) has described vividly the eerie feeling of doing export and import business with China in the 1970s.

(1) The state monopolized trade through state trade corporations. No firm or individual could export or import goods without the intermediation of one of these corporations. (2) There was no close link between the world and domestic prices of tradable goods. A state trade corporation purchased imports at the world price and sold them domestically at a price determined by a state plan, which typically did not vary with world price or domestic demand. Similarly, a state trade corporation purchased exportable goods from domestic firms at a plan-dictated price and sold them at the world market price. (3) Foreign exchange was tightly controlled by the state. All foreign exchange resulting from exports was retained by the state. All imports had to be part of a state plan to be materialized.

In 1979, China decided to open up to the outside world. Since then, a few important steps have been taken in this effort: (1) The government has decentralized decision making regarding exports and imports to local governments or regional foreign trade corporations. (2) A series of special economic zones and coastal open cities have been designated for the purpose of stimulating exports and attracting foreign investment. (3) Administrative restrictions on exports and imports have been replaced by tariffs, quotas, and licensing. (4) Controls on foreign exchange have been loosened over the years, particularly for foreign-invested/managed firms.

How open has China become after a decade of reform? A common measure of openness is the ratio of trade (exports plus imports) to GNP. If one uses the market exchange rate to convert China's GNP to U.S. dollars, China displays a phenomenal increase in the trade-GNP ratio, from about 9.7 percent in 1978 to 26.8 percent in 1989 (Lardy 1992, 151).

However, as Lardy points out, there are two problems with this ratio. First, the ratio is not useful for a cross-country comparison. Smaller countries tend to have higher ratios even if their government policies are equally favorable (or unfavorable) to trade.[5] Another problem is that using the market exchange rate to convert Chinese GNP may overstate Chinese openness since it underestimates China's true GNP.

Foreign direct investment (FDI) is another manifestation of the open door policy. FDI was virtually nonexistent in the decades preceding 1979. In 1983, the flow of foreign investment was a mere U.S. $1.7 billion. It increased to $5.3 billion in 1988, and to $11.4 billion in 1991. Accumulated FDI from 1979 to 1992 (calculated without depreciation) reached $34.5 billion.[6]

In terms of the source of FDI, Hong Kong is by far the absolutely dominant supplier. Between 1984 and 1990, Hong Kong's share of FDI was above 50

5. To control for the contribution of size or geographic location determinants to trade volume, one may want to use a gravity model to establish a norm of trade volume (e.g., Frankel 1992; Frankel and Wei 1993). Then, the deviation from the norm can be used as a more accurate measure of openness.

6. *Almanac of China's Foreign Economic Relations and Trade* (Hong Kong: China Resources Trade Consultancy, 1990); *People's Daily* (Overseas edition) February 1992, May 31, 1993.

percent for every single year except 1985 when the share was 48.9 percent. Of course, of Hong Kong investment, a fraction is Taiwanese capital in disguise for political reasons, and another fraction is mainland Chinese capital in disguise to take advantage of the preferential treatment of foreign investment in China. But the bulk of it is genuinely from Hong Kong.[7]

Japan is ranked second in terms of its share in total FDI in China, although it is much less significant than Hong Kong (Japan's shares in 1989 and 1990 were 11 and 13 percent). In third place is the United States, which follows Japan closely.

Foreign investment takes several forms. Equity joint ventures, which were an insignificant part of FDI in the early 1980s, accounted for 50 percent of all FDI in 1990. There are also contractual joint ventures, wholly foreign-owned ventures, and joint explorations (mainly in offshore oil explorations). Their shares in FDI in 1990 were 18 percent, 18 percent, and 7 percent, respectively. "Compensation trade," in which foreign firms provide machines or product designs to Chinese firms and obtain part of the output as payment, is also counted as FDI in Chinese statistics, although it is really a kind of barter trade. Compensation trade has become less and less important over time. Its share in FDI has declined from about 20 percent in the early 1980s to less than 5 percent in 1990 (Kueh 1992).

One serious obstacle to China's attracting foreign investment is its imperfect property and contract laws. Legal enforcement is weak in spite of the laws that exist in written form. So far, however, foreign investment has been reasonably robust for two reasons. First, low factor costs and tax concessions can often ensure high returns even in a short time. Second, overseas Chinese can use their connection and familiarity with "Chinese culture" (whatever that is) to get things done without the procedural protection of the laws. The latter is one important reason for Hong Kong's prominence as a source of foreign investment. There is little doubt that foreign investment from other than ethnic Chinese would have been greater had there been a better and more transparent legal environment for business, and improving the creation, and particularly the enforcement, of property and contract laws is important for the continued success of China's open door policy.

Foreign investment, like foreign trade, increasingly exposes Chinese workers and firms to international managerial and technological standards and knowhow. It increases the efficiency, not only of those firms that receive foreign investment or that are under foreign management, but also of those domestic firms that interact with foreign-invested/managed firms through various channels (positive externality), as I will show statistically later. It may also promote growth by alleviating the shortage of domestic savings or foreign exchange.[8]

7. See Kueh (1992), who also provided a comprehensive review of FDI in China and particularly in its coastal areas.

8. Wei and Fan (1993), however, fail to find statistical support for this view using the same 1988–90 city-level data as in this paper.

3.2 A Conceptual Framework

In this section, a minimalist model is set up to guide the subsequent empirical investigation. Let a generic firm j in city k operate with the following production function:

$$Y_{kj} = A_{kj}f(L_{kj}) \equiv A_{kj}Z_{kj},$$

where L_{kj} denotes its labor input and A_{kj} is the productivity shift parameter. $f(\cdot)$ is a twice-differentiable concave function. Capital stock is left out of the production function because no city-level data are available.

Assume that the firm maximizes its profit, taking all prices as given. That is, it maximizes

$$A_{kj}f(L_{kj}) - w_k L_{kj}.$$

In the equilibrium, the firm's growth is governed by

$$\frac{\dot{Y}_{kj}}{Y_{kj}} = \frac{\dot{A}_{kj}}{A_{kj}} + \frac{\dot{Z}_{kj}}{Z_{kj}}.$$

Assume that

$$A_{kj} = A_n A_k,$$

where A_n and A_k are the national and city-level productivity components.[9] Note that for simplicity I have assumed away firm-specific productivity shift. This is to focus attention on those activities whose benefits spill over to other firms or other cities. The growth rate of productivity will then be the sum of the growth rates of the two components.

Assume further that

$$Z_{kj} \equiv f(L_{kj}) = L_{kj}^{\alpha}.$$

Then,

$$\frac{\dot{Z}_{kj}}{Z_{kj}} = \alpha \frac{\dot{L}_{kj}}{L_{kj}}.$$

Let g denote any growth rate. The growth rate of city k can be expressed as a weighted average of the growth rates of all the firms in the city, that is, as

$$\begin{aligned} g_k &\equiv \sum_j s_{kj} g_{kj} = \sum_j s_{kj} g_{A_{kj}} + \sum_j s_{kj} g_{z_{kj}} \\ &= g_{A_n} + g_{A_k} + \alpha\, g_{L_k}, \end{aligned}$$

where s_{kj} is firm j's share in city k's output.

We will focus on a few variables that affect the productivity increase. Let

$$g_{A_k} = f(\text{FDI}_k, \text{Exp}_k, Y_{k0}, H_k),$$

9. This specification is similar to that in Glaeser et al. (1992).

where FDI_k and Exp_k are foreign direct investment in city k and exports by city k, respectively, Y_{k0} is the initial size of the industrial sector in city k, and H_k is the stock of human capital in city k.

Assuming a linear version of $f(\cdot)$, we have the following equation as the basis of our subsequent statistical analyses:

$$g_k = g_{A_n} + \beta_1 \mathrm{FDI}_k + \beta_2 \mathrm{Exp}_k + \beta_3 Y_{k0} + \beta_4 H_k + \alpha\, g_{L_k} + e_k,$$

where e_k is a city-specific error term. The error term is assumed to be independent across cities, but can have different variances.

Having the initial size of an industrial sector, Y_{k0}, in $f(\cdot)$ is a crude way to capture the notions of increasing returns to scale as advanced by Romer (1986), or of learning by doing as emphasized by Young (1991). The larger the initial scale of production, the more productive future production will be.

FDI is a primary mechanism for the transfer of technology from developed countries to developing countries. In the context of China, it is also a primary mechanism for the transfer of foreign management methods and worker discipline into the country. Exports expose exporting firms to the rigor of international competition as well as to new techniques in marketing and processing.

FDI can enter the regressions in one of two ways, as a share of the city's total investment or in absolute scale. If the role of FDI is merely as an infusion of capital into a city—that is, the technology it brings with it does not spill over to other firms in the city—then its contribution to the city's growth will be proportional to its share in the city's total capital stock. I will call this as an "intensity effect." On the other hand, there may be a substantial amount of spillover across firms through interactions of workers or managers between the foreign-owned/managed firms and those that do not receive foreign investment directly. The actual channels of spillover may include dinner table conversations of friends or family members who work in different firms. The physical presence of foreign firms in the city facilitates the transfer. Suppose all domestic firms that do not receive foreign investment directly always obtain a constant fraction of the benefits (in terms of extra growth rates) that foreign-invested firms obtain and suppose further that foreign-invested firms accounted for a small fraction of total output, then the contribution of FDI to a city's growth will be proportional to the total FDI the city receives. I will refer to this as a "scale effect." In other words, the presence of a scale effect signals the existence of positive spillover across firms in the same city.[10]

Similarly, exports can also enter regressions in two ways. Exporting firms can learn new ideas about marketing, design, or technology from interacting with buyers in the world market. If the benefits of learning are confined to those firms who actually do the exporting, then its contribution will be proportional to the share of exports in a city's total output. On the hand, the newly

10. The terminology of intensity vs. scale effects is borrowed from Backus, Kehoe, and Kehoe (1992), who used it to represent the absence or presence of externality in human capital.

learned ideas are likely to travel to other firms that may not do any exporting at all. This transfer of ideas can also be accomplished through dinner table conversations, or formal business meetings. Alternatively, nonexporting firms can simply imitate the management or marketing concepts exporting firms have demonstrated. As far as this spillover is concerned, the benefit of exports to the city is more closely related to the total exports of all the firms in the city collectively than to the share of exports in total industrial output. That is, one can also use the scale effect to detect the presence of positive spillover from exports.

The H_k variable captures the contribution of human capital to growth, as emphasized by Lucas (1988) and others. If an educated person is counted passively as one unit of skilled labor, then the contribution of skill workers is limited to their share in the total labor force. But as the theory emphasizes, there are tremendous positive externalities associated with human capital: I become more productive if my colleagues are more educated. Under this hypothesis, more scientists facilitate more and faster cross-fertilization of ideas. The contribution of scientists or skilled workers is likely to be greater, the greater the absolute number of scientists or skilled workers in the city.

It is important to point out that an increase in city *k*'s exports, foreign investment, or the other two variables may improve the entire nation's productivity (cross-city spillover). But any such increase will simply be reflected in the intercept of regressions, because it does not generate cross-city differences in growth.

3.3 Data Sets

I employ two city-level data sets in this paper. The first has 434 cities for 1988–90, and the second 74 cities for 1980–90 (China State Statistical Bureau 1989, 1990, 1991). The first sample has a reasonably large number of observations. Furthermore, many variables of interest, such as shares of private and foreign firms in total industrial output, have been systematically collected in this period. On the other hand, a shortcoming of the data set is its short time period, which makes it more likely to be dominated by cyclical factors. Indeed, the period is one of the low-growth stages in a generally fast-growing decade.

The second sample covers essentially the entire reform period, which makes it ideal for examining the contribution of the open door policy to Chinese growth in a systematic way. The results from this decade-long sample are less likely to be influenced by cyclical factors. However, the sample size is considerably smaller than in the first data set. Furthermore, data on many variables of interest were not collected in the first half of the 1980s. Even for those variables that were collected in 1980, there is a large number of missing values for many cities, rendering the effective sample size much smaller than 74. Overall, one should not rely exclusively on either sample when drawing general lessons about Chinese growth.

3.4 Regression Results from 434 Cities during 1988–90

3.4.1 Initial Industrial Size and Population Growth

In table 3.1, the coefficients on the level of 1988 output are negative although not statistically significant except for one. In other words, for this two-year sample, there is no evidence that a larger initial industrial scale of the city helps it to grow faster.

The coefficient for the population growth rate is 0.60 and significant at the 5 percent level.

3.4.2 The Open Door Policy

Exports and FDI are used as measures of the open door policy. The export variable enters the regressions in two ways: in absolute scale or as a percentage of total output. If exports and FDI are entered separately, both are positive (although only the scale of exports is statistically significant at the 10 percent level). This is a finding often reported in some form in cross-country studies: openness correlates with high growth.[11] Here, a 1 percent increase in the scale of exports is associated with a two-year growth rate higher by 2.5 percentage points.

If the growth rate of exports is used as an explanatory variable, its estimated coefficient is 0.046 and is significant at the 10 percent level. Because of the possibility of reverse causality, I will not read too much into this result.

We next turn to the effect of FDI. Ideally, we would like to use the stock of FDI, but the data are not available at the city level, so we use flow data.[12] Similar to the export variable, the FDI variable can enter the regression in one of two ways: in absolute scale (in U.S. dollars) or as a percentage of total fixed capital investment.

If the two measures of FDI are entered into the regression separately, only the absolute scale of FDI is significant. A 1 percent increase in the size of FDI is associated with a 1.3 percentage point higher growth rate for the two-year period. This lends some support to the notion of an externality effect of FDI. Extra growth by 1.3 percentage points is not negligible, but neither is it overwhelming for Chinese cities. The growth rate of FDI over 1988–90, when included as an explanatory variable, is not significant.

Table 3.2 examines the effect of including measures of FDI and exports in the same regressions. If the absolute scales of both FDI and exports enter the

11. See Edwards (1989) and papers cited therein.

12. The problem may not be fatal, for two reasons: First, there is probably a large serial correlation in the spatial pattern of FDIs. The simple correlation between FDI in 1988 and in 1990 is 0.64. Second, FDI in virtually every city started in the early or mid-1980s. The annual flows of FDI in earlier years were considerably smaller than in later years. Judged from national data, the 1988 flow of FDI was slightly smaller than the combined FDIs of all previous years.

I plan to construct stock data for a subset of cities based on their annual flow data and to reexamine some of the issues here in a subsequent analysis.

Table 3.1 Exports, Foreign Investment, and Industrial Growth, 1988–90

Variable	(1)	(2)	(3)	(4)	(5)	(6)
LY88	−.043**	−.016	−.015***	−.007	−.009	.006
	.023	.011	.009	.013	.008	.011
GPop	.598*	.604*	.617*	.271	.618*	.274
	.230	.231	.258	.201	.233	.203
LExp88	.025**					
	.015					
RExp88		.685***				
		.422				
GExp			.046**			
			.027			
LFDI88				.013**		
				.008		
RFDI88					.289	
					.192	
GFDI88						.008***
						.005
N	347	347	342	.142	341	124
SEE	.19	.19	.19	.13	.18	.13
Adjusted R^2	.18	.20	.21	.07	.19	.06

Notes: Numbers below coefficient estimates are heteroscedasticity-consistent standard errors. All regressions have an intercept which is not reported.

*Significant at the 5 percent level.

**Significant at the 10 percent level.

***Significant at the 15 percent level.

regression, only FDI is statistically significant. If one also adds the growth rates of FDI and exports to the last regression, both the scale and growth rate of FDI are statistically significant, but neither measure of exports is.

To summarize, during 1988–90, foreign investment contributed more to cross-city differences in industrial output than did exports. Furthermore, the scale effect of foreign investment is significant and supports the hypothesis of spillover of technological or managerial knowhow across firms within cities.

3.4.3 Other Reform Policies

One often-mentioned aspect of the Chinese reforms is the vitality of China's nonstate sector.[13] Here, we will quantify the contribution of the nonstate sector to overall industrial growth, and will do so in connection with examining the open door policy.

13. In the Chinese context, the nonstate sector is not exactly the same thing as a private sector. The majority of nonstate firms are what are called collectively owned enterprises. They are community-based firms, but the relevant local governments often have the power to appoint or dismiss managers. Among the collectively owned firms, the TVEs have been developing particularly fast.

Table 3.2 Exports, Foreign Investment, and Industrial Growth, 1988–90: FDI and Exports Together

Variable	(1)	(2)	(3)
LY88	−.001	−.003	
	.027	.025	
GPop	.271	.262	
	.202	.197	
LExp88	−.006	−.028	−.028*
	.021	.022	.010
GExp		.005	.004
		.020	.021
LFDI88	.014**	.029*	.031*
	.008	.007	.008
GFDI88		.021*	.021*
		.006	.007
N	142	123	123
SEE	.13	.12	.12
Adjusted R^2	.07	.15	.09

Notes: Numbers below coefficient estimates are heteroscedasticity-consistent standard errors. All regressions have an intercept which is not reported.

*Significant at the 5 percent level.

**Significant at the 10 percent level.

The first regression in table 3.3 includes as an explanatory variable the ratio of nonstate firms' output to total output. Here the nonstate firms are defined as private firms, township and village enterprises (TVEs), and foreign-owned/managed firms. Urban collective firms are excluded because no data are available. We find this ratio to be positive and significant at the 1 percent level. A 1 percent rise in the output share of the nonstate firms is associated with a 0.19 percent higher growth rate.

If we decompose the nonstate firms into private firms, TVEs, and foreign-owned/managed firms, we see an interesting pattern. Only TVEs and foreign firms have made a positive contribution to overall city growth. A 1 percent increase in the output share of TVEs is associated with a 0.22 percent higher growth rate. Cities with a 1 percent higher share of foreign firms tend to grow 0.55 percent more rapidly. Since the share of foreign-invested/managed firms in total output circumvents the issue of stock versus flow of FDI, the relatively high contribution of the foreign firms may be a better testimony to the contribution of the open door policy to Chinese growth.

The share of private individual firms has a negative coefficient (it is insignificant when it enters the regression alone). The lack of a positive contribution by private firms is not intuitive. In search of an explanation, one may note that private firms in China are typically family-based small businesses (with fewer than eight employees) and were newly started during the reform years. The

Table 3.3 **Nonstate Sector and Industrial Growth, 1988–90**

Variable	(1)	(2)	(3)	(4)	(5)	(6)
LY88	−.004	.020	−.004	−.008	−.019	−.008
	.006	.025	.010	.006	.025	.010
GPop	.676*	.255	.296	.676*	.223	.248
	.251	.342	.347	.252	.344	.347
LExp88		−.028			−.027	
		.018			.018	
GExp			−.004			.002
			.023			.018
LFDI88		.010			.003	
		.007			.007	
GFDI88			.005			.005
			.005			.005
RYNS88	.194*	.274	.227*			
	.070	.075	.075			
RYIND88				−.824*	−.417*	−.426*
				.339	.204	.151
RYTVE88				.219*	.249*	.174*
				.080	.070	.066
RYFOR88				.550*	.731*	.672*
				.101	.138	.106
N	330	138	120	330	138	120
SEE	.16	.12	.12	.16	.12	.11
Adjusted R^2	.25	.13	.12	.26	.19	.21

Notes: Numbers below coefficient estimates are heteroscedasticity-consistent standard errors. All regressions have an intercept which is not reported.

*Significant at the 5 percent level.

regression result may simply reflect a pervasive underreporting of output by private firms in order to evade taxes. Indeed, it is possible that cities with better-performing TVEs and foreign firms find it financially less necessary to strictly enforce tax payment by their private firms.

If one adds the absolute scales of exports and FDI to the above regression, neither variable is statistically significant. The lack of significance can be due to a high collinearity between the FDI and output share of foreign firms.

A second way to measure the extent of reform in a particular city is to look at its share of retail sales conducted on the free market. Before 1978, almost no retail sales were on the free market. The share of the free market has increased gradually as the reform deepens. The rate of increase is certainly uneven across the country. This variable can signal the initiative of city governments in pushing certain reform measures, particularly price liberalization, holding other things constant. Of course, other things are not constant. In particular, different cities have different sized rural areas under their jurisdictions. For example, the city government of Shanghai has a jurisdiction of 10 small surrounding counties, while the city governments in Sichuan control more and larger counties. To the extent that a significant portion of free market trading is in agricultural goods, the free market share of total retail sales may not give a precise measure of reform initiatives related to industrial production. We have to take this into account in interpreting the regression results.

In any case, when the free market share of total retail sales in 1988 is included in the regression, it actually has a negative sign (see table 3.4). In other words, we cannot find a positive effect of price liberalization on industrial growth as measured by the initial free market share. The growth in the share of the free market, when included as an explanatory variable, is positive and statistically significant. But the magnitude of the contribution to overall city growth is modest: 1 percent higher growth of the free market is associated with 0.09 percent higher industrial growth.

A third way to gauge the impact of reform on city growth is to look for evidence of better growth performance by cities that have been granted greater authority to conduct localized reform experiments.

In August 1980, the Beijing government declared four cities, Shenzhen, Zhuhai, Shantou, and Xiamen, "special economic zones" (SEZs).[14] In an SEZ, investment decisions are made largely outside the state plan. Special tax concessions and less restrictive regulations on foreign exchange and land use are adopted in order to attract foreign investment. For foreign-owned/managed firms, there is a two-year tax holiday, followed by another three years of low tax rate (7.5 percent). After the initial five years, foreign firms then pay a 15 percent tax rate. In comparison, outside the SEZs, the tax rate is 33 percent for foreign firms and 55 percent for domestic state-owned firms. Encouraged by the rapid development in the four SEZs, the central government further declared in 1983 that the entire island province of Hainan, close to the size of Taiwan, would be a "special area open to foreign investment" and, in 1988, made it the largest SEZ.

In May 1984, the Beijing government announced that 14 cities spread along the entire Pacific coast had been granted "open coastal city" status. The explicit purpose of this is also to attract foreign capital and technology. In contrast to most of the SEZs, these cities all have an established industrial base and a well-educated labor force. With their new status, they can offer essentially all the preferential policies toward foreign investment of an SEZ except for the special income tax rates. Typically, foreign-owned/managed firms must pay tax at a rate of 24 percent, somewhere between the rates in an SEZ and those

14. Shekou, the part of Shenzhen close to Hong Kong, was declared an "industrial export zone" in January 1979.

elsewhere in the country. Manufacturing firms, however, are taxed at a concessionary 15 percent rate.[15]

Starting in 1981, the central government (and provincial governments) has designated 72 cities "comprehensive reform experimenting cities." The governments of these cities have gained more authority in managing firms inside the city boundaries, have greater access to the revenue originating in them, and can take over certain firms previously managed directly by the ministries in Beijing. Notice that the creation of this status largely entails bureaucratic decentralization (i.e., a transfer of some regulatory authority from the central government to the city governments) and hence does not automatically imply that more market-oriented reforms will be implemented in these cities.

To estimate the effects of these localized reform experiments, I have constructed three dummy variables. They are SEZ for the special economic zone, COAST for the fourteen coastal open cities, and RFM for the comprehensive reform experimenting cities.

The results with the RFM dummy are in table 3.4, and those with SEZ and COAST in table 3.5. The coefficients for the RFM and SEZ dummies are not significant. This indicates that, at least during 1988–90, there was no systematic difference in the growth performance for cities with or without those forms of special status from the central government. In contrast, the COAST dummy does have a positive and significant coefficient: a coastal open city on average grows faster than other cities by 9.2 percent over the two years. However, the dummy is no longer significant once scales of FDI and exports, or growth rates of the two, are included in the same regression. Among the newly added variables, only the scale of FDI or its growth rate are significant. This means that the entire above-the-norm growth rate in the coastal open cities is due to their ability to attract foreign investment.

To summarize, cities with a larger share of the nonstate sectors tend to grow faster. The contribution of the nonstate sectors comes mainly from the TVEs and particularly foreign-owned/managed firms. The coastal open cities do grow faster than the national average, primarily because of their superb record in attracting foreign investment.

3.4.4 Human Capital

Recent growth theories have stressed the importance of human capital for growth (Romer 1986; Lucas 1988). This section examines the contribution of

15. Starting in the mid-1980s and accelerating after 1988, there have also been policies to open the entire Pacific Basin, particularly the Liaoning and Shandong peninsulas, the entire provinces of Guangdong and Fujian, and parts of Guangxi and Hebei provinces. Since April 1990, the Pudong New Area of Shanghai, the largest city in China, has been developed into an "open economic zone" with preferential policies even broader in scope than for an SEZ. I have not attempted to formally incorporate these developments in the statistical work of this paper. For a survey of these developments, see Bell and N'guiamba (1993).

Table 3.4 Reform Experiments and Industrial Growth, 1988–90

Variable	(1)	(2)	(3)	(4)	(5)	(6)
LY88	−.017	−.003	.001	−.017	−.006	.010
	.011	.029	.028	.014	.027	.025
GPop	.614*	.275	.265	.601*	.273	.264
	.232	.199	.194	.232	.200	.196
LExp88		−.005	−.026		−.007	−.030
		.022	.024		.021	.022
GExp			.006			
			.021			
LFDI88		.014**	.028*		.014*	.029*
		.007	.008		.007	.007
RFDI88					.289	
					.192	
GFDI88			.020*			.021
			.006			.006
RMKT88	−160**	−.046	−.027			
	.094	.086	.086			
RFM				.005	−.035	−.025
				.026	.022	.022
N	346	142	123	347	142	123
SEE	.19	.13	.12	.19	.13	.12
Adjusted R^2	.18	.06	.14	.17	.07	.15

Notes: Numbers below coefficient estimates are heteroscedasticity-consistant standard errors. All regressions have an intercept which is not reported.

*Significant at the 5 percent level.

**Significant at the 10 percent level.

human capital to Chinese growth and asks whether this addition may change our earlier conclusions. Our choice of variable for human capital is largely dictated by data availability. We measure the stock of human capital by what is called "scientific and technical personnel" in the Chinese source, both in absolute numbers (to examine the scale effect) and as a percentage of the non-agricultural population (to examine the intensity effect).

It is important to point out that the definition of "scientific and technical personnel" in the Chinese source is broad enough to include essentially all skilled workers. The ratio of scientific and technical personnel to the total labor force offers a more direct measure of the average skill/education level of the labor force than primary and secondary school enrollment, since there is a time lag between school enrollment and labor force entry. School enrollment is often used as a measure of the average human capital level in cross-country studies because the more direct measure is not available.[16]

16. I thank John Page for pointing out that the general education/skill level of the labor force is probably more important than the number of high-level scientists for a country's economic development.

Table 3.5 **Coastal Areas and Industrial Growth, 1988–90**

Variable	(1)	(2)	(3)	(4)	(5)	(6)
LY88	−.016	.001	.003	−.020**	−.000	.004
	.011	.026	.025	.012	.027	.025
GPop	.599*	.268	.256	.613*	.282	.268
	.233	.202	.197	.229	.194	.190
LExp88		−.006	−.022		.008	−.029
		.021	.023		.021	.021
GExp			.009			.004
			.018			.019
LFDI88		.012**	.023*		.013**	.028*
		.007	.008		.008	.008
GFDI88			.018*			.020*
			.006			.006
SEZ	.044	.028	.088			
	.111	.010	.068			
COAST				.092**	.029	.016
				.056	.040	.040
N	347	142	123	347	142	123
SEE	.19	.13	.12	.19	.12	.12
Adjusted R^2	.17	.06	.16	.18	.14	.14

Notes: Numbers below coefficient estimates are heteroscedasticity-consistent standard errors. All regressions have an intercept which is not reported.

*Significant at the 5 percent level.

**Significant at the 10 percent level.

In the original data source, there is a separate variable, "mid or higher level scientific and technical personnel," which is a subset of all "scientific and technical personnel" with advanced training and sophisticated skills. I have also used this variable in the regressions and found essentially the same results.

The statistical results are reported in table 3.6. Unfortunately, neither the scale nor intensity measure of human capital is statistically significant when included alone in the regression, and some even have a negative coefficient. When the growth of the number of scientific personnel is included in the regression alone, it is positive and significant at the 10 percent level. A 1 percent increase in the growth rate of scientific personnel is associated with a 0.06 percent increase in the industrial growth rate. However, when the scales of exports and FDI are included in the same regression, the growth rate of scientific personnel loses its statistical significance (at the 10 percent level). The scale of FDI is positive and significant at the 10 percent level.

To summarize, the scale or average level of human capital does not appear to contribute to the cross-city differences in industrial growth rates during 1988–90. The contribution of the open door policy (in particular, that of foreign investment) identified in earlier subsections is not altered.

Table 3.6 **Human Capital and Industrial Growth, 1988–90**

Variable	(1)	(2)	(3)	(4)
LY88	−.013	−.016	−.016	−.004
	.023	.011	.011	.026
GPop	.603*	.636*	.600*	.283
	.234	.239	.227	.205
LSCNT88	−.005			
	.021			
RSCNT88		−1.03		
		.682		
GSCNT			.063**	.037
			.035	.047
LExp88				−.003
				.021
LFDI88				.014**
				.008
N	346	346	346	142
SEE	.19	.19	.19	.13
Adjusted R^2	.17	.18	.19	.07

Notes: Numbers below coefficient estimates are heteroscedasticity-consistent standard errors. All regressions have an intercept which is not reported.

*Significant at the 5 percent level.

**Significant at the 10 percent level.

3.4.5 Robustness Checks

In this section, I examine the robustness of the statistical results. To ensure that the earlier results are not driven by a few outliers, I am prepared to err on the side of omitting too many observations.

The mean growth rate for 1988–90 is 0.29. But the variation among the cities is enormous. Langfang and Ankong were growing at the rates of 217 percent and 203 percent, respectively, while Jingzhou and Yunchen were growing at −36 percent and −29 percent. I will delete all observations that are outside a two standard deviation band from the mean. This criteria deletes eight supergrowing cities and the six slowest-growing ones. When all the regressions are redone on this restricted sample, the earlier results essentially have survived. In particular, the positive association between FDI and industrial growth is strengthened, while the weak association between exports and growth becomes even weaker.

Because in the main regressions the key regressor (FDI) is at its beginning-of-sample value, the problem of simultaneous bias is probably not serious. Nevertheless, I have also tried to estimate a system of two simultaneous equations for output growth and FDI, in which FDI is assumed to be a function of the trade-output ratio and reform dummies. The scale of FDI continues to have a significant and positive effect on industrial growth.

3.5 Statistical Results for the 1980–90 Sample

A few observations are eliminated because data errors are suspected. The data on Nanchong is omitted because it records an extremely high export-output ratio (0.58) in 1980. Although the city is not known for its openness, the recorded ratio was the highest in the sample. Furthermore, the ratio is substantially higher than the second highest (Weihai, 0.23) and is more than three standard deviations (0.09) away from the mean (0.08).

The second group of omitted data are for Haikou, because it is the only city that is reported to have had a negative growth rate over 1980–90 in the absolute scale of exports. In spite of many news stories about how Haikou has become substantially more open than a decade ago, its reported total growth rate of exports is −29 percent over 1980–90.

Shenzhen is omitted in all regressions because there are no data on its exports in 1980. It is worth pointing out that Shenzhen is the fastest-growing city in the sample in terms of its industrial output. Its 10-year growth rate over 1980–90 is a phenomenal 545 percent, twice as high as the second highest growth rate in the sample,[17] and more than six standard deviations (0.61) above the mean (155 percent). As an SEZ, the city is known to have been extremely outward oriented. Had it been included in the sample, it would undoubtedly have reinforced any finding of a positive contribution of exports or foreign investment to city growth.

We would like to replicate all the key regressions performed on the other sample. Unfortunately, the data on FDI and the ownership composition of industrial output are not available for 1980. The corresponding data for 1990 are used as substitutes. As an admittedly weak justification for this, we note that those variables are likely to be serially correlated. The simple correlation of the scale of FDI between 1988 and 1990 is 0.64, and that of the share of FDI in total investment is 0.68. The correlations for the output shares of the private firms, TVEs, and foreign-invested firms between 1988 and 1990 are 0.74, 0.94, and 0.62, respectively.

Because of this substitution, one has to interpret the regression results with caution. In particular, the use of the end-of-sample values of these variables tend to underestimate their contribution to growth (relative to using the beginning-of-sample values). For example, if the foreign firms grow faster than domestic firms, then cities that have a lot of foreign firms also tend to grow faster. The end-of-sample share of the foreign firms in total output will be larger than the beginning-of-period share, even if the number of foreign firms and other things are held constant. A larger end-of-sample share relative to the beginning-of-sample share is needed to explain the same growth rate. Hence, the resulting coefficient estimate will be smaller.

17. The city with in second highest growth rate in the sample is Guiling, with a 10-year growth rate reaching 267 percent.

Table 3.7 **Exports, Foreign Investment, and Industrial Growth, 1980–90**

Variable	(1)	(2)	(3)	(4)	(5)
LY80	−.242*	−.076**	−.047	−.147*	−.064**
	.099	.039	.040	.064	.037
GPop	.549**	.548*	.625	.662*	.703*
	.297	.271	.402	.329	.332
LExp88	.155*				
	.070				
RExp80		2.171*			
		1.032			
GExp			.128		
			.131		
LFDI90				.048*	
				.022	
RFDI90					2.143*
					.641
N	43	43	43	38	38
SEE	.32	.32	.33	.32	.31
Adjusted R^2	.17	.17	.12	.20	.23

Notes: Numbers below coefficient estimates are heteroscedasticity-consistent standard errors. All regressions have an intercept which is not reported.

*Significant at the 5 percent level.

**Significant at the 10 percent level.

On the other hand, with this substitution, the possibility of reverse causality is also more serious. Imagine that the initial size of FDI has nothing to do with growth, but that new FDI always goes to cities that grow rapidly. By the end of the sample, fast-growing cities may have more FDI. Hence, this can produce a correlation between FDI and growth. For whatever they are worth, regressions similar to those for the 1988–90 sample have been run.

3.5.1 Initial Size of the Industrial Sector

From tables 3.7 and 3.8, one may notice a somewhat surprising result. The coefficient on the level of 1980 output is negative and statistically significant, suggesting a tendency to convergence in growth rates in Chinese cities. One percent higher 1980 output tends to be associated with a reduction of the 10-year total growth rate by 24 percentage points (or of the annual growth rate by 2.4 percentage points). Notice that the convergence result would also have been strengthened if Shenzhen and Haikou were included in the regression, because they both started with a small industrial base but enjoyed phenomenal growth.

The negative coefficient suggests that increasing returns to scale is not operative at the city level in China. This need not be puzzling if one recognizes that much of the industrial sector in prereform China was extremely inefficient, burdened with obsolete technology, inadequate management, and poor worker

Table 3.8 **Exports, Foreign Investment, and Industrial Growth, 1980–90: FDI and Exports Together**

Variable	(1)	(2)
LY80	−.302*	−.351*
	.137	.147
GPop	.504**	.238
	.305	.336
LExp80	.154	.217*
	.102	.105
GExP		.187
		.117
LFDI90	.023	.004
	.028	.025
N	38	38
See	.31	.31
Adjusted R^2	.23	.25

Notes: Numbers below coefficient estimates are heteroscedasticity-consistent standard errors. All regressions have an intercept which is not reported.

*Significant at the 5 percent level.

**Significant at the 10 percent level.

discipline. Furthermore, in selecting cities to experiment with reform measures, particularly in the early 1980s, the Chinese government was often systematically biased against large industrial cities for fear of losing control of the state-owned sector. This can lead to a negative association between initial size and subsequent growth.

3.5.2 Exports and FDI: Scale versus Intensity Effects

The first set of results is in table 3.7. As expected, the growth rate of the nonagricultural population has a positive impact on growth rates. The coefficient on population growth is about 0.55, which is close to the corresponding estimate for the 1988–90 sample (0.60).

The scale of exports in logarithm, when included as an independent variable, has an estimated coefficient of 0.16, which is significant at the 5 percent level. A 1 percent increase in the scale of exports of a city is associated with a 16 percentage point increase in its 10-year growth rate.

If the ratio of exports to output is included in the regression, a much larger estimate is obtained. A 1 percent increase in this ratio is associated with a 2.17 percent higher growth rate. If the growth rate of exports over the decade is used as an independent variable, it is not significant.

Foreign direct investment again can enter the regressions in two ways. In terms of the scale effect of foreign investment, the coefficient is positive and significant at the 5 percent level. A 1 percent increase in the absolute scale of

Table 3.9 Nonstate Sector and Industrial Growth, 1980–90

Variable	(1)	(2)	(3)	(4)	(5)	(6)
LY80	−.131*	−.277*	−.128*	−.299*	−.203*	−.339*
	.031	.124	.033	.138	.053	.120
GPop	−.049	−.073	−.066	−.141	−.310	−.353
	.226	.202	.244	.228	.250	.237
LExp88		.107		.137		.114
		.081		.091		.074
GExp			.027	.077		
			.086	.099		
LFDI90		.002		−.004		−.001
		.021		.022		.024
RYNS90	1.30*	1.04*	1.28*	.962*		
	.321	.319	.331	.352		
RYIND90					−13.35**	−19.12*
					7.20	9.18
RYTVE90					1.36*	1.13*
					.292	.272
RYFOR90					2.07*	1.49*
					.426	.480
N	43	38	43	38	43	38
SEE	.28	.29	.29	.29	.27	.27
Adjusted R^2	.36	.36	.34	.35	.41	.43

Notes: Numbers below coefficient estimates are heteroscedasticity-consistent standard errors. All regressions have an intercept which is not reported.

*Significant at the 5 percent level.

**Significant at the 10 percent level.

FDI is associated with a rise in the 10-year growth rate by 4.8 percentage points. There is a positive intensity effect as well. A 1 percent increase in the FDI-output ratio is associated with a rise in the city's growth rate by 2.14 percent.

If we include both the levels of exports and FDI, and the growth rate of exports in the regression (table 3.8), only the scale of exports is significant at the 5 percent level. Unlike the 1988–90 sample, the contribution of exports appears more important than that of FDI for the decade. Furthermore, the scale effect of exports suggest that the contribution of exports is also through some positive spillover.

3.5.3 Contribution of Other Reforms

As with the sample over 1988–90, we measure the impact of reforms in three ways: (1) the role of the nonstate sectors, in particular, TVEs and foreign firms, (2) the ratio of free market sales to total retail sales, and (3) dummies indicating enhanced authority that cities have received from the central government to experiment with more reforms.

In table 3.9, the estimated coefficient on the nonstate sector is positive and

Table 3.10 **Reform Experiments and Industrial Growth, 1980–90**

Variable	(1)	(2)	(3)	(4)	(5)	(6)
LY80	−.071	−.408*	−.490*	−.051	−.283*	−.330*
	.048	.125	.135	.038	.130	.139
GPop	.752*	.457	.139	.707**	.458	.185
	.341	.296	.326	.372	.354	.398
LExp80		.168**	.264*		.128	.191**
		.095	.095		.105	.100
GExp			.218**			.190
			.123			.116
LFDI90		.044	.021		.028	.009
		.031	.028		.027	.022
RMKT90	−.623	−.636	−.445			
	.597	.528	.577			
RFM				−.089	−.079	−.084
				.117	.160	.151
N	41	36	36	43	38	38
SEE	.34	.31	.30	.33	.32	.31
Adjusted R^2	.10	.27	.30	.11	.22	.24

Notes: Numbers below coefficient estimates are heteroscedasticity-consistent standard errors. All regressions have an intercept which is not reported.

*Significant at the 5 percent level.

**Significant at the 10 percent level.

statistically significant: A 1 percent increase in the share of the nonstate sector in total output is associated with an increase of 1.3 percent in the 10-year growth rate.

If we decompose the nonstate sector into private individual firms, TVEs, and foreign-invested firms, we observe a result similar to the other sample: the shares of TVEs and foreign firms in total output have a positive and statistically significant impact on the growth rate. A 1 percent higher share of TVEs is associated with a 1.36 percent higher growth rate. A 1 percent higher share of foreign-invested/managed firms is associated with a 2.07 percent higher growth rate. The scale of FDI and the growth rate of exports, when added to the above regression, are not significant.

Second, the share of the free market in the city's total retail sales is used as a proxy for price liberalization and related reforms (table 3.10). Because no such data are available for 1980, the 1990 data are used. Similar to the other sample, this ratio is not significant (and the point estimate is even negative).

Third, the dummies COAST and RFM are added as regressors (table 3.11). The SEZ dummy is not added because there are some missing values for each of the special economic zones. The COAST dummy is positive and significant when added alone to the regression. That is, the 14 coastal open cities do grow faster than the national average. However, when the scales of exports and FDI

Table 3.11 Coastal Areas and Industrial Growth, 1980–90

Variable	(1)	(2)	(3)
LY80	−.070**	−.311*	−.373*
	.040	.143	.153
GPop	.641**	.511**	.242
	.427	.295	.320
LExp80		.160	.234*
		.110	.113
GExp			.195
			.121
LFDI90		.026	.010
		.028	.023
COAST	.178**	−.026	−.060
	.107	.124	.112
N	43	38	38
SEE	.33	.32	.31
Adjusted R^2	.14	.21	.23

Notes: Numbers below coefficient estimates are heteroscedasticity-consistent standard errors. All regressions have an intercept which is not reported.

*Significant at the 5 percent level.

**Significant at the 10 percent level.

are added, COAST is no longer significant. At the same time, the scale of exports is significant. This suggests that, over 1980–90, the extra growth rate that the coastal cities enjoyed was largely due to their above-average export performance. (In comparison, during the last two years of the 1980s, the extra growth is more likely explained by the above-average FDI presence in these cities.)

3.5.4 Human Capital

As a measure of human capital, the number of (broadly defined) "scientific and technical personnel" and the ratio this number to the total population are included separately in the regressions.[18] As can be seen from table 3.12, neither measure is positive, contrary to what the human capital strand of new growth theory would have suggested (one estimate is even negative and significant). However, when the growth in scientific personnel is used as a regressor, it turns out to be positive and significant. Note that, because there are only 17 cities that have data on the number of scientists in 1980, these estimates should be treated with caution.

18. As in the 1988–90 sample, "scientific and technical personnel" is defined broadly enough to encompass essentially all skilled workers, not just high-level scientists and technicians.

Table 3.12 Human Capital and Industrial Growth, 1980–90

Variable	(1)	(2)	(3)	(4)	(5)	(6)
LY80	−.079	−.104*	−.115**	−.096	−.111**	−.090
	.112	.041	.066	.122	.060	.127
GPop	1.371**	.606	.124	.564	.157	.182
	.812	.676	1.029	.611	1.030	.984
LSCNT80	−.004					
	.191					
RSCNT80		−9.45*				
		4.46				
GSCNT			.824*	.499*	.580*	.589*
			.347	.207	.250	.261
LExp80				−.023		−.024
				.128		.130
GExp					.190	.190
					.285	.288
LFDI90				−.050	−.054	−.049
				.073	.075	.073
N	17	15	17	14	14	14
SEE	.43	.38	.38	.38	.38	.41
Adjusted R^2	.16	.41	.35	.35	.36	.27

Notes: Numbers below coefficient estimates are heteroscedasticity-consistent standard errors. All regressions have an intercept which is not reported.

*Significant at the 5 percent level.

**Significant at the 10 percent level.

3.6 Conclusion

Using two city-level data sets, this paper has examined the contribution of the open door policy to Chinese growth. There is clear evidence that during 1980–90 more exports were positively associated with higher industrial growth across the cities. In comparison, in the late 1980s, the cross-city growth differences are explained by foreign investment rather than by exports. The contribution of foreign investment comes in the form of technological or managerial spillover across firms, as opposed to the infusion of new capital.

Cities with a larger share of nonstate sectors grow faster. The contribution of the nonstate sectors comes mainly from the TVEs, and particularly foreign-invested/managed firms. The coastal cities do grow faster than the national average, but the extra growth comes almost entirely from their ability to attract more foreign investment. To the extent that inland areas can also attract foreign investment and export via coastal cities, they also benefit from the open door policy.

Finally, it is important to point out that the contribution of the open door policy to Chinese growth is likely to be underestimated. As noted earlier, much of the benefit of export expansion or a foreign investment boom in one city may spill over to other cities. The portion of growth that is generated by the cross-city spillover is reflected only in the intercept of the kind of regressions reported in this paper. Even though the open door policy may substantially raise overall Chinese growth, this may not be picked up by the coefficient estimates for city-level foreign investment or export variables.[19]

Appendix
Definition of Variables in the Regressions

All data refer to cities and surrounding counties in their jurisdiction.

Y = gross value of industrial output
Pop = nonagricultural population
Exp = purchase for exports in RMB yuan
FDI = foreign direct investment in U.S. dollars
IV = total fixed capital investment by all ownership types
RFDI = FDI/IV
RYIND = share of individual/private firms in total industrial output
RYTVE = share of TVEs in total industrial output
RYFOR = share of foreign-owned/managed firms in total industrial output
RYNS = share of private firms, TVEs, and foreign-owned/managed firms in total city industrial output
RMKT = share of free market in total retail sales
SCNT = scientific and technical personnel
MHSCNT = middle or higher levels of scientific and technical personnel
SEZ = dummy for four special economic zones
COAST = dummy for 14 coastal open cities.
RFM = dummy for 72 "comprehensive reform experimenting cities"

G and L prefixes to a variable denote, respectively, the growth rate and logarithmic value of that variable.

19. One channel through which cross-city spillover takes place is labor (and manager) movement across cities. So far, this channel is only marginally operative. Intercity job mobility has changed from virtually zero in prereform years to a small positive number in the 1980s. The diminished and eventually abolished use of food coupons in the 1980s has facilitated this increase in mobility. But the household registration system still in place, the underdevelopment of housing markets, and the social safety net continue to impede labor mobility across cities (Davis 1992).

References

Backus, David K., Patrick J. Kehoe, and Timothy J. Kehoe. 1992. In search of scale effects in trade and growth. Staff Report no. 152. Federal Reserve Bank of Minneapolis.

Bell, Michael, and Simon N'guiamba. 1993. China's open economic zones are speeding its transformation to a market economy. *IMF Survey,* April 19.

Cheng, Hang-Sheng. 1992. China's foreign trade reform, 1979–91. Pacific Basin Working Paper no. PB92–01. Federal Reserve Bank of San Francisco.

China State Statistical Bureau. 1989, 1991. *China urban statistics.* London: Longman.

———. 1990. *The forty years of Chinese urban development.* Beijing: China State Statistical Bureau.

Davis, Deborah. 1992. Job mobility in post-Mao cities: Increases on the margins. *China Quarterly,* December.

Edwards, Sebastian. 1989. Openness, outward orientation, trade liberalization, and economic performance in developing countries. NBER Working Paper no. 2908. Cambridge, Mass.: National Bureau of Economic Research.

Frankel, Jeffrey. 1992. Is Japan creating a yen bloc in Pacific Asia? In *Regionalism and rivalry: Japan and the U.S. in Pacific Asia,* ed. Jeffrey Frankel and Miles Kahler. Chicago: University of Chicago Press.

Frankel, Jeffrey, and Shang-Jin Wei. 1993. Trade bloc and currency bloc. NBER Working Paper no. 4335. Cambridge, Mass.: National Bureau of Economic Research.

Glaeser, Edward, Hedi Kallal, Jose Scheinkman, and Andrei Shleifer, 1992. Growth in cities. *Journal of Political Economy* 100 (6): 1126–52.

Kamm, John. 1989. Reforming Foreign Trade. In *One step ahead in China: Guangdong under reform,* ed. Ezra F. Vogel. Cambridge: Harvard University Press.

Krugman, Paul, and Maurice Obstfeld. 1991. *International economics: Theory and policy,* 2d ed. New York: HarperCollins.

Kueh, Y. Y. 1992. Foreign investment and economic change in China. *China Quarterly* 131:637–90.

Lardy, Nicholas. 1992. *Foreign trade and economic reform in China, 1978–1990.* Cambridge: Cambridge University Press.

Lucas, Robert., Jr. 1988. On the mechanics of economic development. *Journal of Monetary Economics* 22:3–42.

Rivera-Batiz and Paul Romer. 1991. Economic integration and endogenous growth. *Quarterly Journal of Economics* 106:531–55.

Romer, Paul. 1986. Increasing returns and long-run growth. *Journal of Political Economy* 94:1002–37.

———. 1990. Endogenous technological change. *Journal of Political Economy* 98:S71–S102.

Sung, Yun-Wing. 1991. *The China-Hong Kong connection: The key to China's Open-Door Policy.* Cambridge: Cambridge University Press.

Vogel, Ezra F., ed. 1989. *One step ahead in China: Guangdong under reform.* Cambridge: Harvard University Press.

Wang, Tao. 1993. Market and reform: The growth of Chinese urban industries. New York University, May. Unpublished.

Wang, Fang-Yi, and Ashoka Mody. 1993. Industrial growth in coastal China: Economic reforms . . . and what else? Washington, D.C.: World Bank, April. Unpublished.

Wei, Shang-Jin, and Xiong Bai Fan. 1993. Hard currency versus positive externality: A statistical X-Ray of foreign capital in China. Harvard University, June. Unpublished.

World Bank. 1992. *World development report 1992: Development and the environment.* Oxford University Press.

Young, Alwyn. 1991. Learning by doing and the dynamic effects of international trade. *Quarterly Journal of Economics* 106: 369–405.
Zou, Gang. 1993. Modelling the enterprise behavior under the two-tier plan/market system in the PRC. Washington, D.C.: World Bank.

Comment Yun-Wing Sung

This paper has skillfully utilized city-level data to analyze the very important question of the contribution of exports and foreign investment to the phenomenal industrial growth in China. Analysis of the very successful growth of China is difficult because the reform period has been relatively short and quarterly data is mostly unavailable. Fortunately for economists, China is a land of vast regional variations, and the sample size of a regional data set can be quite large. Regional studies of the Chinese economy are becoming fashionable partly because of flourishing powerful regional economies, and partly because of rich data.

Wei uses two city-level data sets: The first has 434 cities for 1988–90, and the second has 74 cities for 1980–90. It is found that, during 1980–90, more exports are positively associated with higher growth rates across Chinese cities. In the late 1980s, the contribution to growth comes mainly from foreign investment. Furthermore, the contribution of foreign investment comes in the form of technological or managerial spillovers across firms, as opposed to an infusion of new capital.

While I agree with the main points of the paper, there are some weaknesses. First, the author should give more prominence to the problem of reverse causality. While the author noted that reverse causality can be a problem when he substituted 1990 end-of-sample values for some variables (foreign direct investment and ownership composition), he should warn the reader that reverse causality is a general problem since the paper does not use simultaneous equation estimation. The positive association between industrial growth on the one hand, and exports and foreign direct investment on the other, may be accounted for by a positive impact of industrial growth on exports and direct foreign investment.

Second, the term "city" or *shi* in China refers to a jurisdictional and administrative unit which may be largely rural, though populous cities such as Shanghai and Beijing contain substantial urban areas. The fact that cities are administrative units means that they can be amalgamated or split for administrative reasons. For example, the jurisdiction zones of many Chinese cities were substantially enlarged in 1983, with the result that the proportion of the Chinese

Yun-Wing Sung is professor of economics at the Chinese University of Hong Kong.

population living in "cities" and "towns" (*shizhen zongrenkou*) rose from 20 percent in 1981 to 32 percent in 1984, and rose further to 50 percent in 1988. The 1983 enlargement of the jurisdiction zones of many Chinese cities has obviously affected the 1980–90 sample, probably substantially.

In China's city-level data sets, data for urban areas are often reported separately from data for the whole administrative district, and so data for the urban area should be reasonably free from the problem of enlargement in jurisdiction. Unfortunately, city-level trade data are only reported for the administrative districts, and regressions involving exports cannot be free from the problem of changes in jurisdiction. For foreign investment, industrial growth, and other variables, the author did not specify whether the data refer to the entire city or to the urban area only. He seems to have swept these problems under the rug.

Third, the second sample of 74 cities contains primarily the more populous cities with large urban areas, whereas the first sample of 434 cities contains largely less populous cities with small urban areas and large rural populations. This difference may be important for the contributions of exports and foreign direct investment to industrial growth. If Robert Lucas is correct in his assessment that spillover benefits are particularly important in urban areas due to the ease of communication, spillover effects should be more prominent in the second sample than in the first.

The difference in the two samples may also be important for exports at the city level. In the Chinese system of foreign trade, exports of a city usually refer to exports of the foreign trade corporations of that city. These include both goods made in that city and goods made elsewhere purchased by the foreign trade corporations of that city for export. The goods of less populous cities are usually sold to foreign trade corporations in large urban areas, especially large ports, for export and are thus regarded as exports of the large cities instead of the small cities of origin. This implies that exports will be prominent in the second sample, which is dominated by large, populous cities, whereas exports will be relatively unimportant in the first sample. This may account for the empirical finding in the paper that exports do not contribute to growth in the first sample, though exports are highly significant for growth in the second sample.

The rerouting of exports to other cities will cause strange fluctuations in exports. For instance, it is noted in the paper that Haikou's exports decreased by 29 percent from 1980 to 1990 despite the fact that Haikou has become substantially more open during the decade. This can probably be attributed to rerouting of exports to other cities.

Finally, there are some loose ends. In the text covering the regressions in table 3.4, it is mentioned that growth in the share of the free market is a statistically significant variable for explaining industrial growth, but the results are reported neither in table 3.4 nor elsewhere.

Despite the above shortcomings, the paper is undoubtedly an important work in the rapidly growing literature on empirical studies of the Chinese economy relying on regional data.

Comment John Page

China's extraordinary growth since undertaking its program of gradual economic reform arguably places it among the other East Asian "superstars." In two important respects—the rapid growth of manufactured exports and the significant role of direct foreign investment (DFI)—China in the 1980s and 1990s share common characteristics with other rapidly growing East Asian economies. The importance of export growth and DFI in engendering the East Asian Miracle has become a subject of intense, and frequently polemical, debate.[1] Thus, further work which helps to enlighten us on the contribution of these factors to growth and on the mechanisms by which they may carry out their growth-augmenting role is especially welcome. Because much of the academic debate on the role of exports and DFI has been argued in the context of cross-country growth regressions, it is also very useful to have a country study in which cross-sectional, time-series data are used to test a number of hypotheses concerning the contribution of exports and foreign investment to growth at the subnational level. In these two respects Wei's paper is an important addition to a literature which in general has been long on theory and argumentation and short on serious empirical analysis.

The debate over growth in East Asia centers on the sources of its rapid increase in per capita incomes. A "growth fundamentalist" school emphasizes the significance of East Asia's unusually high rates of physical and human capital deepening; while "growth mystics" tend to stress the importance of total factor productivity (TFP) change.[2] Wei clearly leans toward the mystic camp. His empirical results lead him to conclude that *both* exports and DFI increase growth rates in per capita income across cities in China through the impact of learning and competition on productivity change, rather than through increased rates of accumulation. A central question, then, is whether, given the limitations of the data, the empirical results support such a view unambiguously.

John Page is chief economist of the Middle East and North Africa Region of the World Bank.

1. See, e.g., Young (1993), Rodrik (1994), and the exchange between Pack and Page (1994) and Young (1994).

2. For an exposition of these quasi-religious views and an attempt to assess their validity see Page (1994).

The Analytical Underpinnings

Any concise paper inevitably must select among the arguments and evidence to be presented. Wei chooses to place emphasis on the description of China's economic reforms of the 1980s and gives rather short shrift to analytical discussion of the possible channels by which either exports or DFI may enhance productivity change. The absence of an explicit analytical framework and/or review of other literature relating export performance to productivity change leaves Wei open to the frequently heard criticism that the causality in his regressions may run from the dependent to the independent variable.

This is most frequently argued in the case of exports. Is it not equally plausible that rapid productivity growth due to some, perhaps unmeasured, factor results in increasing price competitiveness of tradable goods and improved export performance? But a similar case could be made for DFI. Rapid growth in income per capita may make cities more attractive as destinations for DFI. This uncertainty is compounded by the fact that in the interpretation empirical results Wei identifies the productivity-enhancing role of both variables with their absolute size, the "scale effect." I am sympathetic to the implicit model which underlies Wei's specification of the causal relationship, but in the absence of a more thorough discussion of the mechanisms by which exports—as opposed, say, to outward orientation, the impact of both imports and exports—or FDI enhance learning and productivity growth, I suspect that the skeptics will remain unconvinced.[3]

The lack of precision in specifying the mechanisms by which exports and DFI enhance productivity growth is reflected also in the interpretation of the alternative definitions of the two variables. Wei defines both his export and DFI variables in relative (share of output or investment) and absolute terms. The former he calls the "intensity effect" and the latter the "scale effect." He further associates only the scale effect with spillovers; the larger the absolute size of the variable, the greater the potential spillover. The rationale for this distinction is not entirely clear from the discussion in the paper.

Consider the case of DFI. If learning outside the foreign firm takes place by means of spillovers, why should these occur as a "constant fraction of the benefits . . . that foreign-invested firms obtain"? Why should they not be equally related to the probability that the new investment activity observed by an incumbent domestic firm will be of foreign origin? The first interpretation argues in favor of the absolute variable; the second in favor of the relative measure. Similarly for exports, if a high proportion of a city's output is concentrated in exports, does this not increase the probability that nonexporting firms will observe and learn from exporters? Without greater precision with respect to the means by which both within-firm learning and spillovers are realized, the case

3. For a discussion of the mechanisms by which exports may increase TFP growth rates at the firm level, see Pack and Page (1994).

for preferring the absolute to the relative definition of the variable is not as clear-cut as Wei's exposition would suggest.

A second analytical problem derives from a data problem. Wei notes that the city-level data he employs lacks estimates of the capital stock. Thus, he defines the production function in natural units of labor only and proceeds to interpret the residual of output growth net of labor's contribution as TFP growth. Wei is frank about the limitations imposed by such an assumption, but he is perhaps insufficiently cautious in interpreting his results. He has in effect specified a "Barro-type" cross-city regression without specifically using the concept of the endogenity of the capital stock. Moreover, because human capital enters his regressions in a rather ad hoc manner as one of the factors "explaining" productivity change, it is not clear on what basis the investment rate is omitted from the regression.

While Wei's discussion of his data leaves unclear whether total investment and the investment share in output are available, the fact that he can construct a variable which gives the share of DFI in total investment at the city level suggests that they are. If this is the case, a cross-city regression including the share of investment in output would place Wei's specification more squarely in the mainstream of the literature on cross-country growth regressions, would permit comparison with other work, and perhaps most significantly would bolster his arguments concerning the productivity-enhancing role of exports and DFI.

Without some attempt to control for differences in the rate of capital accumulation, the results remain open to the criticism that the export and (especially) the DFI variables—particularly when they are measured in absolute terms—reflect differences in rates of accumulation. In its simplest form the argument would run as follows: because DFI is an important component of total investment, cities with high levels or rates of growth of DFI have high total investment. Output per person increases as a consequence of capital deepening for which the DFI variable is a proxy, not as a consequence of more rapid productivity growth.

The Role of Human Capital

Wei's results are disappointing for those observers of the East Asian Miracle who stress the role of human capital.[4] His human capital variable consistently fails to explain variations in growth of output per person across cities. One problem may be definitional. In cross-country regressions, levels of educational attainment appear to be a more satisfactory definition of human capital than skill categories such as "scientific and technical personnel." In the cross-city context, however, there may be little variance in education stocks and the available variable relates to a broad definition of skilled labor, hence Wei's

4. See, e.g., World Bank (1993).

choice. But, some discussion of the cross-city variation in education stocks would have been welcome to buttress the choice of the skill variable.

A second problem may be conceptual. If, as Wei argues, the principal impact of exports and DFI on growth is through increased mastery of technology and productivity change, human capital may interact with these variables to accelerate growth. Thus, some attempt to explore interactions between skill levels and the other two variables should be attempted, as well as tests of their joint significance in explaining variations in per capita output growth.

The results may, however, continue to disappoint. A least one strand of human capital interpretations of success in Asia (Birdsall and Sabot 1993) emphasizes that it is high cognitive skills in the bottom-end ("low-skill") segment of the labor force which permits the East Asian high performers to adopt and master international best-practice technologies more effectively. According to that view, the interaction between exports, DFI, and human capital might best be captured by using measures of educational attainment in the bottom end of the wage distribution. This proposition cannot be tested with the data available to Wei, but it suggests a fruitful area for future, microeconomic research.

The Lessons

Academic readers looking for a definitive resolution of the fundamentalist-mystic debate on the origins of rapid growth in China will be disappointed. Wei's results are consistent with the view that TFP growth caused by DFI and rapid export expansion was a major engine of growth in China's coastal cities. But the data limitations and the absence of a tight analytical link between export expansion and productivity change will fail to persuade fundamentalist skeptics. Problems with the definition and interpretation of the human capital variable lead to similar problems in presenting a definitive view of its role in China's success.

In a broader sense, however, Wei's results contain important messages for policymakers in other developing economies. Economic liberalization is working in China. Regardless of the precise channel through which it takes place, the net impact of a set of reforms favoring export expansion and DFI has been to increase the growth of per capita income. These results, despite the quibbles, are robust and point out the policy directions for other economies embarking on programs of economic liberalization.

References

Birdsall, Nancy, and Richard H. Sabot. Virtuous circles: Human capital growth and equity in East Asia. Background paper for *The East Asian Miracle.* Washington, D.C.: World Bank.

Pack, Howard, and John M. Page, Jr. 1994. Reply to Young. *Carnegie-Rochester Conference Seminar on Public Policy* 40, forthcoming.

Page, John M., Jr. 1994. The East Asian Miracle—Four lessons for development policy. *NBER Macroeconomics Annual* 9, forthcoming.

Rodrik, Dani. 1994. Miracle or design? Lessons from the East Asian experience. Policy Essay no. 11, 13–53. Washington, D.C.: Overseas Development Council.

World Bank. 1993. *The East Asian Miracle.* Washington, D.C.: World Bank.

Young, Alwyn. 1993. Lessons from the East Asian NICS: A contrarian view. NBER Working Paper no. 4482. Cambridge, Mass.: National Bureau of Economic Research.

Young, Alwyn. 1994. Accumulation, exports and growth in the high performing Asian economies. *Carnegie-Rochester Conference Seminar on Public Policy* 40, forthcoming.

4 Old and New Development Models: The Taiwanese Experience

Ji Chou

The neoclassical growth model, pioneered by Robert Solow (1956), has as its basic features a closed economy with competitive markets and a production technology exhibiting diminishing returns to capital and labor separately and constant returns to all inputs jointly. In this model, population growth and the propensity to save, which affect the per capita level of income, are only affected by exogenous factors. Exogenously determined technology is the only force accounting for growth in per capita income. Therefore the model assigns a comparatively small role to other factors.

There have been calls for modification of these restrictive assumptions since the model's introduction.[1] The recent "new" growth theory includes the role of increasing returns to scale (Romer 1986), the learning-by-doing effects of human capital (Lucas 1988), and the dynamic spillover effects of export expansion (Grossman and Helpman 1991). It emphasizes that, when investment takes place under increasing returns to scale, the marginal product of capital need not decline over time. Hence the incentive to accumulate capital may persist for successive periods, sustaining a steady state of growth.

Recently, Mankiw, Romer, and Weil (1992, henceforth MRW) tested the neoclassical model and found that including human capital accumulation lowers the estimated effects of savings and population growth to roughly the value predicted by the Solow model. Moreover, the differences in savings, education, and population growth can explain about 80 percent of cross-country differences in income per capita. Two points are raised about their study. First, the study tests the neoclassical growth model by estimating the determination of a steady state level of income per capita rather than directly estimating the pro-

Ji Chou is a research fellow of the Chung-Hua Institution for Economic Research.

1. For instance, Solow (1959) himself introduced a model that allowed for the embodiment effect between investment and technical progress. Arrow (1962) suggested the potential of learning by doing as a way of accounting for economic growth.

duction function as conventional approaches do. Second, the study, maintaining the old-fashioned assumptions of the neoclassical model, treats the determinants as exogenous and leaves technological change unexplained. Nevertheless, MRW's study stimulates us in this paper to ask the following questions:

1. Can a country's specific data be applied to MRW's model? Paul Romer (1987) argued that a production function regression using data such as postwar annual time series for a single country yields estimates that are ambiguous, since they cannot be justified in the context of a model for business cycles. Most recent empirical studies employ cross-country data to test growth theory. However, MRW's approach does not test the production function directly and might avoid the problem that Romer raised.

2. Is the exogenous assumption for savings ratio, population growth, and human capital accumulation valid? As MRW demonstrate in their paper, higher savings and lower population growth lead to a higher level of income and thus a higher level of human capital. Following from this consequence, the higher level of human capital accumulation will also lead to a higher level of income and thus a higher savings ratio or a slower growth of population. This implies that there is a contemporaneous feedback from income to the income determinants. Therefore, the exogenous assumption might not be valid. From an empirical viewpoint, both the least squares estimation method and the instrumental variable method should be employed and the estimation results compared to check the validity of the exogenous assumption.

3. What is the possible explanation for technological change? The beauty of the MRW approach is that the parameters of the production function are implied in the income determination function. The determinants of income, i.e., savings ratio and population growth, find their correspondent variables in the production function. The relaxation of the exogenous assumption in income determinants is equivalent to the relaxation of exogeneity of factor inputs in the production function.

The endogeneity of factor inputs might give more of a rationale to the embodiment hypothesis which Solow (1988) suggested; that is, a strong positive association exists between the growth rate of total factor productivity (which Solow called the rate of technical progress in the broad sense) and investment speed in intermediate-run transactions, even if the steady state of growth is not affected. If the interaction between total factor productivity and factor inputs can be applied to physical capital, the interaction between total factor productivity and other factor inputs, i.e., labor force and human capital, should also be taken into consideration.

4. What is the role of exports in growth in the above context? It has been found that there is a strong positive correlation between economic growth and export growth. There are numerous factors which explain this correlation, but how they can be linked within this context is the question. As Solow reminds us, "rapid technical progress and high investment could both be the result of some third factor, like the presence of conditions that encourage entrepreneurial activity. High investment and fast technical progress will then go together" (Solow 1988, 315).

Export expansion, which stimulates the derived demand of factor inputs and enlarges the scale of operations, could serve as the third factor encouraging entrepreneurial activity to enhance the interaction effect which we discussed in the context of question 3.

5. What additional economic implications can be obtained by including human capital accumulation as the third factor input in the production function? In this study, we examine whether including human capital accumulation corrects the overestimated impact of savings on income. Furthermore, we also test Lucas's assertion that human capital accumulation has both internal and external effects. The internal effect is the private marginal product paid to the person endowing the human capital. The external effect is that people interact with others who are more educated in the production process and thereby learn by doing. This has a social value which the private individual may not realize at all.

In order to tackle the problems raised, this paper is divided into two parts. First, we examine the MRW empiric on time-series data for Taiwan for the period 1953–92. The level of income per capita is determined by savings ratio, population growth, and human capital accumulation. The weighted enrollment rate of high schools and universities is compiled as the proxy for human capital accumulation. The aggregate physical capital stock is also compiled for measurement of the depreciation rate and to account for the impact of physical capital on growth of output.

Second, we examine the growth of technological change from the interaction effect between total factor productivity and factor inputs. The parameters of production, which are the implied parameters from the income determinant, are used for the calculation of total factor productivity. The simple interaction effect is rejected. We then propose a modified interaction effect in which the interaction effects of factor inputs coexist with the scale effect generated by export expansion. The implied parameters for the production function show a constant return to scale, and the externality of factor input cannot be separated from scale effect. In this regard, we conclude that the old, neoclassical development model is valid in the sense that the input factor owners are paid by their own marginal productivity. However, the new development model provides an explanation for technological change, in which external effects, factor inputs, and export expansion interact each other.

4.1 Taiwan's Growth Experience: 1953–92

Over the past 40 years, Taiwan's economy has achieved spectacularly rapid growth. Although only a small island of 13,900 square miles with few natural resources and a very high population density,[2] Taiwan realized a 10-fold increase in real GDP per capita with an average annual growth rate of 6.27 percent between 1953 and 1992. As shown in table 4.1, real GDP per capita increased from NT$19,942 in 1953 to NT$213,910 in 1992.[3] During the same period, the population growth rate dropped from 3.81 percent to 0.95 percent and the savings ratio increased from 14.45 percent to 28.42 percent. Therefore, Taiwan's growth has followed the prediction of established growth theory, i.e., high savings and lower population growth lead to a higher level of income.

Before World War II, Taiwan was occupied by the Japanese, and the colonial government regarded Taiwan as a source of agricultural products for their own country. In order to raise output, the Japanese invested in such infrastructure as irrigation and elementary education. After World War II, there was a severe scarcity of materials and foreign exchange due to acute inflation and the withdrawal of the Nationalist forces from mainland China to Taiwan. Faced with these conditions, the government imposed stringent import restrictions and encouraged import substitution industries to invest. However, since Taiwan is a small island, the domestic market reached its saturation point around the mid-1950s, and enterprises had to compete fiercely for the limited domestic market. Real GDP per capita grew only 3.68 percent over 1953–62. The import share was 16.8 percent of GDP, while the export share was only 10.43 percent. This was the only decade during the 1953–92 period that Taiwan's economy suffered a trade deficit and had domestic investment higher than domestic savings. To make up the current account deficit, U.S. aid filled the gap.

When the emphasis of trade policy shifted gradually from import restriction to export promotion following the Nineteen-Point Economic and Financial Reform of 1958,[4] the average growth rate for exports increased from 9.23 percent to 25.42 percent in the 10 years before and after 1963. Consequently, the high growth in exports brought about high growth in investment and imports during the 1963–72 period. The average annual growth rate of real GDP per capita also reached its highest level—7.89 percent—over the past 40 years with declining population growth.

In the period 1973–82, in spite of two oil crises in 1974 and 1979, the export growth rate remained at 9.23 percent, quite high for a period during which most developed countries suffered from stagflation. Meanwhile, mass public investment projects were implemented to raise the investment ratio to 30.73

2. The population density was 568 persons per square kilometer for Taiwan in 1991. This density is higher than in Japan (333 persons) and South Korea (439 persons). Although Hong Kong (5,550 persons) and Singapore (4,750 persons) are highest among the East Asian countries, they are city-states. The most notable high-density country among the industrialized economies is the Netherlands with 369 persons per square kilometer in 1991.

3. In current U.S. dollars, the GNP per capita was $169 in 1953 and $10,215 in 1992.

4. For a description of the background and implementation of export-led policy, see Lee and Liang (1982).

Table 4.1 Economic Growth Indicators in Taiwan, 1953–92

Indicator	1953	1953–62	1963–72	1973–82	1983–92	1992
GDP per capita (NT$ at 1986 prices)	19,942	24,973	43,542	87,794	165,281	213,907
Annual growth rate (%)		3.68	7.89	5.56	6.23	5.59
Population growth rate	3.81	3.51	2.82	1.91	1.11	0.95
Gross domestic saving/GDP (%)	14.45	15.15	23.78	31.81	33.45	28.42
Gross domestic investment/GDP (%)	14.04	16.86	23.25	30.73	21.80	23.91
Current account/GDP (%)	0.40	−1.71	0.54	1.08	11.65	4.51
Export/GDP (%)	8.64	10.43	26.05	48.75	52.47	44.24
Import/GDP (%)	13.81	16.87	26.06	47.26	42.21	41.90
Export growth rate (%)		9.23	25.42	9.36	10.59	6.39
Import growth rate (%)		6.59	21.44	7.95	12.92	10.89
Literacy rate (%)[a]	56.01[b]	62.88	76.84	87.84	91.92	93.59
Secondary school enrollment rate (%)[a]	17.73[c]	29.28[c]	54.79[c,d]	66.52	81.33	85.20
Higher education enrollment rate (%)[a]	1.35[c]	2.73[c]	14.86[c,d]	17.85	25.27	38.62

Sources: Directorate-General of Budget, Accounting and Statistics (DGBAS), *National Income Account* (Taipei, 1993); DGBAS, *Social Indicators of the Republic of China* (Taipei, 1992).

[a]Figures for 1956, 1966, 1976, and 1986 are given for the decades 1953–62, 1963–72, 1973–82, and 1983–92; respectively.

[b]This figure is for 1950.

[c]Military servicemen are not included in the age cohort.

[d]Age cohorts are 15–19 and 20–24 rather than 12–17 and 18–22, since population data for single ages are not available for 1965.

percent. Shares of both exports and imports increased to around 48 percent of GDP, which slightly favored the current account. Real GDP per capita grew at 5.56 percent during this period.

During the period 1983–92, real GDP per capita growth rose to 6.23 percent due to the dramatic depreciation of the U.S. dollar in 1986 accompanied by the relatively slow appreciation of the local currency. Both exports and imports grew quickly during this period; however, that the export share of GDP was 10 percent greater than the import share implied that a great portion of available resources could not be absorbed for domestic use. Although the savings ratio increased to 33.45 percent, the investment ratio dropped to 21.80 percent due to the sluggish growth of public investment and the decline of labor-intensive industries because of the rise in wage rates and appreciation. In order to solve the problem of excess savings, the government implemented the so-called Six-Year National Development Plan in 1991 to boost public infrastructure construction. Furthermore, tremendous effort has been made by the government to encourage private investment.

There is a puzzle as to the growth in the period 1983–92. While the conventional factor inputs such as capital stock and employment grew relatively slowly, they still supported the fast growth of output. This implies that some factors beyond those studied in traditional growth theory should be considered. However, capital is only one factor which has been suggested to make a significant contribution to economic growth. Advances in knowledge and the diffusion of new ideas and objectives are necessary to remove economic backwardness and instill human abilities and motivations that are favorable to economic achievement. Secondary school enrollment was 17.73 percent in 1953 and 85.23 percent in 1991. Compulsory education was extended from six years to nine years in 1968, raising the secondary school enrollment rate from 29.28 percent in 1960 to 54.79 percent in 1970. The increase in income has also increased the demand for higher education. The enrollment ratio of higher education was only 1.35 percent in 1953, but jumped to 33.49 percent in 1991. This factor was very important when Taiwan began to emphasize labor-intensive industries and needed large numbers of skilled laborers in the 1960s to 1980s. And later, this helped Taiwan develop technology-intensive industries in the 1980s.

Compared with other middle-income developing countries, the human capital level in Taiwan is relatively high. In terms of adult literacy, the primary school enrollment ratio, and the secondary school enrollment rate, all of Taiwan's figures are higher than those for countries in the same income group, as shown in table 4.2. In fact, Taiwan's GNP per capita was even lower than the average for middle-income economies in 1970. However Taiwan's GNP per capita increased to twice the average for middle-income economies in 1989. A further observation should be made: the export growth rate is also high and this could enhance the international knowledge spillover effect and hasten economic growth, as outlined in Grossman and Helpman's (1990) paper.

4.2 The MRW Empirics of Growth Model

In this section we use Taiwanese data to test the MRW argument that (1) Solow's growth model predicts that increasing the rate of savings and decreasing population growth will raise the steady state level of per capita income, (2) the influence of the rate of savings is biased in the standard Solow model, (3) the inclusion of human capital in the production function could correct this bias, and (4) the exogenous assumption of income determinants is valid. We begin by reviewing the MRW Solow growth model with implications for a country's specific data.

Table 4.2 **Education Level, Per Capita GNP, and Export Growth Rate: An International Compensation**

Countries	Adult Literacy Rate 1961	Adult Literacy Rate 1981	Primary School Enrollment Rate 1961	Primary School Enrollment Rate 1981	Secondary School Enrollment Rate 1961	Secondary School Enrollment Rate 1981	Per Capita GNP (U.S. $) 1970	Per Capita GNP (U.S. $) 1989	Average Export Growth Rate 1961–89
Taiwan	74.1	90.1	96.0	99.8	33.1	82.6	392	7,201	16.2
Middle-income economies	48.1	65.2	75.2	100.0	14.1	38.9	490	3,190	4.8
High-income economies	98.0	98.9	113.9[a]	101.5[a]	63.9	89.2	2,050	19,240	5.4

Sources: For Taiwan, education data is from DGBAS, *Social Indicators of the Republic of China* (Taipei, 1992); export growth rate is from DGBAS, *National Income Account* (Taipei, 1992). For middle-income and high-income economics, education data is from World Bank *World Table. Volume II, Social Data* (Washington, D.C., 1983); export growth rate is calculated from World Bank, *World Table* (Washington, D.C., 1991).

Note: GNP per capita for Taiwan is calculated according to the World Bank Atlas method of converting data in national currency to U.S. dollars.

[a]The primary school enrollment rate is the enrollment of all ages in primary schools as a percentage of the population of primary school age, which normally covers all children from ages 6–11. The enrollment rate may exceed 100 percent because some pupils are below or above the official school age.

4.2.1 Models

MRW present two growth models. One is the standard Solow growth model with two inputs, capital and labor, which are paid their marginal products. The other adds human capital accumulation to the Solow model.

In the first model, it is assumed that a Cobb-Douglas production function at time t is given by[5]

$$(1) \qquad Y(t) = A(t)K(t)^{\alpha}L(t)^{1-\alpha}, \quad 0 < \alpha < 1,$$

where Y is output, K capital, L labor, and A the level of technology.

The model assumes that L grows exogenously at rate n and that a constant fraction of output s is invested. Through derivation of the evaluation of capital per capita, the standard Solow model indicates that the steady state income per capita is[6]

$$(2) \qquad \ln\left(\frac{Y(t)}{L(t)}\right) = \ln A(t) + \frac{\alpha}{1-\alpha}\ln(s(t)) - \frac{\alpha}{1-\alpha}\ln(n(t) + \delta(t)),$$

where δ is the rate of depreciation.

5. MRW assume the production function is labor augmented. In contrast, we do not assume this initially, but discuss the possibility of labor augmentation in the next section.

6. We specify $\ln A(t)$ rather than $\ln A(0) + gt$ as shown in MRW's eq. (6) because we apply the model for time-series analysis rather than cross-sectional analysis.

Equation (2) states that the steady state income per capita is related positively to the rate of saving and negatively to the rate of population growth. Because the model assumes that factors are paid their marginal products, it predicts not only the signs but also the magnitudes of the coefficients on savings and population growth. However the magnitudes of the coefficients on savings and population growth will be biased if the important input factor is omitted in equation (2). Therefore, the second model is introduced.

The second model expands the Solow model to include human capital. With the production function adding the stock of human capital, *H,* as the third production input, we can go through a similar derivation. Assuming that human capital depreciates at the same rate as physical capital, combining the determination equation with the level of human capital yields an equation for income as a function of the rate of investment in physical capital, the rate of population growth, and the level of human capital:

$$(3) \qquad \ln\left(\frac{Y(t)}{L(t)}\right) = \ln A(t) + \frac{\alpha}{1-\alpha}\ln(s(t)) - \frac{\alpha}{1-\alpha}\ln(n(t) + \delta(t)) + \frac{\beta}{1-\alpha}\ln(H(t)).$$

Equation (3) and equation (2) are different because of the additional variable *H,* which is omitted in equation (2). The omitted human capital term biases the coefficient on savings and population in equation (2).

4.2.2 Specification

Although equations (2) and (3) claim that the higher savings rates and human capital, the higher the level of income per capita, and that the higher the population growth, the lower the income per capita, there is another factor which could influence income level in both equations, i.e., $A(t)$, the technological level. Since the $A(t)$ term reflects not just technology but international and domestic shocks, as well as cyclical fluctuation, it may therefore be determined by

$$\ln A(t) = a + \varepsilon(t),$$

where a is a constant and ε is a random variable which is independent of the savings rate, human capital, and population growth rate.

Therefore equations (2) and (3) can take the stochastic forms:

$$(4) \qquad \ln\left(\frac{Y(t)}{L(t)}\right) = a + \frac{\alpha}{1-\alpha}\ln(s(t)) - \frac{\alpha}{1-\alpha}\ln(n(t) + \delta(t)) + \varepsilon(t),$$

$$(5) \qquad \ln\left(\frac{Y(t)}{L(t)}\right) = a + \frac{\alpha}{1-\alpha}\ln(s(t)) - \frac{\alpha}{1-\alpha}\ln(n(t) + \delta(t)) + \frac{\beta}{1-\alpha}\ln(H(t)) + \varepsilon(t).$$

Equations (4) and (5) are the empirical specification of MRW's version when applied to the time-series data.

In reality, however, the income level could affect savings and population growth (e.g., see Tsiang 1964). Furthermore, higher savings and lower population growth lead to a higher level of income and hence a higher level of human capital. This implies that *s*, *n*, and *H* are endogenous. Using ordinary least squares would lead to a potentially inconsistent estimation result.

In order to deal with this problem, we utilize both the ordinary least squares estimation method and the instrumental variable method.

4.2.3 Data Source and Compilation

The empirical study is conducted using annual data for Taiwan from 1953 to 1992 subject to the availability of data. We measure *n* as the annual growth rate of the working population aged 15–64. We measure *s* as the share of real investment in real GDP,[7] and *Y*/*L* as real GDP at 1986 constant prices divided by the working-age population in that year. To measure the depreciation rate, we measure the aggregate capital stock for Taiwan, then take the depreciation allowance over the capital stock. The measurement of capital stock is described in the appendix.

In measuring human capital to implement the model, we restrict our focus to formal education and, as MRW did, (1) ignore investment in health and on-the-job training, (2) ignore the forgone labor earnings which measured GDP fails to include, and (3) ignore primary education and the input of teachers. However, we include higher education in human capital.

The Harbison-Myers index, which is derived from the secondary school enrollment rate plus five times the university enrollment rate in the respective age cohorts, is used as the proxy of human capital accumulation (see Harbison, Maruhnic, and Resnick 1970). However, data for the single age cohorts for the periods 1963–68 and 1972–73 in Taiwan are not available. We are forced to use the population aged 15–19 and aged 20–24 as the denominator to derive the student population in secondary schools and higher education. Although this variable is not perfect since the age ranges in the two sets of data are not exactly the same, the variable might reflect the concept of stock which lagged the enrollment rate by several years to distinguish the stock of human capital from the flow of human capital.

4.2.4 Time-Series Data Considerations

The difficulties of using annual macrodata to analyze economic growth has been raised by Romer (1987, 186) in at least three respects. They are serially

7. Using the share of investment in GDP rather than the savings share in GDP has special significance for Taiwan. In the 1980s, Taiwan experienced excess savings of over 20 percent of GDP, which could have been used to invest to raise the income level, but which were not absorbed domestically.

correlated disturbances, cyclical fluctuation, and contemporaneous feedback. Since we will estimate the model using both the ordinary least squares method and the instrumental variable method, the third problem has been taken into account. The first two difficulties are discussed here with respect to the stationarity of time-series data with serially correlated disturbance and the addition of a cyclical variable to the equations.

Stationarity

Since the macroeconomic data are generally nonstationary, we have tested the hypothesis of unit roots for the variables studied in this paper to find stationarity. To test for a unit root, we ran both DF and ADF regression at the level and at the first-order difference of the variables.[8]

Table 4.3 shows that all variables except population growth n accept the unit root hypothesis at the level; all variables other than human capital and physical capital reject the unit root hypothesis at the first-order difference. Although the cointegration approach is one way to deal with the unit root problem in the model, variables in equations (4) and (5) are not integrated to the same order and the length of sample is not long enough. This approach is not appropriate for this study. We tried the first-order difference form to estimate equations (4) and (5), but the results do not make any economic sense. We used the Plosser-Schwert-White (1982) differencing test and found the difference regression, indeed, leads to different results.

The low power test for the unit root hypothesis leads us to scrutinize the time property of per capita income $\ln(Y/L)$. The F-test for the hypothesis $\beta_1 = 0$, $\beta_2 = 1$ for the model

$$\ln\left(\frac{Y(t)}{L(t)}\right) = \beta_0 + \beta_1 t + \beta_2 \ln\left(\frac{Y(t-1)}{L(t-1)}\right) + \beta_3\left[\ln\left(\frac{Y(t-1)}{L(t-1)}\right) - \ln\left(\frac{Y(t-2)}{L(t-2)}\right)\right] + e_t$$

is 6.12, which is rejected at the 10 percent significance level.[9]

8. For a discussion of stationarity and the DF and ADF regression for unit test, see Maddala (1992, 258–63, 578–602).

9. The ordinary least squares estimates of the model are

$$\ln\left(\frac{Y(t)}{L(t)}\right) - \ln\left(\frac{Y(t-1)}{L(t-1)}\right) = \underset{(0.18)}{0.64} + \underset{(0.005)}{0.02t} - \underset{(0.07)}{0.23} \ln\left(\frac{Y(t-1)}{L(t-1)}\right) + \underset{(0.15)}{0.29}\left[\ln\left(\frac{Y(t-1)}{L(t-1)}\right) - \ln\left(\frac{Y(t-1)}{L(t-1)}\right)\right],$$

$$\text{RSS} = 0.021228,$$

$$\ln\left(\frac{Y(t)}{L(t)}\right) - \ln\left(\frac{Y(t-1)}{L(t-1)}\right) = \underset{(0.01)}{0.04} + \underset{(0.16)}{0.31}\left[\ln\left(\frac{Y(t-1)}{L(t-1)}\right) - \ln\left(\frac{Y(t-2)}{L(t-2)}\right)\right],$$

$$\text{RSS} = 0.028876,$$

where RSS denotes the residual sum of squares and the numbers in parentheses are standard errors. The F-test for the hypothesis $\beta_1 = 0$, $\beta_2 = 1$ is 6.12, while the 90 percent point of the distribution is given in table VI of Dickey and Fuller (1981) as 5.47.

Table 4.3 **Tests of Unit Roots**

	Level		First-Order Difference	
Variable	DF	ADF	DF	ADF
$\ln(Y/L)$	−3.12	−3.36	−4.45	−4.16
$\ln(I/Y)$	−1.28	−1.58	−4.38	−3.50
$\ln(n+\delta)$	−4.59	−3.88	−8.12	−6.64
lnH	−2.45	−1.88	−2.75	−2.53
$\ln(I/Y) - \ln(n+\delta)$	−3.05	−2.35	−7.98	−6.41
$\ln H - \ln(n+\delta)$	−2.98	−2.36	−7.99	−6.27
lnK	−0.40	−3.26	−1.50	−1.80

Notes: For variable X_t, DF and ADF are the *t*-statistics for b in the regressions $\Delta X_t = a + bX_{t-1} + ct + U_t$ and $\delta X_t = a + bX_{t-1} + c\Delta X_{t-1} + dt + U_t$, respectively.
At the 5 percent significance level with sample sizes 25 and 50, the critical values are −3.60 and −3.50, respectively, for both DF and ADF.

Therefore, we are forced to use the conventional approach and tolerate the low Durbin-Watson (DW) statistic. The occurrence of a low DW value might be due to the fact that omitted variables other than human capital should be considered.[10]

Cyclical Fluctuation

To account for cyclical fluctuation, we added the manufacturing capacity utilization rate, commonly considered the best candidate for cyclical variation, to equations (4) and (5). Only data since 1976 are available. We ran the regression with the additional capacity utilization rate for the period 1976–92 and found the additional variable is not significant. Although this might be caused by the short sample observation, another reason is that the model deals with income per capita at the steady state level rather than the product output of the conventional production model. Therefore, the model is not sensible with respect to cyclical fluctuation.

4.2.5 Results

Table 4.4 shows the estimation result of the Solow model with and without human capital in the case of Taiwan. Both the ordinary least squares estimation method (OLS) and the instrumental variable method (INST) are reported. The sample period is from 1953 to 1992. Equations are estimated with and without imposing the constraint that the coefficient of $\ln(n + \delta)$ is equal to $\ln s$ in the case without human capital, and the constraints that the coefficient of $\ln(n + \delta)$ is equal to $\ln s$ and is equal to $\ln H$ in the case with human capital.

Equation (a) is the neoclassical growth model without human capital estimated by OLS. The result supports the model in two respects. First, the coeffi-

10. The omitted variable might be the export variable, which will be discussed in the next section.

Table 4.4 **Estimation of the Solow Model with and without Human Capital in Two Estimation Methods, Annual Data 1953–92 (NOB=40) (Dependent Variable: log real GDP per working-age person)**

	OLS		INST	
Variable	(a)	(b)	(c)	(d)
CNST	3.43	0.87	2.17	0.29
	(4.58)	(1.79)	(2.33)	(−0.45)
$\ln(I/Y)$	1.22	−0.10	1.19	−0.22
	(9.81)	(−0.66)	(8.66)	(−1.09)
$\ln(n+\delta)$	−1.38	−1.38	−1.87	−1.76
	(−5.31)	(−9.79)	(−5.74)	(−9.85)
$\ln H$		0.81		0.84
		(9.49)		(7.84)
$\bar{R}^2$	0.82	0.95	0.82	0.94
DW	0.44	1.01	0.81	1.30
SSR	2.82	0.81	3.10	0.97
	Restricted Regression			
CNST	3.80	2.59	3.75	2.68
	(49.48)	(15.47)	(47.01)	(14.49)
$\ln(I/Y) - \ln(n+\delta)$	1.26	0.20	1.34	0.36
	(13.48)	(1.35)	(13.64)	(2.00)
$\ln H - \ln(n+\delta)$		0.71		0.64
		(7.59)		(5.98)
$\bar{R}^2$	0.82	0.93	0.82	0.93
SSR	2.84	1.11	2.90	1.14
F	0.25	6.81	−2.41	3.18
Implied α	0.56	0.17	0.57	0.26
β		0.42		0.39

Note: Numbers in parentheses are t-statistics.

cients for savings and population growth have predicted signs and are highly significant. Second, the restriction that the coefficients on $\ln s$ and $\ln(n + \delta)$ are equal in magnitude and opposite in sign is not rejected. The estimated impacts of savings and labor force growth (0.56) are similar to the MRW results and imply the estimate is much higher than the model prediction that $\alpha = 1/3$.

Equation (b) presents regressions of the log of income per capita on the log of the investment rate, the log of $n + \delta$, and the log of human capital. The human capital measure enters significantly and improves the fit of the regression compared with equation (a). The DW statistic rises from 0.44 to 1.01, indicating that human capital is the important factor dominating income per capita—which is itself autocorrelated—and has been omitted from equation (a), the standard neoclassical growth model. Although the unrestricted form of equation (b) exhibits the multicollinearity problem, which makes the coefficient of $\ln(I/Y)$ insignificant and of the wrong sign, the implied value of α in the restricted regression has been reduced from 0.56 to 0.17. The other implied parameter β shows that the impact of human capital on income per capita, 0.42, is still higher than the model prediction. Nevertheless, the *F*-statistic, 6.81, rejects at the 5 percent level the equal impact of physical capital and human capital.

Equations (c) and (d) take into account the endogeneity of the income determinants by employing two-stage least squares estimation procedures, using lagged values of all variables shown in table 4.4 as instruments.[11] For the case without human capital, the results of equation (c) are similar to those of equation (a) for the biased value of α, but with an improvement in the DW statistic.

When human capital is included in the consideration of endogeneity, as shown in equation (d), the autocorrelation problem is almost solved since the DW statistic, 1.30, is close to the lower limit for significance. Furthermore, the implied values of α and β are closer to 1/3, as MRW proposed. We conclude that the MRW proposal of the income per capita model, i.e., adding human capital to the Solow model, can be tested in country-specific time-series data with consideration of endogeneity. The relaxation of the exogeneity assumption on the determinants leads us to move from the old development model to the new development model.

4.3 Interaction between Factor Inputs and Productivity Growth

We have examined a Solow model which includes accumulation of human as well as physical capital using country-specific data. The results are derived from a Cobb-Douglas production function implying that factor inputs are paid by their own marginal productivities. Although the results explain the determinants of the long-term level of output per worker, they do not explain the fast productivity growth and the strong positive association between trade and growth. For the study of productivity growth, Jorgenson (1990) carefully distinguishes the contribution of capital and labor quality from the contribution of capital stock and hours worked based on the strict neoclassical assumption of constant returns to scale. Boskin and Lau (1992) employ the meta–production function to identify separately the degree of returns to scale, the rate of technical progress, and the bias of technical progress. While the time-series and cross-sectional analyses of growth by Jorgenson, as well as Lau and his coauthors, have the flavor of a well-specified theory, they do not take into account the externality factor of input and trade.

Economists including Solow argued that a factor input could generate externalities and contribute to economic growth in excess of what the factor itself earns. We examine this possibility through the interaction effect between total factor productivity (TFP) and factor inputs first, then show the importance of

11. The alternative set of instruments, which includes government consumption, public investment, exports, and imports, as well as the lagged values of these four variables plus the constant term, gives a similar result.

trade and the importance of the trade and factor externalities in the consequent context.

4.3.1 The Simple Interaction Effect

There are three potential interaction effects. First, the embodiment effect suggests that substantial capital accumulation is necessary to put new inventions into practice and to affect widespread employment (Solow 1988; Nelson 1964; Wolff 1991). Second, the improvement in labor quality, due to both the changing age-sex composition of the work force and the decline of work hours,[12] could affect TFP[13] (Nelson 1964; Denison 1979). Third, there is an interaction between human capital and TFP. Lucas (1988) argued that human capital accumulation is a social activity: the more educated workers interact with other educated people, the more new ideas come about which improve productive efficiency. Therefore human capital exerts two effects on the production process: one is the internal effect of an individual's human capital on his own productivity; the other is the external effect that no individual human capital accumulation decision can take into account.

The TFP level is defined as the ratio of total output (Y) to a geometrically weighted average of physical capital input (K), human capital input (H), and labor input (L):

$$\text{TFP} = Y / (K^{\alpha} L^{1-\alpha-\beta} H^{\beta}). \tag{6}$$

Total factor productivity growth can then be defined as

$$\widehat{\text{TFP}} = \hat{Y} - \alpha\hat{K} - (1 - \alpha - \beta)\hat{L} - \beta\hat{H}, \tag{7}$$

where the "hat" (^) indicates the relative rate of change.

In general, a production function associated with the interaction effect in the paper could be expressed as

$$Y = AK^{\alpha} L^{1-\alpha-\beta} H^{\beta} X^{\gamma}, \quad \gamma > 0, \tag{8}$$

where X could be either physical capital, labor input, or human capital. The rate of growth of TFP is then defined as

$$\widehat{\text{TFP}} = \hat{A} + \gamma\hat{X}. \tag{9}$$

Equation (9) is used as the specification for testing the interaction hypothesis by positing a positive association between the rate of growth of TFP and

12. The conventional argument for labor improvement includes improvement in educational attainment in the production function of two inputs (i.e., capital and labor). Since we add human capital as another factor input, an improvement in educational attainment will contribute directly to human capital.

13. The common practice with regard to labor improvement in growth analysis is the labor augmentation approach which treats labor input exogenously and uses another exogenous variable (e.g., production efficiency) as a proxy for labor improvement. If labor input is endogenous, there is no difference between the labor augmentation and the labor interaction effects.

the rate of growth of factor inputs. In this simple version of the interaction effect, there is no other effect involved.

The results of the estimation are shown in table 4.5. All three equations reject the hypothesis. In the case of human capital, the sign of the estimated interaction coefficient is opposite at a significant level. Both physical capital and labor input show statistically insignificant results, while the sign for the capital growth coefficient is also opposite. The results are similar to Dollar's (1991) study on the convergence of South Korean productivity to West German levels, where the hypothesis of the interaction effect between TFP and capital accumulation was also rejected.

4.3.2 The Role of Exports

The rejection of the simple interaction effect is a result of ignoring the export expansion which has played an important role in the economic growth of a small economy like Taiwan's. Exports can be substituted for import goods which either are scarce in nature or for which Taiwan has no advantage in domestic production. Furthermore, it has been found that there is a statistically significant correlation between export expansion and output growth as shown in equation (d) of table 4.5. The relation between export performance and economic growth has been a subject of considerable interest to development economists for various reasons, including economies of scale, efficiency of resource allocation, and international knowledge spillover.[14]

However, Chen and Tang found that "export expansion leads to scale enlargement, thereby contributing to productive growth. But aside from its indirect contribution to the scale of output, export expansion has a rather ambiguous and weak linkage to productivity growth in Taiwan" (1990, 583). Apparently, the scale effect of export expansion can enlarge other external effects which are generated by factor inputs. We attempt to make up for Chen and Tang's gap, and postulate the hypothesis that export expansion will generate economies of scale which coexist with and enhance the externalities of factor inputs in productivity growth.

4.3.3 The Modified Interaction Effect

Our modified version of the interaction effect is derived from a production function

$$Y = AK^{\alpha} L^{1-\alpha-\beta} H^{\beta} X^{f(\hat{E})}, \tag{10}$$

where the interaction effect of factor input X will be enhanced by the scale

14. The proponents of externalities from trade include Bhagwati (1978) who considers scale economies the largest benefit of the export promotion trade strategy, Feder (1984) who argues for the reallocation of existing resources from the less efficient nonexport sector to the higher productivity export sector, and Grossman and Helpman (1991) who see the international knowledge spillover generated by trade coexisting with the externality of domestic innovation.

Table 4.5 Interaction Effect, 1953–92 (Dependent Variable: $\hat{\text{TFP}}$)

Variable	(a)	(b)	(c)	(d)
CNST	0.03	0.02	0.05	0.00
	(0.97)	(0.87)	(5.46)	(0.42)
$\hat{K}$	−0.6			
	(−0.25)			
$\hat{L}$		0.21		
		(0.40)		
$\hat{H}$			−0.35	
			(−4.01)	
$\hat{E}$				0.11
				(3.39)
$\bar{R}^2$	−0.02	−0.02	0.28	0.22
DW	1.87	1.86	1.86	1.94
SSR	0.04	0.04	0.03	0.32
ρ	0.46	0.46	0.21	0.49

Notes: Numbers in parentheses are *t*-statistics. All equations are corrected for serial correlation.

effect of export expansion $f(\hat{E})$. For simplicity, we assume the scale effect is proportional to export growth, $f(\hat{E}) = \gamma\hat{E}$. Thus, the specification for the hypothesis test of the modified version of the interaction effect will be

$$\hat{\text{TFP}} = \hat{A} + \gamma\hat{E}\hat{X}. \tag{11}$$

The modified interaction effect shows that the factor interaction effect "interacts" with the scale effect generated by export expansion. This can be seen from the derivative of $\hat{\text{TFP}}$ with respect to $\hat{X}$:

$$\frac{d\hat{\text{TFP}}}{d\hat{X}} = \gamma\hat{E}. \tag{12}$$

Therefore, the impact of factor growth on productivity is not independent of export growth.

The results of the regression of the modified interaction effects are shown in equations (a)–(c) of table 4.6. The rates of growth of the physical capital and labor inputs now show significant positive effects on the rate of growth of total factor productivity, while human capital still shows an insignificant negative effect without any explanatory power for TFP.

We check the human capital series and find there is a structural break in 1968 (see fig. 4.1.). In that year, the length of compulsory education in Taiwan was extended from six years to nine years. However, the effect of the extension of the length of compulsory education in the human capital series was offset by including servicemen in the population statistics beginning in 1969. Because most servicemen are in the 20–24 age cohort, the exclusion of servicemen leads to a calculation of the higher education portion of the human capital index which is more heavily weighted prior to 1969. Therefore, the data structures for the human capital index before and after 1969 are different.

Table 4.6 **Modified Version of Interaction Effect in Two Different Periods (Dependent Variable: $\hat{TFP}$)**

	1953–92			1970–92		
Variable	(a)	(b)	(c)	(d)	(e)	(f)
CNST	0.00	0.00	0.02	0.00	−0.10	0.02
	(0.15)	(0.72)	(2.69)	(0.16)	(−0.08)	(2.30)
$\hat{E}\hat{K}$	1.14			1.96		
	(4.06)			(7.50)		
$\hat{E}\hat{L}$		2.75			9.48	
		(2.79)			(8.22)	
$\hat{E}\hat{H}$			−0.31			3.95
			(−0.99)			(2.05)
$\bar{R}^2$	0.28	0.15	−0.00	0.72	0.76	0.13
DW	1.95	1.90	1.87	1.87	1.91	1.98
SSR	0.03	0.03	0.04	0.009	0.008	0.023
ρ	0.53	0.52	0.39	0.64	0.70	0.15
F				14.26	24.38	6.42

Notes: Numbers in parentheses are *t*-statistics. All equations are corrected for serial correlation. $F_{1,40}$ at the 5 percent significance level = 4.08.

Table 4.7 **Alternative Version of Interaction Effect in Two Different Periods (Dependent Variable: $\hat{TFP}$)**

	1953–92			1970–92		
Variable	(a)	(b)	(c)	(d)	(e)	(f)
CNST	0.00	0.00	−0.00	−0.00	−0.00	−0.00
	(0.17)	(0.42)	(−0.23)	(−0.54)	(−0.59)	(−0.25)
$\hat{E}\hat{K}$	1.52			−1.02		
	(1.99)			(−1.82)		
$\hat{E}\hat{L}$		−0.46			−5.19	
		(−0.23)			(−1.84)	
$\hat{E}\hat{H}$			−1.90			−1.14
			(−7.89)			(−1.32)
$\hat{E}$	−0.05	0.13	0.28	0.41	0.43	0.30
	(−0.54)	(1.82)	(9.47)	(5.11)	(4.87)	(9.91)
$\bar{R}^2$	0.27	0.19	0.70	0.82	0.82	0.84
DW	1.94	1.93	1.87	1.93	1.94	1.80
SSR	0.03	0.03	0.01	0.01	0.01	0.01
ρ	0.54	0.48	0.47	0.28	0.29	0.56
F				16.93	26.68	4.03

Notes: Numbers in parentheses are *t*-statistics. All equations are corrected for serial correlation. $F_{2,40}$ at the 5 percent significance level = 3.23.

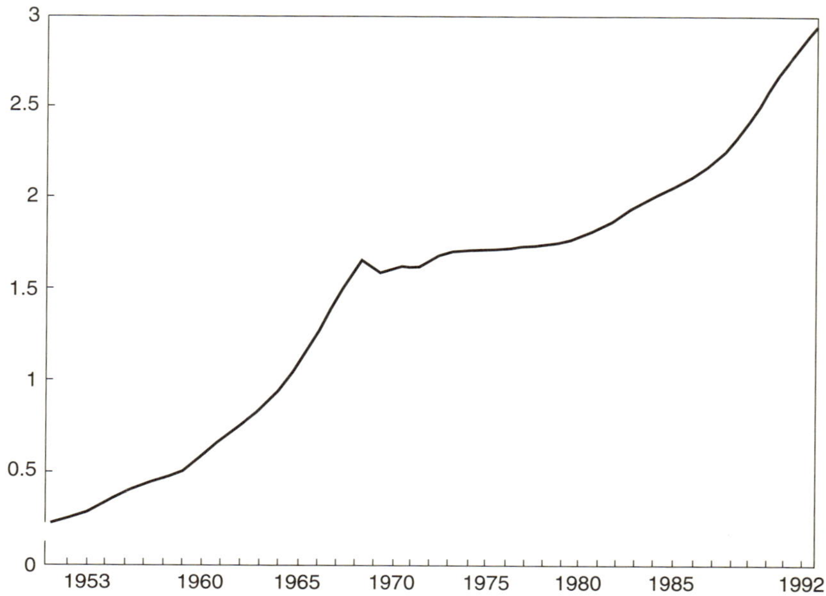

Fig. 4.1 Human capital index

Equations are rerun for the period 1970–92 and are shown in equations (d)–(f) of table 4.6. Chow's F-tests, which are statistically significant at the 5 percent level in all three equations, imply the existence of structural change. All three factor inputs' interaction effects, coexisting with the scale effect, are significantly positively correlated with TFP in the period 1970–92. The explanatory powers of the regressions in the new period have increased from 0.28, 0.15, and 0.0 to 0.72, 0.76, and 0.13 for physical capital, labor input, and human capital, respectively.[15,16]

15. Capacity utilization is another important explanatory variable used to catch the cyclical fluctuation in TFP analysis. However, annual data for Taiwan are available only for 17 years, i.e., 1976–92. Running the regression for that period, we found that the value of adjusted R^2 is raised and the coefficient of the utilization rate is significantly positive. The inclusion of the utilization rate does not alter the importance of export growth on productivity growth, which might imply that export growth generates a scale effect rather than cyclical effects. Since the results do not alter our prediction much, we do not list them here.

16. We tried regression with interactive terms along with the export growth variable, as shown in table 4.7. For the whole period (1953–90), only the interactive term for physical capital is significantly positive, while the additional export growth variable is insignificant. The interactive terms for both labor and human capital are negative with significantly positive export growth. For the period 1970–92, all interactive terms turn negative, while the export growth variable is significantly positive. Five out of six cases show the positive association of export growth with productivity; however, the negative impact of the interactive term on productivity contradicts predicted theory. We are forced to drop the additional export growth variable in table 4.6.

4.4 Conclusion

We find that the neoclassical growth model can be applied to the Taiwanese experience when human capital accumulation is added to physical capital and labor input in the neoclassic production function and when the exogeneity of factor inputs is relaxed. In a perfectly competitive market with constant returns to scale, factors are paid their internal marginal productivity. In other words, the estimated equations in section 4.2 show that, except for population growth and the rate of investment, human capital could change the long-run level of output per worker. This finding essentially supports established growth theory with human capital as the third factor influencing production and with a relaxation of the exogeneity of factor inputs.

However, this finding is not sufficient to explain the rapid growth of the Taiwanese economy in the past 40 years unless we tackle the technological change issue. We examine the interaction effect between technological change and factor inputs and find that in a small open economy like Taiwan's, the interaction effect coexists with the scale effect generated by export expansion. Therefore, our empirical results in section 4.3 show that growth and trade have risen by leaps and bounds as Romer (1986) and Lucas (1988) have suggested.

Our findings stress the importance of trade and human capital accumulation, both of which have been pursued by new growth theory. Because of the coherence of the scale effect from trade for a small open economy and international knowledge spillover from the external effect of human capital and international trade, our empirical findings have empirical and policy implications, i.e., a small country can grow as fast as a large one by introducing international trade and human capital. Therefore, this paper supports the hypothesis that an orientation toward foreign trade is at the heart of the spectacular growth performance of the East Asian economies.

Appendix
Measurement of Aggregate Capital Stock for Taiwan

Although series for capital stock in Taiwan are published by the government statistics agency, the Directorate-General of Budget, Accounting and Statistics (DGBAS), the series start from 1961 and do not yet include aggregate capital stock. We measure the capital stock series in the form

$$K(t) = K(t-1) + I(t) - D(t), \quad \text{(A1)}$$

where $K(t)$ is the real capital stock at period t, $I(t)$ is the real gross fixed investment, and $D(t)$ is the real capital depreciation allowance. The benchmark year is 1951. We calculate the initial stock[17] by

17. The approach of calculating initial capital stock is suggested by William W. F. Chao and Lawrence Lau.

$$K(1) = \frac{I(0)e^{\theta}}{\theta}, \tag{A2}$$

where $I(0)$ and θ are the estimated coefficients of the constant term and TIME in the following form, by ordinary least squares estimation:

$$\ln I(t) = C + \theta\text{TIME}. \tag{A3}$$

The estimation is that (1) the capital stock in the first period is the sum of all past investments:

$$K(1) = \int_{t=-\infty}^{1} I(t)dt; \tag{A4}$$

and (2) the investment series may be approximated by an exponential time trend:

$$I(t) = I(0)e^{\theta t}. \tag{A5}$$

Inserting equation (A5) into equation (A4) yields equation (A2). Taking natural logarithms of equation (A5), we obtain equation (A3) where the constant term c is ln $I(0)$.

References

Arrow, Kenneth J. 1962. The economic implications of learning by doing. *Review of Economic Studies* 24: 155–73.

Azariadis, Costas, and Allen Drazer. 1990. Threshold externalities in economic development. *Quarterly Journal of Economics* 105: 501–26.

Backus, David K., Patrick J. Kehoe, and Timothy J. Kehoe. 1992. In search of scale effects in trade and growth. *Journal of Economic Theory* 58: 377–409.

Bhagwati, Jagdish. 1978. *Anatomy and consequences of exchange control regimes.* Cambridge, Mass.: Bollinger.

Boskin, M. J., and L. J. Lau. 1992. Capital, technology, and economic Growth. In *Technology and wealth of nations,* ed. N. Rosenberg R, R. Landan, and D. Mowery, 17–55. Stanford, Calif.: Stanford University Press.

Chen, Tain-Jy, and De-Piao Tang. 1990. Export performance and productivity growth: The case of Taiwan. *Economic Development and Cultural Change.* 38: 577–85.

Denison, Edward F. 1979. *Accounting for slower economic growth: The United States in the 1970s.* Washington, D.C.: Brookings Institution.

Dickey, David A., and Wayne A. Fuller. 1981. Likelihood ratio statistics for autoregressive time series with a unit root. *Econometrica* 49 (4): 1057–72.

Dollar, David. 1991. Convergence of South Korean productivity on West German levels, 1966–78. *World Development* 49: 263–73.

Feder, Gershon. 1984. On exports and economic growth. *Journal of Development Economics* 12 (February): 241–50.

Grossman, Gene M., and Elhanan Helpman. 1991. Trade, knowledge spillovers, and growth. *European Economic Review* 35: 517–26.

Harbison, F. H., J. Maruhnic, and J. R. Resnick. 1970. *Quantitative analyses of modernization and development.* Industrial Relations Section, Department of Economics, Princeton University.
Jorgenson, D. 1990. Productivity and economic growth. In *Fifty years of economic measurement: The jubilee of the conference on research in income and wealth,* ed. Ernst R. Berndt and Jack E. Triplett, 19–118. Chicago: University of Chicago Press.
Lee, T. H., and Kuo-Shu Liang. 1982. Incentive policies and economic development: Taiwan. In *Development strategies in semi-industrial economics,* ed. Bela Balassa, 310–50. Baltimore: John Hopkins University Press.
Lucas, Robert E., Jr. 1988. On the mechanics of economic development. *Journal of Monetary Economics* 22: 3–42.
———. 1993. Making a miracle. *Econometrica* 61: 251–72.
Maddala, G. S. 1992. *Introduction to econometrics,* 2d ed. New York: Maxwell Macmillan International.
Mankiw, N. Gregory, David Romer, and David Weil. 1992. A contribution on the empirics of economic growth. *Quarterly Journal of Economics* 106: 407–37.
Nelson, Richard R. 1964. Aggregate production functions and medium-range growth projections. *American Economic Review* 54: 575–605.
Plosser, C. I., G. W. Schwert, and H. White. 1982. Differencing as a test of specification. *International Economic Review* (October): 23: 535–52.
Romer, Paul M. 1986. Increasing returns and long run growth. *Journal of Political Economy* 94: 1002–37.
———. 1987. Crazy explanations for the productivity slowdown. *Macroeconomics Annual* 2: 163–210.
Sengupta, Jati K. 1991. Rapid growth in NICs in Asia: Tests of new growth theory for Korea. *Kyklos* 44 (4): 561–79.
Solow, Robert M. 1956. A contribution to the theory of economic growth. *Quarterly Journal of Economics* 70: 65–94.
———. 1988. Growth theory and after. *American Economic Review* 78 (3): 307–17.
Tsiang, S. C. 1964. A model of economic growth in Rostovian stages. *Econometrica* 32 (4): 619–48.
Wolff, Edward N. 1991. Capital formation and productivity convergence over the long term. *American Economic Review* 81: 565–79.

Comment Chia Siow Yue

This paper is a useful contribution to the growing literature on the empirical testing of growth and development models and provides additional insights into Taiwan's miraculous economic performance. Some empirical studies support Solow's neoclassical growth model, and others support the new endogenous growth models. Researchers have found significant relationships between some variables and economic growth, but few results are robust and many could be altered by addition of other explanatory variables. There is no clear distinction between the Solow and endogenous growth models empirically, in part because the two theories complement each other and in part because the

Chia Siow Yue is professor of economics at the National University of Singapore.

existing statistical tests are not powerful enough. The Solow model does not assign any distinctive productive role to human capital or to government policy; growth is due to exogenous technological change. The endogenous growth models complement Solow in explaining technological change and are capable of dealing with issues such as increasing returns to scale, learning-by-doing effects of human capital, and dynamic spillover effects of export growth.

Chou's paper has two parts. The first part uses time-series data on Taiwan to test an extended Solow growth model incorporating human capital accumulation. The second part examines technological change by testing for the interaction effects between total factor productivity and factor inputs. Studies such as this, based on country-specific time series, complement existing studies based on cross-country data and provide more robust relationships. Time-series regressions are more appropriate for studying long-run growth paths. Cross-country studies face the problems of different initial conditions, data of uneven quality and consistency, and comparable quantification of policy variables. However, time-series data face the problems of serially correlated disturbances, cyclical fluctuations, and contemporaneous feedback. Chou used the instrumental variable method in addition to ordinary least squares to take care of contemporaneous feedback, and the manufacturing capacity utilization rate as a proxy for cyclical fluctuations. The problem of serially correlated disturbances remained.

Economists have long stressed the importance of human capital in economic growth, but the role of human capital came into greater prominence with the endogenous growth models. Human capital enhances productivity of both labor and physical capital inputs. Chou's paper explored the effect of adding human capital accumulation to the Solow model. He found human capital to be an important factor in Taiwan's economic growth, and its inclusion in the growth regression improves the fit significantly and corrected for the upward bias in the estimated effects of the savings ratio and population growth. Chou used secondary and tertiary school enrollment as a proxy measure for human capital accumulation. However, enrollment ratios ignore the important role of training and learning by doing and the productivity effect of the educational curriculum. Additionally, labor efficiency depends not only on education and training, but also on labor-management relations and work ethics. In East Asia, Taiwan is noted for its high priority on broad-based education as well as its emphasis on technical and science-based education and training and its absence of industrial strife. Lucas has argued that human capital affects economic growth in two ways, via the internal effect of an individual's human capital on his own productivity and an external effect. For the latter, when educated workers interact, more new ideas emerge to improve productive efficiency. Chou tested the interaction between human capital and total factor productivity in Taiwan but found that the coefficient had an opposite sign which is statistically significant. The implication is that human capital in Taiwan serves the role of accumulating capital, complementing physical capital and labor rather than providing economy-wide externality.

Economists studying East Asia, particularly the Asian newly industrialized economies (NIEs), have stressed the importance of outward orientation in explaining the region's exceptional economic dynamism. However, outward orientation has generally been measured in terms of trade orientation or, more particularly, export orientation. The role of imports, including foreign technology, and the role of foreign investments have been given much less attention. Gains from trade arise from both the static effects of improved resource allocation according to comparative advantage and improved capacity utilization, as well as from positive externalities arising from the exploitation of scale economies and international knowledge spillovers generated by trade coexisting with domestic innovation activity and more efficient management in response to international competition. Evidence of positive level effects does not necessarily imply that trade will lead to faster rates of economic growth. A number of cross-country studies have shown little correlation between economic growth and export-GDP ratios once the growth regressions included other important variables. Chou's study found a statistically significant correlation between export growth and economic growth in Taiwan. Export growth led to productivity growth mainly through the scale effect, which has particularly significant implications for small countries, as represented by the four Asian NIEs. Export growth enhances the externalities of factor inputs in productivity growth. The international spillover effect of exports is unclear.

Chou's paper has demonstrated the importance of human capital and exports in explaining Taiwan's economic growth. However, policy measures affecting human capital formation and exports in Taiwan remain unclear. What are the incentives for education, training, and learning by doing at the individual, household, and firm levels? Is Confucian ethics important in the emphasis on education by individuals and households? Or can the emphasis on education be explained by the reward system, in terms of both earnings and social prestige of the more educated vis-à-vis the less educated? Also, what explains Taiwan's export growth? In particular, given the dominance of small and medium-sized enterprises in the industrial structure, how do these firms achieve export success, and what incentives and assistance are provided by government? Further, in view of the considerable foreign direct investment in Taiwan, what is its role in both human capital accumulation and export performance?

5 Debt Financing, Public Investment, and Economic Growth in Taiwan

Chen-Min Hsu

5.1 Introduction

In December 1990, the R.O.C. Council for Economic Planning and Development announced the Six-Year Plan for Economic Development. According to this plan, the government will issue NT$1,100 billion in bonds to finance public investment. In fact, the government will spend NT$8,238.2 billion over six years to restructure the economy. This amounts to raising public investment by NT$1,370 billion each year. Since public investment in 1990 was about 11 percent of GNP, this means that the ratio of government investment to GNP will be 0.435 if the plan is fully enforced. However, the government claimed that only part of the expenditure will be financed by debt, which will amount to 5 percent of GNP per year. Many controversies have arisen since the plan was announced. The popular view is that the plan is too ambitious and will disturb the economy by crowding out private investment and by worsening the fiscal structure of the government. Moreover, as shown by recent data, only one-third of the plan has been put into effect. This is due to the constraint of the government budget deficit. As we will see in table 5.1, the government budget has worsened during the past three years. Thus, in the following analysis, we will consider the case in which government investment increases by 1.67 percent of GNP per year for six years; in other words, we will take the size of government investment as given.

In the macroeconomics literature, it is well known that in Blinder and Solow's (1974) and Tobin and Buiter's (1976) models, public expenditure will not

Chen-Min Hsu is professor of economics at National Taiwan University.

The author thanks Takatoshi Ito and Anne O. Krueger for their comments and encouragement. Suggestions from Sebastian Edwards, Koichi Hamada, and T. N. Srinivasan were also very helpful, and referees for the National Bureau of Economic Research and the University of Chicago Press pointed out some crucial points related to the Taiwanese empirical data.

cause a large crowding-out effect on private expenditure. And in these models, output and employment effects are positive as long as stability conditions are satisfied. On the other hand, Barro (1989; 1990, chap. 14) showed that, under a neoclassical growth model, debt neutrality or the Ricardian equivalence theorem will not hold under an income tax scheme. In addition, as pointed out by Modigliani (see Haliassos and Tobin 1990), less capital will be accumulated as long as private investment is crowded out. This is also true even though public capital can be accumulated through public investment, as long as the productivity of public capital is less than that of private capital. Moreover, in an open economy foreigners will hold domestic public debt. This will induce more interest payments to foreigners. When the government budget deficit is large, a deficit in the current account is likely to appear.

Barro (1989) suggested that a calibrated equilibrium model be simulated to get more quantitative information about the consequences of fiscal policy (see also King, Plosser, and Rebelo 1988). In this paper, we set up a Solow-Cass-Koopmans growth model (in contrast to Blanchard 1985 and Matsuyama 1987) and follow Barro's suggestion and analyze the effects of public investment with deficit financing using Taiwanese data, given the size of government investment. This extends Barro's (1989) and King, Plosser, and Rebelo's (1988) work to the open economy case. We try to verify several points shown in these models.

This chapter will be organized as follows: In section 5.2, a closed economy model is set up to analyze the effects of deficit-financed public investment. Section 5.3 extends the model to a small open economy. Section 5.4 uses Taiwanese data to calibrate the models described in the preceding sections. Concluding remarks are given in the last section.

5.2 The Basic Model

As shown in table 5.1, the average annual growth rate of real per capita GNP in Taiwan has been about 7 percent during the last 25 years. The unemployment rate has been below 3 percent each year. It is reasonable to regard the Taiwanese economy as growing on the full-employment path. The main contributions to the growth of the economy are the growth of exports and national investment (including government investment). In this section, we follow Barro's neoclassical approach to fiscal policy and consider the effects of public investment through bond financing in a closed economy (see Barro 1989). The economy is divided into three sectors, i.e., households, firms, and the government. Each firm is assumed to be perfectly competitive and to have a Cobb-Douglas production function; i.e.,

$$(1) \qquad Y_t = A_t(K_t^g)^{\theta_g} F(K_t, N_t X_t) = A_t(K_t^g)^{\theta_g} K_t^{\theta_k} (N_t X_t)^{\theta_n},$$

where A_t is temporary technological shock, X_t is labor-augmenting or Harrod-neutral permanent technological shock, K_t^g is public capital, K_t is private capital, and θ_g, θ_n, and θ_k are output elasticities of K^g, NX, and K, respectively. It is

Table 5.1 **Basic Statistics for the Taiwanese Economy**

FY	*r*	Yg	Iy	GCy	GIy	GIi	*u*	BD
1965	11.520	7.9	22.7	16.9	7.1051	31.3	3.3	245
1966	11.520	6.1	21.2	17.4	7.3352	34.6	3.0	975
1967	10.800	7.9	24.7	17.5	9.2625	37.5	2.3	2,281
1968	11.880	6.6	25.2	17.9	9.2232	36.6	1.7	1,249
1969	10.800	6.6	24.5	18.4	10.2410	41.8	1.9	−924
1970	9.800	9.0	25.6	18.3	10.2656	40.1	1.7	866
1971	9.250	10.7	26.3	17.3	10.6252	40.4	1.7	1986
1972	8.500	11.3	25.6	16.1	10.0608	39.3	1.5	291
1973	10.750	10.7	29.1	15.2	10.0977	34.7	1.3	−2,425
1974	12.000	−.7	39.2	14.1	14.9352	38.1	1.5	−20,120
1975	10.750	2.5	30.5	15.9	17.5985	57.7	2.4	125
1976	9.500	11.4	30.8	15.3	16.4164	53.3	1.8	−6,130
1977	8.250	8.1	28.3	15.6	14.3481	50.7	1.8	12,268
1978	8.250	11.9	28.3	15.2	12.7350	45.0	1.7	10,732
1979	11.000	6.4	32.9	15.4	12.9626	39.4	1.3	−21,849
1980	11.000	5.1	33.8	15.9	16.3930	48.5	1.2	4,681
1981	11.750	3.8	30.0	16.2	14.8200	49.4	1.4	21,509
1982	7.750	2.2	25.2	16.9	13.2048	52.4	2.1	39,280
1983	7.250	6.9	23.4	16.2	10.9044	46.6	2.7	37,042
1984	6.750	10.0	21.9	15.7	8.7819	40.1	2.4	3,138
1985	5.250	4.1	18.7	15.9	7.9101	42.3	2.9	21,127
1986	4.500	11.3	17.1	14.5	6.7032	39.2	2.7	47,823
1987	4.500	10.7	20.1	14.1	7.4370	37.0	2.0	11,932
1988	4.500	6.6	22.8	14.8	7.4328	32.6	1.7	−13,509
1989	7.750	6.2	22.3	15.6	8.6524	38.8	1.6	317,979
1990	7.750	3.9	21.9	17.2	10.8405	49.5	1.7	74,346
1991	6.250	6.1	22.2	17.4	11.0778	49.9	1.5	366,694
1992	5.625	5.1	23.9	17.2	11.3286	47.4	1.5	417,809

Source: Council for Economic Planning and Development, R.O.C., *Taiwan Statistical Data Book* (Taipei, 1993).

Note: FY = fiscal year; r = rediscount rate (percent per annum); Yg = annual growth rate of real per capital GNP; Iy = the ratio of gross capital formation to GNP (percent per annum); GCy = the ratio of government investment to GNP (percent per annum); GIy = the ratio of government investment to GNP (percent per annum); GIi = the ratio of the government investment to total gross capital formation; u = unemployment rate (percent per annum); BD = government budget deficit for each fiscal year, starting from July 1 of the preceding year to June 30 of the designated year (million NT dollars).

assumed that $\theta_g + \theta_n + \theta_k = 1$; i.e., the production function gives diminishing returns with respect to total capital ($K + K^g$), but constant returns to scale with respect to total capital and effective labor.

It is assumed that both private and public capital have the same depreciation rate. Their accumulations are

$$K_{t+1} = (1 - \delta)K_t + I_t, \tag{2}$$

$$K^g_{t+1} = (1 - \delta)K^g_t + I^g_t, \tag{3}$$

where I_t and I_t^g are private and public investment, respectively, and δ is the depreciation rate. Let τ_t be the tax rate on the output. The representative firm's net cash flow after taxes is

$$(4) \qquad \Pi_t = (1 - \tau_t)A_t(K_t^g)^{\theta_g}K_t^{\theta_k}(N_t^dX_t)^{\theta_n} - W_tN_t^dX_t - r_{kt-1}K_t,$$

where W_t is the real wage rate and r_{kt-1} is the unit user or rental cost of capital. The quantity r_k is made up of three components: the interest cost, the depreciation cost, and the capital gain or loss of a unit of capital (see Jorgenson 1963). The interest cost is the opportunity cost of retaining earnings used to invest (see Abel and Bernanke 1992, chap. 6). Since the price of capital equals that of the private consumption good, we will not consider the inflation problem. Rather, we will assume no gain or loss on capital. We will also assume that there is no tax on interest income. Thus,

$$(5) \qquad r_{kt-1} \equiv r_{t-1} + \delta,$$

where r is the interest rate of the loanable fund market. The firm maximizes after-tax net cash flows in each period by choosing optimal N_t^d and K_{t+1} (and therefore I_t).

The representative household maximizes its lifetime utility by choosing optimal leisure, labor supply, and consumption. The household consumes private and public goods. Following Barro (1989), we will assume that the household consumes a composite consumption good (C_t^*) which is the linear combination of private consumption (C_t) and public consumption C_t^g) goods. Let L_t and N_t^s be the leisure and labor supplies, and let β and ρ be the discount factor and the time preference rate. The household holds capital (K_t) and public debt (D_t) at the beginning of each period. Let r_d be the interest rate of public debt and S_t be the total real assets held by the household at the beginning of period t. Then, the household's optimization problem can be described by the following:

$$(6) \qquad \max \sum_{t=0}^{\infty} \beta^t U(C_t^*, L_t)$$

such that

$$(7) \qquad C_t^* = C_t + \psi C_t^g,$$

$$(8) \qquad L_t + N_t^s = 1,$$

$$(9) \qquad \beta \equiv (1 + \rho)^{-1},$$

$$(10) \qquad S_{t+1} \equiv K_{t+1} + D_{t+1} = (1 + r_{t-1})K_t + (1 + r_{dt-1})D_t + W_tN_t^sX_t - C_t,$$

where ψ is assumed to be positive and less than one, i.e., $0 < \psi < 1$ (for a detailed discussion see Barro 1989) and equation (10) is the household budget constraint. Following King et al. (1988) and Baxter and King (1990), we will assume that the utility function is in constant relative risk aversion (CRRA) form:

$$(11)\quad U(C_t^*, L_t) = \frac{1}{1-(1/\sigma)}[(C_t^{*\theta}L_t^{1-\theta})^{1-1/\sigma} - 1], \quad \text{for } \sigma \neq 1, \sigma > 0,$$

$$(12)\quad U(C_t^*, L_t) = \theta \ln C_t^* + (1-\theta)\ln L_t, \quad \text{for } \sigma = 1,$$

where $1/\sigma$ is the coefficient of relative risk aversion, while σ is the intertemporal elasticity of substitution in consumption.

The government budget constraint in real terms is

$$(13)\quad Z_t \equiv D_{t+1} - D_t = r_{dt-1}D_t + I_t^g + C_t^g + G_t^b - \tau_t A_t (K_t^g)^{\theta_g} K_t^{\theta_k} (N_t K_t)^{\theta_n}$$

where I_t^g, C_t^g, and G_t^b are, respectively, public investment, public consumption goods, and basic government purchases without providing utility or productive services; D_t is public debt at the beginning of period t; and Z_t is the budget deficit. To avoid indebtedness, we impose a no-Ponzi-game (NPG) condition, i.e.,

$$(14)\quad \lim_{t\to\infty} \prod_{s=0}^{t} (1 + r_s)^{-1} D_{t+1} \geq 0.$$

The economy-wide resource constraint is given by

$$(15)\quad C_t + K_{t+1} - (1-\delta)K_t + I_t^g + C_t^g + G_t^b = A_t (K_t^g)^{\theta_g} K_t^{\theta_k} (N_t X_t)^{\theta_n}.$$

This is also the equilibrium condition for the commodity market. A no-arbitrage condition in the fund market implies that

$$(16)\quad r_{kt} - \delta = r_t = r_{dt}.$$

We make the following definition:

DEFINITION. A *dynamic general equilibrium* is a set of initial conditions D_0, K_0, K_0^g, the process $\{C_t, L_t, N_t, K_{t+1}, S_{t+1}, \tau_t, I_t^g, C_t^g, G_t^b, D_{t+1}, A_t, K_t^g, X_t\}_{t=0}^{\infty}$, and the prices $\{W_t, r_{kt}, r_t\}_{t=0}^{\infty}$ such that

(i) Given the prices $\{r_{kt-1}, W_t\}$, $\{K_{t+1}^d, N_t^d X_t\}$ solves the firm's maximization problem.

(ii) Given the prices $\{r_{t-1}, r_{kt-1}, W_t\}$, $\{C_t, L_t, N_t^s, S_{t+1}\}$ solves the household maximization problem.

(iii) Under $\{W_t, r_t, r_{kt}\}$, all markets are in equilibrium; i.e., $K_{t+1}^d = K_{t+1}$, $N_t^d = N_t^s = N_t$, $D_{t+1}^d \equiv S_{t+1} - K_{t+1} = D_{t+1}$.

(iv) The government budget constraint (15) is satisfied.

Condition (iii) implies that the commodity market is also in equilibrium; i.e., equation (15) is satisfied by Walras's law. As shown by King, Plosser, and Rebelo (1990), labor and leisure will not grow under restrictions on preferences such as equations (11) and (12). In the steady state, C, I, K, Y, I^g, C^g, G^b, and D (all variables are in per capita terms) grow at the same rate as labor-augmenting technical progress. We follow the method used by King et al.

(1988, 1990) by dividing all variables in the system by the growth component X so that we get a stationary model.

In appendix A, we solve the problem and characterize the dynamic general equilibrium.

5.3 Fiscal Policies and the Current Account

The model described in the previous section can be extended to a small open economy such as the Taiwanese economy. In this paper, the exchange rate is assumed to be fixed, since no currencies are formally introduced. We will assume that capital moves perfectly across countries. Foreign and domestic assets are perfect substitutes. However, interest income from foreign assets is taxed at the same rate as that on the capital stock. Let r^{f} be the interest rate in the foreign loanable fund market. Then, a no-arbitrage condition implies that

$$\Omega_t r_t^{\mathrm{f}} = r_t = \Omega_t r_{\mathrm{k}t} - \delta. \tag{17}$$

Following Buiter (1987) and Klundert and Ploeg (1989), we will specify tax rules and spending rules for the government sector so that the solvency of the economy can be satisfied:

$$T_t = \xi_1 f_t + \xi_2 f_{t+1}, \tag{18}$$

$$g_t^{\mathrm{b}} = \xi_3 f_t + \xi_4 f_{t+1}, \tag{19}$$

where f_t is foreign assets held by each household and T_t is the tax on foreign assets per capita. Proportional tax is imposed on foreign assets. Equations (18) and (19) imply that these taxes are used in basic government expenditure—national defense, foreign transfer payments, and so forth. In the following analysis, we will set $\xi_2 = \xi_4 = 0$. The household's budget constraint becomes

$$\begin{aligned} \gamma_x(f_{t+1} + k_{t+1} + d_{t+1}) = {} & (1 + r_t)(k_t + d_t) + (1 + \Omega_t r^{\mathrm{f}} - \xi_1)f_t \\ & + W_t N_t - c_t. \end{aligned} \tag{20}$$

And equation (17) can be rewritten as

$$\Omega_t r_t^{\mathrm{f}} - \xi_1 = \Omega_t r_{\mathrm{k}t} - \delta. \tag{21}$$

Moreover, the government budget constraint becomes

$$\begin{aligned} z_t &= r_t d_t + i_t^{\mathrm{g}} + c_t^{\mathrm{g}} + g_t^{\mathrm{b}} - \tau_t(y_t + f_t) - T_t \\ &= r_t d_t + i_t^{\mathrm{g}} + c_t^{\mathrm{g}} + (\xi_3 - 1)\xi_1 f_t - \tau_t(y_t + f_t). \end{aligned} \tag{22}$$

We define net export as the difference between the accumulation of foreign assets and interest income from foreign assets. That is,

$$e_t = \gamma_x f_{t+1} - (1 + r^{\mathrm{f}})f_t, \tag{23}$$

where e_t is the net export per capita. Thus, from the composition of the national income account, we have

(24)
$$\begin{aligned} \mathrm{GDP}_t \equiv y_t &\equiv c_i + i_t + g_t + e_t \\ &= c_t + i_t + g_t + \gamma_x f_{t+1} - (1 + r^{\mathrm{f}})f_t \end{aligned}$$

and

(25)
$$\begin{aligned} \mathrm{GNP}_t &\equiv y_t + r^{\mathrm{f}} f_t \\ &= c_t + i_t + g_t + \gamma_x f_{t+1} - f_t, \end{aligned}$$

where $\gamma_x f_{t+1} - f_t$ is the current account balance. That is (see Sachs 1982),

(26)
$$\mathrm{CA} \equiv \gamma_x f_{t+1} - f_t = r^{\mathrm{f}} f_t + e_t.$$

The commodity market is in equilibrium under the condition

(27)
$$c_t^* + \gamma_x k_{t+1} - (1 - \delta)k_t + i_t^{\mathrm{g}} + (1 - \psi)c_t^{\mathrm{g}} + g_t^{\mathrm{b}} + \gamma_x f_{t+1} - (1 + r^{\mathrm{f}})f_t = y_t,$$

or

(28)
$$c_t^* + \gamma_x k_{t+1} - (1 - \delta)k_t + i_t^{\mathrm{g}} + (1 - \psi)c_t^{\mathrm{g}} + \gamma_x f_{t+1} - (1 + r^{\mathrm{f}} - \xi_1\xi_3)f_t = y_t.$$

To avoid explosive foreign debt, we impose the NPG condition, i.e.,

(29)
$$\lim_{t\to\infty}(1 + r^{\mathrm{f}})^{-t} f_t \geq 0.$$

Combining equations (27) and (29), we have the intertemporal resource constraint for the economy; that is,

(30)
$$\begin{aligned} f_0 &= \sum_{t=0}^{\infty}(1 + r^{\mathrm{f}})^{-(t+1)}[c_t^* + \gamma_x k_{t+1} - (1 - \delta)k_t + i_t^{\mathrm{g}} + (1 - \psi)c_t^{\mathrm{g}} + g_t^{\mathrm{b}} - y_t] \\ &= -\sum_{t=0}^{\infty}(1 + r^{\mathrm{f}})^{-(t+1)}e_t. \end{aligned}$$

The solution of the model appears in appendix B.

5.4 Numerical Analysis

In the following, we will use Taiwanese data to simulate our model. The sources of the data are from the Directorate-General of Budget, Accounting and Statistics (DGBAS), *Quarterly National Economic Trends, Taiwan Area, The Republic of China* (Taipei, various issues), the *Yearbook of Financial Statistics of the R.O.C.* (Taipei, various issues), and *Aggregate Supply and Demand Quarterly Econometric Model in the Taiwan Area,* no. 8 (Taipei, November 1990) (i.e., DGBAS model no. 8). We use 1990 as the base year. Coefficient data are reported in tables 5.2 and 5.3.

It should be noted that the coefficients are chosen to match Taiwanese factor share data (see DGBAS model no. 8). $\theta_g + \theta_k = 1 - \theta_n = 0.4353$. Since there is no disaggregated data for the sectoral capital stock, we set $\theta_g = \theta_k = 0.21765$. This also matches the data, since in the most recent years the ratio of

Table 5.2 **Parameters and Characteristic Roots for the Closed Economy Case**

Parameters for the production function:
$\theta_g = 0.21765$
$\theta_k = 0.21765$
$\theta_n = 0.5647$
$\delta = 0.0138$
$\gamma_x = 1.07$

Parameters for the utility function:
$\sigma = 1$
$\beta = 0.9953$
$\theta = 0.36956$
$\phi = 0.25$

Other coefficients:
$s_{ig} = 0.11$
$s_{cg} = 0.15$
$s_{gb} = 0$
$d = 0.05$

Characteristic roots:
1.24203; 0.8567076

Table 5.3 **Parameters and Characteristic Roots for the Open Economy Case**

Parameters for the production function:
See table 5.2

Parameters for the utility function:
$\sigma = 1$
$\beta = 0.9953$
$\theta = 0.34982$
$\phi = 0.25$

Coefficients for the feedback rules:
$\xi_1 = -0.028$
$\xi_3 = 0$

Other coefficients:
$s_f = 0.629$
See table 5.2

Characteristic roots:
1.00378867; 0.9733067

investment to GNP in the government sector has been almost 50 percent each year (see table 5.1). We choose β so that the interest rate is 7.75 percent, i.e., $\beta = 0.9953$. This is the 1990 rediscount rate (see table 5.1). And we choose θ so that in the steady state $N = 0.3$, i.e., $\theta = 0.36956$. The tax rate can be found from the government budget constraint. We will assume that the ratio of government expenditure to GNP increases by 1.67 percent each year for six years. Originally, the ratio of government investment to GNP was supposed to have increased 5 percent each year for six years. However, according recent data, the Six-Year Plan has been slowed down because of financial problems. It turned out that only one-third of the plan was realized each year after 1991. Thus, the ratio of government investment to GNP became 1.67 percent each year. Government expenditure is financed through public debt and taxes. The public debts are five-year bonds which each year pay back one-quarter of the par value from the year following the issuing date. Interest payments are financed by taxation.

To see how well the basic structure mimics the actual Taiwanese data, we have examined standard deviations and correlations with output, which are presented in table 5.4. Here the first two columns report statistics for the Taiwanese economy using actual quarterly Taiwanese data for 1966.1–1992.4. These standard deviations are measured relative to the average values, with the departures from the average in percentage form. From these values it is apparent that actual consumption fluctuates less, and both private and public investment much more, than total output in percentage terms.

In the third and fourth columns, comparable figures are reported for a version of the closed economy model that was specified in section 5.2. The magnitude of output fluctuation is governed by the variance of the public investment shock financed by income taxes. From the data in the third column, it is clear that both consumption and private investment vary more than output. The higher fluctuation of consumption is partly due to income tax increases. However, the contemporaneous correlations of the other variables with output reported in table 5.4 show that the basic model matches the actual data rather well.

It should be noted that before 1987 the central bank in Taiwan imposed strict foreign exchange controls on non-trade-related outward remittance by local residents. Both outward and inward remittances of direct capital investment were also subject to approval by the Investment Commission of the Ministry of Economic Affairs. Although the central bank allowed the exchange rate to

Table 5.4 **Comparison of the Taiwanese Economy and the Basic Model**

	Taiwanese Economy[a]		Basic Model	
Variables	Standard Deviation (%)	Correlation with Output	Standard Deviation (%)	Correlation with Output
Output	.65	1	.46	1
Consumption	.61	.99	.60	.99
Investment	.72	.95	.76	.94
Capital stock	.11	.88	.65	.96

[a]The Taiwanese quarterly data used are real GDP, private consumption, gross private investment, and total capital stock (all in 1986 NT dollars).

float in July 1978, it still managed the exchange rate quite tightly. In July 1987, foreign exchange control was released. Since October 1992, each person has been allowed to remit outward and inward up to an annual limit of U.S.$5 million. The central bank went further toward lifting restrictions and raised the ceiling on foreign liabilities of all commercial banks. It is easy to see that during the last few years foreign exchange controls have been almost completely relaxed. This is the reason why we chose the basic model for comparison with the actual data.

5.4.1 Simulation Results for the Closed Economy Case

It is easy to show that the dynamical system described in section 5.2 has two characteristic roots: the absolute value of one characteristic root is greater than one, while the other is less than one. The steady state of the system is thus a saddle point. This is obvious for a dynamical system with one predetermined variable (i.e., capital stock) and an unpredetermined variable (i.e., shadow price of real asset).

Suppose that public investment is financed through public debt. Since all individuals expect that future taxes will be raised to pay current debts, after-tax returns will decline. Private investment will thus be crowded out. As we can see from figure 5.1, taxes rise with public debt accumulation. This results in large crowding-out effects on private investment and consumption. The dynamic paths of the economy will gradually converge to a long-term equilibrium path once the principal of the debts is paid back. As we can see from figure 5.1, when public investment starts to increase initially, output also increases. However, private investment decreases slightly, since the after-tax return on private investment becomes lower. In a closed economy, since output equals total expenditure, total expenditure will go down, and therefore both private consumption and investment are crowded out. Compared to private investment, private consumption declines slowly. This reflects a consumption-smoothing pattern. In addition, labor also decreases with output. This causes higher labor productivity and a higher real wage rate. As consumption goes down, the marginal utility of consumption will rise, and therefore the intertemporal marginal value of assets (λ) also rises. This induces more savings and a greater desire by households to hold bonds. Although the private capital stock decreases with private investment, the real rental rate initially is lowered. This might be due to less labor and output.

We show the effects of tax-financed public investment in figure 5.2. Since it is income taxes rather than lump-sum taxes that are raised to finance government expenditure, there exists an intertemporal substitution effect on labor. Thus, the Ricardian equivalence theorem will not hold. Comparing these two cases in figures 5.1 and 5.2, we find that debt-financed public investment crowds out private expenditure less. In fact, public debt has a tax-smoothing effect and lessens the government's need for unusually high tax receipts when government expenditure increases (see Abel and Blanchard 1983).

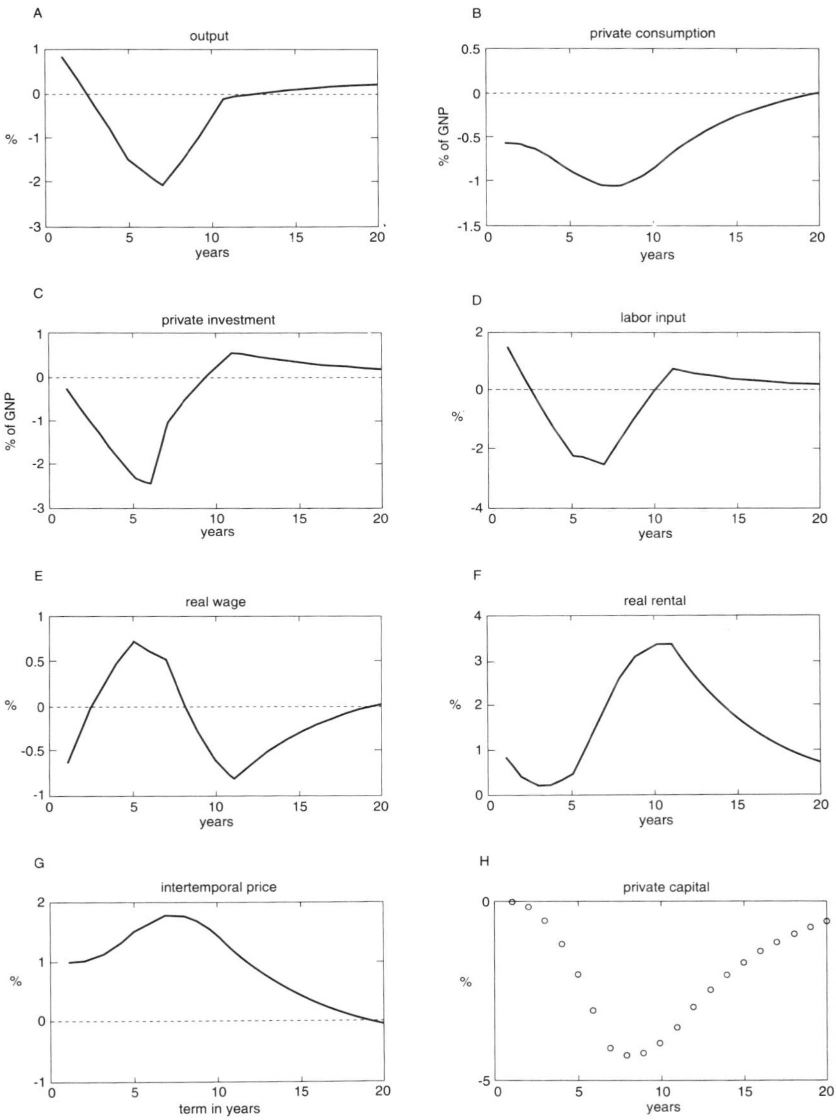

Fig. 5.1 Debt-financed case (closed economy). (*A*) output, (*B*) private consumption, (*C*) private investment, (*D*) labor input, (*E*) real wage, (*F*) real rental, (*G*) intertemporal price, (*H*) private capital.

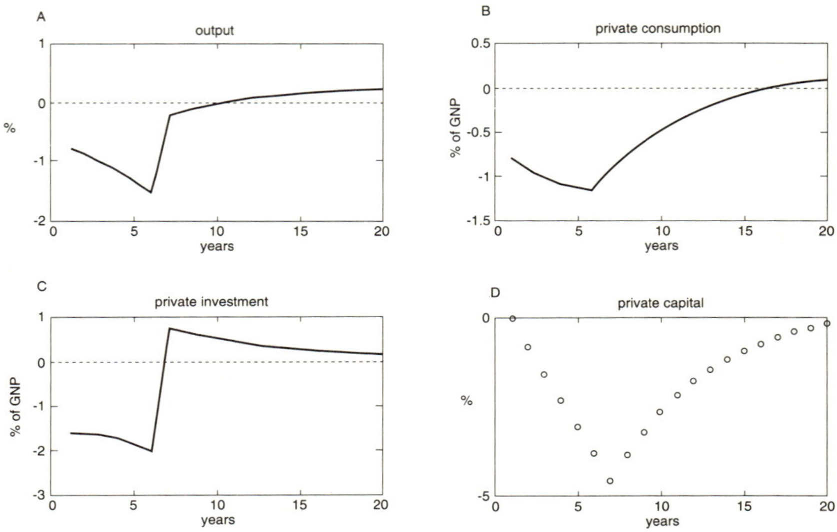

Fig. 5.2 Tax-financed case (closed economy). (*A*) output, (*B*) private consumption, (*C*) private investment, (*D*) private capital.

5.4.2 Simulation Results for the Small Open Economy Case

As shown in figure 5.3, the income tax rate also rises with public debt. Thus, private expenditure will again be crowded out. However, in contrast to the closed economy case, the private sector in an open economy is allowed to borrow abroad and to import foreign goods. Consumption is now smoother, since households can buy foreign goods. Decreases in the marginal utility of consumption imply low intertemporal asset value and thus low savings. Public debt is eventually held by foreigners. This implies a current-account deficit as well as a government budget deficit. Moreover, the intertemporal substitution effect of taxation on labor causes lower labor supply and therefore low productivity of capital.

Comparing this to the closed economy case, we find that output decreases more and the tax rate is higher in an open economy. In an open economy with more foreign debts and more imported goods, the demand for domestic goods will decrease. This will cause output production to decline. And the derived demand for domestic inputs will also fall. Since the tax base has become smaller, the tax rate should be raised so that the government budget can be balanced.

It is hard to compare the welfare levels of two different economies. Even though we choose private consumption as a guideline, we still cannot get a definite answer. Private consumption in the open economy converges after 35 years (not shown in fig. 5.3*B*), while in the closed economy it converges very quickly.

Suppose that public capital is unproductive; i.e., $\theta_g = 0$, while $\theta_k + \theta_n = 1$. This will not change the patterns of output, private consumption, private investment, and private capital. However, all of these variables decrease much more. For example, the lower bound of the output is four times less than in the former case.

Different values of the time preference rate affect the consumption path. The higher the rate of time preference, the lower the discount factor. And people become less patient. Thus, initial private consumption increases more than before and does not decline so quickly after the initial shock. However, the time patterns of other variables do not change significantly.

5.5 Conclusions

We have set up a market-clearing or neoclassical growth model to analyze the effects of public investment with debt financing. By utilizing Taiwanese data to simulate the model we have found that crowding-out effects on private investment do exist in both the open economy case and the closed economy case. Moreover, we have also confirmed a known result, that the Ricardian equivalence theorem does not hold when an income tax system is introduced.

It is also found that consumption is more smoothing and crowds out less in the open economy. However, it is because of capital outflows that private investment is crowded out more in the open economy than in the closed economy. We also found that public investment financed by debt causes both current-account and government budget deficits in the open economy. As for the effects on income and employment, this paper found that in the open economy deficit-financed public investment is more expensive in the long run. All these findings conform to recent Taiwanese experience as more labor shortages prevailed and more funds flowed out, especially to mainland China and south Asian countries.

From the preceding analysis we obtain implications for government policies. The analysis suggests that the government should not intervene too much in production and investment. Most projects of the Six-Year Plan could be opened to investment by private firms, and by foreign investors, since the main purpose of the plan is to induce more private investment and foreign technology transfer. Introducing foreign capital also lessens the stringent fund situation in the short run. However, the analysis also suggests that the government should not borrow abroad, since a lot of foreign reserves are held by the central bank and much of the money stock is still in the hands of the public. Instead, the foreign exchange reserves could be used to finance public investment as long as the domestic interest rate is not much higher than the world interest rate. In addition, this can lessen the fiscal budget deficit as well as the current-account deficit. From recent experience, the government has become aware of this situation. Through a development bank, the central bank has started to lend foreign reserves to the administration sector to purchase foreign goods.

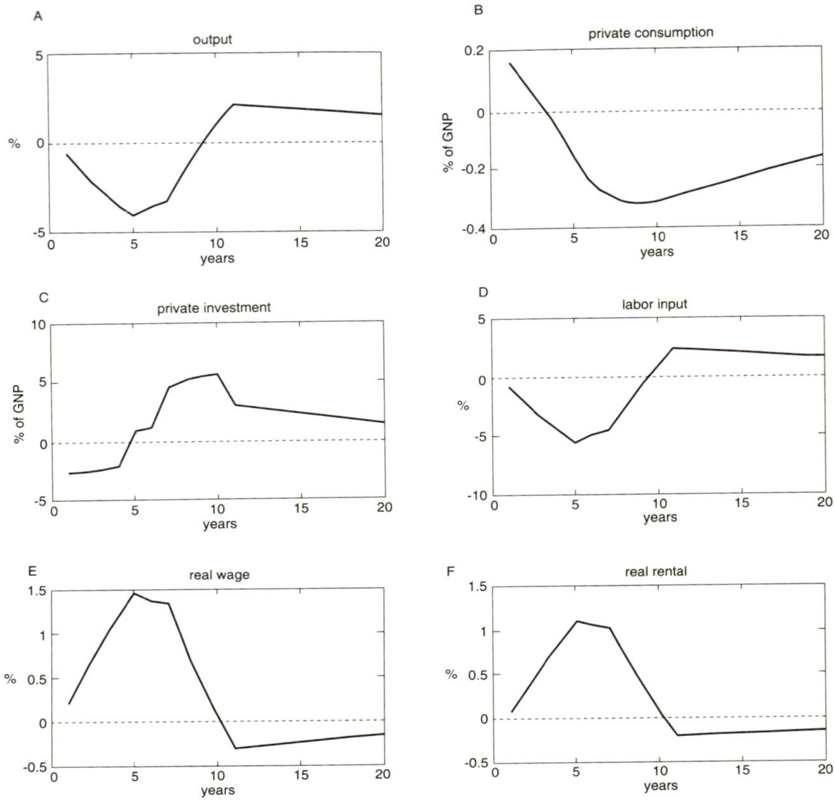

Fig. 5.3 Debt-financed case (open economy). (*A*) output, (*B*) private consumption, (*C*) private investment, (*D*) labor input, (*E*) real wage, (*F*) real rental, (*G*) intertemporal price, (*H*) foreign asset, (*I*) private capital, (*J*) current account.

Appendix A

In this appendix, we will solve the household's optimization problem given in section 5.2. And the dynamic general equilibrium of the model will be log-linearized.

Let $c_t \equiv C_t/X_t$, $k_t \equiv K_t/X_t$, $i_t \equiv I_t/X_t$, etc., and $\gamma_x \equiv X_{t+1}/X_t$. The household's lifetime utility function becomes

$$\sum_{t=0}^{\infty}\beta^t U(c_t^*, L_t) = (X_0)^{\theta(1-1/\sigma)}\sum_{t=0}^{\infty}\{\beta^{*t}\frac{1}{1-1/\sigma}[(c_t^{*\theta}, L_t^{1-\theta})^{1-1/\sigma} - 1] + \sigma V(X_t)\},$$

(A1) if $\sigma \neq 1, \sigma > 0,$

$$= \sum_{t=0}^{\infty}\beta^t[\theta \ln c_t^* + (1-\theta)\ln L_t + \theta \ln X_t],$$

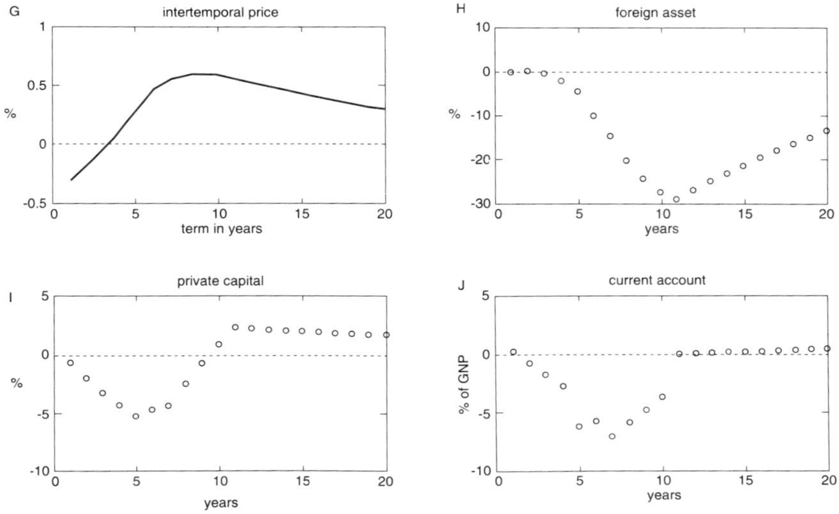

Fig. 5.3 (continued)

if $\sigma = 1$,

where

$$V(X_t) \equiv \beta^t \frac{1}{1 - 1/\sigma}(X_t^{\theta(1-1/\sigma)} - 1),$$

and $\beta^* \equiv \beta\gamma_x^{\theta(1-1/\sigma)}$, while X_0 is given. We will assume that $\beta^* < 1$ so that the expression in equation (A1) is bounded. The transformed optimization problem of the household can be described as follows:

$$\max \sum_{t=0}^{\infty} \beta^{*t}[U(c_t^*, 1 - N_t^s) + V(X_t)]$$

such that

$$\text{(A2)} \qquad \gamma_x s_{t+1} = (1 + r_{t-1})s_t + W_t N_t^s + c_t,$$

$$\text{(A3)} \qquad s_t \equiv k_t + d_t.$$

Let the Lagrangian be

$$\mathcal{L} = \sum_{t=0}^{\infty} \beta^{*t}\{U(c_t^*, 1 - N_t^s) + \lambda_t[W_t N_t^s + (1 + r_t)s_t - c_t - \gamma_x s_{t+1}]\}.$$

The first-order condition becomes

$$\text{(A4)} \qquad U_1(c_t^*, 1 - N_t^s) = \lambda_t,$$

$$\text{(A5)} \qquad U_2(c_t^*, 1 - N_t^s) = \lambda_t W_t,$$

(A6) $$\beta^* \lambda_{t+1}(1 + r_{t+1}) = \lambda_t \gamma_x,$$

(A7) $$W_t N_t^s + (1 + r_t)s_t - c_t - \gamma_x s_{t+1} = 0,$$

(A8) $$\lim_{t\to\infty} \beta^{*t} \lambda_t s_t = 0,$$

where λ_t is the Lagrange multiplier and $U_1(\cdot)$ and $U_2(\cdot)$ are the partial derivatives of $U(\cdot)$ with respect to c_t^* and $1 - N_t^s$. Equations (A4) and (A5) describe the trade-offs among consumption, leisure, and saving. Equation (A6) is the Euler equation or the intertemporal efficiency condition. Equation (A7) is the household's budget constraint. And equation (A8) is the transversality condition.

The production function and the capital accumulation become

(A9) $$y_t = A_t (k_t^g)^{\theta_g} k^{\theta_k} N_t^{\theta_n},$$

(A10) $$\gamma_x k_{t+1} = (1 - \delta)k_t + i_t.$$

The optimization condition for the firm is thus

(A11) $$\Omega_t A_t (k_t^g)^{\theta_g} F_1(k_t^d, N_t^d) = r_{kt-1} = r_{t-1} + \delta,$$

(A12) $$\Omega_t A_t (k_t^g)^{\theta_g} F_2(k_t^d, N_t^d) = W_t,$$

where $\Omega_t \equiv 1 - \tau_t$ and $F_1(\cdot)$ and $F_2(\cdot)$ are the marginal productivities of capital and labor, respectively. Equations (A11) and (A12) are the marginal conditions for the firm.

A dynamic general equilibrium can be described as follows:

(A13) $$U_1(c_t^*, 1 - N_t) = \lambda_t,$$

(A14) $$U_2(c_t^*, 1 - N_t) = \lambda_t \Omega_t A_t (k_t^g)^{\theta_g} F_2(k_t, N_t),$$

(A15) $$\beta^* \lambda_{t+1}[1 + \Omega_{t+1} A_{t+1} (k_{t+1}^g)^{\theta_g} F_1(k_{t+1}, N_{t+1}) - \delta] = \lambda_t \gamma_x,$$

(A16) $$z_t = [\Omega_t A_t (k_t^g)^{\theta_g} F_1(k_t, N_t) - \delta] d_t + i_t^g + c_t^g + g_t^b - \tau_t A_t (k_t^g)^{\theta_g} F(k_t, N_t),$$

(A17) $$c_t^* + \gamma_x k_{t+1} - (1 - \delta)k_t + i_t^g + (1 - \psi)c_t^g + g_t^b = A_t (k_t^g)^{\theta_g} F(k_t, N_t).$$

From equations (A13)–(A17) and the definition of $\Omega \equiv (1 - \tau)$, we can solve for c_t^*, N_t, k_t, λ_t, τ_t, and Ω_t, which are functions of exogenous variables. However, these functions will be nonlinear. In order to do further analysis, we will follow King et al. (1990) by using the log-linearization method. From equation (A16) we can find the wedge function Ω_t. Approximation of Ω_t near stationary levels (k, N, A, B, i^g, c^g, g^b, d, z), where $B \equiv (k^g)^{\theta_g}$, yields

(A18) $$\hat{\Omega}_t = \omega_K \hat{k}_t + \omega_N \hat{N}_t + \omega_A \hat{A}_t + \omega_B \hat{B}_t + \omega_1 \hat{i}_t^g + \omega_2 \hat{c}_t^g + \omega_3 \hat{g}_t^b + \omega_D \hat{d}_t + \omega_Z \hat{z}_t,$$

where the values of ω are elasticities of the wedge function $\Omega_t = 1 - \tau_t$ and $\hat{k}_t \equiv \log(k_t/k)$, etc. Also, we can take the log-linearization of equations (A13), (A14), and (A15) to get

$$\text{(A19)} \qquad \xi_{cc}\hat{c}_t^* - \xi_{cl}\frac{N}{1-N}\hat{N}_t = \hat{\lambda}_t,$$

$$\text{(A20)} \quad \xi_{lc}\hat{c}_t^* - \xi_{ll}\frac{N}{1-N}\hat{N}_t = \hat{\lambda}_t + (\omega_A + 1)\hat{A}_t + (\omega_B + 1)\hat{B}_t + (\omega_K + \xi_{NK})\hat{k}_t + (\omega_N + \xi_{NN})\hat{N}_t + \omega_1\hat{i}_t^g + \omega_2\hat{c}_t^g + \omega_3\hat{g}_t^b + \omega_D\hat{d}_t + \omega_Z\hat{z}_t,$$

$$\text{(A21)} \quad \hat{\lambda}_{t+1} + \eta_A\hat{A}_{t+1} + \eta_B\hat{B}_{t+1} + \eta_K\hat{k}_{t+1} + \eta_N\hat{N}_{t+1} + \eta_1\hat{i}_{t+1}^g + \eta_2\hat{c}_{t+1}^g + \eta_3\hat{g}_{t+1}^b + \eta_D\hat{d}_{t+1} + \eta_Z\hat{z}_{t+1} = \hat{\lambda}_t,$$

where the values of ξ on the left-hand sides of equations (A19) and (A20) are elasticities of marginal utility, while those on the right-hand sides are elasticities of marginal productivities (see King et al. 1990). The values of η in equation (A21) are elasticities of the net after-tax marginal product of capital.

Finally, differentiation of the commodity-market equilibrium condition implies

$$\text{(A22)} \quad \hat{A}_t + \hat{B}_t + s_n\hat{N}_t + s_k\hat{k}_t = s_c\hat{c}_t^* + s_{ig}\hat{i}_t^g + (1 - \psi)s_{cg}\hat{c}_t^g + s_{gb}\hat{g}_t^b + s_i\phi\hat{k}_{t+1} - s_i(\phi - 1)\hat{k}_t,$$

where s_n, s_k, s_c, s_{ig}, s_{cg}, s_{gb}, and s_i are output shares of labor, capital, consumption (c^*), government expenditure, and investment and $\phi \equiv K_{t+1}/I_t$.

Appendix B

The first-order conditions for the household's optimization problem in section 5.3 are

$$\text{(B1)} \qquad U_1(c_t^*, 1 - N_t^s) = \lambda_t,$$

$$\text{(B2)} \qquad U_2(c_t^*, 1 - N_t^s) = \lambda_t W_t,$$

$$\text{(B3)} \qquad \beta^*\lambda_{t+1}(1 + r_{t+1}) = \lambda_t\gamma_x,$$

$$\text{(B4)} \qquad W_tN_t^s + (1 + r_t)s_t - c_t - \gamma_x s_{t+1} = 0,$$

$$\text{(B5)} \qquad W_tN_t^s + (1 + r_{t-1})s_t - c_t - \gamma_x s_{t+1} = 0,$$

where $s_t \equiv k_t + d_t + f_t$. And the firm's optimization conditions are

$$\text{(B6)} \qquad \Omega_tA_t(k_t^g)^{\theta_g}F_1(k_t^d, N_t^d) - \delta = r_t,$$

$$\text{(B7)} \qquad \Omega_tA_t(k_t^g)^{\theta_g}F_2(k_t^d, N_t^d) = W_t.$$

From equations (B1)–(B7) and market equilibrium conditions, we have

(B8) $$U_1(c_t^*, 1 - N_t) = \lambda_t,$$

(B9) $$U_2(c_t^*, 1 - N_t) = \lambda_t \Omega_t A_t (k_t^g)^{\theta_g} F_2(k_t, N_t),$$

(B10) $$\beta^* \lambda_{t+1}[1 + \Omega_{t+1} r^f - \xi_1] = \lambda_t \gamma_x,$$

(B11) $$\Omega_t r_t^f - \xi_1 = \Omega_t r_{kt} - \delta = \Omega_t A_t (k_t^g)^{\theta_g} F_1(k_t^d, N_t^d) - \delta,$$

(B12) $$z_t = (\Omega_t r^f - \xi_1) d_t + i_t^g + c_t^g + (\xi_3 - 1)\xi_1 - \tau_t [A_t (k_t^g)^{\theta_g} F(k_t, N_t) + f_t],$$

(B13) $$c_t^* + \gamma_x k_{t+1} - (1 - \delta) k_t + i_t^g + (1 - \psi) c_t^g + \gamma_x f_{t+1} - (1 + r^f - \xi_1 \xi_3) f_t = A_t (k_t^g)^{\theta_g} F(k_t, N_t).$$

Equations (B8)–(B13) solve the processes $\{c_t^*, N_t, k_{t+1}, \lambda_t, \tau_t, \Omega_t, f_{t+1}\}$. Following the linearization method we used in appendix A, we have

(B14) $$\hat{\Omega}_t = \omega_K' \hat{k}_t + \omega_N' \hat{N}_t + \omega_A' \hat{A}_t + \omega_B' \hat{B}_t + \omega_1' \hat{i}_t^g + \omega_2' \hat{c}_t^g + \omega_f' \hat{f}_t + \omega_d' \hat{d}_t + \omega_z' \hat{z}_t,$$

(B15) $$\xi_{cc} \hat{c}_t^* - \xi_{cl} \frac{1}{1 - N} \hat{N}_t = \hat{\lambda}_t,$$

(B16) $$\xi_{lc} \hat{c}_t^* - \xi_{ll} \frac{1}{1 - N} \hat{N}_t = \hat{\lambda}_t + (\omega_A' + 1)\hat{A}_t + (\omega_B' + 1)\hat{B}_t + (\omega_k' + \xi_{NK})\hat{k}_t + (\omega_N' + \xi_{NN})\hat{N}_t + \omega_1' \hat{i}_t^g + \omega_2' \hat{c}_t^g + \omega_D' \hat{d}_t + \omega_Z' \hat{z}_t + \omega_f' \hat{f}_t,$$

(B17) $$\hat{\lambda}_{t+1} + \eta_A' \hat{A}_{t+1} + \eta_B' \hat{B}_{t+1} + \eta_K' \hat{k}_{t+1} + \eta_N' \hat{N}_{t+1} + \eta_1' \hat{i}_{t+1}^g + \eta_2' \hat{c}_{t+1}^g + \eta_D' \hat{d}_{t+1} + \eta_Z' \hat{z}_{t+1} + \eta_f' \hat{f}_{t+1} = \hat{\lambda}_t,$$

(B18) $$(\omega_A' + \kappa_A)\hat{A}_t + (\omega_B' + \kappa_B)\hat{B}_t + (\omega_K' + \kappa_K)\hat{k}_t + (\omega_N' + \kappa_N)\hat{N}_t + \omega_1' \hat{i}_t^g + \omega_2' \hat{c}_t^g + \omega_D' \hat{d}_t + \omega_Z' \hat{z}_t + \omega_f' \hat{f}_t = 0,$$

(B19) $$\hat{A}_t + \hat{B}_t + s_n \hat{N}_t + s_k \hat{k}_t = s_c \hat{c}_t^* + s_{ig} \hat{i}_t^g + (1 - \psi) s_{cg} \hat{c}_t^g + s_i \phi \hat{K}_{t+1} - s_i(\phi - 1)\hat{k}_t + \gamma_x s_f \hat{f}_{t+1} - (1 + r^f - \xi_1 \xi_3) s_f \hat{f}_t,$$

where the values of ω' are the elasticities of Ω' with respect to its arguments, while

$$1 + \tau_t \equiv \Omega_t = \Omega'(N_t, k_t, f_t; \psi_t'),$$

$$\psi_t' \equiv (A_t, k_t^g, i_t^g, c_t^g, d_t, z_t),$$

the values of η' are the elasticities of $(1 + \Omega_t r^f - \xi_1)$ with respect to each variable, the values of κ are the elasticities of $[r^f - A_t(k_t^g)^{\theta_g} F_1(k_t, n_t)]$ with respect to each variable, and $s_f \equiv f/y$.

References

Abel, Andrew B., and Ben Bernanke. 1992. *Macroeconomics.* Menlo Park, Calif.: Addison-Wesley.

Abel, Andrew B., and Olivier J. Blanchard. 1983. An intertemporal model of saving and investment. *Econometrica* 51, no. 3 (May): 675–92.

Barro, Robert J. 1989. Neoclassical approach to fiscal policy. In *Modern business cycle theory,* ed. R. Barro. Cambridge: Harvard University Press.

———. 1990. *Macroeconomics.* New York: Wiley.

Baxter, Marianne, and Robert King. 1990. Fiscal policy in general equilibrium. Working Paper no. 244. University of Rochester.

Blanchard, Olivier J. 1985. Debt, deficits, and finite horizons. *Journal of Political Economy* 82, no. 6 (December): 1095–1117.

Blanchard, Olivier J., and Stanley Fischer. 1989. *Lectures on macroeconomics.* Cambridge: MIT Press.

Blinder, Alan S., and Robert M. Solow. 1974. Analytical foundations of fiscal policy. In *The economics of public finance,* ed. Alan S. Blinder and Robert M. Solow. Washington, D.C.: Brookings Institution.

Buiter, Willem H. 1987. Fiscal policy in open interdependent economies. In *Economic policy in theory and practice,* ed. A. Razin and E. Sadka. London: MacMillan.

Haliassos, Michael, and James Tobin. 1990. The macroeconomics of government finance. In *Handbook of monetary economics,* vol. 2, ed. B. M. Friedman and F. H. Hahn. Amsterdam: North Holland.

Jorgenson, Dale W. 1963. Capital theory and investment behavior. *American Economic Review* 53: 247–59.

King, Robert, Charles Plosser, and Sergio Rebelo. 1988. Production, growth and business cycles, I. The neoclassical model. *Journal of Monetary Economics* 21: 195–232.

———. 1990. Production, growth and business cycles: Technical appendix. University of Rochester.

Klundert, Theo van de, and Frederick van der Ploeg. 1989. Fiscal policy and finite lives in interdependent economies with real and nominal wage rigidity. *Oxford Economic Papers* 41: 459–89.

Matsuyama, Kiminori. 1987. Current account dynamics in a finite horizon model. *Journal of International Economics* 23: 299–311.

Sachs, Jeffery D. 1982. The current account in the macroeconomic adjustment process. *Scandinavian Journal of Economics* 84(2): 147–59.

Tobin, James, and Willem H. Buiter. 1976. Long run effects of fiscal and monetary policy on aggregate demand. In *Monetarism,* ed. J. L. Stein. Amsterdam: North-Holland.

Comment Ponciano S. Intal, Jr.

Chen-Min Hsu utilizes a Barro-type continuous market-clearing intertemporal one-sector growth model in evaluating Taiwan's planned public investment program under the Six-Year Plan for Economic Development. The simulation re-

Ponciano S. Intal, Jr., is president of the Philippine Institute for Development Studies (PIDS), a government research institution. He was formerly a deputy director-general of the National Economic and Development Authority (NEDA), the Philippines' economic planning agency.

sults are interesting because they are counterintuitive. Specifically, Hsu's simulations indicate that Taiwan's increased government expenditures under the Six-Year Plan would lead to lower growth of national income, albeit not quite contemporaneously. Why?

Hsu's simulation results stem from the crowding out of private expenditures, especially private investment, arising from the government's public investment program. The "crowding-out" result does not conform to the traditional crowding-out literature, however. In the literature, crowding out is caused by a policy-induced rise in the real interest rate, thereby leading to a lower than desired ratio of capital stock to real GNP and lower investment flows. In contrast, Hsu's simulations show declines in the real interest rate in the first few years which, given the marginal condition for the firm in the model, should indicate higher private capital stock and positive private investment. Thus, there appears to be some inconsistency between the results of the simulations and the analytical underpinnings of the standard crowding-out hypothesis.

Hsu's analysis appears to use a different notion or mechanism of crowding out. Specifically, the increased government expenditures crowd out private expenditures because:

1. the reallocation of resources from the private sector to the government sector entails a misallocation of resources (resulting in deadweight productivity and income loss) because the productivity of capital in the government sector is presumed less than the productivity of capital in the private sector, and

2. the concomitant tax rate increases in the future which are needed to pay back loans incurred from increased government expenditures are presumed to have "distortionary effects" on the marginal productivities of labor and capital, thereby resulting in lower than desired capital stock (hence lower private investment flow) and labor input.

It is apparent that given items 1 and 2 above, the magnitude of the public investment program is irrelevant; i.e., any incremental public expenditure will crowd out private expenditure in Hsu's model.

The results of the simulations for the small, open economy case are especially counterintuitive: they indicate that government expenditures reduce income and savings and raise the tax burden in an open economy more than in a closed economy. This is counterintuitive because the general presumption is that the free flow of capital in an open economy reduces the crowding-out effect that government expenditures may have in the domestic capital market. The simulations show decline in the real interest rate, which is inconsistent with the small, open economy case, wherein the domestic interest rate is equal to the exogenously given world interest rate assuming no exchange rate change and uniform taxation between foreign and domestic assets. The behavior of the real interest rate in the simulations can be explained only by currency appreciation during the early years of the simulation period, followed by currency depreciation later on. The paper does not state anything, however, on exchange rate changes. Indeed, by explicitly assuming no inflation and no capital gains, the model implicitly assumes a fixed exchange rate regime.

The above discussion brings out the question of whether the Barro-type one-sector intertemporal model significantly helps clarify the issues related to Taiwan's public investment program. For the most part, the answer is no, because the model, at least as specified in Hsu's paper, assumes away the more important policy issues in Taiwan's expenditure program:

1. Proponents of the government's public investment program emphasize the view that increased government expenditures, which are primarily for infrastructure, have positive externality on private capital. That is, the marginal productivity of private capital would be higher, the higher the level of public capital stock (i.e., infrastructure). The formulation of the production function in the model and the specification of the simulations negate this possibility and hence do not objectively address this critical, if contentious, issue.

2. For a small, export-oriented economy like Taiwan's, the issue of the impact of a significant government expenditure program on its international competitiveness looms large. Taiwan's economic sectors face different degrees of competitive pressures from abroad and have different rates of productivity growth. Given Taiwan's already very tight labor market, there is a danger that large government investment shocks may push Taiwan's wage rates substantially higher than the rate of growth of labor productivity in the tradeable goods sector, thereby endangering Taiwan's international competitiveness unless there is a corresponding depreciation of the NT dollar. In addition, for Taiwan's numerous small-scale firms, the concomitant wage rate pressures may force them to merge or reorganize or to relocate (part of) their operations offshore (e.g., to China or Southeast Asia). It may be noted that Taiwan has started importing contract labor primarily from Southeast Asia in order to dampen wage rate pressures. Nevertheless, this measure can be expected to be merely a palliative since a large expenditure shock can be expected to further raise domestic wage rate pressures. Thus, a two-sector (e.g., tradeable and nontradeable sectors) intertemporal model would provide deeper policy insights into the planned government investment program than a one-sector intertemporal model.

3. With respect to the issue of the magnitude of the government expenditure program, Hsu estimates the program to be equal to 5 percent of GNP per year for six years. Note that during 1986–90, Taiwan's gross domestic saving averaged about 33 percent of GNP, its gross domestic investment averaged about 21 percent of GNP, the central government surplus averaged about 0.5 percent of GNP, and the inflation rate averaged 2.2 percent per year. Taiwan's large domestic saving surplus explains the sharp rise in its international reserves and the growing investment outflows to China, Southeast Asia, and the United States in recent years. Thus, it seems that crowding out is not as important an issue as the issue of whether the productivity of the government's public investment program (funded from international reserve drawdown and domestic saving) is higher than the returns of Taiwan's savings and investments abroad (e.g., international reserves and foreign direct investment).

In sum, the Barro-type continuous market-clearing one-sector intertemporal fiscal model may not be the most appropriate model with which to evaluate the key policy issues surrounding Taiwan's public investment program.

Comment Yun-Wing Sung

Chen-Min Hsu extends Barro's (1989) work to the open economy of Taiwan. The paper is interesting as the very ambitious Six-Year Plan for Economic Development of Taiwan probably has significant macroeconomic impacts.

While the macroeconomic impacts of Taiwan's Six-Year Plan are certainly an important subject, however, the parameter values adopted in the paper artificially cast the public sector in a very unfavorable light. According to the specification of the production function, public capital and private capital are complementary, but the output elasticity of private capital is much higher than that of public capital. As a result, output falls appreciably when the government invests more and the crowding-out effect on private investment is very serious.

The empirical relevance of such a characterization of the Taiwanese economy is doubtful. The congestion and overcrowding of Taiwan's infrastructural facilities are well known to visitors, and Galbraith's famous phrase "private affluence, public squalor" may be applicable to Taiwan. While the productivity of public projects should be analyzed case by case, there are undoubtedly public projects in Taiwan that can be very productive.

As the parameter values of such a highly aggregated model cannot be very accurate, sensitivity analysis would be very important. However, there is no sensitivity analysis in the paper.

Two of the conclusions of the paper, that the projects of the plan should be open to private investors and that the government should use its foreign exchange reserves rather than foreign borrowing, do not follow from the model. In fact, such conclusions cannot be obtained from a one-sector neoclassical growth model.

Public projects must generate revenue in order to attract private investment, but such revenue has not been taken into account in the government's budget constraint (eq. [13]). Opening public projects to private investment would decrease government borrowing to finance the projects, but government revenue would also be decreased. Privatization cannot be recommended unless private investors are more efficient than the government in running such projects. Whether private investors are efficient or not cannot be gauged from a one-sector growth model.

Yun-Wing Sung is professor of economics at the Chinese University of Hong Kong.

If the government uses its foreign exchange reserves rather than borrowing to finance the projects, it may save interest costs, as the borrowing rate is usually higher than the rate of return on the reserves. However, there are good reasons to maintain reserves in case of contingency. Whether Taiwan's reserves are too high cannot be determined from a one-sector growth model.

6 The Role of Trade and Exchange Rate Policy in Korea's Growth

Chong-Hyun Nam

6.1 Introduction

Since the 1960s the Korean economy's rapid growth has attracted attention worldwide. Although Korea's success may be linked to a number of factors, an outward-oriented trade strategy adopted in the early 1960s and onward has often been cited as the most important contributor.

The evolution of economic policies in Korea, however, suggests that the outward-oriented strategy was not instituted by a single stroke of policy, but rather was implemented through a very complicated and continuing process under heavy-handed government intervention. For example, until very recently domestic markets remained highly protected for a supposedly outward-oriented economy, and during the 1970s, the government was actively involved in promoting the so-called heavy and chemical industries (HCIs),[1] with package assistance programs for these "strategic" industries. For these reasons, many—both inside and outside Korea—have questioned whether Korea's success was possible because of, or in spite of, a very activist role for government in both trade and investment activities throughout most of its recent economic development.

The purpose of this paper is to review the evolution of Korea's trade and exchange rate policy and to examine the role it has played in Korea's economic growth over the 1962–91 period. Following this analysis, I will highlight several lessons that developing countries can learn from Korea's experiences.

Chong-Hyun Nam is professor of economics at Korea University.

The author is grateful to Anne O. Krueger, Sebastian Edwards, and Shang-Jin Wei for valuable comments, and to Hong-Sik Lee for research assistance.

1. HCIs include such industries as basic metals, petrochemicals, machinery, electrical and electronic products, and transport equipment.

6.2 Evolution of Trade and Exchange Rate Policies and Growth Performance, 1962–91

6.2.1 Establishing an Outward-oriented Economy through Export Promotion

Prior to 1960, the Korean economy suffered from severe macroeconomic imbalances, such as high unemployment, budget deficits, and balance-of-payments deficits under the high pressure of inflation, all of which could be expected in an immediate postwar period. During the latter half of the 1950s, for example, annual inflation averaged more than 30 percent and the balance-of-payments deficit averaged between 5 and 10 percent of GNP.

The government's efforts were therefore largely directed to alleviating economic pressures on the price level and the balance of payments. As part of the anti-inflationary measures, nominal exchange rates were kept fixed with only insufficient adjustments, resulting in the chronic overvaluation of the Korean won. On the other hand, to bring the balance-of-payments problem under control, the authorities resorted heavily to import restriction measures such as multiple exchange rates, import licensing, and high tariffs on selected items. To be sure, there were some export incentives introduced during the 1950s, including, for example, financing for the purchase of export goods, an export bonus given through preferential foreign exchanges, and discounts on railroad freight (Hong 1979, 53–57). The net result of these policies, however, was discrimination against exports, since incentives given for import substitution were far greater. Thus, until the late 1950s, Korea was a typical inward-oriented economy.

In contrast to the imbalanced economic policies during the 1950s, numerous policy reforms and new plans were put forth during the 1960s, beginning with the first Five-Year Economic Plan (1962–66) implemented in 1962. Issues such as development of key industries and creation of an adequate supply of social overhead capital were especially stressed in this plan, as well as in the succeeding Five-Year Economic Plans.

The major policy shift, however, began with the reform of the payment regime and of the financial sector in 1964 and 1965. After a unified exchange rate was established in 1961, the Korean currency was devalued from 130 won to 255 won per U.S. dollar in May 1964. Following the exchange rate reform, the government raised the interest rates on ordinary loans of banking institutions from 16 to 26 percent per annum in September 1965. Along with these reforms, the government introduced a comprehensive set of export incentives during the 1960s.

The export incentives included a preferential tax system, a preferential loan system, and various administrative support systems. The preferential tax system consisted of tariff exemptions on imported raw materials and intermediate and capital goods for export production, exemptions from indirect taxes for intermediate inputs and export sales, the reduction of direct taxes on profits earned through export activities, the introduction of reserve funds created from taxable income to develop new foreign markets and to defray export losses, and the creation of an accelerated depreciation allowance for fixed capital used directly in export production. The preferential loan system provided exporters with access to subsidized short- and long-term credits for their purchase of inputs and financing of fixed investments. Also, generous wastage allowances were granted on imported duty-free raw materials over and above the requirements of actual export production. An export-import linkage system permitting access to otherwise prohibited imports was put into operation, and preferential rates on several overhead inputs such as electricity were made available.

Some of these export incentives simply enabled exporters to operate under a virtually free trade regime by allowing them to buy their inputs and sell their outputs at world market prices. But others constituted genuine subsidies that helped to enhance the profitability of export sales relative to domestic sales. In fact, given that the effective protection rates for domestic sales were estimated at −1.1 percent for the manufacturing sector and 17.8 percent for the agricultural sector in 1968, the Korean incentive system appears to have favored manufacturing production activities for export sales over domestic sales during the 1960s.[2]

The system of export incentives remained virtually unchanged through the early 1970s. Beginning in 1973, however, some of these incentives were abolished in order to reduce the scope of export subsidies. The 50 percent reduction in taxes on profits from export earnings was abolished in 1973. In July 1975, the system of prior tariff exemptions on imported inputs used in export production was changed into a drawback system. The discount on electricity was abolished in 1976, and wastage allowances were repeatedly reduced, bringing them closer to the actual rate during the 1970s.

As a result, since the mid-1970s, interest rate subsidies and the availability of export-related loans have become the major export incentives. Preferential loans for export activities were steadily expanded throughout the 1970s. For instance, preferential short- and long-term loans to export industries as a proportion of total domestic credit increased from 5.1 percent in 1966 to 20.5 percent in 1978 (Nam 1981b, 193). The average interest rate on all preferential export loans was 7.7 percent in 1966 and 10.6 percent in 1978, whereas the lending rate on ordinary loans from commercial banks was 26.4 percent in 1966 and 19.0 percent in 1978. This interest rate differential between preferential and ordinary loans was gradually reduced and finally abolished with the June 1982 interest rate reform. Simultaneously, the government restricted the availability of export-related loans, so that by 1988, only small firms could

2. See Westphal and Kim (1977, table 2), and further discussion follows in the next section.

Table 6.1 Tariff and Nontariff Import Restrictions in Korea, 1957–91

Year	Simple Average Tariff Rates (%)	Number of Prohibited or Restricted Items	Number of Automatic Approval Items (A)	Total Number of Import Items (B)	Rate of Import Liberalization (A/B)(%)
1957	30.3				
1962	39.9				
1967	39.9	520	792	1,312	60.4
1973	31.5	629	683	1,312	52.1
1975	31.5	668	664	1,312	49.1
1977	29.7	621	664	1,312	52.7
1979	24.8	928	682	1,010	67.5
1981	24.9	1,911	5,649	7,560	74.7
1983	23.7	1,482	6,078	7,560	80.4
1985	21.3	970	6,945	7,915	87.7
1987	19.3	499	7,408	7,911	93.6
1989	12.7	465	9,776	10,241	95.5
1991	11.4	283	9,991	10,274	97.2

Sources: Korean Traders Association, *Annual Report on Foreign Trade* (Seoul, various years); Kim (1988, tables 3 and 4) for 1957 and 1962.

Note: The classification of import items was based on the SITC basic codes through 1977, four-digit CCCN codes for 1979, eight-digit CCCN codes during 1981–87, and 10-digit HS codes during 1989–91.

receive them. This action reduced their share in total domestic credit to less than 3 percent by 1991.

6.2.2 Import Restrictions and Liberalization in an Outward-oriented Economy

Despite the introduction of a comprehensive set of export promotion policies in the early 1960s, the relaxation of import controls did not proceed in any significant way until the latter half of the 1960s. In fact, faced with dwindling U.S. foreign assistance and widening trade deficits, the military government that came into power in 1961 tightened import controls in the early 1960s. As a result, the simple average of legal tariff rates reached a peak of nearly 40 percent in 1962 and stayed at that level throughout the 1960s (see table 6.1). In addition to the regular tariffs, special tariffs were also used between 1964 and 1973. The special tariffs were introduced mainly to soak up some of the excess profits that might accrue to importers of inessential commodities that were subject to quantitative restrictions (QRs). The special tariff rates were estimated at 0.8–3.2 percent of the total value of imports during the 1964–72 period (Kim 1988, 15) before they were abolished in 1973. The average legal tariff rate gradually fell thereafter, reaching 11.4 percent by 1991.

Although the legal tariff rates were generally set very high, they were to a

Table 6.2 Operative Import Tariff Rates in Korea, 1966–91

	1966	1970	1975	1980	1985	1991
A. *Tariffs collected and exempted*						
1. Tariff collected (billion won)	18.0	50.9	181.0	766.1	1,566.1	3,435.5
2. Tariff exempted (billion won)	20.3	107.1	222.7	789.5	2,982.0	3,711.0
3. Total legal tariffs (A.1 + A.2)	38.3	158.0	403.7	1,555.6	4,548.1	7,146.5
4. Total imports (million U.S. $)	716.4	1,194.0	7,274.4	21,598.0	31,135.6	81.524.9
5. Total imports (billion won)	194.4	616.2	3,520.8	13,737.0	27,716.3	62,024.1
B. *Tariff rates*						
1. Actual tariff rates (A.1/A.5)	9.3	8.3	5.1	5.6	5.6	5.5
2. Legal tariff rates (A.3/A.5)	19.7	25.6	11.5	11.3	16.4	11.5

Sources: Ministry of Finance, Office of Taxation; Bank of Korea, *Economic Statistics Yearbook* (Seoul, 1992).

large extent inoperative in Korea. Many imports were exempt from duties, and a number of commodities were subject to prohibitive tariffs. Intermediate goods for export production, for instance, were imported duty free, as were some capital goods for special uses or specific industries. Table 6.2 presents the data on tariffs actually collected and exempted, with the implicit tariff rates calculated on the basis of these data. According to the data, the legal tariff rates for all commodity imports far exceeded the actual tariff rates over the 1966–91 period.[3] During the latter half of 1960s, the legal tariff rate reached 20–26 percent, whereas the actual tariff rate remained at around 8–9 percent. In the 1970s and 1980s, the legal tariff rate fell to 11–16 percent and the actual tariff rate reached around 5–6 percent. These figures for legal and actual tariff rates, however, should not be taken as a measure of protection given to import substitution activities in Korea because, at least until recently, the QRs applied to many import items have been far more important than tariffs in controlling imports.

Indeed, as of the mid-1960s, imports were tightly controlled by the extensive use of QRs in Korea. According to Kim's estimation (1988, 20), as much as 88 percent of all import items were subject to QRs in the first half of 1967, despite the fact that import items liberalized under the "positive list" system increased from 1,447 to 2,950 during the 1965–67 period. A significant import liberalization, however, took place in the second half of 1967, as the earlier positive list system was replaced by a negative list system, in which all import items not listed were automatically approved for importation. As can be seen in the last column of table 6.1, more than 60 percent of the 1,312 basic import items (SITC four-digit) became automatically approved for import in 1967. But since then, the import liberalization rate fell steadily until 1975, when it reached a low of 49.1 percent.

3. Both legal and actual tariff rates calculated here represent an average rate weighted by import shares of individual import items.

This setback in liberalization was partly a result of the government's effort at that time to promote the HCIs. The government began the HCI drive by introducing a series of industry-specific promotional laws in the late 1960s, but it pursued the policy much more vigorously during the 1973–79 period when it instituted package assistance programs for investment.[4]

The government began to relax import controls in 1977, as the current account balance developed a small surplus, mainly due to increased income from oversea construction businesses in the oil-rich Middle Eastern countries. This liberalization was also interrupted by the second oil shock of 1979 and the worsening of the balance-of-payments situation in subsequent years. At the same time, large investment projects in the HCIs encouraged by the government in the 1970s began to produce a number of failures by the late 1970s.

Consequently, the Korean economy underwent a period of serious stagnation in both growth and export performance during 1979–81, registering a negative real growth rate, of 3.7 percent in 1980, for the first time in its postwar history. At the same time, the Korean economy was suffering from a number of structural imbalances, such as underdevelopment of the financial sector, insufficient development of small and medium-sized firms, and an unjustifiable protection structure of the home markets.

The policy reaction of the government to these unfavorable developments was to increase its reliance on market mechanisms. First, a long overdue currency adjustment was made. The Korean won, which had been pegged to the U.S. dollar at 484 won per dollar since 1974, was devalued to 580 won per dollar in 1980. After that, the Korean won was allowed to depreciate gradually to 893 won per dollar by the end of 1985.

The government also stepped up its effort to liberalize import controls and thereby to increase competition in domestic markets and to reduce the cost of protection. In 1983, the government announced a time-phased import liberalization plan for the 1983–88 period. According to the plan, not only was the range of basic tariff rates to be reduced, but the average basic tariff rate was to be lowered from 23.7 percent in 1983 to 18.1 percent by 1988. At the same time, Korea's import liberalization rate was to be increased from 80.3 percent in 1983 to 95.2 percent by 1988. It is notable that this liberalization plan was put into action when the Korean economy was suffering from persistent trade deficits.

After the successful and timely completion of the 1983 liberalization, a new tariff reform plan was prepared for 1989–93. According to this new plan, the average tariff rate was to be decreased from 18.1 percent in 1988 to 7.9 percent

4. There were several reasons for launching the HCI drive in the early 1970s. First, the government feared that Korea would soon lose its international competitiveness in labor-intensive manufactured goods, largely due to the rapid increase in domestic wage-rental ratios at the time. Second, rising protectionism abroad against imports of light industrial products was also viewed as a limit to continued export expansion. Finally, national security concerns worked for the promotion of the HCIs as a way of building a strong defense industry.

in 1993, and the average tariff rate for manufactures from 16.9 percent to 6.2 percent in the same period.

Along with the import liberalization schemes, the government introduced a series of policy reforms in the 1930s. Among other measures, the major commercial banks were privatized, and all interest subsidies were eliminated from "policy" loans, including export loans, in 1982. All industry-specific promotion laws were abolished, and a more general Industry Promotion Law was introduced in 1986. The government also resorted to tighter monetary and fiscal restraints. These policy reforms undoubtedly contributed to the success of the Korean economy in curbing inflation, resuming a high growth rate, and turning the trade balance from red to black in the latter half of the 1980s.

6.2.3 Long-Term Economic Performance

Table 6.3 provides basic data on the growth and transformation of the Korean economy for the 1962–91 period. Real GNP of Korea has increased more than 18-fold during the 1962–91 period, with an average annual growth rate of 10.6 percent. This contrasts with an average growth rate of 3.6 percent during the earlier inward-oriented period of 1954–62. As a result, real per capita GNP in Korea rose from $306 in 1962 to $5,240 in 1991 when measured in 1985 U.S. constant prices. The gradual decline in the rate of population growth, from 2.6 percent for 1962–71 to 1.1 percent for 1981–91, also contributed to this rapid increase in per capita income (Korea's population grew to 43.3 million by 1991, from 25.6 million in 1962).

The policy shift in the early 1960s brought fundamental changes in all sectors of the economy. First of all, rapid expansion of exports was achieved, initially through the rapid increase of labor-intensive production, followed by the expansion of capital- and skill-intensive production as factor endowments shifted with capital and skill accumulation. As seen in table 6.3, the ratio of exports to GNP was only 2.4 percent ($54 million) as of 1962, but rose to 11.6 percent ($1.1 billion) in 1971, and to 25.6 percent ($71.9 billion) in 1991. Moreover, manufactured goods have been the dominant element in export growth: exports of manufactured goods accounted for only 27.0 percent of total exports in 1962, but increased their share to 86.0 percent by 1971, and to 95.4 percent by 1991. As a result, the share of the manufacturing sector in GNP rose from 11.7 percent in 1962 to 27.5 percent in 1991, whereas agriculture's share decreased from 43.6 percent to 8.1 percent in the same period. Likewise, the share of the manufacturing sector in total employment increased from 8.7 percent in 1962 to 26.9 percent in 1991, whereas agriculture's share declined from 63.1 percent to 16.7 percent in the same period.

The rapid expansion of labor-intensive production since the early 1960s has also helped to improve the employment situation: the official unemployment rate, which stood at 8.4 percent in 1962, decreased to 4.4 percent in 1971, and to 2.3 percent in 1991. The labor market has remained at near full employment since 1973, with an unemployment rate never more than 4 percent, except dur-

Table 6.3 **Major Economic Indicators for Korea, 1962–91**

Indicator	1962	1971	1981	1991	Average Annual Growth Rate			
					1962–71	1971–81	1981–91	1962–91
Population (million)	26.5	32.9	38.7	43.3	2.4	1.6	1.1	1.7
GNP (billion won)[a]	7,595	18,564	55,354	141,602	10.4	11.5	9.8	10.6
Per capita GNP								
In thousand won[a]	287	564	1,430	3,270	8.0	9.9	8.7	8.9
In U.S. dollars[b]	306	735	2,074	5,240				
Sectoral share in GNP (%)								
Agriculture	43.6	29.5	15.6	8.1				
Manufacturing	11.7	21.8	31.3	27.5				
Services and social overhead	44.7	48.7	53.1	64.4				
Sectoral share in employment (%)								
Agriculture	63.1	48.2	34.2	16.7				
Manufacturing	8.7	14.2	21.3	26.9				
Services and social overhead	28.2	37.6	44.5	56.4				

Unemployment rate (%)	8.4	4.4	4.5	2.3				
Exports and imports								
Commodity exports[c] (f.o.b.; million U.S. $)	54	1,067	21,254	71,870	39.3	34.8	12.9	28.2
Ratio of exports to GNP (%)	2.4	11.6	31.9	25.6				
Share of manufactures in exports (%)	27.0	86.0	92.9	95.4				
Commodity imports[c] (c.i.f.; million U.S. $)	421	2,394	26,131	81,525	21.3	27.0	12.1	19.9
Ratio of imports to GNP (%)	183	25.2	29.1	29.0				
Investment and saving								
Share of investment in GNP (%)	12.8	25.4	29.1	39.4				
Domestic saving rate (%)	3.3	15.5	21.7	36.2				
Foreign saving rate (%)	10.6	10.8	7.8	3.1				
GNP deflator (1985=100)	3.3	12.8	82.2	145.5	16.3	20.4	5.9	13.9
Wholesale price index (1985=100)	5.6	15.8	93.9	111.3	12.2	19.5	1.9	10.9
Real wage index[d] (1985=100)	21.8	36.8	75.9	180.3	6.0	7.5	9.0	7.6

Source: Bank of Korea, *Economic Statistics Yearbook* (Seoul, various years).

[a]Based on 1985 constant prices.

[b]Based on 1985 U.S. constant prices.

[c]Based on current prices.

[d]For the manufacturing sector.

ing the period of economic stagnation in the early 1980s. In the late 1980s, a labor shortage was acutely felt in some sectors of the economy, due to an overheated domestic construction boom.

During the past 30 years, foreign financing has played an important role in filling the domestic investment and savings gap, to allow for Korea's rapid growth. Table 6.3 indicates that gross investment rose from 12.8 percent of GNP in 1962 to near 40 percent by 1991. The domestic saving rate, however, measured only 3.3 percent of GNP in 1962, but rose rapidly with growth in real incomes, reaching 36.2 percent by 1991. As a result, foreign financing in terms of the ratio to GNP fell from nearly 10 percent in 1962 to 3.1 percent by 1991. In the meantime, however, Korea briefly became a net capital exporter due to a rising surplus in its trade account: between 1986 and 1989 Korea experienced a period of trade surplus, reaching a peak of 8.1 percent of GNP in 1988.

Despite the impressive performance of the Korean economy over the 1962–91 period, a few aspects of the underlying policy management need to be mentioned. First, the HCI promotion drive of 1973–79 scarred the Korean economy for years. It created excess capacities in some unprofitable industries, while depleting investment funds that would have otherwise been available to other export industries.[5] Distortions in the domestic capital market were also severe since preferential loans below market rates became a major instrument in promoting the HCIs.

Second, despite the high domestic inflation rate relative to that of Korea's trading partners during the 1970s, the exchange rate had been pegged at 484 won per U.S. dollar during 1974–80, resulting in a real appreciation of the won against the dollar by more than 20 percent for 1973–79 (see table 6.4 in the next section). Thus, the massive investments in the HCIs, combined with the stagnation in export performance due to unfavorable exchange rates, forced the Korean economy to rely heavily on foreign borrowing to finance its domestic savings gap, raising the external debt, which stood at $16.8 billion in 1978, to $40.1 billion by 1983.

Third, ever since the first Five-Year Economic Plan was launched in 1962, the government had tended to put forward very ambitious investment programs, which were often met by a rapid increase in monetary growth. This in turn helped raise domestic price levels, especially for the first two decades of the 1962–91 period: the average annual inflation rate in terms of GNP deflators was 16.3 percent for 1962–71 and 20.4 percent for 1971–81, but it fell to 5.9

5. The absorption of fixed investment by the HCIs continued to rise from 49 percent of all fixed investment in the manufacturing sector in 1973 to nearly 70 percent in 1979. In the meantime, the capacity utilization rate for certain HCIs fell well below the average rate for the manufacturing sector, resulting in poor business performance. For instance, the average capacity utilization rate averaged only 35 percent for transport equipment, 60 percent for machinery, and 69 percent for electrical appliances in 1979, whereas it was estimated at 82 percent for the manufacturing sector as a whole in the same year. See Nam (1981a, 174, 193).

percent for 1981–91. Of course, such inflation rates could be regarded as modest compared to those experienced by some Latin American countries, but they were much higher than those experienced by Korea's immediate competitors Taiwan, Singapore, and Japan.

Finally, throughout most of the recent development period of 1962–91, the Korean labor market has remained rather undistorted. No minimum wage law was enforced, nor was any disruptive action by labor unions allowed. But with the recent democratization drive launched by the government in 1987, Korea has witnessed rapid growth in union membership and in the number of violent labor disputes.[6] Unions exerted tremendous pressure for a steep wage hike in the late 1980s, in an economy which was already strained by a labor shortage. Moreover, as Korea's trade balance (especially with the United States) turned into a surplus beginning in 1986, the Korean government was hard pressed by the U.S. authorities to alter the won-dollar exchange rate and to reduce Korea's trade surplus with the United States. This led to a rapid, and perhaps too large, appreciation of the won from 881 won per dollar in 1986 to 671 won per dollar in 1989. By 1990, Korea's trade account was again running a deficit and exports stopped growing in real terms. By 1992, the growth rate of real GNP fell to less than 5 percent, the lowest rate since 1980. Undoubtedly, a sharp rise both in real wages and in won values in the late 1980s played an important role in bringing about this outcome, though the extent to which they contributed to is not known.

6.3 The Relation between Trade Incentives, Exchange Rates, and Economic Growth

The single most important feature of Korea's rapid economic growth over the past three decades is that it has been accompanied by even faster growth of manufactured exports. The rapid growth of exports must have served as an important source of employment creation by stimulating domestic production in a multiplied way when the domestic economy was subject to high unemployment, as was the situation in the 1960s and the early 1970s in Korea. The Korean economy must also have benefited from a number of dynamic externalities generated by opening domestic markets to foreign competition, not to mention the static gains from trade expansion itself. As shown in the previous section, a number of policies have been actively pursued by the Korean government in order to make this export-led growth possible. The relative importance of those policies in explaining export growth and their possible links to economic growth will be examined below.

6. The number of labor disputes increased from 276 cases in 1986 to 3,749 cases in 1987. The number has been decreasing since then, to 1,616 cases in 1989 and 234 cases by 1991. See Sakong (1993, 83).

6.3.1 Exchange Rates, Exports, and Economic Growth

Table 6.4 provides summary statistics on the impact of major trade incentives in terms of effective exchange rates for exports and imports. The effective exchange rate for exports includes the subsidy effects of the following: the dollar premium due to multiple exchange rates (1963–64 only), direct subsidy payments (1962–64 only), direct tax reduction (1962–73 only), and interest subsidies due to preferential rates (1962–82 only). The relative importance of these export subsidies was particularly pronounced in the early 1960s when the nominal exchange rate was kept unrealistically low. For instance, the effective export subsidies amounted to as much as 36.6 percent of the official exchange rate in 1963 and 23.1 percent in 1964, but since then, they were never greater than 6.7 percent (in 1971), and in 1982 they were entirely removed.

The effective export subsidies measured above, however, underestimate the true level for several reasons. First, they do not include subsidy effects such as those from accelerated depreciation allowances, reserve funds for developing export markets and export losses, wastage allowances, and preferential rates on some overhead inputs, because either these factors are relatively insignificant in magnitude or the data are not available. Second, the interest subsidy above has been estimated by taking the differential between the interest paid by exporters under preferential rates and the interest payable at nonpreferential rates. The nonpreferential lending rates on ordinary bank loans, however, were also under complete government control and often were set unrealistically low.[7] Finally, although it is impossible to quantify the value, no one can deny that the effect of the informal incentives—such as the rapid processing of government paper work, the assurance of governmental support in the future, etc.—that the government provided to exporters may have been substantial.

More important than the role of effective export subsidies, however, has been the role of exchange rate management itself in keeping Korean exporters competitive in international markets. Given the fact that the Korean inflation rate was much higher than that of its major trading partners, the lack of flexibility in exchange rate management could have grossly undermined Korean exporters' international competitiveness. To show how the exchange rate was managed for the 1962–91 period, table 6.4 provides estimates of various real exchange rates which were obtained by adjusting nominal rates for changes in purchasing power parity (see notes to table 6.4). Several features of the table are noteworthy. First, continuous adjustments in nominal exchange rates, not the extent of export subsidies, played the dominant role in keeping real exchange rates stable and hence maintaining exporters' international competitiveness. For instance, between 1962 and 1982, during which period export subsidies were provided, export subsidies never accounted for more than 7 percent of nominal exchange rates except for a few years in the early 1960s,

7. In fact, Hong's (1979) estimate has shown that all loans through financial institutions in the 1970s were extended, on average, at a negative real rate of interest.

Table 6.4 **Nominal and Real Effective Exchange Rates for Exports and Imports, 1962–91**

	Nominal Exchange Rate[a] (won per U.S. $)			Wholesale Price Index (1985=100)		Real Exchange Rate[d] (won per U.S. $)			
		Effective Rate[b]					Effective Rate		Export-Import Exchange
Year	Official Rate	Exports	Imports	Korea	Major Trading Partners[c]	Official Rate	Exports	Imports	Rate Ratio
1962	130.0	141.8	146.3	5.6	30.1	697.0	762.3	786.5	0.99
1963	130.0	177.6	148.1	6.7	30.2	586.1	800.0	667.1	1.20
1964	213.8	263.1	246.4	9.1	30.8	725.0	891.8	835.3	1.07
1965	266.4	276.3	294.2	10.0	30.9	821.3	852.7	908.0	0.94
1966	270.3	276.7	295.4	10.9	31.8	789.3	809.1	863.7	0.94
1967	268.3	281.3	293.8	11.5	31.6	731.1	766.5	800.5	0.96
1968	276.3	293.3	302.2	12.5	32.8	725.8	769.8	793.2	0.97
1969	288.4	306.4	312.9	13.3	33.6	730.6	773.2	792.2	0.98
1970	310.4	330.6	336.1	14.5	34.3	729.4	776.3	788.9	0.98
1971	350.1	374.1	371.9	15.8	35.7	790.3	844.5	839.5	1.01
1972	394.0	408.6	417.9	19.3	43.1	889.3	912.0	932.8	0.98
1973	398.5	408.5	417.9	19.3	43.1	889.3	912.0	932.8	0.98
1974	406.0	413.2	424.5	27.4	55.8	82.73	841.5	864.6	0.97
1975	484.0	494.1	508.9	34.6	61.2	856.9	841.5	864.6	0.97
1976	484.0	496.3	515.4	38.8	62.3	776.4	796.6	827.3	0.96
1977	484.0	493.4	519.7	42.3	74.6	853.2	870.2	916.6	0.95
1978	484.0	495.0	526.9	47.3	77.1	791.1	808.8	860.9	0.94
1979	484.0	495.0	522.3	56.1	84.6	730.2	746.6	787.8	0.95
1980	607.4	628.0	642.9	78.0	96.3	750.8	776.3	794.7	0.98
1981	681.0	696.0	717.6	93.9	101.0	734.0	750.0	773.3	0.97
1982	731.0	734.0	774.1	98.2	98.7	734.6	737.7	778.0	0.95
1983	775.7	775.7	734.4	98.4	99.0	780.3	780.3	839.4	0.93
1984	805.9	805.9	857.9	99.1	100.2	814.8	814.8	867.4	0.94
1985	870.0	870.0	920.3	100.0	100.0	870.0	870.0	920.3	0.95
1986	881.4	881.4	942.9	98.5	101.8	910.1	910.1	974.0	0.94
1987	822.5	882.5	888.2	99.0	109.5	910.0	910.0	982.5	0.93
1988	731.4	731.4	781.1	101.7	122.4	880.1	880.1	939.9	0.94
1989	671.4	671.4	705.8	103.2	126.7	825.3	825.3	867.1	0.95
1990	707.7	707.7	747.3	107.5	130.6	860.1	860.1	908.0	0.95
1991	733.3	773.3	775.4	113.3	134.7	875.5	875.5	921.9	0.95

Sources: Bank of Korea, *Economic Statistics Yearbook* (Seoul, various years); International Monetary Fund, *International Financial Statistics* (Washington, D.C., various years).

[a]Data for 1962–65 were obtained from Westphal and Kim (1982, 218), and others were calculated by the author.

[b]The effective exchange rate for exports includes exchange premiums due to multiple exchange rates, direct cash subsidies, direct tax reductions, and interest subsidies per dollar of exports, but excludes indirect tax and tariff exemptions. The effective exchange rate for imports includes actual tariffs collected per dollar of imports, but excludes the price effects of QRs on imports.

[c]Major trading partners include the United States, Japan, West Germany, France, and the United Kingdom. The wholesale price index was calculated by a geometric average of those of these five nations using their trade volumes with Korea as weights.

[d]1985 is taken as the base year.

while the nominal exchange rate itself changed from 130 won per U.S. dollar in 1962 to 731 won per U.S. dollar in 1982, almost 600 percent!

Second, adjustments in nominal exchange rates, however, have not always been successful in maintaining stable real exchange rates over time. For instance, until 1973, in the early period of outward orientation, nominal exchange rates had been depreciating fast enough to more than offset inflation differentials between home and abroad, raising the real effective exchange for exports from 762.3 won per U.S. dollar in 1962 to 912.0 won per U.S. dollar in 1973. In 1974, however, the nominal exchange rate was pegged at 484 won per U.S. dollar and remained unchanged through 1979, mainly to dampen domestic inflationary pressure built up by the first oil shock as well as by the excessive investment drive in the HCIs. As a result, the real effective exchange rate for exports again fell back to 746.6 won per U.S. dollar by 1979, and it fell further to a low of 737.7 won per U.S. dollar by 1982 in the wake of the second oil shock. However, it gradually rose to 910.0 won per U.S. dollar by 1986, mainly due to the continuous depreciation of the nominal exchange rate and the slowdown in domestic inflation rates.

Finally, table 6.4 presents estimates of effective exchange rates for imports, which were obtained by adding actual tariffs collected per dollar of imports to the official exchange rates. These estimates, however, do not include the price effects of QRs applied on imports and hence underestimate the nominal protection given to import substitution, especially during the 1960s and 1970s, when the use of QRs was most pronounced. Given this deficiency, the last column of table 6.4 provides the export-import effective exchange rate ratio. As can be seen, it turns out to be very close to one in most years, except for 1963. This suggests that trade incentives as a whole have acted together so as to roughly maintain neutrality between exports and import substitution in Korea. Since 1982, however, import substitution has been slightly favored over exportation—export incentives had been almost completely removed by then.

In order to show the importance of real effective exchange rates in determining exporters' international competitiveness, the movement of real effective exchange rates was plotted against growth rates of real exports for the 1962–91 period, and the result is shown in figure 6.1. As can be seen from the figure, the two variables move together closely, with a correlation coefficient of 0.34. There are, of course, anomalous years in which the two variables moved in opposite directions, such as 1964, 1980, and 1985, and most notably 1975, perhaps as an aftermath to the first oil shock. But more conspicuous is the dismal export performance during 1989–91 with negative real growth rates, which was too bleak to ascribe to the appreciation in real exchange rates alone. This may be explained, however, by the dramatic increase in nominal wages, following the explosive labor disputes, experienced by the Korean economy since 1987. For instance, between 1987 and 1991, nominal wages in the manufacturing sector more than doubled, while labor productivity rose only 28 percent. At the same time, the nominal exchange rate fell from 822.5 to 733.3 won

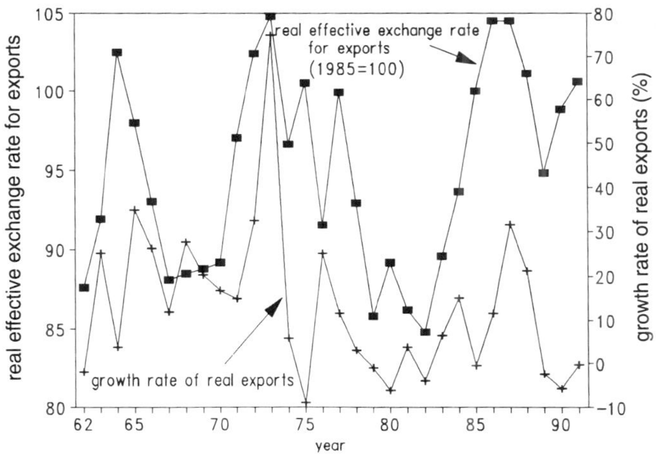

Fig. 6.1 Relation between real effective exchange rates for exports and growth rates of real exports

per U.S. dollar in the same period. As a result, the unit labor cost in terms of U.S. dollars rose by 88 percent in the short span of 1987–91, which undoubtedly undermined Korean exporters' international competitiveness. These findings vividly illustrate the importance not only of exchange rate management but also of labor relations management in order to ensure that domestic exporters can exploit export opportunities up to their potential.

It has already been argued that Korea's economic growth has largely depended on the rapid growth of exports under outward orientation. To show this more explicitly, figure 6.2 presents a regression line obtained by regressing growth rates of real GNP against growth rates of real exports, using the data set over the 1962–91 period. As expected, the result shows a strong positive relation between the two variables, with a correlation coefficient of 0.49 and a R^2 value of 0.24 for the regression equation.

This result is not special to Korea, however. Numerous empirical studies on the relation between the degree of openness, export growth, and economic performance have all produced evidence that there are important links between them.[8] Yet these studies provide little guidance as to the exact routes through which and the extent to which trade policies, or alternatively export expansion, might have affected overall economic growth. This is, perhaps, the reason any attempt to investigate causal links between them may be worthwhile. In the remainder of this section, the allocative efficiency of resources and the sources of economic growth will be briefly examined in relation to trade policies undertaken in Korea.

8. See Edwards (1989) and Roubini and Sala-i-Martin (1991) for a comprehensive survey of studies on the relation between openness and growth.

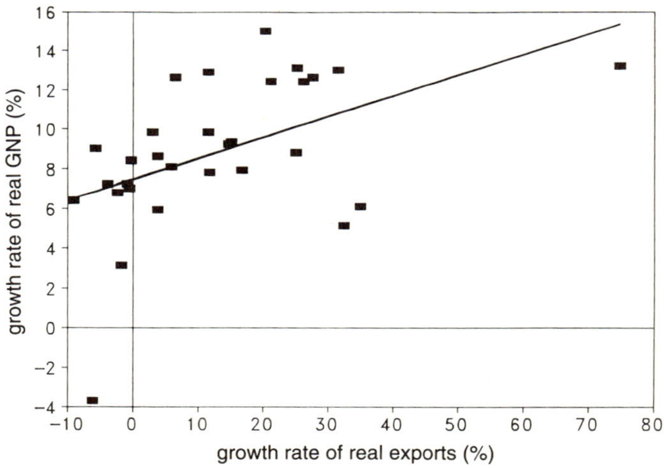

Fig. 6.2 Relation between growth rates of real exports and real GNP

6.3.2 Trade Incentives and the Allocative Efficiency of Resources

Trade reform is mostly undertaken to reduce distortions in the structure of relative prices and thereby to direct scarce resources to sectors that can make the best use of them. In that regard, trade reform has its primary impact on the allocative efficiency of resources, rather than on the rate of resource accumulation.

In any trade reform, the most common course of action includes the simplification of import procedures, the reduction or elimination of import quotas, and the rationalization of the tariff structure along with currency devaluations. However, the trade reform undertaken in Korea in the early 1960s indicates that the shift from inward to outward orientation was not achieved by liberalizing imports outright with currency adjustments (a "free trade" route to outward orientation), but rather by introducing a strong set of export incentives to offset antiexport bias created by import barriers (a "subsidy" route to outward orientation). So until very recently Korea had a very complex system of trade incentives, in which export activities were not only allowed to operate under a free trade regime but were subsidized in addition, while import substitution activities remained under various forms of protection.

It is apparent that the export subsidy route tends to be inferior to the free trade route for a number of reasons. Not only does the former involve substantial administrative costs, but export subsidies and import controls are rarely applied in an industry-neutral manner. Furthermore, QRs of any kind tend to generate large premia which will trigger rent seeking. Many able entrepreneurs may devote much of their energy and resources to privately profitable, but socially wasteful, rent seeking.

There were a few reasons, however, why Korea chose the export subsidy

Table 6.5 Relative Incentive Rates on Exports and Domestic Sales in Korea, 1968 and 1978 (%)

Industry	Legal Tariff Rate		NPR		EPS for Domestic Sales		ESR for Export Sales
	1968	1978	1968	1978	1968	1978	1978
I. Agriculture	36.5	26.7	17.0	55.2	17.9	73.4	15.1
II. Mining and energy	12.5	6.3	8.9	−19.8	3.5	−23.8	10.6
Primary production, total	35.1	24.2	16.5	45.8	17.1	58.7	14.5
III. Processed food	61.5	41.1	2.9	39.8	−14.2	−16.0	16.7
IV. Beverages and tobacco	140.7	133.2	2.2	20.2	−15.5	22.8	10.8
V. Construction materials	32.2	29.5	3.9	−7.2	−8.8	−11.9	15.1
VI-A. Intermediate products I[a]	36.6	23.2	2.8	−2.4	−18.8	−27.4	17.1
VI-B. Intermediate products II[a]	58.7	34.7	21.0	1.3	17.4	5.3	17.6
VII. Nondurable consumer goods	92.3	49.3	11.7	14.9	−8.0	21.9	12.1
VIII. Consumer durables	98.3	44.3	38.5	40.2	39.8	81.0	23.1
IX. Machinery	52.6	27.5	29.9	17.8	29.5	33.2	16.9
X. Transport equipment	62.4	57.0	54.9	30.9	83.2	73.8	16.9
Manufacturing, total	67.6	41.4	12.2	10.0	−1.1	3.7	15.8
All industries	54.3	37.3	14.0	17.8	9.0	24.1	13.9

Source: Nam (1981b, 201, and 206).
[a]Intermediate products I includes products in an earlier stage of fabrication than intermediate products II.

route over the free trade route. First, rapid import liberalization was not feasible, because of political pressure from groups with a vested interest in import protection. Second, the currency devaluation necessary to accompany the reduction in import barriers was often feared as a source of inflationary pressure. Third, import taxes constituted a major source of government revenue. Finally, policymakers were guided by the erroneous belief that both exports and import substitution can be better promoted under the export subsidy than under the free trade route.

It is not possible to quantify the precise impact of Korea's trade reforms on the allocative efficiency of resources, but it is possible to conjecture how resource allocation might have been affected by those trade reforms by examining the resulting structure of protection from the trade incentive system as a whole. If trade incentives affect prices of output or inputs, the best measure of incentives confronting domestic producers is effective protection rates (EPRs), but if trade incentives take the form of direct or indirect subsidies to a specific activity, the best measure of incentives is effective subsidy rates (ESRs). Both EPRs and ESRs measure the degree of protection or subsidy afforded to value-adding processes. These measures also provide an indication of the degree of efficiency gains in resource allocation attainable by the rationalization of the trade incentive system as a whole.

Table 6.5 gives estimates of nominal protection rates (NPRs), which are based on price differentials between home and world markets, and EPRs for domestic sales by industry group for 1978 in comparison with those estimated for 1968. Table 6.5 also provides estimates for ESRs granted to export sales in contrast to EPRs given to domestic sales, for 1978. A number of interesting features can be noted from the table. First, after a bold and significant liberalization effort in the mid-1960s, little progress seems to have been made in liberalizing import controls during the 1968–78 period. Most conspicuous is that protection for agriculture rose to a very high level, with a EPR of 73.4 percent in 1978 compared to 17.9 percent in 1968. The strong protection of agriculture may have been intended partly to ensure security of food supplies but was instituted mainly to support farm incomes, and this was pursued through a high-rice-price policy introduced in the late 1960s. This high-rice-price policy persisted throughout the 1980s, making Korea more like Japan and EC countries than other developing countries, as far as protection of agriculture is concerned.

Second, the average protection rates on manufacturing remained relatively low compared to those in other developing countries during 1968–78 (see Balassa 1971, 1982). The average NPRs declined slightly from 12.2 to 10.0 percent in the 1968–78 period for the manufacturing sector, whereas the average EPRs rose slightly from −1.1 to 3.7 percent in the same period. The main feature, however, is not the low average value of NPRs or EPRs but their dispersion across industries, resulting primarily from QRs. Furthermore, the dispersion in EPRs was even wider in 1978 than in 1968, with some high positive rates and some negative rates, suggesting worsening resource allocation effects of the protection structure. The high protection for consumer durables, machinery, and transport equipment and the negative protection for construction materials and intermediate products I are particularly noticeable. This is not too surprising since HCI products like electronics, heavy machines, and cars were actively promoted in the 1970s, while raw materials like cement, steel, and petroleum products were under complete price control at the time (see Nam 1981b).

In view of Korea's structure of protection, therefore, one may be tempted to conclude that Korea's incentive system certainly failed to bring the same resource allocation result as free trade would have achieved. Indeed, this is true, but the loss due to departures from the free trade result may not have been very significant, mainly because, as of 1978, Korea's trade incentive system as a whole clearly maintained its bias toward exporting (as opposed to import substitution) in most industries, with the notable exception of agriculture.[9]

Korea's export subsidy policy, however, had become increasingly difficult to

9. Even in agriculture, despite high protection, employment changed very little for 1962–81, but declined rapidly at an annual rate of 4.3 percent for 1981–91. High protection for agriculture seems, therefore, to have had the side effect of slowing down the labor migration from rural to urban, or from farm to nonfarm, sectors of the economy, thereby reducing pressure from "too" rapid urbanization or urban unemployment, at least until the 1970s.

maintain by the early 1980s for a few reasons. One is that the export subsidies through preferential loans at below-market rates became increasingly burdensome to Korea's monetary authority due to an ever-increasing export volume. Another is that subsidies by developing countries in general have increasingly become subject to countervailing duties by industrial countries, notably the United States.[10] At the same time, Korea's policymakers realized that the high protection given to HCI products in domestic markets did not guarantee their competitiveness in international markets. For these reasons, most export subsidy measures were removed in Korea by the early 1980s. At the same time, import liberalization was aggressively pursued throughout the 1980s so that the export subsidy route could be successfully replaced by a free trade route. Allocative efficiency of resources would have been improved accordingly.

6.3.3 Sources of Growth in an Outward-oriented Economy

It has long been thought that outward-oriented trade reform has its positive impact on growth through a number of channels other than improved resource allocation—more in line with one's comparative advantage. Among the most frequently cited channels are: the ability to exploit scale economies in production; easier access to better technologies, intermediate inputs, and capital goods; increased efforts toward labor training and research and development, to meet greater competition at home and abroad; and a better chance to have a general policy environment especially conducive to growth.[11]

It has not been possible, however, to measure the absolute or relative importance of these channels as contributing factors to growth. Not only is it difficult to single out the effect of trade policy among a myriad of other policy actions that could have a bearing on these channels, but growth itself can be affected by many factors other than those listed above. Thus, an attempt will be made below to examine the sources of growth estimated for Korea and to explore, though mostly at a conjectural level, their possible links to trade reforms undertaken in Korea.

Table 6.6 provides estimates of the sources of growth, based on Denison's (1967, 1979) approach to growth accounting, for Korea for three subperiods between 1963 and 1988. Table 6.6 also reports estimates of the sources of growth for Japan, West Germany, and the United States for comparison. A number of salient features can be identified from the table.

First, more than half of Korea's output growth is explained by increases in factor inputs—labor and capital—of which the contribution of labor has been persistently greater than that of capital in all three subperiods, accounting for

10. E.g., Korea became one of the four developing countries that were most frequently countervailed against by the United States in the early 1980s. See Nam (1987, 193).

11. For excellent reviews on this subject, see Krueger (1980, 1985), World Bank (1987), and Dornbusch (1992).

Table 6.6 Sources of Economic Growth in Korea, 1963–88

Items	Korea 1963–72	Korea 1972–82	Korea 1979–88	Japan 1953–71	West Germany 1950–62	United States 1948–73
Real national income (growth rate, %)	8.2	8.1	8.0	8.8	6.3	3.8
Total factor input	4.2	5.6	4.8	4.0	2.8	2.1
Labor	3.1	3.5	2.9	1.9	1.4	1.4
Capital	1.1	2.1	1.9	2.1	1.4	0.7
Output per unit of input	4.0	2.5	3.2	4.9	3.5	1.7
Improved resource allocation	0.6	0.7	0.6	1.0	1.0	0.3
Economies of scale	1.5	1.5	1.6	1.9	1.6	0.3
Advances in knowledge and n.e.c.[a]	1.9	0.3	1.0	2.0	0.9	1.1

Sources: Kim and Park (1985, 61–62) for Korea (1963–72 and 1972–82); Hong (1991, 27) for Korea (1979–88); Denison and Chung (1976, 42–43) for Japan and West Germany; Denison (1979, 104) for the United States.

[a]n.e.c. denotes "not elsewhere classified."

more than 30 percent of Korea's growth.[12] The high level of labor's contribution to growth should have been affected by the trade reforms undertaken in Korea in two major ways. One is that the rapid expansion of manufactured exports and the concurrent expansion of the service sector has become a major source of labor absorption in Korea ever since outward-oriented trade reform was undertaken in the early 1960s, reducing first the hidden and unemployed labor force in the rural sector and then the labor force employed by the agricultural sector itself (see table 6.7). The other is that exports became more labor intensive in production and in commodity composition in order to accommodate the shift in comparative advantage with outward-oriented trade reform in the early 1960s. For instance, physical capital intensity declined for exports, while it increased for competitive import replacements for the 1960–66 period (see table 6.8). As a result, the physical capital intensity of competitive import replacements was higher than that of exports by 56 percent in 1966, a sharp increase from 18 percent in 1960. The differential remained roughly the same through 1985. This suggests that, if the rate of capital accumulation was the binding factor on employment, additional investment in the export sector would have created roughly 50 percent more employment than would the same additional investment in the import substitution sector. On balance, it seems

12. These results contrast with the experiences of Japan and West Germany in that more than half of their growth is due to increases in total factor productivity and the contribution of capital is greater than or equal to that of labor.

Table 6.7 Employment Growth in Korea, 1962–91

	Employment (thousand persons)				Average Annual Growth rate (%)			
Sector	1962	1971	1981	1991	1962–71	1971–81	1981–91	1962–91
Agriculture	4,837	4,797	4,801	3,103	−0.1	0.0	−4.3	−1.5
Manufacturing	667	1,413	2,983	5,005	8.7	7.8	5.3	7.2
Services and social overhead	2,158	3,737	6,239	10,468	6.3	5.3	5.3	5.6
Total	7,662	9,946	14,023	18,576	2.9	3.5	2.8	3.1

Source: Bank of Korea, *Economic Statistics Yearbook* (Seoul, various years).

Table 6.8 Factor Intensity in Korean Manufacturing, 1960–85

	Capital-Labor ratio (thousand U.S. $ per worker)[a]			
Sector	1960	1966	1978	1985
Exports (A)	3.3	2.7	6.5	11.8
Competitive import replacements (B)	3.9	4.2	9.5	17.3
(B)/(A)	1.18	1.56	1.46	1.47

Source: Hong (1989, 100).
[a]In terms of 1985 constant U.S. dollars.

clear that the outward-oriented trade reforms undertaken in Korea contributed significantly to expanding employment opportunities in Korea.

Second, another interesting point that can be observed from table 6.6 is that the contribution of capital accumulation to growth was especially low during the 1960s. Of course, this was largely due to a low level of domestic investment in that period. This low domestic investment would have been even lower, however, had foreign savings not been available. As was already seen in table 6.3, gross domestic investment measured only 12.8 percent of GNP in 1962, of which more than 70 percent was financed by foreign borrowing. After then, domestic investment grew very rapidly, with rising domestic income and savings, reaching 25.4 percent of GNP in 1971 and 39.4 percent in 1991. During the 1970s, however, about 20–30 percent of Korean domestic investment was still financed by foreign borrowing. To be sure, this large amount of foreign borrowing would not have been possible had export earnings not been growing quickly under the outward-oriented trade regime.

Third, table 6.6 shows that slightly less than half of Korean output growth was due to growth of total factor productivity (output per unit of input). Three major sources for the growth of total factor productivity have been considered and estimated for their respective contributions to growth: they include improved resource allocation, economies of scale, and advances in knowledge. According to Kim and Park (1985, 58), the contribution of improved resource allocation came primarily from the shift of labor from low-productivity agriculture to high-productivity nonagricultural sectors. The contribution of improved resource allocation to growth has been very steady over the three subperiods between 1963 and 1988, accounting for about 0.7 percentage points of the output growth rate, or about 10 percent of total output growth. Needless to say, labor migration from agriculture to nonagricultural sectors was greatly promoted by the export-promoting trade policy and the concomitant rapid growth of labor-intensive manufactured exports in Korea.

Fourth, according to the estimates shown in table 6.6, the contribution of economies of scale to growth has also been very significant and steady over the three subperiods, accounting for about 1.5 percentage points of output growth rate, or about 20 percent of total output growth. This figure appears to be, however, somewhat less than those experienced by Japan and West Germany during the postwar period. This may be partly due to the high protection given to some import substitution activities in Korea, though exports have been fully liberalized. But the high protection of domestic markets may not have been too inimical to reaping scale economies since protection was often provided to those industries that risked a loss in their export markets.

Finally, a third source of growth of total factor productivity, classified as "advances in knowledge" in table 6.6, represents a residual which is obtained by subtracting the effects of improved resource allocation and economies of scale from the growth rate of total factor productivity. According to Kim and Park (1985, 59), the contribution of this third source of growth comes mostly from improved production technique, distribution, and business organization that occurred in a particular period. The estimates of the contribution of this source of growth show that it has been erratic over the three subperiods between 1963 and 1988. Its highest contribution was obtained during the early period of outward orientation 1963–72, with 1.9 percentage points of the output growth rate, explaining nearly a quarter of output growth in that period. But it fell to a low of 0.3 percentage points of the output growth rate, explaining less than 5 percent of output growth during 1972–82. Of course, this period includes two oil shocks, and a crop failure in 1980, but the massive investment drive in the HCIs may have also contributed to the poor productivity growth obtained in that period.

In conclusion, trade reforms undertaken in Korea for the past three decades have not only led to static efficiency gains in resource allocation but have also generated dynamic growth effects through a number of channels, though it is not possible to single out their effects in quantitative terms as a major factor in economic growth.

6.4 Concluding Remarks

Several policy lessons can be drawn from this study of Korea's trade and exchange rate policies and the role they have played in Korea's growth over the 1962–91 period.

First, an outward-oriented growth strategy was successfully implemented in Korea by an export subsidy rather than a free trade route until the early 1980s. Despite somewhat chaotic government interventions both on the export and on the import substitution side, the net effects largely offset each other, resulting in a good deal less discrimination—or more neutrality—between import substitution and export production than in many other developing countries.

However, other developing countries thinking of emulating Korea's experience with the subsidy route to outward orientation need to be cautioned. For one thing, this route was feasible in Korea mainly because protection of the home market was relatively low to begin with, so that antiexport bias was easily offset by export subsidies.[13] For another, it is hard to avoid economic losses due to distortions in factor and in output markets under the export subsidy route. For example, export subsidies through policy loans at below-market interest rates retarded the financial sector, and the promotion of the HCIs by the government proved very costly in Korea. Also, the wide dispersion of EPRs across industries observed in Korea indicates that further improvement in the allocative efficiency of resources can be achieved. Furthermore, export subsidies combined with import barriers increasingly risk antidumping or countervailing actions by some industrial countries. For these reasons, Korea, too, has shifted from an export subsidy to a free trade route to outward orientation since the early 1980s.

Second, establishing a neutral incentive system between exports and import substitution constitutes an important condition for an outward-oriented growth strategy, but this alone does not guarantee rapid export growth. Korea's experience vividly illustrates that it is vitally important to maintain competitive real exchange rates to secure sustained export growth. In Korea, the real exchange rate for exports (including export subsidies) has been kept very stable over the 1962–91 period, with the exception of a few years between the late 1970s and the early 1980s. In the early 1960s, export subsidies played an important role in keeping the real exchange rate for exports stable, amounting to, for example, as much as 37 percent of the official exchange rate in 1963. But beginning with the 1964 devaluation of the won against the dollar by nearly 100 percent, the government placed increasing reliance on adjustments of nominal exchange rates and less on export subsidies to keep the real exchange rate for exports stable over time, and by 1982 the export subsidies were entirely removed.

Third, a critical precondition for fast growth is a high level of domestic investment. In Korea, foreign borrowing played an important role in financing

13. E.g., large export subsidies did not suffice to offset the high protection of import substitution in countries like Brazil and Mexico.

domestic investment, especially in the early years of outward-oriented growth with very low rates of domestic savings. During the 1960s, for instance, nearly half of gross domestic investment was financed by foreign borrowing, and about a quarter of it was foreign funded in the 1970s, when domestic saving rates averaged more than 20 percent of GNP. The government can be largely credited for this. Not only was mobilizing foreign borrowing a major component of each of Korea's successive Five-Year Economic Plans since 1962, but the government extended its repayment guarantees to loans by the private sector to stimulate foreign borrowing. However, without the rapid growth of export earnings, such a large inflow of foreign capital would not have been possible.

Finally, in order to translate outward-oriented trade reforms effectively into rapid growth of exports and income, it is imperative to have all essential infrastructure in place. Education, transportation, and communication, the maintenance of macroeconomic stability, and a well-defined legal system are, for example, some of the important services needed for efficient market processes. Although the Korean government fumbled in some areas, such as the promotion of the HCIs and the control of the financial sector, it was a relatively efficient provider of these essential services. The successive Five-Year Economic Plans were instrumental in delivering essential infrastructure in Korea.

References

Balassa, Bela, ed. 1971. *The structure of protection in developing countries.* Baltimore: Johns Hopkins University Press.

———, ed. 1982. *Developing strategies in semi-industrial economies.* Baltimore: Johns Hopkins University Press.

Denison, Edward F. 1967. *Why growth rates differ: Postwar experience in nine western countries.* Washington, D.C.: Brookings Institution.

———. 1979. *Accounting for slower economic growth: The United States in the 1970s.* Washington, D.C.: Brookings Institution.

Denison, Edward F., and William K. Chung. 1976. *How Japan's economy grew so fast.* Washington, D.C.: Brookings Institution.

Dornbusch, Rudiger. 1992. The case for trade liberalization in developing countries. *Journal of Economic Perspectives* 6, no. 1 (Winter): 69–86.

Edwards, Sebastian. 1989. Openness, outward orientation, trade liberalization and economic performance in developing countries. NBER Working Paper no. 2908. Cambridge, Mass.: National Bureau of Economic Research.

Hong, Sung Duk. 1991. *Estimation of sources of growth and factor productivity for the Korean economy* (in Korean). Seoul: Korea Development Institute.

Hong, Wontack. 1979. *Trade, distortions and employment growth in Korea.* Seoul: Korea Development Institute.

———. 1989. Factor intensities of Korea's domestic demand, production and trade: 1960–85. *International Economic Journal* 3, no. 2 (Summer): 97–113.

Kim, Kwang-Suk. 1988. Economic impact of import liberalization in Korea. In *Indus-*

trial policies of Korea and the Republic of China. Seoul: Korea Development Institute.
Kim, Kwang-Suk, and Joon-Kyung Park. 1985. *Sources of economic growth in Korea: 1963–1982.* Seoul: Korea Development Institute.
Krueger, Anne O. 1980. Trade policy as an input to development. *American Economic Review* 70 (May): 288–92.
———. 1985. Importance of general policies to promote economic growth. *World Economy* 8, no. 2 (June): 93–108.
Nam, Chong-Hyun. 1981a. Heavy and chemical industry. In *National budget and policy goals* (in Korean), ed. Chong-Kee Park and Kyu-Uck Lee. Seoul: Korea Development Institute.
———. 1981b. Trade and industrial policies, and the structure of protection in Korea. In *Trade and growth of the advanced developing countries in the Pacific Basin,* ed. Wontack Hong and Lawrence B. Krause. Seoul: Korea Development Institute.
———. 1987. Export-promoting subsidies, countervailing threats, and the General Agreement on Tariffs and Trade. *World Bank Economic Review* 1, no. 4 (September): 723–43.
Roubini, Nouriel, and Xavier Sala-i-Martin. 1991. Financial development, the trade regime, and economic growth. NBER Working Paper no. 3876. Cambridge, Mass.: National Bureau of Economic Research.
Sakong, Il. 1993. *Korea in the world economy.* Washington, D.C.: Institute for International Economics.
Westphal, Larry E., and Kwang Suk Kim. 1977. Industrial policy and development in Korea. World Bank Staff Working Paper no. 263. Washington, D.C.: World Bank, August.
———. 1982. Korea. *Developing strategies in semi-industrial economies,* ed. Bela Balassa. Baltimore: Johns Hopkins University Press.
World Bank. 1987. *World Development Report.* Washington, D.C.: World Bank.

Comment Shang-Jin Wei

Chong-Hyun Nam's interesting paper has an ambitious objective. He reviews Korea's four decades of trade and exchange rate policies, assesses their role in Korea's rapid growth, and finally draws four lessons for other developing countries.

His policy review presents a comprehensive and interesting picture of the policy structure supporting Korea's outward growth strategy. Some of his material is not readily available outside Korea.

I also agree with most of the lessons he draws for other developing countries, such as his emphasis on the importance of maintaining a competitive exchange rate and investing in infrastructure. However, I would like to add some qualifications to one of his lessons: Nam has expressed skepticism about the desir-

Shang-Jin Wei is assistant professor of public policy at the John F. Kennedy School of Government, Harvard University, and faculty research fellow of the National Bureau of Economic Research.

ability and feasibility of other developing countries' following Korea's lead in an outward-oriented growth strategy via export subsidy. This conclusion does not follow very well from the body of his paper. Furthermore, the outward-oriented strategy via export subsidy is both feasible and, under certain circumstances, desirable for other developing countries.

That pursuing an outward-oriented strategy via export subsidy to achieve high growth is feasible can be seen from the recent example of Chinese growth. Moving away from a rigid version of import substitution, China has since 1980 embarked on an impressive path of opening up to the outside world. Export subsidies, explicitly or implicitly, have been extensively used in order to spur export growth. Over the 1980s, the average annual growth rate of Chinese external trade was above 15 percent, three times higher than the growth in world trade. In some sense, export subsidy may be the way for a large country to rapidly increase its exports in a short time, although the threat of foreign antidumping duties places some limit on export subsidy.

As for desirability, one can certainly find an efficiency-based justification for export subsidy. For example, if one believes in the existence of positive externality from export activity to the rest of the economy, then one would favor policies that encourage exports. Of course, this does not imply that *any* kind of export subsidy is necessarily beneficial. If the nature of the externality is such that the larger the total exports the better for the economy, then one would want policies that do not discriminate among various export activities. An example of this policy is an artificially undervalued domestic currency. In Korea's case, the government's policy in the 1960s and early 1970s of rewarding firms based on their export volume is close to a nondiscriminatory one. Its drive to support the heavy and chemical industries during 1973–79 involved subsidies skewed toward a particular industry and later proved to be a mistake.

I would like to suggest that, even in the absence of positive spillover from export activity, there is often a political economy argument for export subsidy for countries that are trying to get out of an import substitution trap. That is, free trade may be politically unattainable, but export subsidy (together with preservation of some old import protection) is attainable. In fact, Korea's case is illuminating on this point. As Nam points out in this paper, one important reason that Korea chose the export subsidy route over the free trade route was "political pressure from groups with a vested interest in import protection." As Nam's review of Korea's policies indicates, various policies of import protection took a long time (two decades) to phase out even though Korea is regarded as a highly outward-oriented economy. I would like to elaborate on Nam's observation in a way that may or may not suit his taste.

Fernandez and Rodrik (1991) have taught us how, if an economy is initially dominated by import protection, free trade, though it may be able to muster a majority's support if ever implemented, can be rejected in a political process. Because no one knows for sure how costly it will be for her to switch jobs if free trade is indeed implemented, the ex post gainers do not realize they are gainers ex ante. Hence, import protection may be politically preferred to free trade even though a majority may benefit from free trade.

Suppose the costs of switching jobs are uneven among people in the protected sectors but are known to everyone. Would export subsidy with some import protection be preferred to pure import protection? The answer is yes if there are enough people in the protected sector who have a relatively low cost of switching jobs. In this case, export subsidy operates like job-switching assistance or a job-training fee that will greatly relieve the reservations that the low switching cost people have about leaving the inefficient but protected industries. Because they benefit as consumers in a less distorted economy and now need not worry about income loss, they will side with people in the efficient export industries to move away from pure import protection toward export promotion. If the number of low switching cost people plus those originally in the export industries is large enough, they can exert strong enough pressure to materialize a shift in the trade regime. Therefore, although free trade is difficult to attain directly, export promotion can nevertheless be preferable to the original import protection. A formalization of the above story can be found in Wei (1993).

To summarize, export subsidy is still feasible and can be desirable by both efficiency and political economy arguments.

References

Fernandez, Raquel, and Dani Rodrik. 1991. Resistance to reform: Status quo bias in the presence of individual-specific uncertainty. *American Economic Review* 85, no. 5 (November): 1146–55.

Wei, Shang-Jin. 1993. Switching from import substitution to export promotion: A note. John F. Kennedy School of Government, Harvard University.

7 The Role of the Government in Promoting Industrialization and Human Capital Accumulation in Korea

Joon-Kyung Kim, Sang Dal Shim, and Jun-Il Kim

7.1 Introduction

Korea's economic growth performance in the past 30 years has been cited as an exemplary model of rapid economic development and has been termed an "economic miracle." Lucas (1993) even constructed a model for the occurrence of economic miracles based on the Korean growth example.

Korea started its process of economic development in the early 1960s with a small industrial base and little accumulated capital and technology. The postwar division of the country severed whatever industrial link existed between the north and south, and the Korean War (1950–53) almost completely destroyed the production facilities and infrastructure of the economy. In the 1950s, many foreign observers regarded the Korean economy as hopeless. Until the early 1960s, the economy depended on foreign economic aid, and its per capita income was less than $100, which lagged behind that of many African countries (including Ghana and Kenya), not to mention most Latin American countries. Korea, perhaps with Taiwan, is one of the few countries that grew from poverty to industrial strength comparable to advanced OECD countries.

Identifying the factors behind Korea's fast growth is a task of paramount interest to both policymakers and academic researchers. In academic circles, there has been a renewal of interest in identifying the factors that determine growth after the publication of Romer's paper (1986), which sparked a significant amount of research on "endogenous growth." According to the theory of endogenous growth, one of the key factors generating fast growth is human capital accumulation through learning by doing, or on-the-job training, as well as education. The accumulation of human capital can be accelerated through

Joon-Kyung Kim, Sang Dal Shim, and Jun-Il Kim are research fellows at the Korea Development Institute.

international trade, which expands and diversifies the production frontier and hence provides excellent opportunities for fast learning. Grossman and Helpman (1989, 1990) identified knowledge spillovers from advanced to developing countries as the most important gains from trade. Lucas (1993) stressed the importance of becoming a large-scale exporter, as it allows workers and managers to continue taking on new tasks, which enables sustained learning on the job.

Government assistance can also affect the speed of human capital accumulation. In order to maintain a high rate of learning, people need to change jobs, which necessitates the continuous introduction of new industries and new products, requiring different skills and technologies. But the creation of these new industries is subject to high risks. The government's assistance can encourage private industrialists to undertake new projects by reducing the risk they face. Thus, the diversification of the industrial structure with governmental assistance enables the learning process to continue without being subject to diminishing returns.

The role of governmental assistance has been given little attention in the endogenous growth theory literature. In practice, the most successful economies, such as those of the East Asian countries, were not only big exporters but were those whose governments extensively supported exports and industrialization. This paper attempts to identify the factors behind the rapid Korean growth and interpret the Korean experience within this framework, while giving special attention to the contribution that Korean government policies made in accelerating economic growth. It will also explore the negative side effects of such policies.

The paper is organized as follows: Section 7.2 will discuss the socioeconomic factors that contributed to the Korean work ethic and heightened educational zeal. Section 7.3 will discuss policy measures that were adopted from the 1960s to the 1970s to promote exports and industrialization. Section 7.4 evaluates the effectiveness of these policy measures in accelerating human capital accumulation and economic growth in Korea. It also discusses distributional issues and other side effects of such government interventions, which need to be addressed for the formation of future developmental policies.

7.2 Socioeconomic Factors and Human Capital Accumulation

The socioeconomic environment can affect human capital accumulation. Unlike countries like India, where there is a caste system which precludes a person from advancing in social status, the class distinction between the noble and ordinary people was largely destroyed in Korea during Japanese colonial rule (1910–45). The destruction of the traditional social hierarchy played a major role in motivating Koreans to invest in human capital.

Just before liberation in 1945, 90 percent of industrial assets were under

Japanese ownership, and the rest belonged to a handful of Korean landowners. Between 1949 and 1951, land was distributed to poor farmers through the Land Reform Bill and large landowners disappeared. As mentioned before, most of the industrial and capital base was devastated during the Korean War, resulting in the extreme poverty of all people. As a result, Korea saw an unusual equalization in assets and income in the 1950s and became a rare case among developing countries.

Korea has maintained one of the world's most competitive educational systems, in which access to higher education is determined by a uniform standard. With few exceptions, access is determined by the applicant's score on a national exam—unlike in Western countries where multiple standards such as family background, extracurricular activities, alumni connections, and leadership skills are considered.

Such an environment of equal status with fair competition created great potential for vertical mobility in society: the general public was given almost equal opportunity and strong incentives to move up the "status ladder" by investing in human capital or by entrepreneurial activities.[1] Of course, human capital accumulation and active business promotion at the individual level would have been unlikely if the government had initiated the economic development process within a socialist framework, rather than a capitalist one.[2]

7.3 Government Policies for Industrialization

7.3.1 Export Promotion

From the beginning of the first Five-Year Economic Development Plan in 1962, the Korean government has adopted an export promotion strategy rather than an import substitution policy.[3] The government strongly supported exporting firms with various incentive measures, including favorable treatment in the allocation of credit and in the taxation system.

The system of export financing played a critical role in supporting export industries until the mid-1980s when the Korean current account recorded a surplus. The essence of the system was the Bank of Korea's (BOK's) automatic rediscounting policy, which supplied credit via commercial banks to exporting firms who received letters of credit (L/C). The central bank's discount loans

1. This argument resembles the convergence results in neoclassical growth models in which poor economies with lower capital-labor ratios grow faster than rich countries, converging to the same steady state, other things being equal. In endogenous growth models, however, absolute convergence results are not obtained because steady state growth itself depends on saving rates and other model parameters.

2. In 1960, North Korea dominated South Korea in terms of production capacity and per capita GNP. Such dominance, however, was reversed in the early 1970s.

3. Export promotion was largely dictated by the need to finance the imports required to build up industrial capacity.

Table 7.1 Export Loans by Domestic Money Banks (%)

	1961–65	1966–72	1973–81	1982–86	1987–91
Export loans by BOK (as a share of export loans by DMBs)	n.a.	75.4	90.1	65.8	45.3
Export loans by DMBs (as a share of total loans by DMBs)	4.5	7.6	13.3	10.2	3.1
Export loans by DMBs (as a share of total policy loans[a] by DMBs)	n.a.	n.a.	20.4	16.5	4.5
Export loan interest rate (A)	9.3	6.1	9.7	10.0	10–11.0
General loan interest rate (B)	18.2	23.2	17.3	10–11.5	10–11.5
B − A	8.9	17.1	7.6	0–1.5	0–0.5
Financial subsidy ratio for exports[b]	n.a.	1.6	0.6	0.5	0.2
Annual export growth rate[c]	40.3	37.7	35.1	10.5	16.4
Export/GNP	3.5	9.9	26.2	32.5	30.7

Source: Bank of Korea, *Economic Statistics Yearbook* (Seoul, various issues).

[a]The size of policy loans is estimated for earmarked credit such as export credits, National Investment Fund loans, housing loans, and credit for agriculture, fisheries, and small and medium-sized companies.

[b]The financial subsidy ratio is estimated by dividing the total amount of financial subsidy for exports by the total export value. The amount of financial subsidy is calculated by multiplying the size of export-related loans by the interest rate differential between the average borrowing rate for the manufacturing industry and interest rates for export-related loans.

[c]Annual export growth rate during 1953–60 was 8.2 percent.

were also extended to preshipment exports, as well as to imports of raw materials and intermediate goods for export use and to the purchase of export content from local suppliers.[4]

Table 7.1 shows that most of the export credit extended by domestic money banks (DMBs) were supported by the central bank. Between 1966 and 1986, the annual average ratio of BOK export credits to DMB export loans was 79.4 percent. In particular, the ratio reached 90.1 percent in the 1973–81 period. Table 7.1 also shows DMB export loans as a share of total DMB loans. Between 1961 and 1965, the annual average share was only 4.5 percent. The share increased to 7.6 percent in the 1966–72 period and further, to 13.3 percent, in the 1973–81 period. The share, however, has decreased significantly since the mid-1980s, when the current account surplus began accumulating.

The interest rate on export loans was also heavily subsidized. Until 1981, export loans were provided at rates of 6–10 percent even though general loan rates were 17–23 percent. After 1982, the differential disappeared (see table

4. In addition to this explicitly earmarked export credit program, the government guided the banks through moral suasion, directives, or communication to lend to exporters to support their fixed investment as well as working capital. See Rhee (1989) and Cho and Kim (1993) for a detailed description of Korea's export credit policy.

7.1). Given the facts that the availability of credit was what mattered and that the curb-market rates usually exceeded 30 percent, the preferential treatment given to exporters was far greater than that implied by the above-mentioned differentials alone.

It is interesting to see in table 7.1 that there is some positive correlation between export growth and export loan support, in terms of its availability and the extent of preferential treatment. Between 1961 and 1981, exports grew about 35–40 percent per annum and their share in GNP increased by more than seven times. However, the growth rate has dropped to the 10 percent level since 1982.

Such fast export growth in the 1960s and 1970s was not due solely to these export credit programs. The government also provided substantial tax incentives to exporting firms by reducing business and corporate taxes on export income by 50 percent and exempting tariffs on materials or intermediate goods imported as export content. Furthermore, exporters were exempted from tax investigations, which motivated business firms to restlessly participate in exporting.

In addition to these incentives, there was also a long list of governmental measures for export activity promotion at the microlevel. Since export marketing has substantial fixed costs in the beginning stages, the government established the Korea Trade Promotion Corporation (KOTRA) mainly to explore foreign markets. To assist Korean exporters in effectively filling foreign orders, the government also subsidized projects to improve the wrapping and design of products, the expansion of inspection facilities for export goods, the opening of foreign-language training centers, and traveling expenses for delegations to overseas expositions and trade shows.[5]

The government also initiated close consultation with the export industries and monitored the performance of supported firms through "monthly export promotion expansion meetings," chaired by the president. Ministers with trade-related duties, representatives from business, banking institutions, and shipping companies, and labor-union leaders participated in these meetings to review export performance broken down according to product and destination, and to discuss international market trends and emerging problems. For instance, if export performance was weak, the president urged relevant government officials and bankers to provide enhanced support to achieve a target volume of exports as planned. Through the process of consensus building in these meetings, export promotion policies were systemized (Kim 1990).[6]

Another salient feature of Korean export promotion policies was that the

5. These broad projects were financed from a sort of semitax on domestic exporter's imports, which was operated by the Korea Trader's Association (KTA).

6. The term "Korea Incorporated" was coined mainly because of this unique feature of Korea's export promotion policy implementation: banks acted as a treasury unit, the industrial sector as production and marketing units, and the government as a central planning and control unit (Cho and Hellmann 1993).

government's support to exporting firms was based on export performance. Exporters eligible to receive support were limited to those whose past year's exports exceeded a target amount.[7] To get more privileges, exporters had to work hard to compete with each other and foreign businesses. In this way, the Korean government maintained an efficient allocating device for picking winners and was able to reduce the risk of an "interventionist approach" (Cho and Kim 1993). Furthermore, this strategy compelled Korean firms to compete with foreign firms and brought tremendous externalities of accelerated learning on the job and, thus, a shortened learning curve.

There seems to be little controversy over the fact that these comprehensive export promotion policies contributed to the remarkable expansion of the Korean export sector by stimulating learning by doing. But one may remain doubtful whether the full extent of government subsidies used by Korean policymakers was necessary to kick off export growth.

7.3.2 Promotion of the Heavy and Chemical Industries

From the beginning of economic development, the Korean military government made deliberate efforts to upgrade the industrial structure by promoting the heavy and chemical industries (HCIs). It believed that the build up of the HCIs would lead to a "wealthy country and a strong army." The promotion of the HCIs was carried out despite many critical obstacles: (1) Korea lacked capital and Korea's market was very small, while the HCIs require huge capital investments with long gestation periods and they are sensitive to scale. (2) Technical skills necessary to efficiently produce HCI products were absent in Korea. The Korean government designated the steel industry, along with the petrochemical industry, strategic industries to be given top priority in the second Five-Year Economic Development Plan (1967–71).[8]

In the early 1970s, the promotion of the HCIs was further pushed to sustain export growth. The Korean industrial structure had rapidly transformed during the 1960s from an agrarian economy to a light manufacturing sector–dominated economy. But the government suspected that export-led growth would not be sustained when the light industries' production reached the "effective minimum scale" and their position of comparative advantage in the international market deteriorated.

The HCI drive was also largely motivated by national security concerns, magnified by the Carter administration's plan to completely withdraw U.S. ground forces from Korea and by the fall of South Vietnam to communist rule. In response, the Korean government announced in 1973 that it would promote the HCIs simultaneously with the defense industry.

7. The general trading companies introduced in 1972 had favorable access to various government supports. But their licenses had to be renewed every year. Those that had not exported beyond a certain amount found their licenses revoked. (Cho and Kim 1993).

8. Pohang Integrated Steel Mill (POSCO) and Wulsan Petrochemical Complex were built during the second Five-Year Plan.

The government's key strategy for developing the HCIs was raising factory sizes to international standards, in order to promote their competitive edge. Since the domestic market was too small for these large factories, the government decided that the HCIs were to be promoted as strategic export industries to solve marketing problems and to practice economies of scale (Kim 1990).[9]

The HCI policy was implemented through subsidized credit and special tax policies, selective protection, entry restrictions, and direct government involvement in industrial decision making. The government picked *chaebols* (conglomerates) or firms to enter specific industries.

Among various government supports, financing was the most critical factor since the HCIs required huge amounts of capital. With limited domestic saving, the government had to actively seek foreign capital. At that time, the ability of Korean entrepreneurs to attract foreign capital was very limited due to the low creditworthiness of domestic firms. The government, in response, took two big steps. It began to guarantee the reimbursement of all foreign loans, whether they were initiated by public companies or by private companies. Much more important, the government normalized relations with Japan, despite very strong anti-Japan sentiment and popular protest.[10] These measures facilitated large inflows of foreign capital and technology, especially from Japan.

Table 7.2 shows the allocation of foreign loans by industry. From 1959 to 1982, commercial loans were mostly allocated to the manufacturing industries, especially to the HCIs, while public loans went mainly to the service industry (mostly for infrastructure). During this period, 59 percent of all commercial loans were distributed to manufacturing industries, of which 73.8 percent were allocated to HCI-related projects, indicating that, without easy access to international commercial lending, the HCI plan which required mammoth investment could not have been implemented.

The government also established a special system called the National Investment Fund (NIF) in 1973 to facilitate the financing of long-term investment in plants and equipment for the HCIs. The sources of the NIF were a combination of domestic funds from private financial intermediaries such as commercial

9. In particular, the HCI build-up in parallel with the defense industry was a challenge because production capacity could stay idle in peacetime. In order to prevent unnecessary idle capacity, the Korean government devised a scheme to make use of portions of the capacity of private-operated factories in the HCIs to produce certain parts of weapons. In fact, the government designated 82 large- and medium-sized firms as part-producing factories. Behind this plan lay the government's basic principle that "any weapon could be turned into parts when taken apart," and "when any standard parts were assembled, they turned into weapons with good performance." In order to maintain the sound financial structure of parts-producing factories by not letting production capacity stay idle in peacetime, firms followed a rule that 20 percent of their total production capacity was to be for military use and the rest for civilian use (Kim 1990).

10. The construction of POSCO, which has grown to become the third largest steel company in the world, could not have begun without the reparation fund settled in the normalization treaty with Japan. See Cho and Kim (1993) for the details of the government's financial support of POSCO.

Table 7.2 Composition of Public and Commercial Foreign Loans by Industry (on the basis of arrival; %)

	Agriculture, Forestry, and Fisheries	Manufacturing		Service	Total
		HCIs	Light Industries		
1959–66					
Public loan	7.5	11.7	8.3	72.5	100.0
Commercial loan	22.3	43.4	31.4	2.9	100.0
1967–71					
Public loan	42.2	6.8	1.6	49.4	100.0
Commercial loan	3.6	31.6	23.9	40.8	100.0
1972–76					
Public loan	18.2	6.1	0.0	75.8	100.0
Commercial loan	2.2	42.4	23.7	31.7	100.0
1977–82					
Public loan	17.0	1.5	0.3	81.2	100.0
Commercial loan	0.6	46.0	10.6	42.8	100.0
1959–82					
Public loan	19.0	3.0	0.4	77.6	100.0
Commercial loan	1.6	43.6	15.4	39.5	100.0
Total	9.6	24.9	8.5	57.0	100.0

Source: Cha (1986).

banks and insurance companies and government funds, but predominantly the former. During 1974–81, the NIF mainly supplied equipment loans to facilitate construction of the HCIs, specifically the steel, petrochemical, and shipbuilding industries.[11] As shown in table 7.3, the share of NIF equipment loans to HCIs in total equipment loans supplied from the banking sector reached 70 percent at the end of 1970s. Since the mid-1980s, as the construction of the HCIs was mostly completed, the share of NIF equipment loans gradually declined to 11.4 percent at the end of 1991. The NIF also provided a sizeable amount of equipment loans to the electric power industry in order to meet the sharp increase in demand for electricity related to the construction of the HCIs.

Along with massive credit supports, the government overhauled the education and training systems to promote and secure engineers and skilled workers for the HCIs. Training centers, technical high schools, and engineering col-

11. After 1982, most of the NIF loans were supplied to many unspecified firms for the purchasing of domestically produced machinery and postshipment export financing. This change in allocation was caused by the following two factors: First, the need to support factory construction diminished as the HCI plants were mostly completed by the early 1980s, while it was still necessary to support sectors that marketed HCI-related products. Second, as the government's direct promotion of "strategic" firms and industries with preferential credits gave way to more indirect and functional support of unspecified firms after the early 1980s, the mode of NIF operation also changed from firm- and industry-specific support to function-specific support (Cho and Kim 1993).

Table 7.3 **Share of NIF Loans in Total Loans by the Banking Sector (%)**

	HCIs		Power and Gas Industries
Year	Total Loans	Equipment Loans	Total Loans
1974	6.1	25.3	10.8
1976	16.6	54.2	38.2
1978	25.1	70.6	52.7
1980	21.4	67.3	59.9
1982	21.2	64.1	67.3
1984	20.3	55.9	49.5
1986	15.2	36.7	30.7
1988	12.3	26.6	24.7
1990	7.1	14.8	18.1
1991	4.9	11.4	8.1

Sources: Bank of Korea, Overview of the National Investment Fund (Seoul, 1989); Bank of Korea, Monthly Bulletin (Seoul, various issues); Korea Development Bank, Monthly Bulletin (Seoul, various issues).

Note: Loans reported are those oustanding at the end of each year and include loans from the DMBs and the Korea Development Bank.

leges were expanded both in quality and quantity. Specifically, the government imposed vocational training requirements on private sector firms to expand the supply of skilled labor for the HCIs. As a result, the number of in-plant vocational trainees drastically increased in 1976, reaching an annual level of almost 100,000. Large numbers of workers continued to be trained from 1977 to 1980, averaging about 70,000 annually (see table 7.4). The government also introduced a skills licensing system to encourage every Korean worker to possess at least one skill. In addition, for each field of engineering the government actively recruited outstanding Korean scientists abroad and established a modern laboratory where research on the improvement of production technologies was conducted in collaboration with industry researchers and university professors. Industrial parks were built to house the HCIs because (1) HCIs have strong forward and backward linkages among themselves, (2) they require large-scale social overhead capital for water, electricity, and transportation networks, and (3) some of the factories produce a great deal of pollution (Kim 1990).

These concerted efforts by the government helped to institute a rapid change in the industrial structure toward the HCIs. As shown in table 7.5, the share of the HCIs in GDP was only 11.9 percent in 1970, but increased to 26.3 percent in 1980, which exceeded the share of light industry, and the HCI share further increased to 31.3 percent in 1988. The HCI drive also contributed in stimulating import substitution of HCIs. The import coefficient dropped from 36.9 percent in 1970 to 23.7 percent in 1980, and further decreased to 21.6 percent in 1985. Furthermore, the share of HCI products in total exports rose substantially from 12.8 percent in 1970 to 51.4 percent in 1988. These results indicate

Table 7.4 **Vocational Training in Korea (thousand persons)**

Year	Public Vocational Training	In-Plant Vocational Training
1967	1.5	3.9
1968	7.9	8.1
1969	9.7	8.8
1970	11.5	13.6
1971	15.6	14.7
1972	16.1	11.3
1973	25.1	14.5
1974	27.1	13.2
1975	32.6	42.7
1976	28.8	96.8
1977	14.9	58.7
1978	19.2	73.0
1979	28.6	91.0
1980	31.1	66.2
1981	26.3	48.4
1982	28.1	30.1
1983	24.7	21.0
1984	22.8	20.8
1985	22.6	23.9
1986	22.9	19.0
1987	22.6	14.2
1988	20.7	18.2
1989	20.1	15.0
1990	24.4	25.7
1991	26.0	43.3

Source: Lee (1992).

that Korea has achieved a sort of miracle by developing a full set of industries (the light industries, HCIs, and defense industry) in the short period since 1962, the year of the light industry take-off.

Such a drastic transformation of industrial structure could be regarded as an engine of Korea's high sustained economic growth. It introduced new products in the market and generated technology spillovers to other industries, which accelerated the process of human capital accumulation. Since the HCI drive was pursued with a view to building strategic large-scale export industries, the manufacturers could enjoy scale economies and enhanced technology spillover.

The effect of the HCI drive on growth, however, is not free from controversy. Prevalent criticisms include inappropriate scale choices, excessively capital-intensive investments in targeted sectors, and the retardation of trade and financial liberalization. Nonetheless, the HCIs became the leading export sector in Korea starting in the mid-1980s and large-scale industrial firms with international reputations—POSCO, Samsung, and Hyundai—were developed within

Table 7.5 **Trend of Development of the HCIs (%)**

Industry	1970	1975	1980	1985	1988
		Industrial Structure			
Agriculture/fishery	17.0	12.8	8.3	7.7	6.3
Mining	1.1	0.9	0.8	0.7	0.6
Manufacturing	40.3	50.4	51.0	50.0	52.7
Light	28.4	29.5	24.7	21.7	21.4
HCIs	11.9	20.9	26.3	28.3	31.3
Petrochemical	5.9	10.8	12.6	11.4	10.0
Basic metal	2.0	3.4	5.1	4.9	5.3
Metal/machinery	4.0	6.7	8.6	12.0	16.1
Power/gas/construction	9.8	7.7	10.2	10.4	9.3
Service	31.8	28.2	29.7	31.2	29.4
Total	100.0	100.0	100.0	100.0	100.0
		Import Coefficients[a]			
Light	9.2	10.6	7.3	7.0	8.5
HCIs	36.9	29.5	23.7	21.6	22.5
Petrochemical	23.5	19.7	14.9	17.0	19.1
Basic metal	35.1	27.6	18.9	17.6	20.4
Metal/machinery	50.5	41.7	35.8	26.9	25.1
		Composition of Exports			
Light	49.4	45.6	35.2	30.0	29.1
HCIs	12.8	29.0	38.3	47.5	51.4
Petrochemical	5.4	9.2	9.9	12.4	11.0
Basic metal	1.5	4.0	8.1	5.8	5.1
Metal/machinery	5.9	15.8	20.3	29.3	35.4

Source: Bank of Korea, *Input-Output Tables* (Seoul, various issues).
[a]Import coefficient = (total import/total supply of goods to the market) × 100.

such a short period in part because of the drive. Many also think that, if Korea had not built the HCIs in the 1970s, it may not have been able to take full advantage of the appreciation of the Japanese yen and the world economic boom in the second half of the 1980s.

7.3.3 Government Risk Sharing with Private Industries

Risks and uncertainties have far-reaching implications for economic growth as private firms are not able to invest in high-risk projects. In the absence of a well-functioning financial market which allows the pooling of risk involved in capital investment, one bad draw from a random experiment will drive the investor off the scene. The Korean experience suggests how risk sharing between the government and private firms can affect the process of rapid industrialization and product diversification.

The Korean government has acted as an active risk partner for all industrial firms chosen to participate in strategic projects. In practice, the risk-sharing scheme was established by the state's control over finance. The government

Table 7.6 **Financial Indicators in the Manufacturing Industry (%)**

Year	Ratio of Debt to Equity[a]	Ratio of Interest Expenses to Net Sales	Ratio of Net Profits to Net Sales
1963	92.2	3.0	9.1
1964	100.5	4.9	8.6
1965	83.7	3.9	7.9
1966	117.7	5.7	7.7
1967	151.2	5.2	6.7
1968	201.3	5.9	6.0
1969	270.0	7.8	4.3
1970	328.4	9.2	3.3
1971	394.2	9.9	1.2
1972	313.4	7.1	3.9
1973	272.7	4.6	7.5
1974	316.0	4.5	4.8
1975	339.5	4.9	3.4
1976	364.6	4.9	3.9

Source: Bank of Korea, *Financial Statements Analysis* (Seoul, 1981); quoted from Kim (1991).
[a]Total liabilities/net worth.

owned all major banks, set their interest rates at levels far below market rates, and tightly controlled the allocation of their loans and foreign loans.

As mentioned before, the government fully guaranteed private firms' repayment of foreign borrowing. It revised the Foreign Capital Inducement Act in 1965 to allow government-controlled banks to provide debt guarantees without the approval of the National Assembly. In this way, large inflows of foreign capital were promoted without political interruption, and risky ventures that could not be undertaken by private companies alone could be undertaken with government support.

Furthermore, the government, by controlling financial markets, did not hesitate to bail out whatever strategic firms were financially insolvent. In an economy like Korea's, where the initial accumulation of capital was poor and rapid investment expansion had to be financed by bank credit and foreign loans, firms had highly leveraged financial structures: during the period of initial take-off (1963–71), the Korean manufacturing sector's debt ratio increased more than four times, from 92 percent to 394 percent (see table 7.6). In such a credit-based economy, financial crises would occur with major economic downturns unless some risk-sharing schemes between creditors and borrowers existed.[12]

The most dramatic example of the government's direct involvement in risk sharing with business firms is the Presidential Emergency Decree of August 1972, which declared a moratorium on the payments of corporate debt to curb-

12. In Japan, the "main bank" system helped risk sharing between creditors and borrowers.

market lenders. All corporate loans from the curb market were converted to long-term loans to be paid on an installment basis over a five-year period with a grace period of three years, at a maximum interest rate of 16.2 percent, when the prevailing curb-market rate was over 40 percent per annum. In addition, approximately 30 percent of the short-term high-interest (15.5 percent per annum) commercial bank loans to businesses were converted to long-term loans to be repaid on an installment basis over a five-year period at an 8 percent annual interest rate with a three-year grace period.

Behind this drastic measure was strong pressure from business firms amid the worldwide recession at the end of the 1960s. The situation was aggravated extremely by the devaluation of the Korean currency by 18 percent in 1971. This devaluation, which was prompted by the sharp slowdown in export growth, caused a sudden increase in the cost of foreign debt servicing and created severe financial constraints on firms, especially those who had borrowed heavily from abroad.[13]

The August 1972 decree sharply reduced the interest burden of many debt-ridden firms. The ratio of interest expenses to sales volume for manufacturing firms dropped from 9.9 percent in 1971 to 7.1 percent in 1972 and then to 4.6 percent in 1973 (see table 7.6). As the financial situation of the corporate sector improved, so did the problem of nonperforming loans of banks.[14]

The decree firmly demonstrated that the government would take measures to relieve financial distress when necessary. The government's commitment to risk partnership largely motivated private entrepreneurship and allowed the credit-based economy and its highly leveraged firms to explore risky investment opportunities with long-term objectives in mind.

The decree, however, also had adverse effects. It raised social equity issues as the wealth of the depositors in the curb market and banks was transferred to the corporate sector, especially large firms. The fact that there was no profit-sharing arrangement in return for the wealth transfer created discontent among the public, although this dissatisfaction was suppressed under the authoritarian regime. The problem of moral hazard for corporate firms and banks was no less serious. The government's excessive risk partnership with selected firms caused these firms not only to overinvest but also to depend heavily on the government's protection and support, leading them to give insufficient attention to their investment appraisals. The efficient development of the banking system was also hampered, because as long as the government was willing to rescue firms, banks had little incentive to screen projects and monitor firms.

13. The amount of the debt service increased from $160 million in 1970 to $230 and $455 million in 1971 and 1972, respectively.

14. The economy recovered quickly. Total investment grew by 40 percent, and export growth was almost 100 percent in 1973. The real growth of the economy in the first quarter of 1973 increased to 19.3 percent from 6.4 percent for the same period in 1972.

7.4 Appraisal of Korean Industrialization Policy

We have seen that the remarkable economic growth of Korea was largely a result of rapid human capital accumulation driven by on-the-job training. Government policies greatly contributed to accelerating this process. Export promotion has led to substantial technological spillover, which in turn stimulated learning by doing. Specifically, the promotion of the HCIs as strategic export industries expanded the spectrum of the product mix of the economy and provided domestic producers with an excellent ground for practicing scale economies, which enabled economic growth to be sustained. The government's active risk sharing with private firms significantly contributed to this successful implementation of these policies.

Korean economic success is also a result of strong market competition among private firms. As is well known, the Korean system of resource allocation has used government interventions more extensively than any other successful mixed economy, including other newly industrialized countries. Target industries and firms in Korea were selected by the government rather than by the market. Such government intervention can cause distortive allocations and foster moral hazard problems. But, as exporting firms were competing in the international market, they had strong incentives to remain cost effective. The potential inefficiencies that may arise from the government's extensive interventions were reduced because those selected firms needed to pass market tests to survive in the international market. In addition, the government tried to link the amount of assistance to the performance of individual firms in the market. This practice of picking winners has helped to avoid adverse incentives that may arise along with the provision of governmental assistance.

Although the Korean approach in the 1960s and 1970s has been effective in achieving rapid expansion of industrial investment and development of private entrepreneurship, it was not costless. The government's excessive risk sharing and assistance to target industries raised social equity issues. It also put a heavy burden of nonperforming loans on the banking system. The seriousness of such adverse effects, which had been boiling beneath the surface, was recognized by the government by the end of 1970s. It prompted the government to shift its policy stance from unbalanced to balanced growth.

In early 1980s, the government first reduced the scope of its financial support for exporting industries. Interest subsidies on export loans, mainly for large firms, as well as the number of qualified large firms eligible for policy loans were reduced. On the other hand, the support for previously disadvantaged sectors such as small and medium-sized companies (SMCs) and housing were substantially increased.[15] In particular, the emergence of a current account surplus and the political democratization during the second half of the

15. The government tightened the required ratio of the SMC loans out of banks' total loans (see table 7.7) and introduced the National Housing Fund (in 1981) to finance investment in housing for low income class households.

Table 7.7 Domestic Money Bank Required Ratio of SMC Finance (%)

Bank Type	1965	1976	1980	1985	1986	1992
Nationwide commerical banks	30[a]	30[b]	35[c]	35	35	45
Local banks	30[a]	40[b]	55[c]	55	80	80
Foreign bank branches				25	25	25

[a]Ratio in terms of total loans outstanding.
[b]Ratio in terms of increase in total loans.
[c]Ratio in terms of increase in total loans in won.

Table 7.8 Loans to SMCs and 30 Largest *Chaebols* by Domestic Money Banks (%)

Loan Destination	1983	1985	1988	1989	1990	1991
Loans to SMCs	33.1	31.5	48.1	50.1	55.5	56.8
Loans to 30 largest *chaebols*	n.a.	n.a.	23.7	20.7	19.8	20.4

Source: Bank of Korea, internal memorandum.

1980s spurred social demand for equity, which forced the government to further assist the SMC sector while abolishing policy loans for large corporations.[16] This step led to a sharp increase in the portion of bank loans to the SMCs as a percentage of total bank loans, from 33.1 percent in 1983 to 56.8 percent in 1991, while gradually reducing the share of bank loans to the *chaebols* (see table 7.8).

Such a reversal of policy to one with more a political than an economic orientation was caused by the absence of a prearrangement for sharing the returns realized from privileges bestowed to selected sectors by the previous government. The presumed strategy was to enlarge the pie first and distribute it later. But the strong authoritarian government (1961–79), which was able to promote growth actively, collapsed before the completion of a fair distribution of the pie. Because the democratic government was faced with difficulties in redistributing the returns, it allowed privileges to new interest groups with strong voices. Such rent-seeking behavior by interest groups discouraged competition in the market and directed resources away from productivity growth. Furthermore, it significantly undermined the traditional values and work ethics

16. Since 1988, large corporations have been completely excluded from export credit programs. At the same time, reflecting severe public criticism against the economic concentration within the *chaebols,* the government began to strictly restrict *chaebols'* financing and investment. For instance, the basket control of the credit system (credit ceilings) on large business groups was introduced in 1987 to limit the share of bank loans going to the nation's 30 largest *chaebols.* On the other hand, the BOK applied a preferential rate of rediscounting the SMC bills, and the government established a structural adjustment support program for the SMCs in 1988 to promote R&D and business transformation of the SMCs.

which have been crucial for the accumulation of human capital. These two adverse effects eventually led to a significant erosion of international competitiveness of the Korean economy starting in the late 1980s.

Lucas (1993) claimed that the quicker the introduction of new products into the economy, the quicker the process of learning by doing. The Korean experience strongly suggests that a government can play an important role in sustaining human capital accumulation through learning on the job and economic growth. Such dynamic gains in growth, however, may be at least partially offset by distributional problems that arise in the industrialization process unless a profit-sharing or ownership-sharing scheme is prearranged. From a long-term view, a second-best welfare-enhancing scheme would be to design industrial policies along with an adequate tax policy for income redistribution at the outset. Kim (1988) showed that in the presence of credit market failures, lump-sum taxes-cum-transfers along with governmental direct financial support for private firms can generate an economic growth rate that is higher than it would be without collective efforts by the government and the private sector.

References

Cha, Dongse. 1986. *An analysis of the effect of foreign capital in-flow* (in Korean). Seoul: Korea Institute for Economics and Technology.

Cho, Yoon-Je, and T. Hellmann. 1993. Government intervention in credit markets in Japan and Korea—An alternative interpretation from a new institutional economics perspective. PRE Working Paper Series. Washington, D.C.: World Bank.

Cho, Yoon-Je, and Joon-Kyung Kim. 1993. Credit policies and industrialization of Korea. Paper presented at the World Bank Symposium on the Effectiveness of Credit Policy: Japanese and Korean Experiences, Washington, D.C., February 26.

Grossman, Gene M., and Elhanan Helpman. 1989. Comparative advantage and long run growth, NBER Working Paper no. 2809. Cambridge, Mass.: National Bureau of Economic Research.

———. 1990. Trade, knowledge spillovers and growth. NBER Working Paper no. 3485. Cambridge, Mass.: National Bureau of Economic Research.

Kim, Chung-Yum. 1990. *A thirty year history of Korean economic policy: A memoir* (in Korean). Seoul: Joongang Ilbo-Sa.

Kim, Joon-Kyung. 1988. *The role of money in economies with imperfect capital markets: Theory and empirical evidence.* Ph.D. dissertation, University of California, San Diego.

Kim, Wan-Soon. 1991. The president's emergency decree for economic stability and growth. In *Economic development in the Republic of Korea: A policy perspective,* ed. Lee-Jay Cho and Yoon Hyung Kim. Hawaii: East-West Center.

Lee, Ju-Ho. 1992. Vocational training and industrial competitiveness. In *The 1992 national budget and policy goals* (in Korean). Seoul: Korea Development Institute.

Lucas, Robert E. 1993. Making a miracle. *Econometrica* 61: 251–72.

Rhee, Yung Whee. 1989. Trade finance in developing countries. Policy and Research Series, no. 5. Washington, D.C.: World Bank.

Romer, Paul. 1986. Increasing returns and long run growth. *Journal of Political Economy* 94: 1002–37.

Comment Chia Siow Yue

This is a very interesting paper, containing many insights on the Korean economic miracle. The paper aimed at identifying the factors behind Korea's rapid economic growth, relating the Korean growth experience to endogenous growth theory, and evaluating the role of government policies, particularly export promotion and industrial policies.

My comments focus on a number of areas. First, there appears to be considerable overlap between this paper and Chong-Hyun Nam's paper (chap. 6 in this volume) on the role of trade and exchange rate policy in Korea's economic growth. To minimize overlap, perhaps the authors could focus less on export promotion policies and more on policies pertaining to human capital accumulation and investment. And it would have been enlightening if the authors had provided some quantitative evidence on the sources of economic growth in Korea and had shown the importance of human capital accumulation and economies of scale as stressed by endogenous growth theory. Nam's paper showed that, using Denison's growth-accounting approach, more than half of the economic growth in Korea could be explained by increases in labor and capital factor inputs. He did not estimate the contribution of human capital accumulation, as distinct from labor, but found that economies of scale accounted for about 20 percent of economic growth.

Second, discussion on the factors explaining Korea's economic success could be expanded to provide greater insight, in view of the widespread interest in the economic performance of Asia's newly industrialized economies (NIEs), and possible lessons for the developing world. The paper left unclear the role of extensive government intervention in Korea's success, nor was there evaluation of the appropriateness of various government policies pertaining to industrial targeting, manpower development, and technology acquisition and development.

Third, the authors attempted to correlate human capital accumulation and international trade and concluded that Korean economic growth was well explained by sustained human capital accumulation plus strong export promotion. What remains unclear is the role of foreign direct investment and technology imports. Also, what explains the Korean zeal for education? Part of the incentive structure for human capital accumulation, as described by the authors, is the government's role in providing vocational training as well as imposed training requirements on private firms. The emphasis on vocational training is reflected in the high percentage of trained craftsmen among blue-collar workers. Secondary school enrollment is an inadequate indicator of human capital accumulation, as it omits the role of training and falls short of measuring the efficiency of the formal educational system. Based on years of schooling alone, the Philippines should have a better record of economic

Chia Siow Yue is professor of economics at the National University of Singapore.

growth performance among East Asian countries. Labor efficiency also depends on the educational curriculum, on-the-job and off-the-job training, labor-management relations, and work ethics. It is to be noted that the Asian NIEs placed high priority on vocational, technical, science-based education and training to produce an efficient industrial work force. Commentators have also drawn attention to the absence of industrial strife as a factor contributing to labor productivity and competitiveness in the Asian NIEs. Education expenditure ratios probably underestimate human capital accumulation, as they ignore forgone labor earnings of students and private expenditures by families to supplement the educational services provided by formal schools, such as on private tuition.

Fourth, Lucas was cited as emphasizing the dynamic gains from trade in accelerating the learning process through continuing introduction of new tasks for workers and managers; the speedier the introduction of new products and industries into the economy, the speedier the learning and growth. Is there an optimal learning path? Would accelerated industrial upgrading through industrial policy lead to premature obsolescence of skills? Does the age profile of Korea's industrial work force affect worker attitudes toward industrial restructuring and commitment to training? How prevalent is job hopping in Korea and do high labor turnovers affect management's commitment to providing training?

Fifth, the authors rightly drew attention to the advantages of the export orientation strategy in opening up larger markets for Korean firms, so that they benefitted from scale economies, while access to technology and a more competitive environment promoted efficiency. The discussion on export promotion policy is enlightening in showing the extent to which the Korean government used macro- as well as microtools. The latter may be unique to Korea among East Asian economies, extending to measures of export targeting by product and country and to conferring decorations and medals on outstanding performers. A key to the success of export subsidies in inducing Korean firms to improve performance is the direct linkage of subsidies to export performance, thus ensuring that subsidies go to the most efficient rather than the least efficient exporters. For a more complete picture of the export promotion policies pursued by Korea, the authors may wish not only to focus on the system of subsidized credit allocation, but also to make reference to the roles of the preferential tax system and exchange rate policy.

Sixth, the authors pointed out that the policy of promoting heavy and chemical industries (HCIs) in the early 1970s was greatly motivated by national security concerns and described the comprehensive financial and market support measures to divert resources to the HCIs, resulting in the rising shares of HCIs in GDP, import substitution and exports, and the technological spillover to other industries. Critics of East Asian industrial policy have drawn attention to the high cost of the HCI program to Korea. The negative experience with the HCIs and growing concern with economic concentration and social equity as well as external pressures have led the Korean government to reorient its industrial policy away from industry- and firm-specific credit and tax measures and support of *chaebols* to function-specific measures such as support of R&D and support of small and medium-sized enterprises.

Seventh, the authors emphasized the importance of risk sharing between government and private enterprises and highlighted the role of the Korean government in guaranteeing the foreign debt repayments of the private sector and bailing out financially insolvent firms. Apart from the issue of economic concentration and social equity, the poser is how Korea managed to provide such support for its industries and firms without undermining its economic performance, while many countries have gotten into serious economic difficulties for doing likewise.

Finally, will the convergence postulated by the neoclassical growth model lead to a slowing down of the Korean growth rate? Will political democratization and the greater demand for social equity in the 1990s hasten the process of slowdown? The authors noted that noneconomic factors have dominated Korean economic decision making, with rent-seeking behavior by new interest groups and erosion of work ethics undermining Korea's international competitiveness. They advocated the design of industrial policies with a pie-splitting arrangement at the outset. The unanswered question is how the pie sharing is to be decided. Perhaps the authors could elaborate in what they meant by the "design [of] industrial policies along with adequate tax policies for income redistribution at the outset."

Comment Hak K. Pyo

Kim, Shim, and Kim's paper reviews the past development policies taken by the Korean government in the context of new growth theory. In the first part of the paper, the authors emphasize the positive role played by the Korean government in accelerating human capital accumulation and promoting knowledge spillover through export promotion. In the second part, they discuss risk sharing between the government and firms in Korea and sectoral balance and redistribution policy during the period 1982–92 and attempt to draw the implications of this changing policy direction to the future course of economic growth in Korea. The paper concludes by arguing that industrial policies need to be designed along with a pie-splitting arrangement at the outset.

The linkage of the first part to endogenous growth models is straightforward. However, the paper lacks a statistically meaningful analysis of how the Korean government initiated investment in both education and export industries in the

Hak K. Pyo is professor of economics at and a research associate of the Institute of Economic Research at Seoul National University.

early period of economic development with scarce resources. The question remains as to why only Korea and Taiwan succeeded while many other developing countries failed. What was the nature of Korea's endowed human capital at the beginning of economic development?

In addition, the authors need to update their literature survey with both new growth-theoretic empirical studies such as Sengupta (1991, 1993) and more recent growth accounting results on Korean data such as Kim and Park (1988) and Pyo et al. (1993). An empirical analysis of human capital accumulation and on-the-job training at the industry level or firm level would greatly strengthen the authors' argument.

The main problem I find with the paper is its second part. The linkage of the analysis to endogenous growth theories is ambiguous and confusing. The authors need to explain how risk sharing between the government and firms and the redistribution policy recently pursued by the Korean government would fit into the framework of *new growth models.* There are neither theoretical explanations nor empirical references in the paper.

For example, the authors claim that the government should establish at the initial stage a transparent system of fair distribution of returns realized from the selected projects. I cannot find any endogenous growth theory which addresses this dilemma—the government selecting projects while ensuring a fair distribution scheme. At the end of the paper, they also argue that government support should be financed from the budget, minimizing as much as possible the risk of rent seeking by interest groups. They need to explain why budget financing necessarily minimizes the risk of rent seeking and, if so, how it fits into the framework of endogenous growth theories.

References

Kim, K. S., and S. R. Park. 1988. *Productivity change and factor analysis in South Korean manufacturing* (in Korean). Seoul: Korea Institute of Economics and Technology.

Pyo, H. K., B. H. Gong, H. Y. Kwon, and E. J. Kim. 1993. *Sources of industrial growth and productivity estimates in Korea (1970–1990)* (in Korean). Seoul: Korea Economic Research Institute.

Sengupta, Jati K. 1991. Rapid growth in NICs in Asia: Tests of new growth theory for Korea. *Kyklos* 44 (4): 561–79.

———. 1993. Growth in NICs in Asia: Some tests of new growth theory. *Journal of Development Studies* 29 (2): 342–57.

8 Japan's Development Cooperation and Economic Development in East Asia

Hirohisa Kohama

8.1 Introduction: Japan's Postwar Development Experience and Its Influence on Japan's Aid Policy

An objective of this paper is to explain the characteristics of Japan's official development assistance (ODA) and the philosophy behind it. Special attention will be paid to the question of whether Japan's ODA is actually intended to foster the growth and development of recipient countries or whether it is motivated by the commercial goal of Japanese export promotion. I will outline the characteristics of Japan's ODA program and its impact on East Asian countries and put forward the contention that Japan's aid philosophy is based on its own development experience.

The Japanese ODA program started in 1954 when Japan joined the Colombo Plan, and the ODA loan program started in 1958. At that time Japan faced constraints on its balance of payments and export expansion was crucially important; all ODA loans were tied loans intended to promote Japan's exports to developing countries. This aim is clearly mentioned in the government document describing the program (Ministry of International Trade and Industry [MITI] 1959, 129).

As it was starting its ODA program, Japan borrowed money from the World Bank throughout the 1950s, and even in the early 1960s. World Bank loans to Japan were for infrastructure and basic industry investments as shown in table 8.1.

I believe that the experience of economic development and the development policy in postwar Japan has had a substantial influence on Japan's aid policy. The connection is not direct but is important in determining the Japanese government's basic aid policy.

Hirohisa Kohama is professor of economics at University of Shizuoka.

Table 8.1 **World Bank Loans to Japan**

Year	Project	Loan (thousand U.S. $)
1953	Power plant	21,500
	Power plant	11,200
	Power plant	7,500
1956	Steel plant	5,300
	Steel plant	2,600
	Machine tools for car plant	2,350
1957	Ship engine plant	1,650
	Ship engine plant	1,500
	Steel plant	20,000
	Agricultural land development	1,330
	Agricultural land development	1,133
	Non-project	984
	Non-project	853
	Irrigation	7,000
1958	Steel plant	8,000
	Power plant	37,000
	Power plant	25,000
	Steel plant	33,000
	Steel plant	10,000
	Power plant	29,000
	Steel plant	22,000
1959	Power plant	10,000
1960	Steel plant	24,000
	Steel plant	20,000
	Freeway	40,000
1961	Steel plant	6,000
	Steel plant	7,000
	Power plant	12,000
	Shinkansen (bullet train)	80,000
1962	Freeway	40,000
1963	Freeway	75,000
1964	Freeway	50,000
1965	Freeway	25,000
	Power plant	25,000
	Freeway	75,000
	Freeway	25,000
1966	Freeway	100,000
Total		862,900

Source: World Bank (1991, 114–17).

Many observers outside Japan argue that the Japanese government, in particular the MITI, played a crucial role in the rapid industrialization and export expansion in postwar Japan. It is true that the Japanese government (in particular the MITI) implemented various postwar industrial and export promotion policy measures. For a comprehensive analysis of Japan's industrial policy, see

Table 8.2 **Investment Financing by Source in Postwar Japan (%)**

	1952–54	1955–59	1960–64	1965–67
Bank loans	52.2	62.1	63.5	73.5
Government loans	28.4	20.5	15.0	16.8
Bond	5.6	3.4	5.6	5.5
Stock	13.8	14.1	15.9	4.1
Total	100.0	100.0	100.0	100.0

Source: Kodama (1994).

Komiya, Okuno, and Suzumura (1988) and Itoh et al. (1991). However, the MITI did not always lead the private sector, and private companies did not always respond as the MITI expected. Relevant anecdotes on Japan's industrial policy are presented in Ohkawa and Kohama (1989, chap. 8).

The most important factor in explaining Japan's rapid economic growth was not industrial policy but the dynamism of the private sector and the limited role played by the government. Industrial policy was successful only when it assisted the efficiency-oriented management of the economy based on the dynamism of the private sector, or, in other words, the market mechanism. The Japanese government simply provided the basic infrastructure and a competitive economic environment. This is the secret of Japan's postwar economic success.

In order to realize the above-mentioned private initiatives, political stability, continuity of economic policy, and provision of basic infrastructure are indispensable. Table 8.2 shows investment financing by source. This table shows that the weight of government loans for investment was less than 20 percent during the postwar rapid growth period. Moreover government loans for financing manufacturing investment were relatively small compared with the government loans for infrastructure and mining (table 8.3). These figures indicate that government loans, one of the major tools of industrial policy, were used indirectly for industrialization through the provision of public goods. I think this fact is very important in understanding the role of government in the process of economic development.

In the following section, the characteristics of Japan's ODA are outlined. In section 8.3, economic cooperation with East Asia and the expansion of Japan's ODA are discussed. In section 8.4, I will outline my view of East Asian dynamism, and the role of development cooperation is presented. Major conclusions are summarized in the final section.

Table 8.3 Allocation of Government Loans for Investment in Postwar Japan (%)

	1952–54	1955–59	1960–64	1964–67
	Allocation for Investment			
Agriculture	18.5	15.3	13.8	15.0
Mining	3.8	4.0	4.8	4.8
Manufacturing	n.a.	22.8	31.7	27.7
Electricity/gas/water	41.1	33.0	15.9	5.9
Transportation/communication	17.5	14.4	20.0	27.7
Others	6.1	10.4	13.7	18.8
Total	100.0	100.0	100.0	100.0
	Relative Share of Allocation for Investment			
Agriculture	74.6	72.0	92.9	111.6
Mining	120.3	172.8	339.5	468.6
Manufacturing	71.8	78.3	94.4	85.1
Infrastructure[a]	590.3	445.6	327.4	323.9
Others	n.a.	28.4	35.1	44.3
Total	100.0	100.0	100.0	100.0

Source: Kodama (1994).

Note: Relative share is the raito of allocation of government loans for investment (data in panel A) to value-added share of each setor.

[a]Electricity/gas/water/transportation/communication.

8.2 Japan's ODA and Its Characteristics

8.2.1 A Motif of ODA Policy

The officially stated principle of ODA has undergone substantial changes over time depending on the economic status and condition of Japan. As mentioned in section 8.1, the purpose of extending ODA loans in the late 1950s was to promote Japan's exports. Later, in the 1970s and 1980s, the Japanese government stated only two aid principles, those of "humanitarian consideration" and "recognition of interdependence" (Ministry of Foreign Affairs 1990, 25–27). These two aid principles were too broad, however, and tantamount to no principle at all. Moreover, it seems that Japan's aid is not always derived from a stated principle and implemented deductively from it, and it is often derided as a compromise reached through the complicated power politics among various bureaucratic systems and political factions. This may be a very Japanese way of policy making.

However, despite the vagueness of these aid principles, the administration of Japan's aid has consistently shown a strong, though implicit, motif. To clarify the basic motif behind Japan's aid policy: aid should be conducive to the long-term economic development of recipient countries, based on Japan's development experience. Although never stated explicitly, this motif of contributing to the recipient's long-term development has comprised the background of Japan's policy formation and seems to have been broadly accepted among policymakers in the Japanese government. The government announced the ODA Charter in June 1992.

8.2.2 The Relationship between ODA and Development Policy

Four basic characteristics of Japan's ODA have been identified (Kohama and Teranishi 1992):

1. low share of grants,
2. emphasis on project financing, although the share of policy-based lending (PBL) is increasing, in cooperation with the World Bank adjustment lending,
3. emphasis on the request principle, or the principle of extending aid on a request basis, and
4. emphasis on the self-help efforts of a recipient country.

Needless to say, it is important to note that these characteristics stand in close relationship to the Japanese view of economic development policy described in the previous section and, in a sense, could be regarded as logical consequences of it. The relationship is most apparent in the emphasis on the request principle. Since the degree of underdevelopment of markets and the accumulation of learning capability differs among countries for reasons other than their relative phases of development, Japan's aid policy puts special emphasis on maintaining a different approach for each recipient country. The policy not only avoids the application of a uniform development strategy, it recommends that a recipient country devise its own methods of coping with obstacles to development. Consequently, emphasis on self-help constitutes another characteristic of Japan's approach, and as for the choice of objectives of aid, the basic stance is passively reacting to the request emanating from the recipient's own initiatives.

In this regard, Japan's aid is expected to support the developing countries' initiatives for development and is based on the understanding that economic development be promoted by self-help efforts. Therefore, it is implicitly understood among technocrats in Japan that it is not desirable to force policy reforms by placing conditions on the recipients of aid money. I am not saying that policy reforms are unnecessary. But compared with forced reforms without substantial policy dialogue, policy reform efforts following the recipient's own initiatives are much more effective in promoting economic development.

The Japanese preference for project aid and reluctance to pursue PBL also reflect its views on development policy. From the viewpoint of organizational efficiency, project aid seems to be the most suitable instrument for the effective implementation of aid, since it contributes directly to the enhancement of individual organizations or production units, either by transferring technology or by breaking particular bottlenecks.

The high share of ODA *loans* from Japan also merits special attention. Compared with grants, recipient countries tend not to abuse ODA loans because they must be repaid in the future. From this viewpoint, the low share of grants in Japan's aid is nothing to be ashamed of, but has its own positive effect in offsetting the shortcomings of grants.

8.3 Economic Cooperation with East Asia and Japan's Presence: Description

8.3.1 Development Cooperation

Japan started giving aid in the 1950s. Japan's ODA was less than $500 million in the 1960s but started to increase in the 1980s. It is reported that by 1992 Japan's ODA had increased to more than $11 billion (for a per capita ODA budget of about $100).

The presence of Japan's ODA in developing countries is becoming more and more apparent. In 1970, there were six countries for which Japan's ODA was the largest among bilateral donors. In 1991, there were 31 (table 8.4). In 1989 Japan was the top donor for 30 developing countries. Among these 30, Japan's ODA was larger than the financial flow from international organizations, except in the cases of Ghana, Kenya, St. Vincent, India, Nepal, and Laos.

It is often suggested that the quality of Japan's ODA is low. For example, DAC review of Japan's ODA in 1993 stated that the terms of Japan's ODA were more severe than those of other DAC member countries due to the low grant ratio. Indeed, Japan's grant ratio and grant element (GE) are among the lowest of DAC member countries. The tied-aid ratio is also an indicator of aid quality. When Japan started giving ODA loans in the late 1950s, its tied-aid ratio was almost 100 percent, which meant all aid money was used to import Japanese goods. However, the ratio of tied aid among Japanese ODA loans has declined remarkably and is now one of the lowest of DAC member countries.

The geographical distribution of Japanese ODA is shown in table 8.5. The share of Japan's ODA that went to Asian countries was more than 70 percent in the 1970s, but it decreased to 60 percent in 1990. This reflects the fact that Japan's aid is extended to those countries with which it has close economic relations such as trade and direct investment.

Some economists have conducted regression analyses in order to find the determinants of Japan's bilateral ODA distribution. Teranishi (1983) investigated the determinants of Japan's ODA distribution for 1975–79. He found that this distribution bears a strong relation to Japan's exports to and the per capita GNP of recipient countries. Okamoto and Yokota (1992) also empirically analyzed the determinants of Japan's bilateral ODA distribution for the period 1975–89 with five subperiods. They found that the coefficients of Japan's exports to, income level of, and population of recipient countries show a statistically significant correlation with expected signs for total ODA and grant distribution. But in the case of Japan's ODA loan share, no estimated coefficients of

Table 8.4 Countries for Which Japan's ODA is the Largest among Bilateral Donations

1970	1980	1985	1989	1990	1991
Iran	Sierra Leone	Ghana	Ghana	Ghana	Kenya
Kuwait	Paraguay	Zambia	Kenya	Nigeria	Peru
Qutar	Iran	Brazil	Nigeria	Brazil	Bahrain
Burma	Saudi Arabia	Guyana	Zambia	Bolivia	Turkey
Cambodia	UAE	Paraguay	Mexico	Paraguay	Jordan
Philippines	Buram	Iraq	St. Vincent	Grenada	Syria
	Maldives	Saudi Arabia	Brazil	Bahrain	Yemen
	Nepal	UAE	Bolivia	Turkey	Saudi Arabia
	Pakistan	Burma	Paraguay	Qatar	UAE
	Bangladesh	Maldives	Qatar	Saudi Arabia	Burma
	Indonesia	Nepal	Saudi Arabia	Brunei	Sri Lanka
	Korea	Burnei	Bahrain	Bhutan	Nepal
	Philippines	China	Yemen	Burma	Singapore
	Malaysia	Indonesia	Bhutan	Sri Lanka	Pakistan
	Thailand	Singapore	Burma	Nepal	India
		Philippines	Sri Lanka	Bangladesh	Butan
		Malaysia	India	Pakistan	Brunei
		Thailand	Maldives	Maldives	Indonesia
		Laos	Nepal	Indonesia	Philippines
			Bangladesh	Philippines	Malaysia
			Burnei	Malaysia	Thailand
			China	Thailand	Laos
			Indonesia	Laos	China
			Korea	China	South Korea
			Philippines	South Korea	Mongolia
			Malaysia	Cyprus	Malta
			Thailand	Tonga	Maldives
			Laos	Western Samoa	Pacific Islands
			Solomon Islands		Kiribati
			Tuval		Solomon Islands
					Western Samoa
(6 countries)	(15 countries)	(19 countries)	(30 countries)	(28 countries)	(31 countries)

Source: Ministry of Foreign Affairs (1992, 29); Government of Japan (1993, 25).

income level of recipient countries show a statistically significant correlation in the five subperiods.

In order to investigate recent determinants of Japan's bilateral ODA distribution, the average Japanese ODA shares to the 79 countries where data was available for the period 1990–92 were regressed on the following variables of recipient countries as they existed in 1991, in six different specifications:

1. ODA share = const. + a N + b YN + c FR + d X
2. ODA share = const. + a N + b YN + c X
3. ODA share = const. + a N + b YN + c FR + d XM

Table 8.5 Geographical Distribution of Japan's ODA, 1990 (net disbursement; million U.S. $)

	Financial Grant	Technical Assistance	ODA Loans	ODA Total
Asia	639.16	707.39	2,770.00	4,116.55
East Asia	38.61	275.51	520.59	834.72
Southeast Asia	273.00	351.24	1,755.00	2,379.24
South Asia	327.55	76.30	494.41	898.25
Others	4.34	4.34	0.00	4.34
Middle East	113.24	96.06	495.35	704.65
Africa	423.23	124.89	243.63	791.75
Latin America	117.17	199.10	244.92	561.20
Oceania	61.40	32.00	20.13	113.53
Europe	0.00	11.85	146.11	157.96
Eastern Europe	0.00	5.38	147.73	153.12
Others	19.85	474.06	0.00	493.91
Total	1,374.05	1,645.35	3,920.16	6,939.56

Source: Ministry of Foreign Affairs (1991).

4. ODA share = const. + a N + b YN + c XM
5. ODA share = const. + a N + b YN + c FR + d XM + e AD
6. ODA share = const. + a N + b YN + c XM + d AD

ODA share: Gross disbursement of Japan's total ODA, or net disbursement of Japan's total ODA
N: Population (million; 1991)
YN: Per capita GNP (U.S.$; 1991)
FR: Gross international reserves (months of import coverage; 1991)
X: Japan's exports (million U.S.$; 1991)
XM: Japan's exports to and imports from the recipient country (million U.S.$; 1991)
AD: Asian dummy (Asian developing countries = 1, other developing countries = 0)

Shares of Japan's ODA categories (gross disbursement of total ODA, net disbursement of total ODA; 1990–92 average) are regressed in the six specifications shown above. Estimated results for all specifications are presented in tables 8.6 and 8.7. Although all estimated coefficients of FR are not statistically significant, other variables are significant. Income levels are all significantly negative, and foreign trade variables are significantly positive. Japan's ODA shares are higher for lower-income countries and for countries with closer foreign trade relations. All Asian dummies except for technical assistance share are significantly positive. Japan's ODA shares to Asian developing

Table 8.6 **Determinants of Japan's ODA Distribution, 1990–92: Gross Disbursement of Total ODA**

Specification	Constant	Population (N)	Per capita GNP (YN)	Reserves (FR)	Exports (X)	Exports + Imports (XM)	Asian Dummy (AD)	Adjusted R^2
1	0.89923**	0.00546*	−0.00029*	0.02728	0.00033*			0.4059
	(2.6061)	(3.9083)	(−3.0260)	(0.3615)	(4.2551)			
2	0.98085*	0.00558*	−0.00028*		0.00033*			0.4128
	(3.7807)	(4.1369)	(−3.0366)		(4.2653)			
3	0.87732*	0.00367*	−0.00033*	0.03014		0.00024*		0.4925
	(2.7506)	(2.6560)	(−3.7267)	(0.4329)		(5.8167)		
4	0.96780*	0.00381*	−0.00032*			0.00023*		0.4980
	(4.0289)	(2.8485)	(−3.7386)			(5.8329)		
5	0.62788**	0.00271**	−0.00029*	0.04622		0.00015*	2.27308*	0.5655
	(2.0731)	(2.0749)	(−3.5048)	(0.7157)		(3.3323)	(3.6650)	
6	0.76927*	0.00293**	−0.00027*			0.00015*	2.24293*	0.5684
	(3.3622)	(2.3217)	(−3.4423)			(3.3181)	(3.6368)	

Sources: Ministry of Foreign Affairs of Japan (1993); World Bank (1993); IMF (1993).

Notes: Japan's ODA shares to 79 countries (1990–92 average) are regressed on the independent variables in 1991. Numbers in parentheses are *t*-values.

*Significant at the 1 percent level.

**Significant at the 5 percent level.

Table 8.7 **Determinants of Japan's ODA Distribution, 1990–92: Net Disbursement of Total ODA**

Specification	Constant	Population (N)	Per capita GNP (YN)	Reserves (FR)	Exports (X)	Exports + Imports (XM)	Asian Dummy (AD)	Adjusted R^2
1	0.84018**	0.00655*	−0.00025**	0.02865	0.00022*			0.3936
	(2.4827)	(4.7759)	(−2.6296)	(0.3871)	(2.9169)			
2	0.92590*	0.00667*	−0.00024**		0.00022*			0.4005
	(3.6383)	(5.0412)	(−2.6223)		(2.9089)			
3	0.82069**	0.00501*	−0.00029*	0.03355		0.00018*		0.4641
	(2.5791)	(3.6359)	(−3.3437)	(0.4830)		(4.3997)		
4	0.92140*	0.00517*	−0.00028*			0.00018*		0.4695
	(3.8530)	(3.8720)	(−3.3330)			(4.3965)		
5	0.61053***	0.00420*	−0.00026*	0.0471		0.00010**	1.91505*	0.5169
	(1.9692)	(3.1451)	(−3.0897)	(0.7124)		(2.2874)	(3.0163)	
6	0.75462*	0.00443*	−0.00025*			0.00010**	1.88433*	0.5201
	(3.2220)	(3.4270)	(−3.0183)			(2.2692)	(2.9848)	

Sources: Ministry of Foreign Affairs (1993); World Bank (1993); IMF (1993).

Notes: Japan's ODA shares to 79 countries (1990–92 average) are regressed on the independent variables in 1991. Numbers in parentheses are *t*-values.

*Significant at the 1 percent level.

**Significant at the 5 percent level.

***Significant at the 10 percent level.

Table 8.8 **Countries Receiving the Most Japanese Bilateral ODA, 1992 (net disbursement; million U.S. $)**

Country	ODA Total	Financial Grant	Technical Assistance	ODA Loans
1. Indonesia	1,356.71	85.73	141.72	1,129.26
2. China	1,050.76	72.05	187.48	791.23
3. Phillippines	1,030.67	112.34	73.32	845.01
4. India	425.20	23.94	16.62	384.64
5. Thailand	413.97	42.69	116.79	254.50
6. Vietnam	281.24	0.21	5.22	275.81
7. Pakistan	173.33	59.39	12.85	101.09
8. Bangladesh	163.44	163.59	28.48	−28.63
9. Malaysia	157.12	6.42	63.80	86.90
10. Peru	154.80	40.13	15.02	99.65
Total	5,207.24	606.49	661.30	3,939.46
Bilateral ODA total	8,484.23	1,732.81	2,131.50	4,619.92

Source: Ministry of Foreign Affairs (1993).

countries are higher than to developing countries in the other regions when adjusted for the population size, income level, and foreign trade transactions.

Major recipient countries of Japan's ODA are shown in table 8.8. The ASEAN-4 and China are the countries receiving the most Japanese bilateral ODA aid. When we look at the cumulative figures of Japan's bilateral ODA loans up to 1991, Indonesia, India, the Philippines, China, Thailand, Korea, Pakistan, Malaysia, Bangladesh, and Egypt are the top 10 recipient countries. East Asian countries such as the ASEAN-4 and China are the chief recipient countries of Japan's ODA loans in terms of cumulative value. Although causality is not clear, economic growth rates are relatively high for these 10 countries.

The share of Japan's ODA loans in its total bilateral ODA was 50 percent in 1991 (Government of Japan 1993, 42). This is much higher than the DAC average (11.7 percent). This fact is related to the first characteristic of Japan's ODA mentioned in section 8.2.2. Table 8.9 shows the sectoral distribution of major DAC member countries. This table shows that the share of ODA for economic infrastructure is quite high for Japan.

8.3.2 A Background for Aid Policy

The share of ODA loans in Japan's total ODA is much higher than the DAC average because Japan's ODA is partly financed by the Fiscal Investment and Loans Program.[1]

The request basis principle emanates from the shortage of information about recipient countries and the lack of a concrete Japanese policy design. ODA

1. Some observers believe that Japan, by emphasizing infrastructure, presents an alternative to "the World Bank/IMF approach." For example, the Overseas Economic Cooperation Fund of Japan (OECF 1991) holds a skeptical view of the World Bank approach. They note four points:

Table 8.9 **Sectoral Distribution of ODA, 1991 (commitment; %)**

Sector	Japan	United States	United Kingdom	France	Germany	Italy	Canada	Australia	Sweden	DAC Average
Social infrastructure	17.5	23.0	27.2	49.0	28.3	15.4	22.2	36.1	15.6	25.7
Economic infrastructure	31.7	4.7	22.7	20.6	25.8	26.4	12.3	19.9	22.5	19.1
Agriculture	10.0	8.3	8.8	6.9	10.5	19.3	11.1	18.2	9.1	11.3
Industry	8.7	6.2	4.5	10.7	20.1	19.2	7.8	5.7	10.7	9.8
Food aid	0.6	13.2	1.5	0.9	2.9	4.4	7.0	7.3	0.2	5.9
Program aid	31.5	44.6	33.3	21.9	11.4	15.4	39.6	13.0	44.6	26.0
Total	100.0	100.0	100.0	100.0	100.0	100.0	100.0	100.0	100.0	100.0

Source: Ministry of Foreign Affairs (1992).

policy is determined through negotiation among four agencies (Ministry of Finance, Ministry of Foreign Affairs, MITI, and Economic Planning Agency) and, by and large, is a product of compromise among the interests of these agencies.

When things are determined by consensus among four agencies, aid policy of a controversial nature is not easily realized, and instead those policies that everyone agrees with tend to be chosen. Thus the above-mentioned humanitarian considerations are important in ODA policy in Japan since no one could effectively oppose this philosophy. A quarter of Japan's bilateral ODA is issued to satisfy basic human needs (BHNs) or to alleviate poverty. The policy objective of economic development in recipient countries is likewise easily accommodated. Since this is related to improving the living standards of the poor, there would be no effective objection to this.

Moreover, the future of the Japanese economy depends heavily on the maintenance of the free trade system and the expansion of world trade. ODA as a tool for expanding world trade as well as bringing about political stability in developing countries conforms, in this sense, with Japan's "national interest."

8.3.3 Current Issues in ODA Policy

Although Japan's ODA policy is based on the country's past experiences with economic development, new important elements are emerging, reflecting the rapid changes in global conditions and in the Japanese position therein. Two topics will be taken up below: strategic aid and environmental considerations.

Strategic Aid

There exists a movement in the Ministry of Foreign Affairs and in the former ruling Liberal Democratic party (LDP) to increase the emphasis on "strategic considerations" in ODA.

In a Diet debate on April 10, 1991, Toshiki Kaifu, then prime minister of Japan, announced the existence of ODA policy considerations relating to strategic factors such as military expenditure in recipient countries. This is not a

---

1. Structural adjustment is not sufficient for sustainable development. It is necessary to introduce investment promotion measures.
2. It is necessary to protect the domestic industry to some extent to allow a viable export industry to develop.
3. It is indispensable to have development financing institutions lending with a subsidized interest rate, under some circumstances, in order to maximize the social welfare.
4. We must carry out privatization only when adequate conditions, such as the existence of well-functioning markets, are achieved.

However, emphasis on project financing does not imply that Japan has a well-defined alternative development model.

new policy meant to replace the two basic philosophies of ODA mentioned in section 8.1—humanitarian considerations and recognition of interdependence. However, the following four points were new considerations announced in April 1991. The Japanese government now takes the following into consideration in providing bilateral ODA:

1. military expenditure in recipient countries,
2. the development and production of arms in recipient countries,
3. exports and imports of arms in recipient countries,
4. the trend of democratization, introduction of a market-oriented economic system, basic human rights, and freedom in recipient countries.

Based on these four points, the ODA Charter, adopted by the Cabinet on June 30, 1992, states four principles and geographical and sectoral priorities. The four principles of the ODA Charter are:

1. Environmental conservation and development should be simultaneously pursued.
2. Any use of ODA for military purposes or for aggravation of international conflicts should be avoided.
3. Full attention should be paid to trends of military expenditure and trade in arms of recipient countries for Japan's aid giving.
4. Full attention should be paid to efforts for democratization and introduction of a market economy of recipient countries for Japan's aid giving.

Regional priorities for Asian developing countries are clearly stated in the ODA Charter. Five sectoral priorities are (1) environmental problems, (2) basic human needs, (3) human resource development, (4) infrastructure development, and (5) structural adjustment.

It is desirable to implement development aid based on an explicit policy. However, once the policy is announced, there should not be too many exceptions. This poses interesting questions with regard to aid to China. Was resuming ODA to China consistent with the above four points? Is China not a large exporter of arms? Are human rights and freedom maintained in China?

Japan's ODA by the Ministry of Foreign Affairs of Japan (1992, 30–34; 1993, chap. 2) discussed the issues related to the above four points and the ODA Charter. It pointed out various cases where ODA was stopped due to a coup d'etat or other human rights violations. But nothing is mentioned about China. If China's case is to be an exception, the Japanese government should present the reasons for the exceptional treatment of China. Without explicit reasoning it is difficult to understand the inconsistency between China's situation and resumption of Japanese aid to China.

Environment and Development Aid

The OECD ministerial meeting on the environment and development was held in December 1991, and the U.N. Conference on the Environment and Development (UNCED) was held in Rio de Janeiro in June 1992. The central issue was how to balance economic development and environmental protection, in other words, how to achieve sustainable development.

During the long process of economic development, people in industrialized countries paid little attention to environmental issues. For developing countries, economic development is a policy of first priority. It is hard for such countries to pay more attention to environmental issues, but deterioration of the environment in developing countries has external diseconomies for everyone.

We should recognize the fact that industrialized countries have attained economic development without due consideration to environmental issues by present-day standards. Donor governments should make compensation. It is our view that, in order to cope with the issue of external diseconomies, we should provide more aid to a recipient country which plans to pay more attention to environmental issues in its development planning.

8.3.4 Financial Flow to East Asia

As is well known, in its initial phase of industrialization Korea depended heavily on external financing. When Korea started its first five-year plan in 1962, nearly 80 percent of gross domestic fixed capital formation (GDFCF) was financed by external sources. Even in its third five-year plan period (1972–76), which marked the start of heavy industrialization in Korea, the ratio of foreign capital to GDFCF was still higher than 20 percent.

Accumulated foreign borrowing in Korea was an important policy issue around 1980. In terms of external debt Korea was among the worst 10 in 1980. But nobody claims that Korea has an external debt problem now. Due to its high economic growth and export expansion, Korea's external debt in relation to its economic size declined sharply. This is often attributed to the shift to an export-oriented development strategy in Korea. In certain phases of economic development, developing countries often depend on external sources for financing investment. The crucial point of external financing is how to use foreign savings efficiently.

Financial flow to East Asian countries in 1991 is shown in Table 8.10. Panel A shows the absolute value of the selected categories of external financing, and Panel B compares the ratio of external financial flow to investment.

Ratios of financial flow to investment in Hong Kong and the ASEAN-4 were higher than 12 percent in 1991, higher than those of all Asian NICs, except Hong Kong. Dependence on official flow increased in the 1980s for East Asian countries. The figures in the table seem to suggest that external financing, both official and private, makes substantial contributions to capital accumulation and economic development in East Asia.

8.4 East Asian Dynamism and Development Cooperation

Some East Asian developing countries, such as Indonesia, China, and Vietnam, are in the process of structural adjustment. Indonesia's economy is shifting from oil-based to industry-based, by a series of deregulation policies. China and Vietnam are in the midst of the transition from centrally planned economies to market economies.

Table 8.10 **Financial Flows to East Asia, 1991**

A. Amount (million U.S. $)

Country	Total Receipt Net	ODA Net	ODA Gross	OOF Net	Total Official Gross	Private Flows
Hong Kong	2,860.1	36.1	39.0	−7.7	39.2	2,831.7
Korea	2,230.0	54.7	309.2	−440.6	517.5	2,615.9
Singapore	913.7	7.8	32.7	114.6	183.6	791.3
Taiwan	35.8	3.4	4.4	−2.1	4.6	34.5
Indonesia	5,225.9	1,877.3	2,499.8	2,129.8	5,706.1	1,218.8
Malaysia	1,910.1	289.0	433.2	163.9	819.8	1,457.2
Philippines	1,641.8	1,055.2	1,142.0	801.7	2,404.2	−215.1
Thailand	3,581.5	721.0	887.8	338.5	1,740.2	2,522.0
China	5,933.6	2,007.2	2,160.8	993.3	3,756.2	2,933.1
Vietnam	250.1	218.5	235.8	2.5	242.0	29.1

B. Financial Flows/Investment Ratio (%)

Country	Total Receipt Net	ODA Net	ODA Gross	OOF Net	Total Official Gross	Private Flows	Current Account (million U.S. $)
Hong Kong	12.4	0.2	0.2	0.0	0.2	12.3	n.a.
Korea	2.1	0.1	0.3	−0.4	0.5	2.4	−4,080
Singapore	5.7	0.0	0.2	0.7	1.2	5.0	4,208
Taiwan	0.1	0.0	0.0	0.0	0.0	0.1	10,769
Indonesia	12.8	4.6	6.1	5.2	14.0	3.0	−8,726
Malaysia	13.8	2.1	3.1	1.2	5.9	10.5	−4,530
Philippines	18.3	11.8	12.7	8.9	26.8	−2.4	−1,034
Thailand	12.6	2.5	3.1	1.2	6.1	8.9	−7,564
China	n.a.	n.a.	n.a.	n.a.	n.a.	n.a.	13,272
Vietnam	n.a.	n.a.	n.a.	n.a.	n.a.	n.a.	n.a.

Sources: OECD, *Geographical Distribution of Financial Flows to Developing Countries* (Paris, 1988/1991); IMF, *International Financial Statistics* (Washington, D.C., April 1993); Asian Development Bank, *Key Indicators of Developing Member Countries of the Asian Development Bank* (Manila, 1992).
Note: Figures are net disbursements except ODA Gross and Total Official Gross.

East Asia is the most dynamic region in the world. By "dynamic" we mean that the economic growth rate and the speed of structural change are high. Maintaining East Asian dynamism is crucially important not only for the East Asian countries themselves but also for the world economy. I believe that the most important factor in explaining high growth in East Asia is that they are very clever followers, in the sense of the catching-up product cycle. They utilize the diffusion of dynamism: from Japan to the Asian NICs, from the NICs to the ASEAN countries, then from the ASEAN countries to China and Vietnam. For China and Vietnam the shift from centrally planned economies to market economies and open economic policy are important to their becoming successful followers. They understand the mechanisms to promote development and the role of government. In spite of popular misunderstanding of Japan's industrial policy (Johnson 1982), technocrats in East Asia understand that the crucial point is to utilize private dynamism. The role of government is not to intervene in the market directly, but to maintain a competitive economic environment and provide basic infrastructure. Further, in East Asia, competition among countries is quite fierce. When one country announces a deregulation policy for foreign direct investment, neighboring countries try to deregulate their foreign investment policies as well.

Foreign direct investment played a crucial role in the diffusion of dynamism. Many companies from Japan, Korea, Taiwan, and other more developed countries are rushing to Thailand, Indonesia, China, and Vietnam. For example, many export-oriented firms have rushed into Indonesia since the start of a series of deregulation policies in the mid-1980s. Since then, the change in the Indonesian export structure has been remarkable. In 1985 more than two-thirds of Indonesia's exports were oil and gas. By 1993, manufactured exports had increased sharply to more than 60 percent. Relatively open trade and foreign investment policies have become widespread in East Asian countries recently. However, the shortage of basic infrastructure, such as electricity and port facilities, is a serious problem for these countries.

Generally speaking, the contribution of aid for economic development in developing countries is limited. But the contribution of aid is not so small in some Asian cases. Table 8.11 shows the contribution of Japan's ODA loans to the selected economic infrastructure in East Asia. For example in Thailand 20 percent of the total electricity supply and 29 percent of irrigation facilities were financed by Japan's ODA loans. Although it is difficult to verify the contribution of aid with a rigorous quantitative model, the figures in table 8.11 are very important supporting evidence in understanding the positive role of aid in economic development in East Asia.

It is difficult to identify the impact of ODA, especially bilateral ODA, on the economic development of recipient countries. As shown in table 8.10, official resources for financing investments in East Asian countries are not small. Japan's ODA is expanding, and Japan lays special emphasis on Asia in its ODA distribution, as shown in tables 8.5 and 8.8.

Systematic development plans with well-balanced private and public investment programs and efficient economic management are crucially important to promoting economic development. The Japanese government implicitly pledges an annual disbursement of ODA to selected developing countries. In such cases, recipient countries can utilize Japan's ODA money for infrastructure investment. With a sufficient supply of infrastructure and human capital, developing countries can expect sustained economic development.

Table 8.11 Contribution of Japan's ODA Loans to Economic Infrastructure in East Asia (%)

	China	Korea	Indonesia	Malaysia	Philippines	Thailand
Electricity	4		31	51	5	20
Rural electrification						21
Telephone	10					
Rural telephone network					11	
Railway	8		12	20		
Port	5					
Freeway			18			100[a]
Dam		82				
Rural water supply					13	
Irrigation			4			29
Pumping station					70[b]	

Source: OECF (1992).

Note: Contribution of Japan's ODA loans to total supply of infrastructure service.

[a]Freeway in Bangkok.

[b]Pumping station for flood control in Manila.

8.5 Concluding Remarks

In this paper, I have described characteristics of Japan's ODA. I shall summarize the major findings of the paper.

In the 1950s and 1960s, Japan's major purpose in providing ODA was to promote its exports to recipient countries. However, the ratio of tied aid to total ODA loans from Japan has declined remarkably and has become one of the lowest among DAC member countries. In 1991 Japan's untied-aid ratio (the ratio of untied ODA to total bilateral ODA) was 79.7 percent, the third highest among the 20 DAC member countries. This means that export promotion has become much less important to Japanese ODA policy.

Geographically speaking, about 60 percent of Japan's bilateral ODA is provided to Asian developing countries. This geographical priority is clearly stated in Japan's ODA Charter, announced in June 1992, and is also confirmed by the regression analysis in section 8.3.

The major sector of Japanese bilateral ODA is economic infrastructure investment. The DAC average share of economic infrastructure investment was less than 20 percent. However, more than 30 percent of Japan's bilateral ODA was intended for this sector in 1991.

The four basic characteristics of Japan's ODA—the low share of grants, the emphasis on project financing, the emphasis on the request principle, and the emphasis on the self-help efforts of a recipient country—have been identified. I have argued that these characteristics of ODA policy are rooted in Japan's postwar development experience.

References

Government of Japan. 1993. *Wagakuni no Seifu Kaihatsu Enjo no Jisshi Jokyo* (Japan's ODA in fiscal year 1992). Tokyo: Government of Japan.

Inoue, Ryuichiro, Hirohisa Kohama, and Shujiro Urata, eds. 1993. *Industrial policy in East Asia.* Tokyo: Japan External Trade Organization.

International Monetary Fund (IMF). 1993. *Direction of trade statistics yearbook.* Washington, D.C.: IMF.

Itoh, Motoshige, Kazuharu Kiyono, Masahiro Okuno-Fujiwara, and Kotaro Suzumura. 1991. *Economic analysis of industrial policy.* San Diego: Academic.

Johnson, C. 1982. *MITI and the Japanese miracle: The growth of industrial policy, 1925–1975.* Stanford, Calif.: Stanford University Press.

Kodama, Toshihiro. 1994. Seifu no Yakuwari: Sangyo Seisaku (The role of government: Industrial policy). In *Meido in Japan* (Made in Japan), ed. Hiroyuki Yoshikawa and Japan Commission on Industrial Performance. Tokyo: Daiyamondo-sha.

Kohama, Hirohisa, and Juro Teranishi. 1992. Japan's ODA policy and economic development of recipient countries. Revised version of paper presented at conference on Development Cooperation Policies of Japan, the United States, and Europe, Institute of Developing Economies, Tokyo, January 29–30.

Kohama, Hirohisa, and Shujiro Urata. 1993. Industrial policy and development strategy in East Asia. In *Industrial policy in East Asia,* ed. R. Inoue, H. Kohama, and S. Urata. Tokyo: Japan External Trade Organization.

Komiya, Ryutaro, Masahiro Okuno, and Kotaro Suzumura, eds. 1988. *Industrial policy of Japan.* San Diego: Academic.

Ministry of Foreign Affairs of Japan. Annual. *Wagakuni no Seifu Kaihatsu Enjo* (Japan's ODA). Tokyo: Association for Promotion of International Cooperation.

Ministry of International Trade and Industry of Japan (MITI). 1959. *Keizai Kyoryoku no Genjo to Mondaiten* (White Paper of Japan's Economic Cooperation). Tokyo: MITI.

Overseas Economic Cooperation Fund of Japan (OECF). 1991. Issues related to the World Bank's approach to structural adjustment—Proposal from a major partner. OECF Occasional Paper no. 1. Tokyo: OECF, October.

———. 1992. *ODA loans today* (in Japanese). Tokyo: OECF.

Ohkawa, Kazushi, and Hirohisa Kohama. 1989. *Lectures on developing economies—Japan's experience and its relevance.* Tokyo: University of Tokyo Press.

Okamoto, Yumiko, and Kazuhiko Yokota. 1992. Nihon no Enjo Seisaku no Suryo Bunseki (Empirical analysis of Japan's aid policy). *Kokusai Kaihatsu Kenkyu* (Japan Society for International Development) 1, no. 2.

Teranishi, Juro. 1983. Wagakuni no Seifu Kaihatsu Enjo (ODA) Seisaku ni tsuite (On Japan's ODA policy). *Keizai Kenkyu* (Institute of Economic Research, Hitotsubashi University) 34, no. 2.

World Bank. 1991. Segin Shakkan Kaiso (World Bank loans to Japan). Tokyo: World Bank.

———. 1993. World development report. Washington, D.C.: World Bank.

Yanagihara, Toru. 1990. Policy-based lending and Japanese policy. Paper presented at the conference on Japan's Surplus and Implications for Growth in Developing Countries, Washington, D.C., March 9.

Comment Chong-Hyun Nam

This is an interesting paper. I enjoyed it very much and I learned a lot from it. At the same time, I must say that I found it rather difficult to comment on, partly because it covers a wide range of issues and partly because it develops arguments based on facts about Japan's postwar experience with which I am not too familiar. I will, however, talk about questions and issues that I would liked to have seen in a paper under the same title.

This paper gives a very good description of two major issues that are both important but only thinly related to each other. One concerns the development mechanism experienced by Japan during the postwar period, and the other concerns Japan's development cooperation with developing nations in recent years.

I wholly agree with Kohama that Japan has been able to achieve its high degree of industrialization by finding the proper mix of infant-industry protection and import liberalization during the postwar period, an extremely difficult task both in theory and in practice. Flexibility in the interaction mechanism between the private sector and the government and a preannounced liberalization plan have been effective in establishing a competitive environment.

I also agree with Kohama that developing nations are often burdened with underdeveloped domestic markets, lack of organizational efficiency, and so forth, and hence government intervention is often called for.

But Kohama goes one step further to claim that a competitive environment can be enhanced even in a protected and oligopolistic market such as postwar Japan's because entrepreneurs will have a strong incentive to improve productivity and international competitiveness under protection. Indeed, this may well be true in Japan, but I doubt the same argument will hold for other developing nations. I wonder whether one might find counterexamples even in Japan. It seems to me Japanese entrepreneurs did their best to improve productivity and international competitiveness whether protection was given or not. This might have been especially the case when protection was perceived by entrepreneurs to be only a temporary measure. I hope there will be no misunderstanding on this point, especially in other developing nations who contemplate emulating Japan's experience of import protection. In addition, I think Japan has become trapped by prolonged protection in agriculture, as well as in some service sectors such as the distribution system.

As for the second issue, that of Japan's development cooperation with developing nations, Kohama presents a rather lengthy description of the positive contribution of Japan's official development assistance (ODA). No one can dispute the importance of ODA in terms of capital financing in developing nations. But it is also true that there are a number of issues of importance overriding ODA in relation to Japan's role in developing economic cooperation with developing nations. For example, I would liked to have seen a description of

Chong-Hyun Nam is professor of economics at Korea University.

the possibility of trade expansion, direct investment (including joint ventures), technology transfers, and the problem of leadership in the ongoing Uruguay Round negotiations for developing nations. But then that would be another paper.

Finally, Kohama addresses Korea's development issues in one section of the paper. He talks about the importance of foreign capital in financing domestic investment and about Korea's trade orientation with an ultra–export bias. This will be discussed more in detail in my paper presented in chapter 6 of this volume.

Comment John Page

Careful analyses of the design strategies underlying bilateral aid and their possible impact on the development strategies of recipient countries are rare. This is especially true in the case of the successful East Asian economies, where the focus of attention has been primarily on the roles of domestic resource accumulation and activist public policies in explaining their exceptional growth.[1] Kohama's paper is therefore welcome on two counts. First, it represents an attempt to explain which elements of Japan's own development experience had the greatest impact on the design of aid strategy. And second, it tries to link aid strategy to some of the origins of success in other East Asian economies. This is an ambitious task, and while the paper does not wholly succeed, it provides some interesting insights into a very poorly understood aspect of the Asian success story, regional contagion.

East Asia has a remarkable record of high and sustained economic growth. Most of this achievement is attributable to seemingly miraculous growth in just eight economies: Japan; the "four tigers," Hong Kong, Republic of Korea, Singapore, and Taiwan; and the three newly industrializing economies (NIEs) of Southeast Asia, Indonesia, Malaysia, and Thailand. Since 1960, these eight have grown more than twice as fast as the OECD and the rest of East Asia, roughly three times as fast as Latin America and South Asia, and 25 times faster than sub-Saharan Africa. Between 1960 and 1985, real income per capita increased more than four times in Japan and the four tigers and more than doubled in the Southeast Asian NIEs. If growth were randomly distributed, there is roughly one chance in 10 thousand that success would have been so regionally concentrated.

Relative geographical proximity is the most obvious shared characteristic of the successful Asian economies. East Asian economies have clearly benefited

John Page is chief economist of the Middle East and North Africa Region of the World Bank.

1. See, e.g., World Bank (1993) which devotes little attention to the role of external assistance in East Asia.

from the kind of nonformal economic linkages geographic proximity encourages, including those in trade and investment flows. Despite the substantial development assistance flows to the region shown by Kohama, private capital flows dominate as a source of investment in all of the East Asian economies except Indonesia and the Philippines. Private capital flows have accelerated in the last decade, as northeast Asian manufacturers of labor-intensive exports moved their factories south to take advantage of lower wages. The share of foreign investment in total investment has increased over the decade, in contrast to the share of development assistance. From the policy viewpoint, these linkages have been encouraged by macroeconomic stability and the generally liberal treatment of foreign investment. But even where foreign investment policies have been restrictive, informal credit and information networks have helped investors to move capital relatively freely.

Kohama identifies one central factor, both as an essential principle underlying Japan's aid strategy and as a major source of East Asia's dynamism. In Kohama's words, "technocrats in East Asia understand that the crucial point is to utilize private dynamism." The extent to which the developing, high-performing Asian economies (HPAEs) have succeeded in tapping this dynamism is shown in figure 8C.1, which gives private and public investment as a share of GDP for a sample of 47 low- and middle-income economies (LMIEs) (including five of the developing country HPAEs).[2] Private investment is about 7 percentage points higher in the HPAEs than in other middle-income economies. It rose from about 15 percent of GDP in 1970 to nearly 22 percent in 1974, then declined and held at about 18 percent between 1975 and 1984. Private investment contracted sharply between 1984 and 1986 reflecting the global recession, then recovered by 1988.[3] In contrast, private investment in other LMIEs has remained relatively stable at about 11 percent of GDP. Indeed, virtually all of the difference in investment rates between the HPAEs and other developing countries is due to differences in private investment.

The central unanswered question of Kohama's paper is, To what extent was the aid design and strategy of Japan relevant to the widespread adoption of private investment–driven development strategies in other HPAEs? The basic characteristics of official development assistance (ODA) identified in the paper—low grant share, emphasis on project financing, emphasis on the "request basis" for lending, and emphasis on self-help—appear to differ little from the objectives expressed by many other bilateral and multilateral donors and to be tangentially related at best to the development of the high levels of private investment described above. The answer may lie in two seemingly unrelated observations in the paper: first, that Japan "not only avoids the application of

2. The data are drawn from Pfeffermann and Madarassy (1992).

3. This basic pattern is observed in four individual economies—Korea, Thailand, Singapore, and Malaysia. The pattern for Indonesia differs; real private investment declined continuously during the 1980s from a peak of 20 percent of GDP to a low of 13 percent in 1989.

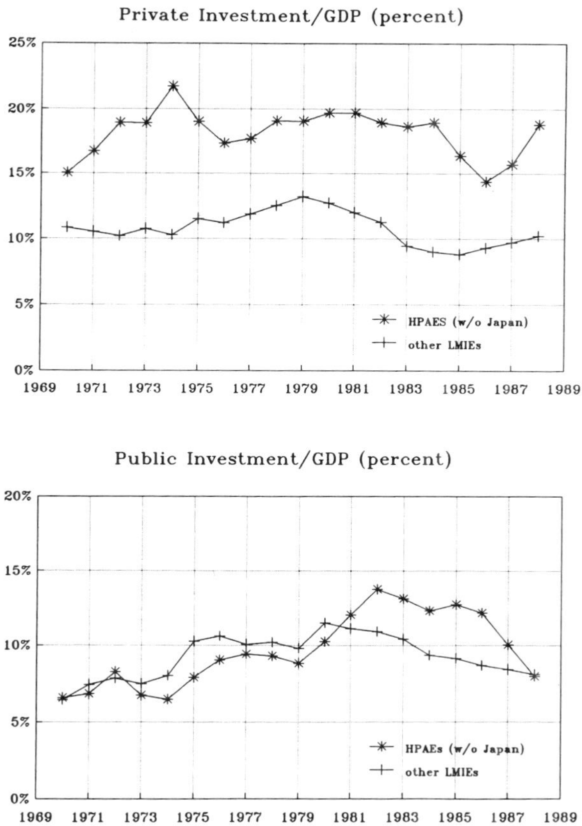

Fig. 8C.1 Public and private investment
Source: World Bank data.
Note: LMIEs = low- and middle-income economies.

a uniform development strategy, it recommends that a recipient country devise its own methods of coping with obstacles to development," and second, that in the case of East Asia Japan's ODA loans were heavily concentrated in the provision of economic infrastructure.

The HPAEs encouraged private investment by several means. First, they did a better job than most developing economies at creating infrastructure which was complementary to private investment. Second, they created an investment-friendly environment through a combination of tax policies favoring investment and policies that kept the relative prices of capital goods low, largely by avoiding the effects of high tariffs on imported capital goods.

Third and more controversial, most HPAE governments controlled deposit and lending rates below market-clearing levels. Japan, Korea, Malaysia, Thailand, and Taiwan, had extended periods of mild financial repression. Governments were able to mildly repress interest rates on deposits with a minimal impact on saving and pass the lower rates to final borrowers, thus subsidizing corporations. This transfer of income from households to firms may have increased the volume of savings. It also changed the form in which savings were held, from debt to corporate equity, increasing the risk-bearing capacity of the economy (Stiglitz 1993). Tests of the relationship between interest rates and growth suggest that in the cases of Japan, Korea, and Taiwan, the negative relationship between interest rate repression and growth found in cross-economy analyses is not present (World Bank 1993).

Finally some governments, especially in the northeastern Asian tier, spread private investment risks to the public. In some economies the government owned or controlled the institutions providing investment funds, in others it offered explicit credit guarantees, and in still others it implicitly guaranteed the financial viability of promoted projects. Relationship banking by a variety of public and private banking institutions in Hong Kong, Japan, Korea, Malaysia, Singapore, Thailand, and Taiwan involved the banking sector in the management of troubled enterprises, increasing the likelihood of creditor workouts. Directed credit programs in Japan, Korea, and Taiwan signaled directions of government policy and provided implicit insurance to private banks.

At least some of these policy initiatives, while reflecting successful Japanese experience, were contrary to the lending criteria of multilateral institutions such as the World Bank and to those of many bilateral aid agencies. Seen in this light, the combination of lack of a prior model with regard to appropriate development policy and a focus on economic infrastructure which was complementary to private investment led growth in the HPAEs. It is also likely that geography facilitated the adoption of imitative strategies, in both public and private-sector activity. Policy imitation—specifically of Japan's industrial strategy—was an explicit objective in Korea, Indonesia, and Malaysia.

Some economists and political scientists have argued that the East Asian Miracle is due to the high quality and authoritarian nature of the region's institutions (Johnson 1982). They describe East Asian political regimes as "developmental states" in which powerful technocratic bureaucracies, shielded from political pressure, devise and implement well-honed interventions. But Kohama asserts correctly that the most broadly applied lesson of Japan's experience "was not the industrial policy but the dynamism of the private sector."

Developmental state models overlook the central role of government–private-sector cooperation. While leaders of the HPAEs have tended to be either authoritarian or paternalistic, they have also been willing to grant a voice and genuine authority to a technocratic elite and key elements in the private sector. Unlike authoritarian leaders in many other economies, leaders in the HPAEs realized that economic development was impossible without cooperation.

Leaders needed institutions and mechanisms to reassure competing groups that each would benefit from growth. The first step was to recruit a competent and relatively honest technocratic cadre and insulate it from day-to-day political interference. The power of these technocracies has varied greatly. In Japan, Korea, Singapore, and Taiwan, strong, well-organized bureaucracies wield substantial power. Other HPAEs have had small, general-purpose planning agencies. But in each economy, economic technocrats helped leaders to devise a credible economic strategy.

Leaders in the HPAEs also built a business-friendly environment. A major element of that environment was a legal and regulatory structure which was generally hospitable to private investment, and the investment-friendly public policy framework outlined above. But beyond this, the HPAEs have with varying degrees of formality and success focused on enhancing communications between business and government. Japan, Korea, Malaysia, and Singapore have established forums, called deliberation councils. These forums have enabled private-sector groups to influence the formulation and implementation of government policies relevant to their interests.

In Japan and Korea, technocrats used deliberation councils to coordinate behavior among firms. Because the private sector participated in drafting the rules and because the process was transparent to all participants, private-sector groups became more willing participants in the leadership's development efforts. One byproduct of this process was a tendency to minimize private resources devoted to wasteful rent-seeking activities rather than productive endeavors. Deliberation councils also facilitated information exchanges between the private sector and government, among firms, and between management and labor. The councils thus supplemented the market's information transmission function, enabling firms to respond more quickly than in other economies to changing markets. In Malaysia the councils appear to be increasing in importance and scope. In Thailand the formal mechanisms of communication have generally been used to present businesses' positions to government and reduce suspicion of the private sector.

Kohama notes that "the most important factor to explain high growth in East Asia is that they are very clever followers, in the sense of the catching-up product cycle." Although he intends this to refer to the diffusion of technology, it could equally well be applied to the diffusion and adaptation of policies and institutions. Institutions of business-government communications were undoubtedly due more to the impact of geography promoting imitation—it is no accident that Prime Minister Mahatir of Malaysia calls his institution-building strategy "Look East"—than a conscious product of aid policy or institution building by Japan. The general model of Japanese success undoubtedly impressed policymakers throughout East Asia and provided a sense of the feasibility, as well as potential instruments, of growth. Aid policy, importantly however, supported rather than suppressed local initiatives.

As Japan becomes more geographically diversified in its aid program, there will be new challenges for ODA policy. Japan is now the largest bilateral donor to Africa. To what extent can it rely on the "request principle" to guide aid allocations toward appropriate economic infrastructure outside of East Asia? Will policies to promote private investment work in the institutional settings of other developing countries? Does Japan need to play a more active role in institution building and development of the private sector? Will the lessons of Japan's experience diffuse adequately without the benefit of geographical proximity? These are questions both Kohama and Japanese aid policy leave unanswered.

References

Johnson, Chalmers. 1982. *MITI and the Japanese miracle.* Stanford, Calif.: Stanford University Press.

Pfeffermann, Guy P., and Andrea Madarassy. 1992. *Trends in private investment in developing countries.* IFC Discussion Paper no. 14. Washington, D.C.: World Bank and IFC.

Stiglitz, Joseph E. 1993. Some lessons from the Asian miracle. Background paper for *The East Asian miracle,* Policy Research Department. Washington, D.C.: World Bank.

World Bank. 1993. *The East Asian miracle.* New York: Oxford University Press.

III Relevance of Endogenous Growth Theory for Understanding East Asia

9 A Time-Series Test of the Endogenous Growth Model with Human Capital

Hak K. Pyo

9.1 Introduction

The endogenous growth model developed by Romer (1986) and Lucas (1988) has focused on the role of human capital from the outset as a main source of increasing returns and divergence in growth rates between developed and underdeveloped countries. The model has been refined and extended further by Romer (1990) himself, Rebelo (1991), and Stokey (1991).

It has also been subject to empirical testing. Barro (1991) initiated it by regressing cross-country per capita income growth on a set of ancillary variables including the primary school enrollment ratio as a proxy variable for human capital. He found the initial level of human capital to be a significant determinant for economic growth. Kyriacou (1991) has constructed a cross-country human capital index from data on average school years in the labor force and school enrollment ratios. From the cross-country regression of per capita income growth, he finds the coefficient of initial human capital stock to be positive and significant but that of human capital growth to be negative and insignificant. However, Kyriacou's index is still another proxy variable limiting the validity of his empirical findings.

The convergence hypothesis implied by the Solow-type (1956) neoclassical model has been questioned by endogenous growth theories mainly in the context of a long-run growth path. Therefore, the hypothesis calls for an empirical test using time-series data rather than cross-country data. In a recent article, Lucas (1993) refers to the fact that, from 1960 to 1988, GDP per capita in South Korea grew at 6.2 percent per year, doubling the living standard every 11 years. He views the growth miracle as a productivity miracle made possible

Hak K. Pyo is professor of economics and a research associate of the Institute of Economic Research at Seoul National University.

by the accumulation of human capital. In fact, South Korean labor productivity has been converging to West German and U.S. levels as estimated by Dollar (1991) and Szirmai and Pilat (1990), respectively. However, the latter study notes that while South Korean labor productivity increased from 11.9 percent of U.S. productivity in 1975 to 19.2 percent in 1985, it is still less than one-fifth of the U.S. level. From this point of view, the prospect for full convergence even by the most successful industrial exporter is quite uncertain and inconclusive.

The purpose of this paper is to provide an empirical test of the endogenous growth model using country-specific time-series data on human capital stocks rather than cross-country data on proxy variables. The estimates of human capital stocks by Kendrick (1969) for the United States and those by the author (Pyo 1993) for South Korea are used in the estimation of an aggregate Cobb-Douglas production function. In particular, we explicitly test the model of Romer (1990) and Rebelo (1991), which behaves just like the neoclassical model with labor and human capital augmenting technological change and which exhibits the usual constant or diminishing returns to capital accumulation, warranting a steady state growth path. We have estimated significant positive coefficients of human capital stocks for both countries. But, while diminishing returns to capital is estimated for South Korea, near-constant returns to capital is estimated for the United States. Therefore, the convergence hypothesis implied by neoclassical theory is rejected while the new growth theory with human capital is validated.

In the following section, I review alternative specifications of the endogenous growth model with human capital. Section 9.3 discusses time-series data used in the regression and presents parameter estimates of the alternative Cobb-Douglas production specifications for the United States (1940–69) and South Korea (1955–90). Section 9.4 compares the regression result with previous empirical studies in the context of the significance of human capital stocks and the convergence hypothesis. Conclusions are reported in section 9.5.

9.2 Aggregate Production Function with Human Capital

In order to examine the significance of human capital and the convergence hypothesis in the context of time-series data, let us consider the following Cobb-Douglas specification:

$$Y_t = AK_t^a L_t^b, \quad 0 < a < 1, 0 < b < 1, \tag{1}$$

where Y_t, K_t, and L_t are output, capital, and labor, respectively, and A is a technology factor. The conventional neoclassical production model assumes that A is exogenously determined and the law of diminishing marginal returns prevails.

The convergence hypothesis implied by the model can be revisited by deriving the rate of return (r) as the difference between marginal product and the depreciation rate (d):[1]

$$r = aAK_t^{a-1} L_t^b - d. \tag{2}$$

If the growth rate of labor is exogenously given as n, the following condition must be satisfied to keep r at a constant level:

$$(dK/dt)/K = bn/(1 - a), \tag{3}$$

which implies the steady state growth rate of capital stocks. If capital stocks are low relative to the population and, therefore, a higher rate of return prevails, then the growth rate of capital will be higher. As capital is accumulated, the rate of return will fall to the steady state level. In short, a developing economy with lower per capita capital stocks is expected to grow faster and to "converge" to the steady state achieved by advanced economies.

The new growth theory, which focuses on the role of human capital, such as the first model in Lucas (1988), Stokey (1991), and Tamura (1991) endogenizes the technology factor as follows:

$$A_t = BH_t^c, \quad 0 < c < 1, \tag{4}$$

where H_t is the level of human capital stocks. Therefore, if H_t increases by 1 percent, A_t is assumed to increase by c percent.

Now suppose that labor input is allocated between physical output production and human capital production by xL_t and $(1 - x)L_t$, respectively. Then the production function of equation (1) can be respecified as

$$Y_t = BK_t^a H_t^c (xL_t)^b. \tag{5}$$

In this model, endogenous growth is possible as long as there is continuous investment in human capital even if it keeps being accumulated. In other words, models of this kind introduce a critical assumption that there is no diminishing returns in the production of human capital. The assumption is embodied in the following form of the human capital production function:

$$\begin{aligned} dH/dt &= j(1 - x)L_t(H_t/L_t) \\ &= j(1 - x)H_t, \end{aligned} \tag{6}$$

where $(1 - x)L$ is the labor input into the production of human capital and j is a productivity parameter. In addition, the productivity in human capital production is assumed to be proportional to the level of per capita human capital stocks (H_t/L_t) at time t.

Both Romer (1990) and Rebelo (1991) have shown that sustained growth can be made compatible with technologies that display constant returns to scale by assuming that there are constant returns to factors that can be accumulated.

1. See an excellent review of the convergence hypothesis by You and Chang (1991).

If physical capital and human capital are such factors ($a + c = 1$), then non-converging growth is feasible.

Consider an alternative endogenous growth model which also departs from the assumption of exogenous technology factors but defines capital as total capital, which is the sum of physical capital and human capital.[2] Therefore, the Cobb-Douglas function is respecified as

$$Y_t = A_t (K_t + H_t)^a L_t^b, \quad 0 < a < 1, 0 < b < 1. \tag{10}$$

Suppose the accumulation of total capital induces the accumulation of technology as follows:

$$A_t = B(K_t + H_t)^c, \quad 0 < c < 1, \tag{11}$$

which assumes that 1 percent growth of total capital increases technology by c percent. The substitution of the above equation to into equation (10) gives

$$Y_t = B(K_t + H_t)^{a+c} L_t^b. \tag{12}$$

The rate of return is given by

$$r = (a + c)B(K_t + H_t)^{a+c-1} L^b - d. \tag{13}$$

If there is increasing returns to total capital ($a + c > 1$), the rate of return will increase as the capital stocks grow, as discussed in Romer (1986). This provides an explanation of why the convergence of growth rates among different economies is not universally observed, but it rules out the possibility of steady state equilibrium. Therefore, the later model of Romer (1990) and Rebelo (1991) assumes constant returns to total capital ($a + c = 1$).

Under the assumption of constant returns to capital, the rate of return will be given as constant regardless of the level of total capital stocks. In this case, the growth rate of total capital will also be constant and equal to the growth rate of per capita income. The economy is always at the steady state.

9.3 Estimation of Alternative Endogenous Growth Models with Human Capital

From a brief review of endogenous growth models with human capital, the following equations are derived for estimation from the alternative Cobb-Douglas specifications of equations (1), (5), and (12):

$$\log Y_t = \text{constant} + a \log K_t + b \log L_t + u_t, \tag{1a}$$

$$\log Y_t = \text{constant} + a \log K_t + c \log H_t + b \log (xL_t) + u_t, \tag{5a}$$

$$\log Y_t = \text{constant} + (a + c) \log (K_t + H_t) + b \log (L_t) + u_t. \tag{12a}$$

2. Kendrick (1976) defines this as "total capital," which is the sum of nonhuman and human capital stocks.

First, I proceed to test $a + b = 1$ from equation (1a) to check the convergence hypothesis implied by the conventional neoclassical growth model. Second, the statistical significance of the coefficient of human capital stocks in equation (5a) is tested, and the hypothesis of constant returns to capital ($a + c = 1$) is tested. Third, the same hypothesis ($a + c = 1$) is tested from the estimation result of equation (12a). Further, if the hypothesis of constant returns to capital ($a + c = 1$) is accepted from the estimation results of equations (5a) and (12a), it may be necessary to reestimate equations (5a) and (12a) by imposing the linear constraint $a + c = 1$.

9.3.1 Data

In order to estimate a production function, we must define capital stocks and labor input. Miller (1983) distinguishes gross capital stock and net capital stock as the concepts of the capacity to produce output and the ability to produce income, respectively. I use the net concept which measures capital stocks net of depreciation since GDP, not gross output, is used as output and income.

The sample period for an empirical analysis using time-series data is naturally conditioned by the availability of human capital stock data. Kendrick (1976) has estimated human capital stocks for the United States for the period 1929–69 using a backward-looking approach.[3] The methodology is basically a cumulative accounting of past investment in human tangibles (rearing costs) and intangibles (education, health, and mobility costs). Instead of extending the data beyond 1969, the present study uses the original estimate by Kendrick to avoid possible errors in computing human capital stocks. Since Kendrick (1976) provides a consistent accounting framework for estimating both human and nonhuman capital stocks, his estimate of nonhuman capital stocks is used as the data for physical capital for the United States. Since Kendrick's estimate is available in 1958 constant prices, the U.S. GDP in 1958 constant prices has been generated from the U.S. Income and Product Accounts using GDP deflators.

For labor input data, I use "hours worked by full-time and part-time employees" (L) reported in the National Income and Product Accounts of the United States, 1929–74 for the period of 1948–69. Since the data is not available but the data for "full-time equivalent employees" (FEE) are available for the period 1929–74, I estimated hours worked for the period 1940–47 by the following regression equation for the period 1948–69, without a constant term:

$$L = \underset{(0.005)}{2.037}\text{FEE}, \quad \bar{R}^2 = 0.98,$$

3. An alternative method of estimating human capital is the present value or forward-looking approach mainly introduced by Graham and Webb (1979). This approach regards human capital as a discounted stream of future returns and estimates the present value of discounted lifetime earnings from cross-sectional data.

where the figure in parenthesis is the standard error of the estimated coefficient.

The data for South Korea's physical and human capital stocks have been estimated by the author and are available for the period 1955–90 in Pyo (1992) and Pyo (1993), respectively. The estimation of human capital stocks follows Kendrick's method closely, and the estimation of physical capital stocks combines the polynomial benchmark method and the perpetual inventory method utilizing Korea's three-time national wealth survey in 1968, 1977, and 1987. The detailed description of the estimation method and estimates by industries and types of goods are presented in Pyo (1992). The GDP data for South Korea published by the Bank of Korea is available in National Income Accounts (1984) and National Accounts (1991).

Next, in order to obtain stable estimates, I excluded a decade of the post-Depression era (1929–39) from the sample period for the estimation of the U.S. production function. For South Korea, the data for hours worked by full-time employees are available only after 1970, and those for total number of employees are available after 1955. Therefore, the period for estimation of the Korean production function for the present study is reduced to 36 years (1955–90).

The summary statistics for the basic data used for estimation are reported in table 9.1. During the post-Depression era 1940–69, the U.S. economy grew at 4.3 percent per year in real GDP terms, with the growth of physical capital (3.8 percent), human capital (3.6 percent), and employment (2.4 percent) in terms of hours worked by full-time and part-time employees.

The correlation coefficients reported in table 9.1 indicate a high degree of correlation among the U.S. GDP, physical capital stocks, and human capital stocks. The ratio of human capital stocks to total capital stocks remained rather stable, from 0.63 in 1940 to 0.62 in 1969.

The growth miracle achieved by South Korea as discussed recently by Lucas (1993) is well reflected in the growth rates of GDP (7.9 percent), physical capital (9.8 percent), and human capital (10.3 percent) reported in table 9.1. In particular, that the accumulation of human capital exceeds that of physical capital lends support to the conjecture that human capital may be an important determinant for attracting physical capital and for achieving economic growth. The ratio of human capital stocks to total capital stocks in South Korea has increased steadily from 0.47 in 1955 to 0.52 in 1990 even though it has not yet reached the U.S. level.

The convergence of South Korean productivity to the level of industrial nations is well documented in the cross-country growth accounting literature. Summers and Heston (1988) estimated that South Korea's per capita GDP in 1954 was about 10 percent of the U.S. level but reached 25 percent by 1979. Pilat (1993) reports that South Korea's labor productivity in manufacturing was only 6.4 percent of the U.S. level in 1967 but reached 26.3 percent by 1987. Dollar (1991) argues that South Korea's labor productivity in manufac-

Table 9.1 Summary Statistics for Basic Data

Statistics	United States (1940–69)	South Korea (1955–90)
Growth Rates (%)		
GDP (Y)	4.3	7.9
Physical capital (K)	3.8	9.8
Human capital (H)	3.6	10.3
Total capital ($K+H$)	3.7	10.0
Employed labor (L)	2.4	2.5
Per capita GDP (Y/L)	1.9	5.4
Per capita physical capital (K/L)	1.4	7.3
Per capita human capital (H/L)	1.2	7.8
Per capita total capital ($(K+H)/L$)	1.3	7.5
Correlation Coefficients		
r_{YK}	.98	.99
r_{YH}	.98	.99
r_{YL}	.96	.97
r_{KH}	.99	.98
r_{KL}	.92	.94
r_{HL}	.91	.97
Human capital ratio ($H/(K+H)$)	(1940) .63	(1955) .47
	(1969) .62	(1990) .52

Notes: Physical capital is defined as net nonhuman capital stocks excluding land and inventory stocks from Kendrick (1976) and Pyo (1992). Human capital is also defined as net stocks in constant prices. Employed labor is measured by hours worked by full-time and part-time employees for the United States and by total number of employees for South Korea.

turing had reached two-thirds of the West German level by 1978. All of these estimates support the catch-up or convergence hypothesis, but at the same time, they also indicate that South Korea has not yet achieved full convergence to the industrial nations level.

9.3.2 Estimation Results

The results for regressions using the ordinary least squares estimation method run on log GDP are reported in table 9.2 and table 9.3. Table 9.2 is an unrestricted version, while table 9.3 is a restricted version after imposing constant returns to all factor inputs. To account for wartime effects, a dummy variable (D) for the years 1942–45 was included in the regression for the United States. (Estimation results for U.S. data over a shorter period, 1948–69, appear in the appendix.)

Looking at the estimation results for the U.S. data, we find estimated coefficients of all three alternative models have correct signs and high significance. The degree of fitness is high, and the degree of autocorrelation is rather mild. It is interesting to note that the coefficient of human capital stocks in equation (2) and the coefficient of total capital stocks in equation (3) are significant at

Table 9.2 **Parameter Estimates of the Cobb-Douglas Production Model: Unrestricted Estimates (Dependent Variable: log GDP)**

Equation	Constant	log *K*	log *H*	log (*K*+*H*)	log *L*	*D*	$\bar{R}^2$	D-W	Auto-correlation
				United States (1940–69)					
(1)	−8.144	0.570			0.884	0.034	0.99	0.99	
	(0.611)	(0.033)			(0.071)	(0.013)			
(2)	−8.309	0.374	0.212		0.881	0.045	0.99	1.28	
	(0.581)	(0.099)	(0.102)		(0.067)	(0.013)			
(3)	−8.974			0.588	0.897	0.049	0.99	1.28	
	(0.545)			(0.032)	(0.067)	(0.013)			
				South Korea (1955–90)					
(1)	3.138	0.550			0.210		0.99	1.67	AR(1):0.974
	(6.264)	(0.298)			(0.119)				(0.087)
(2)	−0.153	0.381	0.399		0.199		0.99	1.51	AR(1):0.776
	(0.932)	(0.112)	(0.134)		(0.131)				(0.112)
(3)	−0.914			0.784	0.215		0.99	1.57	AR(1):0.766
	(0.775)			(0.050)	(0.126)				(0.106)

Notes: Standard errors in parentheses. Estimates for South Korea were obtained with the first-order autoregressive (AR(1)) adjustment on the software package Micro TSP. Parameter estimates of first-order autocorrelation coefficients with their standard errors are reported in the last column.

Table 9.3 **Parameter Estimates of the Cobb-Douglas Production Model: CRS Restricted Estimates (Dependent Variable: log GDP/*L*)**

Equation	Constant	log *K*/*L*	log *H*/*L*	log (*K*+*H*)/*L*	*D*	$\bar{R}^2$	D-W	Auto-correlation
				United States (1940–69)				
(1)	−1.396	0.883			0.128	0.95	0.85	
	(0.185)	(0.039)			(0.024)			
(2)	−1.394	0.858	0.028		0.130	0.95	0.86	
	(0.190)	(0.231)	(0.257)		(0.029)			
(3)	−2.021			0.940	0.161	0.95	1.01	
	(0.172)			(0.046)	(0.027)			
				South Korea (1955–90)				
(1)	0.110	0.647				0.99	1.56	AR(1):0.915
	(0.213)	(0.072)						(0.061)
(2)	−0.346	0.370	0.406			0.99	1.51	AR(1):0.778
	(0.142)	(0.098)	(0.129)					(0.110)
(3)	−0.918			0.784		0.99	1.57	AR(1):0.767
	(0.115)			(0.039)				(0.104)

Notes: Standard errors in parentheses. Estimates for South Korea were obtained with the first-order autoregressive (AR(1)) adjustment on the software package Micro TSP. Parameter estimates of first-order autocorrelation coefficients with their standard errors are reported in the last column.

the 5 percent significance level with a one-tail test. The estimated coefficient of labor is very high (around 0.88) and highly significant.

Note that in all three equations the hypothesis of constant returns to capital is rejected, and instead decreasing returns ($a + c < 1$) is accepted at the 5 percent significance level with a one-tail test. But, increasing returns to all factors ($a + b + c > 1$) is accepted for all three equations. Therefore, it is necessary to impose the restriction of constant returns to scale (CRS) and reestimate three equations, the results of which are reported in table 9.3.

Under the CRS restriction, the coefficient of per capita human capital is almost zero (0.028) and quite insignificant. But the estimated capital coefficient is very high with $a = 0.883$ in equation (1) and $a + c = 0.886$ in equation (2). Against the formal hypothesis of constant returns to capital ($a = 1$ or $a + c = 1$), both results reject the null hypothesis with t-values of -3.0 and -3.56, respectively, but it can be seen that they show near constant returns to capital. In particular, when capital is defined as total capital by equation (3), the estimated capital coefficient (0.94) accepts the null hypothesis ($a + c = 1$) with a t-value of -1.30. The above results partly support the hypothesis of constant returns to a broad concept of capital that includes human capital advanced by the recent models of endogenous economic growth. Barro and Sala-i-Martin (1992, 246) note that the neoclassical model requires a coefficient value of about 0.8 for a broadly defined concept of capital to fit the observed speeds of convergence from the 98-country group data. The estimated coefficient of broadly defined capital for the United States is consistent with their conjecture.

The last estimation results, reported in table 9.4, are estimates of parameters using the growth accounting equation. Benhabib and Jovanovic (1990) argue that estimation of the production function using levels is subject to all the caveats. Following this argument, Benhabib and Spiegel (1991) advance the view that, if stochastic shocks to the production function are random walks, estimating the coefficients using growth rates can overcome such difficulties.

For the U.S. results, it can be seen that the magnitude of the estimated labor coefficient has been reduced to the level of 0.46–0.50. It can be also noted that the pure neoclassical production equation (1) has produced a capital coefficient (0.63) and a labor coefficient (0.47) which are roughly consistent with the results of U.S. growth accounting. While the estimated coefficient of human capital in equation (2) is negative and insignificant, that of total capital in equation (3) is positive and significant.

Finally, it is noted that the growth accounting equation did not fit well to the South Korean data, resulting in very low degree of fitness and relatively lower t-values for the estimated coefficients.

Next, turning to the estimates from the South Korean data, table 9.2 presents significant estimated coefficients for all three equations including the coefficient of human capital stocks in equation (2) and that of total capital in equation (3). The notable difference from the U.S. results lies in the magnitude of

Table 9.4 **Parameter Estimates of Growth Accounting Equations (Dependent Variable: RGDP)**

Equation	Constant	*D*	R*K*	R*H*	R(*K*+*H*)	R*L*	$\bar{R}^2$	D-W
			United States (1940–69)					
(1)	−0.004	0.005	0.626			0.466	0.93	1.72
	(0.008)	(0.009)	(0.227)			(0.038)		
(2)	0.006	0.003	0.692	−0.339		0.459	0.93	1.73
	(0.016)	(0.009)	(0.236)	(0.458)		(0.039)		
(3)	−0.010	0.010			0.757	0.502	0.92	1.62
	(0.014)	(0.009)			(0.406)	(0.035)		
			South Korea (1955–90)					
(1)	0.043		0.312			0.229	0.19	1.76
	(0.015)		(0.144)			(0.123)		
(2)	0.068		0.262	−0.194		0.230	0.20	1.83
	(0.031)		(0.154)	(0.211)		(0.123)		
(3)	0.047				0.249	0.275	0.10	1.60
	(0.034)				(0.339)	(0.129)		

Notes: RGDP is defined as the growth rate of GDP: $(\text{GDP}_t - \text{GDP}_{t-1})/\text{GDP}_{t-1}$. Other variables are similarly defined.

the estimated labor coefficient and the estimated returns to scale. The estimated labor coefficients (around 0.21) are smaller than those from the U.S. data. The estimated returns to broadly defined capital is around 0.78 and the estimated returns to both broadly defined capital and labor is around 0.98–1.0. Therefore, for the South Korean data, the CRS restriction to all inputs is not necessary but is imposed to compare with the U.S. result as reported in the bottom of table 9.3. The result is almost identical to table 9.2, as it should be. It is noted that the estimated capital coefficients are smaller than those from the U.S. data.

It is important to note that the estimated coefficient for human capital from the South Korean data is around 0.4 and very significant in both the unrestricted and the restricted estimations. Therefore, it lends support to a conjecture that, for a growing economy which has not yet arrived at a long-run steady state and has not completed its productivity convergence to the industrial nation level, human capital plays the role of accumulating capital, complementing physical capital and labor rather than providing economy-wide externality as hypothesized by the endogenous growth models. The low estimates for the labor coefficient indicate that human capital is accounting partly for labor embodiment and partly for capital embodiment.

9.4 The Role of Human Capital and the Convergence Hypothesis

The estimation results of the Cobb-Douglas production function in level form using time-series data for the United States and South Korea reveal quite different results from those using cross-country data. Human capital is found to be a significant factor in aggregate production. It complements both physical capital and labor, and therefore, income growth cannot be explained by physical capital and labor only. On the other hand, the recent results of cross-country growth accounting regressions such as Kyriacou (1991) and Benhabib and Spiegel (1992) reported negative coefficients for the growth of human capital but a positive significant coefficient for the initial level of human capital stocks. Kyriacou's explanation of this puzzling result is that there could be high fixed costs in the production of human capital stocks, high opportunity costs for acquiring education in countries with low per capita human capital, and transaction, interaction, communication, and other costs when educated workers have to operate in a poorly educated environment. However, if this interpretation is correct, a developing economy can converge, or catch up, only after a certain level of human capital is endowed or created.

The difference in the magnitude of estimated capital coefficients between the U.S. data and the South Korean data provides us with a conjecture for the debate on the convergence hypothesis. The diminishing returns to capital estimated for South Korea implies that Korea started from a lower level of capital, and therefore, with a higher rate of return prevailing, the growth rate of capital has been higher. Convergence or catch-up has been occurring, as evidenced by cross-country studies of productivity comparison such as Summers and Heston (1988), Szirmai and Pilat (1990), and Dollar (1991). The accumulation of human capital is found to be an important determinant of the growth of the South Korean economy, but it has not yet arrived at a certain threshold as discussed in Azariadis and Drazen (1990) at which human capital starts providing economy-wide externality. The estimated near constant returns to broadly defined capital from the U.S. data indicates that the U.S. economy has passed the threshold and is already at a steady state.

In summary, convergence will be observed for developing economies which make use of human capital as a productive input. On the other hand, divergence will be observed between developing economies which could not make use of human capital as a productive input and developed economies which enjoy an economy-wide externality from accumulated human capital stocks. In this regard, the growth miracle of South Korea is not a miracle but the result of sustained accumulation and use of human capital. It also implies that until a converging economy's human capital reaches a certain threshold point, the externality implied by endogenous growth models cannot be expected. Until that stage, human capital will serve as a productive input rather than as a source of externality.

9.5 Conclusion

In this paper, I first estimated three Cobb-Douglas specifications of an aggregate production function suggested by the endogenous growth model with human capital. Instead of using cross-country growth data with proxy variables for human capital, the direct estimates of human capital stocks for the United States and South Korea are used for regression.

The estimation results in level form confirm the proposition that human capital plays a significant role in economic growth. However, I estimated different returns to capital between the United States and South Korea. Near-constant returns to capital estimated from the U.S. data lends support to the nonconvergence hypothesis advanced by endogenous growth models. On the other hand, decreasing returns to capital estimated from the South Korean data supports the convergence hypothesis implied by the conventional neoclassical model.

From the viewpoint of endogenous growth theory, these findings provides us with an explanation for observed divergence between rich countries and poor countries. The explanation is a conjecture that developing economies which make use of human capital as a productive input and continue to accumulate it can converge, while those which cannot may diverge. Only after the accumulation of human capital reaches a certain threshold can the broadly defined capital provide the economy with externality.

However, evidence from two-country time-series data is too fragile to test the convergence hypothesis. In addition, it can be concluded that a lot more theory and empirical evidence are required to explain why the accumulation and the utilization of human capital cannot begin in the bulk of developing countries.

Appendix

Estimation for U.S. Data, 1948–69

Table 9A.1 Parameter Estimates of the Cobb-Douglas Production Model: Unrestricted Estimates (Dependent Variable: log GDP)

Equation	Constant	log K	log H	log $(K+H)$	log L	$\bar{R}^2$	D-W
(1)	−8.264	0.592			0.873	0.99	0.87
	(0.840)	(0.040)			(0.095)		
(2)	−7.793	0.349	0.276		0.805	0.99	0.96
	(0.805)	(0.121)	(0.132)		(0.093)		
(3)	−8.164			0.632	0.794	0.99	0.93
	(0.763)			(0.038)	(0.090)		

Table 9A.2 **Parameter Estimates of the Cobb-Douglas Production Model: CRS Restricted Estimates (Dependent Variable: log GDP/L)**

Equation	Constant	log K/L	log H/L	log $(K+H)/L$	$\bar{R}^2$	D-W
(1)	−1.651	0.860			0.95	0.53
	(0.189)	(0.042)				
(2)	−1.672	0.326	0.564		0.96	0.72
	(0.173)	(0.243)	(0.253)			
(3)	−2.272			0.888	0.96	0.71
	(0.141)			(0.039)		

References

Azariadis, Costas, and Allan Drazen. August 1990. Threshold externalities in economic development. *Quarterly Journal of Economics* 105: 501–26.

Barro, Robert J. 1991. Economic growth in a cross section of countries. *Quarterly Journal of Economics* 56: 407–43.

Barro, Robert J., and Xavier Sala-i-Martin. 1992. Convergence. *Journal of Political Economy* 100: 223–51.

Benhabib, Jess, and Boyan Jovanovic. 1991. Growth accounting and externalities. *American Economic Review* 81: 82–113.

Benhabib, Jess, and Mark M. Spiegel. 1992. Growth accounting with physical and human capital accumulation. C. V. Starr Center Working Paper no. 91–66. New York University.

Dollar, David. 1991. Convergence of South Korean productivity on West German levels, 1966–1978. *World Development* 19 (2/3): 263–74.

Graham, John, and Roy Webb. 1979. Stocks and depreciation of human capital: New evidence from a present-value perspective. *Review of Income and Wealth* 25: 209–24.

Kendrick, John W. 1976. *The formation and stock of total capital.* New York: Columbia University Press.

Kyriacou, George. 1991. Level and growth effects of human capital. C. V. Starr Center Working Paper no. 91–26. New York University.

Lucas, Robert. 1988. On the mechanics of economic development. *Journal of Monetary Economics* 22: 3–42.

———. 1993. Making a miracle. *Econometrica* 61: 251–72.

Miller, E. M. 1983. Capital aggregation in the presence of obsolescence-inducing technical change. *Review of Income and Wealth* 29: 283–96.

Pilat, Dirk. 1993. The economics of catch up: The experience of Japan and Korea. Groningen Growth and Development Centre Monograph no. 2. University of Groningen.

Pyo, Hak K. 1992. A synthetic estimate of the national wealth of Korea, 1953–1990. KDI Working Paper no. 9212. Seoul: Korea Development Institute.

———. 1993. A comparative analysis of national wealth: Korea with Japan and the United States. Paper presented at the Allied Social Science Associations, Anaheim, Calif., January 5–7.

Rebelo, Sergio. 1991. Long-run policy analysis and long-run growth. *Journal of Political Economy* 99: 500–21.

Romer, Paul. 1986. Increasing returns and long-run growth. *Journal of Political Economy* 94: 1002–37.
———. 1990. Endogenous technological change. *Journal of Political Economy* 98: S71–S102.
Solow, Robert M. 1956. A contribution to the theory of economic growth. *Quarterly Journal of Economics* 70: 65–94.
Stokey, Nancy L. 1991. Human capital, product quality and growth. *Quarterly Journal of Economics* 106: 587–616.
Summers, R., and A. Heston. 1988. A new set of international comparisons of real product and price levels, estimates for 130 countries, 1950–1985. *Review of Income and Wealth* 34: 1–25.
Szirmai, A., and D. Pilat. 1990. Comparisons of purchasing power, real output and labor productivity in manufacturing in Japan, South Korea and U.S.A., 1975–1985. *Review of Income and Wealth* 36 (1): 1–31.
Tamura, R. 1991. Income convergence in an endogenous growth model. *Journal of Political Economy* 99: 522–40.
You, J., and H. Chang. 1991. New growth theory: A critical assessment with a special reference to the question of convergence (in Korean). *Korean Economic Journal* 30: 691–711.

Comment Geoffrey Carliner

The final conclusion which Hak Pyo makes in his paper is certainly correct, that evidence from time-series data on two countries is too fragile to test the convergence hypothesis. It does not require a sophisticated model to see that Korea's per capita output, physical capital stock, human capital stock, and productivity have been converging to U.S. levels with amazing speed. However the differences between the two economies are still so large that we would not want to estimate a date of convergence or overtaking, or even whether it will happen, based on the two countries' experiences over the past 35 years. It is impossible to know if Korea will be able to sustain its extraordinary rates of increase in physical and human capital, or what will happen to changes in total factor productivity as the Korean economy continues to grow.

Furthermore, the annual time-series data which Pyo uses to estimate his production functions also do not seem well suited to answering questions about convergence, since much of the movement in dependent and independent variables is due to cyclical factors rather than long-run growth. This may explain some of his results. The coefficients on human capital are not at all robust in different specifications. The increasing returns to all factors found for the United States in the unconstrained equations hardly seems consistent with low U.S. productivity growth. In any case, this finding is not repeated in the other regressions.

Geoffrey Carliner is executive director of the National Bureau of Economic Research.

Pyo observes that not all developing countries can make use of human capital as a productive input. This is supported by Helliwell (1994), who finds that high levels of human capital did not help Sri Lanka or the Philippines to grow rapidly, and low levels did not prevent Pakistan, Indonesia, and Thailand from achieving relatively high growth. Helliwell concludes that openness and investment in physical capital contributed more to rapid growth in Asia than investment in education. Perhaps inappropriate employment or education policies can sharply lower the social return on human capital.

Topel and Kim (1992) provide a more detailed look at Korean labor markets and human capital. During the 20 years they examine, the Korean economy has undergone a very rapid transformation out of agriculture into manufacturing, and from unskilled low-tech industries to higher-skilled medium and even high-tech industries. In spite of the greatly increased demand for educated labor which these shifts imply, Topel and Kim find that Korean wage differentials by education have been falling over time. This presumably is the result of the 10+ percent annual increase in the stock of human capital, estimated elsewhere by Pyo (1992). Korea's achievement in maintaining or decreasing its wage inequality while growing at a very high rate and transforming its economy is certainly remarkable.

Another recent study of Korea's path to convergence toward developed country levels of output and productivity is Young (1994). He finds that most of Korea's growth has been due to shifts from low- to high-productivity sectors, massive investment in physical and human capital, and an increase in the labor force. Although increases in total factor productivity also contributed to Korea's growth, it played a smaller role than these other factors.

References

Helliwell, John. 1994. International growth linkages: Evidence from Asia and the OECD. In *Macroeconomic linkage: Savings, exchange rates, and capital flows,* ed. T. Ito and A. O. Krueger, 7–28.

Pyo, Hak K. 1992. A synthetic estimate of the national wealth of Korea, 1953–1990. KDI Working Paper no. 9212. Seoul: Korea Development Institute.

Topel, Robert, and Dae-Il Kim. 1992. Labor markets and economic growth: Lessons from Korea's industrialization, 1970–1990. Manuscript.

Young, Alwyn. 1994. The tyranny of numbers: Confronting the statistical realities of the east Asian growth experience. NBER Working Paper no. 4680. Cambridge, Mass.: National Bureau of Economic Research.

Comment Shin-ichi Fukuda

Hak K. Pyo has presented a very interesting paper. Instead of using cross-country data, Pyo used time-series data for South Korea and the United States and tested the role of human capital in economic growth. The comparison of the results for South Korea and the United States showed several differences in the role of human capital between the two countries and has several significant implications for economic development. I have four comments.

My first comment is on the over-time stability of the estimated coefficients. Assuming the Cobb-Douglas production function, the paper estimated the one-sector growth model with human capital as one of the inputs. The approach is standard. However, when we consider the economic growth of developing countries, this approach may be misleading. For example, in the case of Japan, labor-intensive textiles were one of the main products in the early stage of postwar economic growth. Thus, in this stage, the coefficient of log labor input was very large when we estimated equations like equations (1a) and (5a). However, the share of the labor-intensive textile industry gradually declined as the Japanese economy sustained its high rate of growth. Instead, the capital-intensive steel industry and, more recently, the capital-intensive electronic and automobile industries became the main ones in the most recent stage of Japanese economic development. Thus, as a consequence of high economic growth, the coefficient of log labor input became smaller in Japan. The situation is probably quite similar in Korea, implying the possibility of biased estimations in the paper.

In fact, if we look at table 9.1, we can easily see that the growth rates of per capita physical capital and per capita human capital are very high in Korea. Of course, this result is consistent with the capital accumulation process in the one-sector growth model. However, it also implies the possibility that the leading industry in South Korea changed from a labor-intensive one to a capital-intensive one. This is a testable hypothesis, which is possibly correct. One way of testing the hypothesis is to check the time-series property of the wage-rental ratio. This is because, under a standard Cobb-Douglas production function, the wage-rental ratio is proportional to the capital-labor ratio when the factor markets are competitive.

My second comment is on human capital measurement errors. Following the method of Kendrick, the paper carefully estimated human capital stocks based on a cumulative accounting of past investment in human tangibles (rearing costs) and intangibles (education, health, and mobility costs). The estimates will be a good proxy variable for some kind of human capital. However, the estimates are not sufficient in that they have difficulty capturing accumulation of human capital through on-the-job training. In the stage of economic

Shin-ichi Fukuda is associate professor at the Institute of Economic Research, Hitotsubashi University.

development considered here, human capital accumulation through on-the-job training is very important and deserves to be taken into account.

In addition, the estimates of human capital in the paper probably neglect the accumulation of knowledge by imitating foreign technology. In a closed economy model, we do not need to take into account this kind of human capital accumulation. However, since the export-oriented economic growth of South Korea is well known, human capital accumulation through imitating foreign technology is much more relevant in South Korea than in the United States. Thus, in comparing the role of human capital between the two countries, we have to pay more attention to different styles of human capital accumulation.

My third comment is on the econometric methods in the paper. Except for the estimates in table 9.4, Pyo ran regressions without differencing the raw data. However, it is quite possible that the levels of output, capital, and labor have unit roots. If so, the estimated t-value will be biased and the standard hypothesis test cannot be applied. In fact, if we look at the Durbin-Watson statistics in the regressions, we can easily see that they are very low in tables 9.2 and 9.3. Furthermore, the AR(1) coefficients of the disturbance terms are very close to one for South Korea, implying the high possibility of unit root problems in the analysis.

In addition to the unit root problems, the estimations in the paper may be subject to the multicollinearity problem. For example, if we look at table 9.1, we can easily see that the independent variables (i.e., physical capital, human capital, and labor input) are highly correlated with each other. If the multicollinearity problem exists, a slight change of the model specification drastically changes the estimates of the regressions. In fact, some parameter estimates of the growth accounting equations for South Korea in table 9.4 (say, a negative coefficient of human capital) are not intuitive, implying the possibility of this multicollinearity problem.

My final comment is on the accumulation of human capital. In the paper, the accumulation process is simply described by equation (6). However, the actual accumulation process of human capital will be more complicated and not automatic. The role of sophisticated government policies is likely to be very important, as is the role of exports. Allowing these elements into the analysis will make the results of the paper more fruitful and comparable to the results of other research.

10 Conditional Convergence in East Asian Countries: The Role of Exports in Economic Growth

Shin-ichi Fukuda and Hideki Toya

10.1 Introduction

One of the main implications of Solow-type neoclassical growth models (Solow 1956) is a notion of "convergence" according to which developing countries grow faster than developed countries given the growth rates of technology and population. In particular, if countries are similar with respect to structural parameters, neoclassical growth models predict that a country's per capita growth rate tends to be negatively related to its starting level of income per person. However, except for the evidence in OECD economies (e.g., Baumol 1986), this convergence hypothesis in neoclassical growth models seems to be inconsistent with various cross-country studies. Moreover, recent endogenous growth models, such as Romer's (1986), show that without diminishing returns to capital, the growth rate of per capita product is independent of the starting level of per capita product.

The purpose of this paper is to investigate whether there is a tendency to convergence in East Asian countries (i.e., the Asian newly industrialized economies [NIEs], the ASEAN countries, and Japan). Our interest in the subject of this paper was originally stimulated by the observation that recent growth in East Asian countries was miraculous. We first present the cross-country evidence that per capita growth rates in East Asian countries have little correlation with the starting level of per capita product even if we allow for the difference in the level of human capital. We then show that, given the export-GDP ratios, subsequent growth rates in East Asian countries are negatively related to the initial level of per capita GDP.

Shin-ichi Fukuda is associate professor at the Institute of Economic Research, Hitotsubashi University. Hideki Toya is a graduate student of economics at Hitotsubashi University.

The authors would like to thank Anne O. Krueger, Koichi Hamada, Sang-Dal Shim, and other conference participants for their helpful comments.

In the previous literature of development economics, a number of studies stressed a special role for exports in economic growth (e.g., Balassa 1978; Krueger 1980; Feder 1982; Edwards 1992). These studies highlighted various beneficial aspects of exports and international trade: greater capacity utilization, resource allocation according to comparative advantage, exploitation of economies of scale, technological improvements and efficient management in response to competitive pressures abroad, and so on. These studies also proposed that, since there are substantial differences in productivities between export-oriented and non–export-oriented industries, countries which have adopted export-oriented policies benefit from closer-to-optimal resource allocation and higher growth (see Edwards 1993 for a survey).

However, in recent studies based on endogenous growth models, the results were mixed on the hypothesis that exports play a special role in economic development. In particular, several theoretical studies showed that the relation between international trade and economic growth was very ambiguous.[1] Even in empirical studies, the cross-country evidence showed that per capita growth rates had little correlation with the export-GDP ratios once the regression included other important variables (see, e.g., Kormendi and Meguire 1985; Levine and Renelt 1992).[2]

Focusing on economic development in East Asian countries, this paper reexamines the role of exports in economic growth models. We show that exports have played a special role in the economic development of East Asian countries. This explains why the role of exports in economic development was ambiguous in previous cross-sectional studies. This result is also consistent with many studies which propose that the successful promotion of exports has been primarily responsible for rapid industrialization in East Asian countries (see, e.g., Park 1988).

In the previous literature, there are several related studies which focused on a unique development pattern of Asian countries based on a recent endogenous growth framework. In particular, Grier and Tullock (1989) and Helliwell (1992) showed that there was little evidence to support the convergence hypothesis in Asian countries. Our result is in marked contrast with these studies in that we support the conditional convergence hypothesis for East Asian countries. That is, once we allow for a special role for exports, our empirical result supports the convergence hypothesis in East Asian countries.

Needless to say, the special role of exports may not be the only important factor explaining East Asian rapid economic development. For example, the increase in foreign direct investment (from, say, Japan) may be another im-

1. While Rivera-Batiz and Romer (1991) showed the positive linkage between international trade and economic growth, several theoretical studies such as Grossman and Helpman (1991) and Young (1991) showed that the relation between international trade and economic growth is very ambiguous (see Roubini and Sala-i-Martin 1991 for a survey).

2. Levine and Renelt (1992) showed that the ratio of exports to GDP is not robustly correlated with growth when investment is included as an explanatory variable.

portant factor in the rapid economic growth. Relatively stable political conditions may be another important source of East Asian growth. This paper does not rule out these possibilities. Instead, our empirical result tries to propose an independent special role for exports, which these other important factors could not play in East Asian economies.

The paper is organized as follows. Section 10.2 presents the cross-country evidence that per capita growth rates in East Asian countries have little correlation with the starting level of per capita product. Section 10.3 shows that, given the export-GDP ratios, subsequent growth rates in East Asian countries are negatively related to the initial level of per capita GDP. Section 10.4 investigates the role of government in East Asian economic development. Section 10.5 explores the ability of our model to predict East Asian rapid economic growth in the 1980s. Section 10.6 summarizes our main results and discusses their implications.

10.2 The Weak Convergence Tendency

This section examines whether the convergence hypothesis in neoclassical growth models has held in East Asia over the last few decades. A basic equation we estimate is the following:

$$(1)\qquad \mathrm{GYP}_{it} = a_1 * \mathrm{RYO}_{it} + a_2 * \mathrm{AD}_i * \mathrm{RY0}_{it} + b * \mathrm{INV}_{it} + c * \mathrm{GN}_{it},$$

where GYP is the growth rate of real per capita income, RY0 is log of the initial level of (Summers-Heston) per capita real income, INV is the log of the share of investment in GDP, and GN is the log of the rate of population growth plus 0.05.[3] AD_i is the East Asian dummy, which is one when country i is one of the nine East Asian countries and zero otherwise. The nine East Asian countries are Hong Kong, Indonesia, Japan, Korea, Malaysia, the Philippines, Taiwan, Thailand, and Singapore.

Except for the use of an East Asian coefficient dummy for the initial level of per capita real income, this type of linear regression with three explanatory variables has been quite common in recent studies of endogenous economic growth (e.g., Barro 1991; Fischer 1991; Mankiw et al. 1992; and Levine and Renelt 1992). We estimated this basic equation by three alternative data sets: cross-sectional and pooled data sets based on the real national accounts constructed by Summers and Heston (1988, 1990), and a pooled data set based on the *International Financial Statistics* (*IFS*) of the International Monetary Fund. In the cross-sectional data sets, we included almost all of the world other than centrally planned economies. In pooling the data, we used five-year averaged data for G7 and East Asian countries. See the data appendix for details.

3. The number 0.05 follows Mankiw, Romer, and Weil (1991).

Table 10.1 Tests of the Convergence Hypothesis in East Asia

Variable	SH-A	SH-B	IFS-B
Constant	0.037	−0.012	0.029
	(1.191)	(−0.167)	(0.418)
RY0	−0.005	−0.006	−0.010
	(−2.574)	(−1.472)	(−2.825)
AD*RY0	0.003	0.002	0.002
	(5.236)	(2.993)	(1.948)
INV	0.022	0.015	0.029
	(6.802)	(1.967)	(3.319)
GN	−0.021	−0.037	−0.045
	(−1.927)	(−1.365)	(−1.899)
Adjusted R^2	0.517	0.230	0.376

Notes: SH-A is a cross-sectional regression of 99 countries based on the Summers-Heston data set. SH-B and IFS-B are pooled regressions of G7 and East Asian countries based on the Summers-Heston data set and *IFS*, respectively. Numbers in parentheses are t-values.

Table 10.1 summarizes our regression results. Except for the estimates of a_2, all estimates were consistent with previous studies and most were significant. In particular, regardless of the choice of data set, the estimates of a_1 were negative; that is, there was evidence of strong convergence in the world economy. However, the estimates of a_2 were significantly positive in all cases. This implies that even if we allow for the rate of investment and population growth, there is a much weaker tendency to convergence in East Asian countries.

The basic results do not change even if we allow for human capital, which plays an important role in most recent endogenous growth models. We ran a regression for the following equation:

$$(2) \qquad \mathrm{GYP}_{it} = a_1 * \mathrm{RY0}_{it} + a_2 * \mathrm{AD}_i * \mathrm{RY0}_{it} + b * \mathrm{INV}_{it} + c * \mathrm{GN}_{it} + d * \mathrm{HC}_i,$$

where HC is the investment rate for human capital, which is proxied by the log of the secondary school enrollment rate (see the data appendix for details about HC_i).

Except for the use of an East Asian coefficient dummy, the estimated equation is essentially the same as that estimated in Barro (1991) and Mankiw et al. (1992). A higher school enrollment rate means a higher accumulation of human capital. Thus, if higher human capital means higher economic growth, a higher school enrollment rate may lead to higher economic growth. Table 10.2 reports the regression results. Inclusion of a proxy for human capital substantially improved the fit of the model, especially the significance level of the negative coefficient of RY0. However, the estimates of a_2 were still significantly positive in all cases, implying much weaker convergence in East Asian

Table 10.2 **Tests of the Convergence Hypothesis Given the Level of Human Capital**

Variable	SH-A	SH-A	SH-B	SH-B	IFS-B	IFS-B
Constant	0.074	0.074	0.067	0.073	0.044	0.048
	(2.251)	(2.239)	(0.844)	(0.908)	(0.632)	(0.729)
RY0	−0.009	−0.009	−0.010	−0.011	−0.010	−0.015
	(−3.784)	(−3.772)	(−2.387)	(−2.435)	(−2.826)	(−3.872)
AD*RY0	0.003	0.003	0.002	0.003	0.002	0.004
	(4.054)	(1.041)	(3.032)	(2.437)	(2.297)	(3.613)
INV	0.019	0.019	0.017	0.013	0.028	0.029
	(5.797)	(5.745)	(2.291)	(1.611)	(3.182)	(3.494)
GN	−0.025	−0.025	−0.029	−0.024	−0.041	−0.053
	(−2.329)	(−2.321)	(−1.076)	(−0.882)	(−1.684)	(−2.251)
HC	0.006	0.006	0.011	0.003	0.005	−0.006
	(2.795)	(2.781)	(2.058)	(0.232)	(1.314)	(−1.022)
AD*HC		0.002		0.011		0.022
		(0.243)		(0.884)		(2.724)
Adjusted R^2	0.531	0.526	0.259	0.257	0.381	0.426

Notes: SH-A is a cross-sectional regression of 98 countries based on the Summers-Heston data set. SH-B and IFS-B are based on the same data sets as in table 10.1. Numbers in parentheses are *t*-values.

countries. Furthermore, the essential result did not change even if we added an East Asian coefficient dummy on the human capital variable.[4]

In previous studies such as Barro (1991) and Mankiw et al. (1992), it was shown that, once we allowed for differences in human capital, the cross-country evidence supported the convergence hypothesis in neoclassical growth models. Our result is in marked contrast with these previous studies because the data still showed little supporting evidence for the convergence hypothesis given the level of human capital. The following sections explore why the data do not support the convergence hypothesis in East Asian countries.

10.3 Exports and Conditional Convergence

In Asian NIES, it is widely believed that the successful promotion of exports has been primarily responsible for rapid industrialization. For example, in Korea, the phenomenal increase in export earnings accounted for about one-third of the increase in output growth between 1955 and 1975. Although the period of rapid economic growth may be different, similar evidence can be found for the other Asian NIES, i.e., Taiwan, Hong Kong, and Singapore. Even in the ASEAN countries, similar evidence is found, conspicuously for Thailand and

4. In the cross-sectional studies based on Summers and Heston's data, Taiwan was excluded from the sample because data on human capital are not available in the data set of Mankiw et al. (1992).

Malaysia in the late 1980s. In these two countries, the growth rate of exports was more than twice as large as the rate of GNP growth between 1987 and 1990. The contribution of exports was less conspicuous in the Philippines and Indonesia. However, even in these countries, the export-GNP ratios were high compared to other developing countries (say, Latin American countries) and they went up steadily in the late 1980s (see table 10.3).

This section examines whether the results indicating weaker convergence in East Asian countries are due to the exclusion of export variable in the regression. We estimated the following equation:

$$\text{GYP}_{it} = a_1 * \text{RY0}_{it} + a_2 * \text{AD}_i * \text{RY0}_{it} + b * \text{INV}_{it} + c * \text{GN}_{it} + e * \text{X}_{it}, \quad (3)$$

where X_{it} is the share of exports in GDP (see the data appendix for details).

We estimated this equation with and without an East Asian coefficient dummy on the share of exports in GDP.[5] Table 10.4 summarizes our regression results. Except for the estimates of a_2, the inclusion of the export variable did not change the basic properties. However, it led to two noteworthy results on the estimates of a_2 and e.

First, the inclusion of the export variable made the estimates of a_2 less significant in all regressions. In particular, when we included an East Asian dummy in the coefficient of the export variable, the estimates of a_2 became far from significant in all cases and were negative in two regressions. This result implies that, given the export-GDP ratios, there is a strong tendency for poor countries to grow faster on average than rich countries, even in East Asia. In other words, given the export-GDP ratios, East Asian countries show conditional convergence, under which their subsequent growth rates are negatively related to their initial level of per capita GDP.

Second, when we included an East Asian dummy in the coefficient of the export variable, the coefficient of the export variable without an East Asian dummy became significantly negative. This result may partly reflect the fact that many Latin American countries experienced a decline of growth rates in spite of export increases in the 1980s. This may also be caused by the data problem that our export variable includes nonmanufactured products. However, since we can significantly reject the hypothesis that the sum of the coefficients of X and AD*X is zero, the total effects of exports on East Asian economic growth were still significantly positive (see T-STAT in table 10.4). Thus, we can see how special a role exports have played in East Asian economic development during the last few decades. We can also make a conjec-

5. In the cross-sectional studies of 98 countries, we also added the coefficient dummy, PD, for exporters of nonfuel primary products and fuels (mainly oil) based on the classification of the World Bank, *World Development Report 1992*. The coefficient of this dummy variable was significantly negative, implying that the exports of nonmanufactured products do not help accelerate the rate of economic growth.

Table 10.3 **Growth Rates of Output and Export**

	Malaysia			Thailand			Indonesia			Philippines		
Year	dY	dEX	EX/Y	dY	dEX	EX/Y	dY	dEX	EX/Y	dY	dEX	EX/Y
1986	1.0	−5.4	51.4	4.8	16.8	26.5	5.7	−7.3	19.5	3.4	15.6	26.3
1987	5.3	23.2	61.6	9.0	25.8	30.0	4.8	40.1	23.9	4.7	12.9	26.6
1988	8.6	18.6	68.1	12.4	31.5	34.2	0.5	14.9	24.4	6.1	21.7	28.2
1989	8.4	20.3	76.7	11.4	23.1	36.5	12.3	20.4	25.4	5.8	15.3	28.5
1990	9.3	17.5	77.3	9.5	15.3	36.8	6.9	20.1	26.4	2.7	12.6	27.9
1991	8.3	17.0	81.8	–	–	–	6.4	18.2	27.4	−1.0	19.7	29.4

Source: IFS.

Notes: dY = rate of real output growth, dEX = rate of export growth, and EX/Y = export as a percentage of output. For real output, we used real GDP for Malaysia and Indonesia, and real GNP for Thailand and the Philippines.

Table 10.3 (continued)

	Korea			Taiwan			Singapore			Hong Kong		
Year	dY	dEX	EX/Y	dY	dEX	EX/Y	dY	dEX	EX/Y	dY	dEX	EX/Y
1986	11.7	25.5	38.6	11.8	27.7	56.7	1.9	−2.4	126.7	10.5	17.1	112.0
1987	11.4	22.3	41.5	11.2	17.8	60.3	9.0	20.7	141.4	13.6	33.9	127.6
1988	10.9	12.6	39.9	7.5	6.6	59.1	10.6	27.1	158.1	8.0	30.3	146.4
1989	6.0	−4.6	34.1	7.1	8.5	58.1	9.0	9.9	153.5	2.8	20.2	155.7
1990	8.8	9.1	37.7	4.9	5.0	56.0	7.8	8.8	149.6	3.2	16.8	164.3
1991	8.1	12.9	29.3	7.0	13.9	57.8	6.5	7.1	148.1	4.1	24.4	182.3

Table 10.4 Tests of the Convergence Hypothesis Given the Export-GDP Ratios

Variable	SH-A	SH-A	SH-B	SH-B	IFS-B	IFS-B
Constant	0.087	0.054	−0.005	−0.045	0.040	0.016
	(2.739)	(1.720)	(−0.064)	(−0.638)	(0.599)	(0.240)
RY0	−0.006	−0.005	−0.008	−0.010	−0.013	−0.014
	(−3.502)	(−2.716)	(−2.052)	(−2.423)	(−3.413)	(−3.656)
AD*RY0	0.002	0.001	0.001	−0.001	0.001	−0.001
	(3.076)	(1.101)	(1.740)	(−0.599)	(0.816)	(−0.859)
INV	0.024	0.024	0.015	0.016	0.029	0.030
	(7.567)	(7.403)	(2.032)	(2.294)	(3.442)	(3.622)
GN	−0.008	−0.019	−0.043	−0.069	−0.051	−0.067
	(−0.753)	(−1.754)	(−1.587)	(−2.389)	(−2.160)	(−2.745)
X	0.015	−0.027	0.012	−0.081	0.013	−0.062
	(1.560)	(−2.375)	(1.648)	(−1.946)	(1.898)	(−1.682)
AD*X		0.050		0.098		0.077
		(3.012)		(2.279)		(2.057)
PD*X	−0.044					
	(−4.162)					
T-STAT		1.871		2.244		2.382
Adjusted R^2	0.586	0.552	0.246	0.283	0.395	0.418

Notes: SH-A, SH-B, and IFS-B are based on the same data sets as in table 10.1. Numbers in parentheses are t-values. T-STAT denotes t-statistics for the hypothesis that the sum of the coefficients of X and AD*X is zero.

ture about why some previous cross-country studies showed mixed evidence on the correlation between growth rates and export-GDP ratios.

10.4 The Role of Government

In recent studies on endogenous growth, the effects of government consumption on the rate of economic growth have been extensively discussed (e.g., Barro 1990). In these studies, it has been shown that an increase in the share of government consumption in GDP has a negative effect on the rate of economic growth. The argument was that government consumption had no direct effect on private productivity, but lowered saving and growth through distortionary effects from taxation.

This section investigates whether including a government consumption variable will change our basic results from the previous sections. We first estimated our basic equation with a government consumption variable but without an export variable. We ran a regression as follows:

$$\text{(4)} \qquad GYP_{it} = a * RY0_{it} + b * INV_{it} + c * GN_{it} + f * GC_{it},$$

where GC_{it} is the share of government consumption in GDP.

We estimated this equation with and without an East Asian coefficient dummy on the share of government consumption in GDP. Table 10.5 summa-

Table 10.5 Role of Government Consumption in East Asia

Variable	SH-A	SH-A	SH-B	SH-B	IFS-B	IFS-B
Constant	0.120	0.082	0.116	0.008	0.120	−0.014
	(3.588)	(2.477)	(2.098)	(0.107)	(2.465)	(−0.192)
RY0	−0.010	−0.008	−0.010	−0.006	−0.013	−0.007
	(−4.476)	(−3.772)	(−2.729)	(−1.353)	(−3.702)	(−1.821)
INV	0.029	0.026	0.018	0.013	0.038	0.025
	(8.712)	(7.803)	(2.447)	(1.733)	(5.157)	(2.811)
GN	−0.016	−0.021	−0.015	−0.038	−0.029	−0.054
	(−1.371)	(−1.881)	(−0.581)	(−1.341)	(−1.287)	(−2.205)
GC	−0.084	−0.064	−0.103	−0.137	−0.028	−0.077
	(−3.923)	(−3.090)	(−1.994)	(−2.563)	(−0.537)	(−1.411)
AD*GC		0.124		0.092		0.119
		(3.579)		(1.983)		(2.337)
Adjusted R^2	0.464	0.524	0.185	0.213	0.349	0.383

Notes: SH-A, SH-B, and IFS-B are based on the same data sets as in table 10.1. Numbers in parentheses are *t*-values.

rizes the regression results. As in previous studies, the government consumption variable without an East Asian coefficient dummy had a significantly negative effect on the rate of economic growth in many cases. However, when we included an East Asian dummy in the coefficient of the government consumption variable, the estimated coefficients of this dummy variable were significantly positive and their absolute values were greater than those of non–East Asian countries in most cases. This result is consistent with the result of Grier and Tullock (1989), implying that an increase in government service was special in East Asian countries and had some positive effects on the rate of economic growth.

The result, however, no longer carried through when we included both export and government consumption variables in the regression. That is, when we estimated the following regression:

$$\text{(5)} \qquad \begin{aligned} GYP_{it} = a * RY0_{it} + b * INV_{it} + c * GN_{it} + e * X_{it} \\ + f_1 * GC_{it} + f_2 * AD_i * GC_{it}, \end{aligned}$$

the estimated coefficient of AD*GC was significant in no case (see table 10.6). Moreover, the effects of other variables, especially the positive effects of exports on East Asian economies, were essentially the same as what had been obtained without government consumption variables.

This suggests that, in East Asian countries, an increase in government service has some positive effects on the rate of economic growth through increasing export-GDP ratios. This interpretation is consistent with the view that most East Asian countries have achieved rapid economic development by export

Table 10.6 **Role of Government Consumption and Exports in East Asia**

Variable	SH-A	SH-A	SH-B	SH-B	IFS-B	IFS-B
Constant	0.129	0.082	0.001	−0.042	−0.001	0.002
	(3.950)	(2.492)	(0.007)	(−0.551)	(−0.007)	(0.025)
RY0	−0.010	−0.007	−0.008	−0.010	−0.011	−0.014
	(−4.909)	(−3.593)	(−1.866)	(−2.225)	(−2.439)	(−2.961)
INV	0.027	0.027	0.014	0.016	0.026	0.030
	(8.509)	(8.020)	(1.891)	(2.117)	(2.920)	(3.302)
GN	−0.008	−0.020	−0.045	−0.065	−0.059	−0.069
	(−0.758)	(−1.868)	(−1.589)	(−2.271)	(−2.394)	(−2.770)
GC	−0.062	−0.048	−0.076	0.011	−0.042	0.075
	(−3.335)	(−2.388)	(−1.185)	(0.150)	(−0.734)	(0.848)
AD*GC	0.066	0.038	0.068	−0.023	0.079	−0.030
	(1.968)	(0.925)	(1.425)	(−0.374)	(1.433)	(−0.358)
X	0.020	−0.024	0.013	−0.072	0.011	−0.064
	(2.372)	(−2.230)	(1.695)	(−1.926)	(1.741)	(−1.454)
AD*X		0.048		0.087		0.079
		(3.571)		(2.337)		(1.729)
PD*X	−0.048					
	(−4.978)					
T-STAT		2.401		1.966		2.2131
Adjusted R^2	0.618	0.573	0.231	0.272	0.398	0.412

Notes: SH-A, SH-B, and IFS-B are based on the same data sets as in table 10.1. Numbers in parentheses are *t*-values. T-STAT denotes *t*-statistics for the hypothesis that the sum of the coefficients of X and AD*X is zero.

promotion policies rather than import substitution policies (see, e.g., Teranishi 1992). It may also indicate that government policies did not function well to promote exports and economic growth outside East Asia.

10.5 East Asian Economic Growth in the Second Half of 1980s

Throughout the 1980s, the rates of economic growth in the NIEs were miraculous. Even in the ASEAN countries, most economies conquered the slowdown of growth in the early 1980s and achieved rapid economic growth in the second half of the 1980s. For most countries, this was not the first time they accomplished such a high level of economic growth. In fact, most East Asian countries achieved a comparably high growth rate in the 1970s. However, from the viewpoint of economic development, the rapid economic growth in the late 1980s had special meaning. This is because, for most East Asian countries, the export-oriented manufacturing industry became dominant in the late 1980s. That is, before the mid-1980s, the main exports of many East Asian countries were primary products and agricultural products. However, in the late 1980s and the early 1990s, manufactured products came to account for more than half of exports in these countries.

Table 10.7 Mean-Square Errors of the Forecasts by Three Equations

Case	Equation without East Asian Dummy	Equation with East Asian Dummy	Equation with Export Dummy
Case 1	3.938	3.340	2.858
Case 2	3.089	2.582	2.230
Case 3	4.427	3.547	3.210
Case 4	3.651	3.042	2.612

Notes: Case 1 = mean-square errors of the forecasts for nine East Asian countries. Case 2 = mean-square errors of the forecasts for East Asian countries except the Philippines. Case 3 = mean-square errors of the forecasts for East Asian countries except Japan. Case 4 = mean-square errors of the forecasts for five ASEAN countries.

The purpose of this section is to explore the ability of our estimated equations in previous sections to predict the economic development of East Asian countries after the mid-1980s. To make the forecasts, we used three types of equations: a basic equation without an East Asian coefficient dummy, a basic equation with an East Asian coefficient dummy, and an equation with an export variable. We made forecasts of the growth rates from 1985 to 1991 in East Asian countries, based on their per capita real GDP in 1985 and the seven-year averaged data of explanatory variables (i.e., investment ratios, population growth rates, and export ratios). The parameter set we used for the forecasts was estimated by the pooled data of G7 and East Asian countries from 1960 to 1991 in the *IFS*.

Table 10.7 summarizes the mean-square errors of the forecasts by the three types of equations. Figure 10.1 also plots the relation between the actual and predicted growth rates for the nine East Asian countries for equations with and without the export variable. Two interesting results were derived from the table and figure. The first was that the mean-square errors in the forecasts with an East Asian coefficient dummy were smaller than those without such a dummy. This result implies that the weaker convergence tendency in East Asian countries still carries through after the mid-1980s. The second was that the mean-square errors were smallest in the forecasts of equation (3) with the export variable. This result is quite consistent with our proposition that exports are the main source of weak convergence in East Asian countries.

During the 1980s, the export structure in most East Asian countries drastically changed. One reason was the "big push" in the demand side. That is, after the Plaza Accord (in September 1985), the Japanese yen appreciated substantially. This appreciation first increased the demand for manufactured products from the Asian NIEs. The appreciation then increased the demand for export-oriented manufactured products from the ASEAN countries, because the

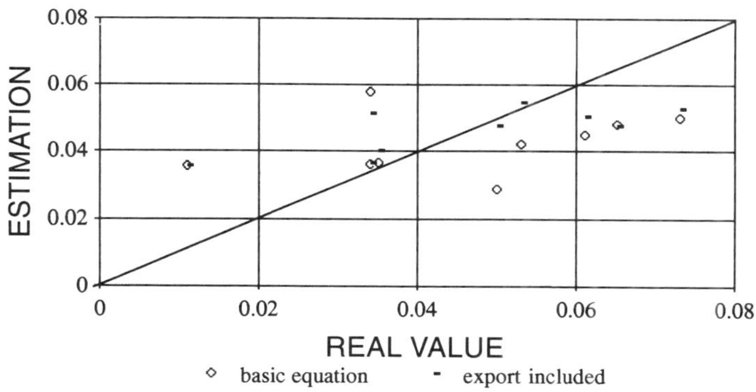

Fig. 10.1 Convergence versus conditional convergence
Note: Estimated values are based on the estimates of equations (1) and (3).

NIEs' currencies also substantially appreciated in the late 1980s. Since this "big push" in the demand side had spillover effects, most East Asian countries achieved rapid economic growth without following the standard steps of endogenous growth models. The above result implies that our basic equation with the export variable clearly tracks such a development process of the East Asian countries in the late 1980s.

10.6 Concluding Remarks

This paper investigated whether there was a tendency to convergence in the East Asian countries (i.e., the Asian NIEs, the ASEAN countries, and Japan) over the last few decades. The paper first presented the cross-country evidence which rejects the strong convergence hypothesis in East Asian countries. Stressing the role of exports in economic growth, the paper then showed that given the export-GDP ratios the cross-country evidence supports the strong conditional convergence hypothesis in East Asian countries.

For the last few decades, the rates of economic growth in East Asia have been miraculous. The result of this paper implies that such miraculous "big push" economic growth is largely attributable to export-oriented economic growth. However, there still remains the question of why East Asian countries achieved export-oriented economic growth but other countries did not. A hint at an answer is the special role of government policy. In section 10.4, we showed that an increase in government service was special in East Asian countries and had some positive effects on the rate of economic growth. As is well known, governments in most East Asian countries have pursued export promotion policies rather than import substitution policies for the last few decades. Investigating the role of such a government policy in detail is an interesting topic for future research.

Appendix

In the text, we ran regressions based on various data sets. The details of the data sets are as follows.

The data on real GDP (if not, GNP) and investment ratios are based on three alternative data sets. The first data set is from the 99 non–oil-exporting country data set in Mankiw et al. (1992), which augmented and implemented the Mark IV data sample described in Summers and Heston (1988). The second data set is from the Mark V data sample described in Summers and Heston (1991). It is composed of five-year averaged data of G7 (i.e., the United States, the United Kingdom, France, Germany, Italy, Canada, and Japan) and East Asian countries from 1960 to 1984 and four-year averaged data of G7 and East Asian countries from 1985 to 1988. The third data set is from the IMF, *International Financial Statistics* (Yearbook) (Washington, D.C., various years) except for Hong Kong and Taiwan. (The data of Hong Kong and Taiwan are taken from the statistical yearbook of each country.) It is composed of five-year averaged data of G7 and East Asian countries from 1960 to 1984 and seven-year averaged data of G7 and East Asian countries from 1985 to 1991.

For the data on human capital, we used two alternative data sets. When we ran a regression based on the data set in Mankiw et al., we used the human capital data in Mankiw et al., which is the percentage of the working-age population that is in secondary school. Data for Taiwan are not available in this set. In other cases, we used the secondary school enrollment rate in 1960, which is available in the World Bank, *World Development Report* (Washington, D.C., various years).

For the data on export-GDP ratios, we used two alternative data sets. In the 99-country cross-sectional regression, the data was taken from Georg P. Muller, *Comparative World Data* (Baltimore: John Hopkins University Press, 1988) (and if not, IMF, *International Financial Statistics* [Yearbook] [Washington, D.C., various years]). In other cases, we calculated the export-GDP ratios based on the IMF, *International Financial Statistics* (Yearbook) (Washington, D.C., various years) by taking the five-year average from 1960 to 1984 and the four- or seven-year average after 1985 of the G7 and East Asian country data.

The data on share of government consumption in GDP are based on three alternative data sets. The first data set is from the 99-country data set in Summers and Heston's Mark V data sample, which is averaged from 1960 to 1985.

The second data set is from Summers and Heston's Mark V data sample, which is composed of the five-year averaged data of G7 and East Asian countries from 1960 to 1984 and the four-year averaged data from 1985 to 1988. The third data set is from the IMF, *International Financial Statistics* (Yearbook) (Washington, D.C., various years), which is composed of the five-year averaged data of G7 and East Asian countries from 1960 to 1984 and the seven-year averaged data from 1985 to 1991.

References

Balassa, B. 1978. Exports and economic growth: Further evidence. *Journal of Development Economics* 5: 181–89.

Barro, R. J. 1990. Government spending in a simple model of endogenous growth, *Journal of Political Economy* 98: 103–25.

———. 1991. Economic growth in a cross section of countries. *Quarterly Journal of Economics* 106: 407–43.

Baumol, W. J. 1986. Productivity growth, convergence and welfare: What the long run data show. *American Economic Review* 76: 1072–85.

Edwards, S. 1992. Trade orientation, distortions and growth in developing countries. *Journal of Development Economics* 39: 31–57.

———. 1993. Openness, trade liberalization, and growth in developing countries. *Journal of Economic Literature* 31: 1358–93.

Feder, G. 1982. On exports and economic growth. *Journal of Development Economics* 12: 59–74.

Fischer, S. 1991. Growth, macroeconomics, and development. In *NBER macroeconomics annual 1991,* ed. O. Blanchard and S. Fischer. Cambridge: MIT Press.

Grier, K. B., and G. Tullock. 1989. An empirical analysis of cross-national economic growth, 1951–1980. *Journal of Monetary Economics* 24: 259–76.

Grossman, G., and E. Helpman. 1991. *Innovation and growth in the global economy.* Cambridge: MIT Press.

Helliwell, J. 1992. International growth linkages: Evidence from Asian and the OECD. NBER Working Paper no. 4245. Cambridge, Mass.: National Bureau of Economic Research.

Kormendi, R. C., and P. G. Meguire. 1985. Macroeconomic determinants of growth: Cross-country evidence. *Journal of Monetary Economics* 16: 141–63.

Krueger, A. 1980. Trade policy as an input to development. *American Economic Review* 70: 288–92.

Levine, R., and D. Renelt. 1992. A sensitivity analysis of cross-country growth regressions. *American Economic Review* 82: 942–63.

Mankiw, N. G., D. Romer, and D. N. Weil. 1992. A contribution to the empirics of economic growth. *Quarterly Journal of Economics* 152: 407–37.

Park, Y.-C. 1988. Korea. In *The open economy,* ed. R. Dornbusch and F. L. C. Helmers. New York: Oxford University Press.

Rivera-Batiz, L. A., and P. M. Romer. 1991. Economic integration and endogenous growth. *Quarterly Journal of Economics* 106: 531–55.

Romer, P. M. 1986. Increasing returns and long-run growth. *Journal of Political Economy* 94: 1002–37.

Roubini, N., and X. Sala-i-Martin. 1991. Financial development, the trade regime, and economic growth. NBER Working Paper no. 3876. Cambridge, Mass.: National Bureau of Economic Research.
Solow, R. 1956. A contribution to the theory of economic growth. *Quarterly Journal of Economics* 70: 65–94.
Summers, R., and A. Heston. 1988. A new set of international comparisons of real product and price levels: Estimations for 130 countries. *Review of Income and Wealth* 34: 1–25.
———. 1991. The Penn World Table (Mark 5): An expanded set of international comparisons, 1950–1988. *Quarterly Journal of Economics* 106: 1–41.
Teranishi, J. 1992. Import substitution policy in Japan's economic development. Discussion Paper Series A, no. 256. Institute of Economic Research, Hitotsubashi University.
Young, A. 1991. Learning by doing and the dynamic effects of international trade. *Quarterly Journal of Economics* 106: 369–405.

Comment Koichi Hamada

This is a neat paper. It is concisely written—I would even say too concisely written to be sufficiently reader-friendly. It requires careful reading.

The Meaning of the Experiment

First, let us consider the meaning of convergence or conditional convergence, and the meaning of the experiments in this paper. I would like to appeal to a modified version of the Swan diagram indicating the relationship between the natural rate of growth and actual economic growth. Rigorously, there is a problem because the natural rate of growth below is defined as a specific type of technical progress—labor-augmenting technical progress. However, as long as most current empirical analysis is conducted by the extensive use of the Cobb-Douglas production function, I think the simplification is justified because in such a world every kind of technical progress can be reduced to labor-augmenting technical progress.

In figure 10C.1, the capital/output ratio is measured on the horizontal axis. This can be regarded as positively related to the income level under a given technology. On the vertical axis, the growth rates of capital and income are measured. The growth rate of labor is given the natural rate of growth, which may be exogenous or endogenous. The growth rate of capital is given in a Solow growth model by

$$\dot{K}/K = (S^Y)/K = S(K/Y)^{-1},$$

Koichi Hamada is professor of economics at the Economic Growth Center, Yale University.

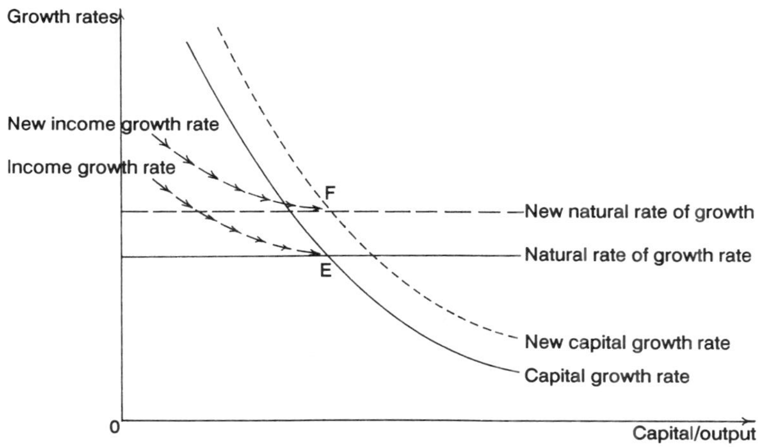

Fig. 10C.1 Conditional and unconditional convergence

where *K, L, Y,* and *S* are, respectively, capital, labor, income, and the propensity to save.

Or, in a Cass-Koopmans optimizing growth model, as well as in the modern endogenous growth model, the growth rate of capital is implicitly given by the Euler equation:

$$\dot{\lambda}/\lambda = -(r - \delta),$$

where λ, r, and δ are the marginal utility of consumption, the rate of interest, and the rate of time preference, respectively. The growth rate of income is given by the convex combination of the growth rate of capital and the natural rate of growth.

In a simple growth model, E is the equilibrium. As the arrows indicate, the growth rate is correlated negatively with the initial level of income. Suppose the natural rate of growth is exogenously given and, in some circumstances, common to all the countries. Then, *the higher* the initial capital-output ratio, *the lower* the income growth rate. This is the case of *unconditional* convergence.

In an endogenous growth model—or some version of the neoclassical growth model with learning by doing and embodied technical progress—the natural rate of growth is affected by investment in physical and human capital. Suppose investment or export rises, then the natural rate of growth will move upward. Government consumption spending may move the natural rate of growth downward. The capital accumulation path depicted by the Euler equation can also be affected in turn by the shift of the natural rate of growth. The growth path will shift from the lower set of arrows to the upper and to a new equilibrium F.

Thus, triggering factors such as equipment investment, government consumption, and investment in human capital have two effects: the effect on the equilibrium rate of growth and the effect on the adjustment path (see fig. 10C.1). If one adjusts the effects of the triggering factors, one can still see the negative correlation between initial income level and rate of growth during the adjustment. This is the case of conditional convergence.

Since the effect of these factors is a combination of the long-run effect on the level of the growth rate and the short-run effect on the adjustment process, the statistical results should be interpreted very carefully. The cross-country comparison of average growth rates over a substantial time span can be interpreted as the long-run effect, but the results of time-series regression contain both kinds of effects. Therefore the result of Fukuda's analysis by pooling time-series and cross-country data needs careful evaluation, because the pooled data trace segments of the convergence process. The only case in which the paper avoids this identification problem completely is the case of the effect of human capital. There, since Fukuda uses only the initial level of human capital—he should be more explicit about it—its effect should be viewed as the effect in the long run.

The Interpretation of the Empirical Results

We shall briefly examine the meaning of the empirical results.

Equations (1) and (2) seem to indicate that convergence is weaker in Asian countries. Dependence on the initial level of income is weak there. Does this mean that the Asian economy is more dynamic than other regions of the world, and that the enduring effects of triggering factors are stronger in East Asia?

In interpreting equation (3), the author claims that it "explains why the role of exports in economic development was ambiguous in previous cross-sectional studies." The explanation is given in section 10.3, but it is just an explanation of statistical reasons and falls short of the clarification of the underlying economic mechanism.

The author states that the estimation results of equations (4) and (5) "suggests that, in East Asian countries, an increase in government service has some positive effects on the rate of economic growth through increasing export-GDP ratios." This is an interesting interpretation but does not seem to be a definite implication derived from the results.

I will not repeat my characterization of the whole exercise as producing black boxes that I mentioned in my comments on Krueger's paper (chap. 1 in this volume): The results are informative, but the clarification of the economic mechanism is missing. Rather I will conclude with two questions:

Is the in-sample comparison of the accuracy in forecasts between equations that have different degrees of freedom a fair comparison? Does an equation with an additional dummy not have an advantage in such a comparison?

Figure 10C.1 is easier to grasp if the actual values are on the vertical axis so that the vertical deviation is the forecasting error. Each point should be identified by a country name. Does this figure suggest that Asian countries have been moving toward more nonconvergence?

11 Explaining Miracles: Growth Regressions Meet the Gang of Four

William Easterly

11.1 Introduction

Like everyone else, economists find success irresistible. The spectacular success of the East Asian economies has attracted a huge literature to explain the success and to examine the prospects for imitation by others. The leading actors in this development drama are the four most successful of the East Asian less developed countries (LDCs): Hong Kong, Korea, Singapore, and Taiwan—known by such encomiums as the Gang of Four, the Four Dragons, the Four Tigers, the Asian miracles, and the newly industrialized countries (NICs). The Four have been used to support each development school's favorite prescriptions, ranging from free market outward orientation to aggressive trade intervention.[1]

It is obvious why the story of the Four is so tantalizing: if only their success could be understood and replicated in other LDCs, the development problem would be solved. The metaphors for the Four recognize that replication is not

William Easterly is principal economist in the Policy Research Department of the World Bank.

The author has benefited from comments by Anne Krueger, Takatoshi Ito, T. N. Srinivasan, and other participants in the NBER East Asian Seminar, from comments by Michael Bruno, Howard Pack, John Page, and other participants in the East Asian Miracle Conference, Stanford University, October 25–26, 1993, from discussions with Lant Pritchett, and from comments and research assistance by Mary Hallward. Views expressed here are not necessarily those of the World Bank.

1. The case for market-friendly and outward-oriented policies is made by Balassa (1991), Krueger (1985, 1990), Thomas and Wang (1993), Chenery (1988), World Bank (1993b), and numerous others. The case for intervention ("getting prices wrong") is made in varying degrees by Amsden (1989, 1991) and Wade (1989, 1990). Somewhere in the middle are Kihwan and Leipziger (1992), Pack and Page (1993), Pack and Westphal (1986), Page and Petri (1993), Stiglitz (1992), and World Bank (1993a). Other authors stress education (Birdsall and Sabot 1993), stable real exchange rates (Kim 1985; Balassa 1978), political stability (Hofheinz and Calder 1982; Haggard 1989, 1990), low inequality (Krueger 1990; Haggard 1989), macroeconomic stability (Collins 1990; Nam 1988), foreign investment (Romer 1993; Parry 1988), and Confucian culture (Kahn 1979; MacFarquhar 1980).

so easy. "Miracles" are unique (the Red Sea was parted *once*); "tigers" are an endangered species. As Lucas (1993) says, "simply advising a society to 'follow the Korean model' is a little like advising an aspiring basketball player to 'follow the Michael Jordan model.' "

Nevertheless, economists find it much more appealing to study what the successes did right than what failures did wrong: from 1969 to the present there have been 717 articles on Singapore in economics journals.[2] On the Central African Republic, a country of similar population size but opposite performance, the number of articles over this period was: 1. It is not really clear why large positive outliers should contain more information than large negative outliers.

The alternative to case studies is to examine the entire range of cross-sectional variation of performance and policies for evidence on what distinguishes successes from failures. This approach was already well established in the development literature (e.g., the large literature on exports and economic growth of Balassa 1978, Feder 1983, and others), but has taken on truly mammoth proportions with the advent of the "new growth literature" inspired by Romer (1986). Numerous empirical studies have examined the relationships between policies and growth predicted by "new" growth models as well as by extended "old" growth models. The studies show strong associations between country characteristics and growth (e.g., Barro 1991), although these relationships are very sensitive to the choice of right-hand-side control variables (Levine and Renelt 1992).

A natural exercise is to examine to what extent this large empirical literature can explain the success of the Four.[3] The Four's per capita growth rates of around 6 percent will be among the largest outliers in any study of growth. This is not surprising: the Four Tigers are Tigers *because* their growth rates were high.[4] This sample selection problem bedevils the analysis of the Gang of Four: we cannot say *how* special are the Four because they were selected because they *are* special. This paper will examine the place of the Four in growth regressions keeping in mind this selection problem. The Four generally have large positive residuals in growth regressions, but this paper will argue that this is not surprising for observations that were known in advance to be at the top of the sample. Growth regressions and, more generally, quantitative measures of "policies" are not very successful at picking out the Four as most likely to succeed.

2. These numbers are taken from the number of references generated by a search request for the country's name in EconLit, the CD-ROM index of articles in economics journals, issued by the *Journal of Economic Literature.*

3. I have benefited from the similar exercise of Barro and Lee (1993) in identifying the best and the worst in economic growth.

4. The others that are ranked as high as the Four are Malta and Japan in the Barro exercise and Botswana and Yemen in the Levine-Renelt data. Japan is not in the Gang of Four because it has a separate, reverential status; Botswana, Malta, and Yemen are presumably less celebrated because they are tiny, not in a coherent region, and/or subject to peculiar circumstances.

Table 11.1 **A Report Card for the Gang of Four, 1960–85 (110 observations)**

Indicator	Hong Kong	Korea	Singapore	Taiwan
Per capita growth (1960–85) higher than:	99	98	100	95
Fitted value of per capita growth from Barro regression higher than:	94	75	99	86
Growth residual from Barro regression higher than:	97	98	99	94
Magnitude of growth residual	2.66	2.91	3.02	2.06
Primary enrollment (1960) higher than:	56	58	91	63
Secondary school enrollment (1960) higher than:	65	71	76	72
Share of government consumption in GDP (1960–85) lower than:	100	61	91	18
Deviation of investment deflator from United States (1960) lower than:	48	16	39	49
Revolutions and coups (1960–85) lower than:	100	19	100	64
Assassinations per capita (1960–85) lower than:	100	36	100	38
Initial per capita income (1960) lower than:	29	73	28	71

Source: Barro (1991).

Note: Table gives percentile rankings of Gang of Four for variables in growth regression, where 100 is the most favorable for growth.

The second, related issue to be examined is to what extent omitted, country-specific fixed factors explain the success of the Dragons. This is the same as asking how permanent is the success of the Asian miracles. Cross-country evidence will show that large positive residuals like those associated with the Dragons have historically been transitory. The natural conclusion is that the miraculous growth rates of the Dragons are unlikely to continue.

11.2 The Gang of Four in Growth Regressions

We examine in this section how the Gang of Four enter into growth regressions. We take two well-known empirical studies as a point of departure: Barro (1991) and Levine and Renelt (1992) (the latter unfortunately omits Taiwan). For each regression, we will examine how much the right-hand-side variables are successful in predicting the high growth of the Gang of Four. Equivalently, we will ask whether the Four were as highly ranked in their policies and other country characteristics as they were in their growth rates.

Table 11.1 shows the ranking of the Four in the right-hand-side variables from the Barro (1991) regression. Some of the policy rankings are considerably less than superlative. All of the Four are in the worst half on a measure of price distortion: the deviation of the investment goods price in dollars from the U.S. price. Hong Kong and Singapore have highly stable political systems, but not so Taiwan and Korea. Primary education is exceptional in Singapore, but only slightly above average in the other three. Government consumption is adversely high in Taiwan (whose many public enterprises are notorious for overstaffing and inefficiency—see Liu 1993). Initial income is low in Korea and Taiwan, so that they benefited from the tendency of poor nations to grow faster (Barro and Sala-i-Martin 1992), but Hong Kong and Singapore were relatively rich. Altogether, the predicted value of growth from the right-hand-side variables is among the highest in the sample for Singapore and Hong Kong; Taiwan is less clearly picked out as exceptional, while Korea just barely makes the top quartile. To put it more graphically, there were 27 countries that were predicted to do better than Korea, including such notable nonsuccesses as Guyana, Jamaica, and Uruguay.

All of the Four Tigers have large positive residuals of 2 or 3 percentage points of growth.[5] The positive residuals are unsurprising: observations at the upper end of the sample are likely to have positive residuals. To illustrate this, suppose that growth had been completely random around a constant term. If we had regressed a large sample of such randomly determined growth rates on a constant term, then by definition the four largest growth rates would have the four largest residuals in such a regression. If we have a model with some predictive power, then the countries with the largest growth rates are likely to have above-average values *both* of the predicted value of growth and of the random error term.[6]

Another way of illustrating how poorly predicted is the growth of the Four in this regression is to calculate the probability that a given country will achieve a "miracle," where a miracle is defined as growth greater than 5 percent per capita. There were seven such miracles in the Barro data: Japan, Malta, Gabon, and the Gang of Four. The probability of reaching such a growth rate is calculated as the probability of a sufficiently large realization of the error term such that the fitted value of growth plus the error term is greater than 5 percent.[7] A country with favorable characteristics will need only a small realization of the error term to reach "miraculous" growth rates, while a country with highly unfavorable characteristics would need an improbably high realization to attain a miracle. Again, we see in table 11.2 that the Barro regression is good at picking out the success of Japan and Singapore, less so the success of Hong Kong and Taiwan, and much less so the miracle of Korea.

5. The regression is (t-statistics in parentheses): **Growth 60–85** = .023 (3.3) −.0000055 (−4.8) **Initial income 1960** + .027 (4.87) **Primary enrollment 1960** + .032 (2.80) **Secondary enrollment 1960** −.0035 (−1.67) **Assassinations per capita 60–85** −.0247 (−4.05) **Revolutions and coups 60–85** −.0688 (−2.66) **Government consumption 60–85** −.0063 (−1.26) **Investment price deviation 1960.** 110 observations, R^2 = .502, standard error = .014. The regression differs slightly from that reported in Barro (1991) because the sample is larger.

6. The lower the predictive power (the lower the R^2) of the growth regression, the larger is the expected magnitude and rank of the residual for the countries that have the largest growth rates in the sample. The expected value of the residuals of the countries with the largest growth rates is always positive for any R^2 less than one.

7. The t-distribution is used for the probability distribution of the residual divided by the standard error of the regression.

Table 11.2 **Probability of Country Attaining a Miracle**

Country	Probability (%)
Most probable	
Japan	**59.98**
Singapore	**34.62**
Malta	**30.95**
Cyprus	29.73
Greece	27.31
Guyana	24.45
Portugal	23.81
Hong Kong	**23.49**
Finland	22.86
Belgium	20.41
France	20.24
Mauritius	18.78
Jamaica	18.57
Malaysia	17.07
Paraguary	16.90
Taiwan	**16.84**
Ireland	15.60
Iceland	15.29
Brazil	14.30
Barbados	12.61
Sri Lanka	11.95
Gabon	**11.82**
Spain	11.27
Austria	11.06
Netherlands	10.35
Germany	9.51
Uruguay	8.98
Korea	**8.80**
Least probable	
Sudan	0.01
Ethiopia	0.00
Angola	0.00
Chad	0.00

Source: Barro (1991).

Note: A "miracle" is defined as greater than 5 percent per capita growth, 1960–85. Actual "miracles" are shown in boldface.

Interpreting Korea's high residual literally is an interesting thought experiment. According to table 11.2, Korea had only about a 1 in 11 chance of attaining the miraculous growth rates that it in fact attained. There would then be nothing special about Korea—it would just be the economy that got lucky out of a larger set of countries with good but not great economic policies. These odds of a miracle still reflect relatively favorable conditions for growth in Korea; by contrast, Chad—with adverse characteristics for growth, to put it

Table 11.3 Another Report Card for the Gang of Four

Indicator	Hong Kong	Korea	Singapore
Per capita growth (1960–89) (World Bank) higher than:	97	98	99
Fitted value from Levine-Renelt regression higher than:	84	87	99
Residual from Levine-Renelt regression higher than:	98	99	92
Magnitude of growth residual	3.13	3.23	1.69
Investment/GDP (1960–89) higher than:	92	80	100
Population growth (1960–89) lower than:	59	65	69
Initial income (1960) lower than:	30	63	36
Secondary enrollment (1960) higher than:	64	70	75

Source: Levine and Renelt (1992).

Note: Table gives percentile rankings of Gang of Four for variables in growth regressions, where 100 is the most favorable for growth.

mildly—had only a 1 in 100,000 chance of attaining "miraculous" growth. The "luck" view would accord with some of the new theoretical views of growth that stress multiple equilibria: countries with very similar characteristics could have widely divergent outcomes.[8]

We could also read the failure of the growth regression to pick out the Gang of Four as yet another indictment of cross-sectional growth regressions. As in the old growth models, the residual is a measure of our ignorance. We might hope that other plausible specifications would drastically reduce the large error term. There are, however, two reasons why this is unlikely. One is that, as we will see in the next section, the feasible R^2 that one can attain with permanent country characteristics in cross-sectional regressions is bounded by the high time-series instability of growth rates. The other, as we will see now, is that other specifications do not appreciably improve our ability to explain cross-country variation in general or the Gang of Four in particular.

The other predetermined specification we examine is the core regression of Levine-Renelt (1992), which was found to be reasonably robust.[9] Table 11.3 shows how the Four (actually the Three, since Taiwan is omitted from the sample) rank according to the right-hand-side variables of this regression. The

8. Among the many examples of models with multiple equilibria: Krugman (1991), Becker, Murphy, and Tamura (1990), and Kremer (1993). The development literature has long described mechanisms for virtuous and vicious circles. Birdsall and Sabot (1993) use the virtuous circle metaphor to describe self-reinforcing processes of rising education, fertility decline, and rapid growth in East Asia.

9. The regression, which is reproduced exactly as in the original source except for scale factors, is (t-statistics in parentheses): **Per capita growth 60–89** = −.0083 (−0.98) −0.385 (−1.72) **Population growth 60–89** + .174 (6.53) **Investment/GDP 60–89** + .032 (2.46) **Secondary Enrollment 1960** −.0035 (−2.52) **GDP per capita 1960.** 102 observations, R^2 = .463, standard error = .0139.

Table 11.4 A Final Report Card for the Gang of Four

Indicator	Hong Kong	Korea	Singapore	Taiwan
War casualties per capita (1960–88; EKPS 1993) lower than:	100	100	100	100
Government education spending/GDP higher than:	16	75	41	45
Ratio of consolidated public sector investment/GDP (Easterly and Rebelo 1993) higher than:	3	23	52	72
Ratio of income earned by top 20 percent to income earned by bottom 20 percent (Clarke 1993) lower than:	51	77	65	87
Ratio of trade to GDP (1960–88; Summers and Heston 1985 international prices) higher than:	98	43	99	n.a.
Ratio of M2 to GDP (1970; King and Levine 1993) higher than:	n.a.	64	93	n.a.
Average black market premium (1960–89; Fischer 1993) lower than:	100	49	77	99
Central government deficit (Easterly and Rebelo 1993) lower than:	n.a.	77	97	n.a.
Inflation (percentage change in the consumer price index, 1970–88) lower than:	74	42	95	n.a.
Terms of trade gain weighted as percent of GDP (EKPS 1993) higher than:	13	39	5	n.a.
Other performance indicators:				
Ratio of private investment to GDP (1960–88; Easterly and Rebelo 1993) higher than:	98	92	91	58
Percentage rate of decline in under-five mortality rates (1965–85; Sen 1993) higher than:	95	81	93	97
Consumption growth per capita (1960–88; World Bank) higher than:	98	92	90	n.a.

Note: Table gives percentile rankings of Gang of Four for variables in growth regressions, where 100 is the most favorable for growth.

most significant difference from the Barro regression is the addition of investment, where Singapore and Hong Kong outrank most of the world and Korea is also well above average.[10] With investment added, the residual for Singapore is much lower than in the Barro regression. This is reminiscent of the results of Young (1992) that total factor productivity growth (i.e., growth controlling for capital and labor growth) is close to zero in Singapore. Like the Barro regression, the Levine-Renelt regression is fairly successful at picking out Singapore as most likely to succeed, and less so at picking out Hong Kong and Korea. Sixteen countries are predicted to do better than Hong Kong, including Jamaica (again) and Suriname.

To conclude this section, the ranking of the Four Dragons for other variables common in growth regressions are considered. Table 11.4 confirms again that

10. As Levine and Renelt (1992) note, investment is likely to be endogenous and so is less an explanation of high growth than a corollary of it.

the Four generally had policies and other characteristics more favorable for growth than the average, but are by no means as extreme outliers in policies as they are in growth. The Four have completely avoided wars over 1960–89, but here they are tied with the three-quarters of the sample that was also at peace. Government spending on education is low in Hong Kong and unexceptional in the other three. Public investment is very different among the Four: very low in Hong Kong, below average in Korea, and above average in Taiwan. As frequently pointed out, inequality is low in the Four and openness is high. The financial system is exceptionally deep in Singapore and less so in Korea. The black market premium is absent in Taiwan and Hong Kong, but nontrivial in Korea and Singapore. Macroeconomic stability is exceptional in Singapore—low government deficits, low inflation—but not in Hong Kong or Korea.[11] Interestingly, the terms of trade changes in Hong Kong and Singapore have been among the most unfavorable in the world.

The last part of table 11.4 shows other performance indicators. Private investment (either a result or a cause of growth) is exceptionally high in all of the Four *except* Taiwan. The improvement in social indicators—specifically the under-five mortality rate—is among the largest in the sample, with the curious exception of Korea. Consumption growth per capita is not as impressive as overall per capita growth in Korea and Singapore, reflecting again the effect of high rates of capital accumulation. The Four's superiority of performance is not completely robust to other performance indicators.

While the Four Dragons do not seem to be striking outliers according to the right-hand-side variables considered here, there are no doubt other characteristics where they would be found to be exceptional; such characteristics could thus "explain" their high growth. The problem with such explanations is that they are too easy to find. It is not that hard to find characteristics that four countries have in common, such as a "Confucian work ethic" or high population density. Such ex post "explanations" are of dubious value. The advantage of predetermined specifications (like the Barro 1991 and Levine-Renelt 1992) is that they were not chosen specifically to explain the Four Dragons.

Of course, the most obvious trait the Four have in common are that they are in the same region: East Asia. The more recent success of other East Asian economies like China, Thailand, Malaysia, and Indonesia have added to the case for East Asian exceptionalism. However, the selection bias problem may be infecting even our regional definitions. Development textbooks written before the onset of the "East Asia Miracle" used a regional breakdown of Asia/

11. However, macroeconomic instability may be poorly measured by average inflation and average government deficits. Analysis of time series of macroeconomic indicators may uncover other dimensions of the quality of macromanagement (like the response to shocks), and the Four may look more exemplary in such an analysis. Bruno (1993) discusses how, in many non–East Asian middle-income developing economies, "the deep crisis of the 1970s (and even more in the 1980s), and the delayed adjustment to the external shocks, had and must still keep having a very marked effect on long-run growth" (40).

Africa/Latin America (see, e.g., Kuznets 1966, 360–61; Meier 1964, 6; Hagen 1968, 23; Higgins 1959, 10; Enke 1963, 48). The "East Asia" regional definition apparently came into use among development economists after the divergence in growth rates became evident.

Even if East Asia is a coherent geographic region, there are other coherent regional breakdowns that could have been used. The choice of which to use is partly endogenous. For example, East and West Africa could be distinguished, but usually are not because they are not dramatically different in performance. Drawing the boundaries of East Asia is also tricky: Is Myanmar (Burma) included? Is Malaysia? Does economic performance influence where we draw the boundary?

Even if exaggerated by endogenous regional definition, it still seems unlikely that the concentration of success in (East?) Asia occurred by chance. It is surprising that the literature does not make more of this concentration (other than to speculate about cultural or other fixed regional traits supposedly favorable for growth). The alternative explanation to a fixed Asia effect is that success is contagious across borders. DeLong and Summers (1991) tested formally for spatial correlation of residuals in a growth regression, but failed to find any correlation based on physical proximity. However, Chua (1993) presents evidence that spillovers exist from countries' right-hand-side variables (particularly investment) to their neighbors' growth performance.

Contagion seems like a more likely explanation than a fixed Asia effect, for the simple reason that Asia's success is relatively recent. As the next section shows, cross-country evidence suggests that episodes of success are short-lived, and so fixed effects like "cultural predisposition to growth" do not fit the evidence for either regions or countries.

11.3 Is the Dragons' Success Transitory?

A recent paper (Easterly et al. 1993, henceforth EKPS) found that success as measured by rapid growth is surprisingly transitory. The correlation of growth rates across successive decades or even longer periods is only about 0.2 to 0.3, implying that only 20 to 30 percent of cross-country differences in growth rates persist from one decade to the next. Figure 11.1 reproduced from EKPS, shows least squares per worker growth (from Summers and Heston 1991) in 1974–88 against growth in 1960–73. The dotted lines show the medians in each period. Many countries are in the off-diagonal quadrants: successes one period are disappointments the next, and vice versa. The boxes indicate the top and bottom deciles in each period. Only four countries are in the top decile in both periods: Botswana and three of the Gang of Four. The fourth gang member—Hong Kong—just misses out on the top decile in the first period. The Four are notable as consistent performers (with tiny Botswana) in the postwar data.

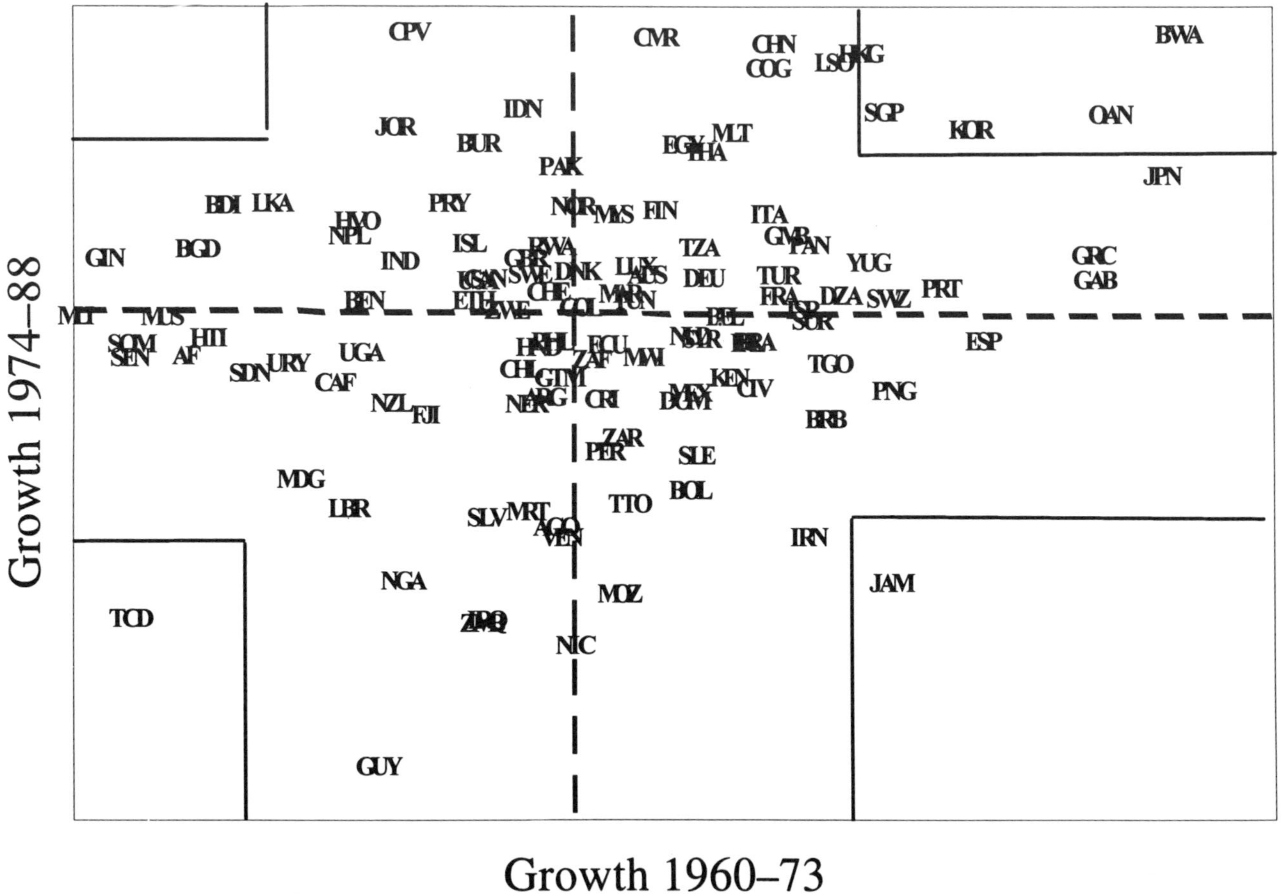

Fig. 11.1 Per capita growth rates, 1960–73 and 1974–88
Note: Three-letter World Bank country codes are used (also used in Summers and Heston 1991).

How unusual is it that four countries would appear in the top decile in two successive periods? EKPS show that the correlation coefficient of growth rates across periods can be interpreted as the ratio of the permanent cross-sectional variance in growth rates to the sum of the cross-sectional variance and the time-series variance in growth rates. A correlation coefficient of growth rates across periods of 0.33 implies that a third of the total variance of growth rates is explained by permanent cross-country differences as opposed to period-to-period variation. EKPS show that this also implies a limit to the R^2 in pure cross-sectional regressions that will be realized with permanent country characteristics on the right-hand side—persistence of 0.33 implies that the upper limit on the R^2 is about 0.6 with cross-sectional regressions covering 30 years. We perform an illustrative Monte Carlo simulation of the variance structure implied by a cross-period correlation of 1/3.[12] Twelve out of 50 simulations show four or more countries in the top decile across successive periods. While not the most likely outcome, it is not all that unusual to find four consistently positive outliers even with relatively small permanent differences in cross-country performance.

Like everyone else, the four NICs cannot count on success lasting very long. The pattern of low persistence of growth rates suggests that their growth is likely to fall in the 1990s.[13]

11.3.1 Before the Miracle: Historical Antecedents for the Four Dragons

While the success of the Four Dragons now seems to have been written in the stars, the Four's promise was not so apparent beforehand. Failure to recognize the low persistence of growth performance often leads to overestimation of the prospects of countries that have been doing well, and the underestimation of countries doing badly.

As table 11.5 shows, the performance of Korea and Taiwan—and of other Asian miracles—was not so stellar before the miracle. None of the later success stories had exceptional growth over the first part of the century (historical growth estimates—which of course should be taken with a grain of salt—are from Maddison 1989).

It is therefore not surprising that most observers before the miracle were pessimistic about East Asia. Enke (1963) presents a table of factors favorable

12. Specifically, we generate a random variable that is the sum of a $N(0,1)$—the cross-country variance—and a $N(0,2)$—the time-series variance. The realization of the cross-country process stays the same between successive periods, while there is a new realization of the $N(0,2)$ each period. The correlation coefficient between the two periods will be 1/3. The simulation was for 120 observations for 100 time periods. We then calculated the number of repeated successes (the same observation twice in the upper decile) for 50 independent pairs of time periods.

13. Other authors also urge caution about the NICs prospects. World Bank (1993a) notes coming infrastructural bottlenecks and the need for financial sector reforms. Krueger (1990) and Balassa and Williamson (1990) argue that continued rapid growth will require greater trade liberalization. Lehmann (1992) suggests that competition from the next tier of NICs will slow down the original Four. Hong (1993) argues that unless tax reforms are instituted in Korea to reduce incentives for speculation and improve distribution, growth will be slowed by internal conflicts and waste of resources.

Table 11.5 Before the Miracle: Historical Statistics on Asian Economies, 1900–50

Country	Per Capita Growth
Dragons	
South Korea	0.10
Taiwan	0.40
Other Asian miracles	
China	−0.30
Indonesia	−0.10
Japan	1.00
Thailand	0.10

Table 11.6 Ranking of Regions in 1963 According to Factors Favorable or Unfavorable for Development

Rank	*Per Capita Income*	*Population Pressure*	*Economic Culture*
Most favorable	Latin America	sub-Sahara Africa	Latin America
	Middle East	Latin America	Middle East
	sub-Sahara Africa	Middle East	sub-Sahara Africa
Least favorable	Southeast Asia	Southeast Asia	Southeast Asia

or unfavorable for development, reproduced here as table 11.6. He ranks four developing regions: Latin America, sub-Sahara Africa (*sic*), Middle East, and Southeast Asia. By the latter, he means all of Asia east of the Middle East and south of Siberia.

Southeast Asia was at the bottom of the list in all three of his categories. It was the poorest region, which was thought to be unfavorable for growth because of the low savings rates (!) of poor countries; it had the highest population pressure; it had the culture most unfavorable for development. The latter is particularly interesting given all that has subsequently been written about the "Confucian ethic" (Kahn 1979; MacFarquhar 1980). Such an ethic was not evident before 1960. An economist in 1952 commented sadly that "the age-long influence of the West . . . failed with only few exceptions to instill its economic activity and enterprise into the minds and habits of these peoples. The Western apparatus of . . . production remained an . . . indigestible element in Southeast Asia . . . the economic energy for a vigorous resurgence [was] lacking."[14]

Nor were the prospects of individual countries clear ex ante. The first World Bank mission to Korea in the early 1960s described the development program as ludicrously optimistic: "There can be no doubt that this development program [GDP growth of 7.1 percent of 1962–66] far exceeds the potential of

14. Quoted in Hoselitz (1952, 215).

the Korean economy. . . . It is inconceivable that exports will rise as much as projected." (In the event, Korean growth was 7.3 percent over that period.) Prominent academic economists also did not detect East Asia's promise. Chenery and Strout forecast in the early 1960s that growth in India and Pakistan over 1962–76 would exceed that of Korea. Rosenstein-Rodan at the same time predicted that Sri Lanka would have a higher per capita income than Taiwan or Korea by 1976. Hong Kong and Singapore, according to the same predictions, would be left in the dust by Argentina and Colombia. Myrdal worried that Singapore "has its own potentially explosive problems [of rapid population growth], which threatens a mounting unemployment burden."[15]

By contrast, the World Bank's economic report in 1957 was optimistic about the Philippines, which had "achieved a position in the Far East second only to Japan. . . . The prospects . . . for sustained long-term growth are good." An even more promising case was Burma, which in 1958 was said by the Bank to have "made remarkable economic progress. . . . Burma's long-run potential compares favorably with those of other countries in South East Asia."[16] (In the event, Burma [Myanmar] and the Philippines have been among the few poor performers in East Asia.)

Asia's prospects looked poor compared to those of Africa, where the World Bank's chief economist in 1967 predicted "the economic future before the end of the century can be bright." He listed seven African countries that "clearly have the potential to reach or surpass a 7 percent rate of growth." All of those he listed had negative per capita growth over 1970–88.[17]

The postwar doubts about Asia's prospects echoed earlier doubts about the most famous Asian success story, Japan. In the nineteenth century, the first Western visitors to Japan held out little hope for the country's future: "Wealthy we do not think it will ever become: the advantages conferred by Nature . . . and the love of indolence and pleasure of the people themselves forbid it. . . . In this part of the world principles, established and recognized in the West, appear to lose whatever virtue and vitality they originally possessed and to tend fatally towards weediness and corruption."[18]

11.3.2 Persistence of the Tigers' Residuals

We have seen that the Four Tigers have large positive residuals in growth regressions, and that their performance has been consistent since 1960. A way of probing deeper into both of these facts is to examine the residuals of the Tigers in pooled cross-section, decade regressions, where each country will have up to three decade-average observations (for the 1960s, 1970s, and 1980s). Regressions will again be run using roughly the Barro (1991) and Lev-

15. The last three predictions are taken from Hicks (1990).

16. The World Bank quotes, including the preceding one on Korea, are taken from World Bank (1993b, 14–15).

17. Kamarck (1967), quoted in EKPS.

18. A quote via Lipton and Sachs (1992, 250).

ine and Renelt (1992) specifications. We will examine the robustness of the results to alternative specifications of the dependent variable: Summers-Heston versus World Bank growth rates, and per capita versus per worker GDP growth rates.

The regressions are reported in the appendix. The "Barro" versions regress decade-average growth rates on time dummies for the 1960s and 1970s, per capita income at the beginning of the decade, primary and secondary enrollment ratios at the beginning of each decade, the average share of government consumption in GDP (decade average), and the decade-average black market premium (which is a substitute for Barro's price distortion variable, since the latter is not available separately for decades). The "Barro" regression uses Summers and Heston (1991) GDP data for two alternative definitions of the dependent variable: least squares per capita growth and least squares per worker growth.[19] The "Levine-Renelt" regression has as right-hand-side variables the investment rate over the decade, secondary enrollment at the beginning of decade, population growth (or labor force growth when per worker growth is the dependent variable), initial per capita income in the decade, and decade dummies. The dependent variable is decade-long least squares growth for either GDP per capita or GDP per worker, using World Bank GDP data.

Table 11.7 shows the resulting residuals for the four alternative specifications. The residuals stay consistently high and positive in the Levine-Renelt regression with per capita growth rates, but somewhat less so in the Barro regression with per capita growth rates. The residuals are more unstable when per worker instead of per capita growth rates are used: Singapore has residuals close to zero for two out of the three decades in both Barro and Levine-Renelt per worker regressions. The other three Tigers also have erratic residuals in the Barro per worker regression.[20]

What is the tendency of residuals to persist for the entire sample? EKPS showed that the low persistence of growth rates is *not* explained by variations in policies or other country characteristics. It follows that the persistence of residuals in pooled growth regressions will be low. In the Barro regression with per worker growth rates, for example, the cross-decade correlation of the residuals is only 0.1 and is statistically insignificant. An equivalent way of stating this low persistence is that residuals for all countries will tend to move back toward zero (i.e., there is regression to the mean, where the mean by construction is zero). With a cross-decade correlation of only 0.1, 1 − 0.1, or

19. The original Barro (1991) regression used the previous version of Summers and Heston (1988). We use the newer one because it goes up to 1988 instead of 1985.

20. Barro and Lee (1993) also show unstable residuals for the Four Tigers in separate regressions for 1965–75 and 1975–85, even using per capita growth rates (based on Summers and Heston 1988—version 4). The particularly low residuals for Singapore in our results are again suggestive confirmation for Young's (1992) conclusion that productivity growth in Singapore was zero. Kim and Lau (1993) fail to reject the hypothesis of zero total factor productivity growth for *all* of the NICs except Taiwan.

Table 11.7 **Growth Residuals of Gang of Four in Pooled Growth Regressions**

Country	1960s	1970s	1980s
Levine and Renelt (1992) Regression with World Bank per Capita Growth Rates			
Hong Kong	2.57	3.98	4.07
Korea	2.02	3.97	3.75
Singapore	2.83	2.24	2.06
Levine and Renelt (1992) Regression with World Bank per Worker Growth Rates			
Hong Kong	1.90	3.35	3.72
Korea	1.86	3.48	4.71
Singapore	2.80	0.19	0.45
Barro (1991) Regression Using Summers-Heston Mark V per Capita Growth Rates			
Hong Kong	3.03	2.70	4.44
Korea	2.17	2.87	3.62
Singapore	0.28	2.06	3.45
Taiwan	1.93	2.33	2.78
Barro (1991) Regression Using Summers-Heston Mark V per Worker Growth Rates			
Hong Kong	2.11	1.35	4.28
Korea	1.28	2.19	2.85
Singapore	−0.43	−0.29	3.85
Taiwan	2.46	1.20	1.68

90 percent of the residual will tend to disappear in the following period.[21] Figure 11.2 shows this as the tendency for the change in the residual from the first to the second decade to be inversely related to the residual in the first decade. We see in the graph that the Four Tigers fit snugly into the overall pattern: the evanescence of the unexplained component of success.[22]

The behavior of the Tigers' residuals (and those of the rest of the sample) implies two important conclusions. One is that the residuals are reduced, and more of the Tigers' success explained, with per worker than with per capita growth rates. Part of the success was simply due to the labor force growing faster than the population (especially notable in Singapore). The second is that the residuals in the sample in general are highly unstable and transitory—

21. If the variance of the residuals is unchanged each period (which appears to be roughly the case), then the expected value of the correlation coefficient across decades is the same as that of the β coefficient from regressing the residual on the lagged residual. The regression of the change in the residual on the level of the lagged residual will yield a coefficient of $\beta - 1$.

22. If we use per capita instead of per worker growth rates, then the Four Dragons would be at the upper boundary of the downward sloping blob of points in the figure. Using the Levine-Renelt residuals does not change the graph or the conclusions. The graph shows the change in decade residuals plotted against the lagged decade residual for each country, so that for any given country there would be two points: the residual's change from the 1970s to the 1980s against the residual in the 1970s, and the residual's change from the 1960s to the 1970s against the residual in the 1960s.

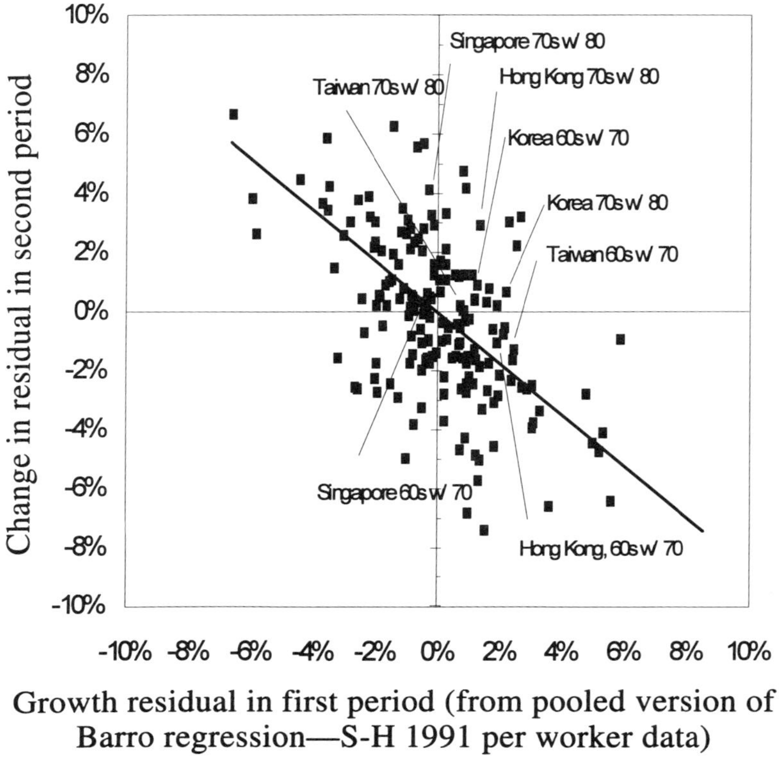

Fig. 11.2 Change in growth residual in second period against residual in first period

country fixed effects do not seem to be an important part of the explanation of the part of growth unexplained by investment, education, price distortions, and so forth. The low persistence of the residuals would rule out those unobservable factors that are relatively fixed over time—like culture, institutions, quality of government—as a large part of the explanation of growth differences.[23]

11.4 Conclusions and Suggestions for Further Research

Nothing in this paper should be taken as denigrating the success of Hong Kong, Korea, Singapore, and Taiwan. How ever it was achieved, the rapid growth of these Four is one of the most remarkable success stories in economic history.

But what should we make of the fact that a significant part of the Dragons'

23. Others have also pointed out that a "Confucian ethic" that has been around for millenia is not a terribly convincing explanation for an economic surge beginning after 1960. Cf. Stiglitz (1992).

success is unexplained? This paper argues: not much. The Four were selected *because* they were highly successful. If there is any random variation in our models at all, then we should not be surprised that the strongest positive outliers in growth have a positive growth residual. The quest to explain the success of the Four is bound to be at least partly futile. The literature has often been unable to resist the temptation to read too much into East Asia's success. The great success of the Gang of Four does not imply a blanket endorsement of all of their policies—they may have made mistakes that were more than offset by other good policies and, probably at least in part, by good luck. As in the story of the man turning 100 who attributes his longevity to generous consumption of whiskey, not all of the Dragons' habits are fit for imitation.

What are the implications for the Dragons of the low persistence of growth rates? It is true that the Four were more consistent good performers than almost anyone else in the sample. It is also true that one would expect some small number of countries to be consistent good performers even with only a modest tendency toward persistence of growth differences. The cross-country evidence suggests that the stratospheric trajectory of the Four should be heading back toward earth soon.

What *may* be unusual about the Four's success is that they were all in one region. The spatial association of success with East Asia (even if the category "East Asia" is partly endogenous) would imply that more attention should be paid to economic geography, as argued by Krugman (1991). The Asian successes look at least casually a lot like growth radiating from poles, with Japan followed by the Gang of Four, followed by China, Thailand, Malaysia, and Indonesia. Wang and Mody (1993) have shown how there are spillovers from Taiwan and Hong Kong to coastal provinces in China. Chua (1993) shows that countries benefit from their neighbors' good policies. It may be that the "something extra" in East Asia is partly the mutually beneficial set of spillovers from high investment and other favorable country characteristics. But this is in itself not sufficient to explain concentration of success—what is also needed is that neighbors influence each other to adopt high investment rates or other "good" characteristics (or that growth itself spills across borders). While past attempts at identifying spatial correlation based on physical proximity have had no success (DeLong and Summers 1991), it may be that more complicated interactions between countries remain to be studied.

Another geographic twist is to notice that Singapore and Hong Kong are really more like cities than countries. Cities are more subject than countries to forces like sectoral shifts from agriculture to industry and externalities from migration and urbanization (which would plausibly have strong effects on cities' per capita growth as well as their population growth rates).[24] One might

24. See Rauch (1993) and Glaeser et al. (1992) for suggestive evidence of strong externalities within cities. Ciccone and Hall (1993) argue that density in itself has a strong productivity effect across U.S. states.

think accordingly that cities have a higher variance of per capita growth rates than do countries, and would be thus more likely to have large positive outliers (as well as negative ones). Mean per capita growth rates of all cities may also be higher than those of rural areas. It follows that the natural comparators to the success of Hong Kong and Singapore would be other cities' economic growth, not growth rates of countries.[25] Other city "miracles" could be hidden in the data by aggregation within countries. For example, the Anaheim, California, metropolitan area (1970 population: 1.4 million) had per capita growth of 5.9 percent in the 1950s (when U.S. growth was only 1.2 percent). But Anaheim did not thereby enter the lore of economic miracles (Anaheim's success probably had more to do with the opening of Disneyland in 1955 than with "good policies" by the city fathers).[26] Data on per capita income growth of developing country metropolises are unfortunately hard to come by.

Finally, when all is said and done, the story of the East Asian successes is consistent with the old prosaic fundamentals—investment, education, financial depth, low budget deficits. The Four were above average in these areas, and regressions do show quantitatively and statistically significant effects of policies on growth. This cross-country evidence has at least as much to say as the case studies that attempt to decipher the meaning of the Four's large growth residuals.

Perhaps the best way to think about good policies is that they make success *likely* sooner or later. Policymakers should be convinced by looking at cross-country evidence that it is a lot better to make miracles feasible through good policy than to make them impossible by bad policy. But the policymakers' lot is not an easy one: it is disturbing how large and transitory is the unexplained element in economic success.

25. I am indebted to Lant Pritchett for making this point.

26. Anaheim's per capita growth is from Greenwood (1981, 74), which gives the nominal growth in median family income (which of course is not exactly "per capita"—if family size was lower in 1960 than 1950, then per capita growth would be higher). I deflate it by U.S. CPI inflation for the 1950s (which may overstate Anaheim's real growth since inflation was probably higher in a booming area).

Appendix

Pooled Versions of Barro (1991) and Levine and Renelt (1992) Regressions

Table 11A.1 Levine-Renelt with World Bank per Capita Growth Rates: Least Squares (Dependent Variable = GYP; 306 Observations)

Variable	Coefficient	Standard Error	*t*-Statistic	Two-Tail Significance
C	0.0123264	0.0165139	0.7464239	0.4560
DUM60	0.0295255	0.0032858	8.9858686	0.0000
DUM70	0.0191983	0.0030524	6.2896584	0.0000
INV	0.1492889	0.0188816	7.9065956	0.0000
SEC	0.0253555	0.0094359	2.6871204	0.0076
GPO	−0.3279395	0.1634988	−2.0057602	0.0458
LRGDP	−0.0052455	0.0023868	−2.1977155	0.0287
R^2	0.365726			
Adjusted R^2	0.352998			
S.E. of regression	0.020685			
Log likelihood	756.1182			
Mean of dependent variable	0.020583			
S.D. of dependent variable	0.025716			
Sum of squared residual	0.127934			
F-statistic	28.73422			
Prob (*F*-statistic)	0.000000			

Variables (decades are 1960–69, 1970–79, and 1980–89):

GYP	Per capita growth, compound rate by decade (World Bank National Accounts)
DUM60	Dummy variable for decade of 1960s = 1, otherwise = 0
DUM70	Dummy variable for decade of 1970s = 1, otherwise = 0
INV	Investment/GDP, average for decade (World Bank National Accounts)
SEC	Secondary school enrollment ratio, beginning of decade (Barro 1991)
GPO	Growth of population, by decade (World Bank Social Indicators)
LRGDP	Log of income (Summers and Heston 1991), initial year of decade

Table 11A.2 Levine-Renelt with World Bank per Worker Growth Rates: Least Squares (Dependent Variable = LGPW; 296 Observations)

Variable	Coefficient	Standard Error	*t*-Statistic	Two-Tail Significance
C	0.0246784	0.0154730	1.5949396	0.1118
DUM60	0.0299728	0.0032674	9.1733685	0.0000
DUM70	0.0154288	0.0029886	5.1624633	0.0000
INV	0.1542238	0.0188695	8.1731867	0.0000
SEC	0.0220750	0.0086438	2.5538607	0.0112
GRLF	−0.4920195	0.1309579	−3.7570816	0.0002
LRGDP	−0.0066414	0.0023710	−2.8010763	0.0054

(continued)

Table 11A.2 (continued)

Variable	Coefficient	Standard Error	*t*-Statistic	Two-Tail Significance
R^2	0.373179			
Adjusted R^2	0.360166			
S.E. of regression	0.020305			
Log likelihood	737.0214			
Durbin-Watson	1.914646			
Mean of dependent variable	0.017675			
S.D. of dependent variable	0.025384			
Sum of squared residual	0.119148			
F-statistic	28.67614			
Prob (*F*-statistic)	0.000000			

Variables:

LGPW	Least squares growth rate by decade, GDP per worker (World Bank National Accounts)
DUM60	Dummy variable for decade of 1960s = 1, otherwise = 0
DUM70	Dummy variable for decade of 1970s = 1, otherwise = 0
INV	Investment/GDP, average for decade (World Bank National Accounts)
SEC	Secondary school enrollment ratio, beginning of decade (Barro 1991)
GRLF	Least-squares growth rate of labor force by decade (World Bank Social Indicators)
LRGDP	Log of income (Summers and Heston 1991), initial year of decade

Table 11A.3 **Pooled "Barro" Regression Using per Worker Growth Rates: Least Squares (Dependent Variable = SLPW; 303 Observations)**

Variable	Coefficient	Standard Error	*t*-Statistic	Two-Tail Significance
C	0.1364398	0.0209900	6.5002292	0.0000
LGDPPC	−0.0188251	0.0030151	−6.2436568	0.0000
PRIM	0.0001987	6.996E-05	2.8403036	0.0048
SEC	0.0003837	9.947E-05	3.8574606	0.0001
SGOV	−0.0741720	0.0219419	−3.3803750	0.0008
BLCK	−0.0297244	0.0044487	−6.6816356	0.0000
DUM60	0.0271613	0.0039898	6.8076529	0.0000
DUM70	0.0198466	0.0035927	5.5241248	0.0000
R^2	0.363949			
Adjusted R^2	0.348856			
S.E. of regression	0.024748			
Log likelihood	694.9134			
Mean of dependent variable	0.017640			
S.D. of dependent variable	0.030669			
Sum of squared residual	0.180679			
F-statistic	24.11416			
Prob (*F*-statistic)	0.000000			

Table 11A.3 (continued)

Variables:

SLPW	Summers and Heston (1991) least squares growth per worker, decade average
LGDPPC	Log of initial per capita income, beginning of decade (Summers and Heston 1991)
PRIM	Primary enrollment, beginning of decade (World Bank)
SEC	Secondary enrollment, beginning of decade (World Bank)
SGOV	Share of government consumption in GDP (Summers and Heston 1991)
BLCK	Black market premium, average over decade (Levine and Renelt 1992; World Bank)
DUM60	Dummy variable for decade of 1960s = 1, otherwise = 0
DUM70	Dummy variable for decade of 1970s = 1, otherwise = 0

Table 11A.4 **Pooled "Barro" Regression Using per Capita Growth Rates: Least Squares (Dependent Variable = LSPC; 283 Observations)**

Variable	Coefficient	Standard Error	*t*-Statistic	Two-Tail Significance
C	0.1015168	0.0197857	5.1308283	0.0000
LGDPPC	−0.0155429	0.0028198	−5.5119951	0.0000
PRIM	0.0002455	6.469E-05	3.7955829	0.0002
SEC	0.0004337	9.322E-05	4.6527473	0.0000
SGOV	−0.0488336	0.0204781	−2.3846737	0.0178
BLCK	−0.0388459	0.0048094	−8.0771068	0.0000
DUM60	0.0278901	0.0037380	7.4611895	0.0000
DUM70	0.0232782	0.0033872	6.8724279	0.0000
R^2	0.435391			
Adjusted R^2	0.421019			
S.E. of regression	0.022256			
Log likelihood	679.3560			
Mean of dependent variable	0.018928			
S.D. of dependent variable	0.029249			
Sum of squared residual	0.136213			
F-statistic	30.29465			
Prob (*F*-statistic)	0.000000			

Variables:

LSPC	Per capita growth rate, least squares by decade (Summers and Heston 1991)
LGDPPC	Log of initial per capita income, beginning of decade (Summers and Heston 1991)
PRIM	Primary enrollment, beginning of decade (World Bank)
SEC	Secondary enrollment, beginning of decade (World Bank)
SGOV	Share of government consumption in GDP (Summers and Heston 1991)
BLCK	Black market premium, average over decade (Levine and Renelt 1992; World Bank)
DUM60	Dummy variable for decade of 1960s = 1, otherwise = 0
DUM70	Dummy variable for decade of 1970s = 1, otherwise = 0

References

Amsden, Alice. 1989. *Asia's next giant.* New York: Oxford University Press.

———. 1991. Diffusion of development: The late-industrializing model and greater East Asia. *American Economic Review* 81 (2): 282–86.

Balassa, Bela. 1978. Exports and economic growth: Further evidence. *Journal of Development Economics* 5 (June): 181–89.

———. 1991. *Economic policies in the Pacific area developing countries.* London: Macmillan.

Balassa, Bela, and John Williamson. 1990. *Adjusting to success: Balance of payments policy in the East Asian NICs.* Washington, D.C.: Institute for International Economics.

Barro, Robert J. 1991. Economic growth in a cross section of countries. *Quarterly Journal of Economics* 106: 407–43.

Barro, Robert J., and Jong-wha Lee. 1993. Losers and winners in economic growth. In *Proceedings of the World Bank Annual Conference on Development Economics, 1993. World Bank Economic Review,* Supplement: 267–315.

Barro, Robert J., and Xavier Sala-i-Martin. 1992. Convergence. *Journal of Political Economy* 100: 223–51.

Becker, Gary, Kevin Murphy, and Robert Tamura. 1990. Human capital, fertility, and economic growth. *Journal of Political Economy* 98: S12–S37.

Birdsall, Nancy, and Richard Sabot. 1993. Virtuous circles: Human capital, growth and equity in East Asia. Paper prepared for the World Bank's project on Strategies for Rapid Growth: Public Policy and the Asian Miracle. Washington, D.C.: World Bank.

Bruno, Michael. 1993. Inflation and Growth in an Integrated Approach. NBER Working Paper no. 4422. Cambridge, Mass.: National Bureau of Economic Research.

Chenery, Hollis. 1988. Industrialization and growth: Alternative views of East Asia. In *Achieving industrialization in East Asia,* ed. Helen Hughes. New York: Cambridge University Press.

Chua, Hak. 1993. Regional spillovers and economic growth. Center Discussion Paper no. 700. Economic Growth Center, Yale University.

Ciccone, A., and R. E. Hall. 1993. Productivity and the density of economic activity. NBER Working Paper no. 4313. Cambridge, Mass.: National Bureau of Economic Research.

Clarke, George. 1993. New evidence on inequality and economic growth. World Bank Working Paper WPS 1064. Washington, D.C.: World Bank.

Collins, Susan. 1990. Lessons from Korean economic growth. *American Economic Review* 80 (2): 104–7.

De Long, J. B., and L. H. Summers. 1991. Equipment, investment, relative prices, and economic growth. *Quarterly Journal of Economics* 106: 445–502.

Easterly, William, Michael Kremer, Lant Pritchett, and Lawrence Summers. 1993. Good policy or good luck? Country growth performance and temporary shocks. *Journal of Monetary Economics* 32: 459–83.

Easterly, William, and Sergio Rebelo. 1993. Fiscal policy and economic growth: an empirical investigation. *Journal of Monetary Economics* 32: 417–58.

Enke, Stephen. 1963. *Economics for development.* London: Dennis Dobson.

Feder, Gershon. 1983. On exports and economic growth. *Journal of Development Economics* 12 (February/April): 59–73.

Fischer, Stanley. 1993. Macroeconomic factors in growth. *Journal of Monetary Economics* 32: 485–512.

Glaeser, E. L., H. D. Kallal, J. A. Scheinkman, and A. Shleifer. 1992. Growth in cities. *Journal of Political Economy* 100 (6): 1126–52.

Greenwood, Michael J. 1981. *Migration and economic growth in the United States: National, regional, and metropolitan perspectives.* New York: Academic.

Hagen, Everett. 1968. *The economics of development.* Homewood, Ill.: Irwin.

Haggard, Stephen. 1989. The East Asian NICs in comparative perspective. *Annals of the American Academy of Political Science Society* 505: 129–41.

———. 1990. *Pathways from the periphery: The politics of growth in the newly industrializing countries.* Ithaca, N.Y.: Cornell University Press.

Hicks, George. 1990. Explaining the success of the Four Little Dragons: A survey. In *Essays in honor of Professor Sinichi Ichimura,* ed. Seiji Naya and Akira Takayama. Singapore: Institute of Southeast Asian Studies.

Higgins, Benjamin. 1959. *Economic development: Principles, problems and policies.* New York: Norton.

Hofheinz, Roy, and Kent Calder. 1982. *The East Asia edge.* New York: Basic.

Hong, Wontack. 1993. Export-oriented growth and equity in Korea. In *Trade and Protectionism,* ed. Anne O. Krueger and Takatoshi Ito. Chicago: University of Chicago Press.

Hoselitz, Bert, ed. 1952. *The progress of underdeveloped areas.* Chicago: University of Chicago Press.

Kahn, Herman. 1979. *World economic development: 1979 and beyond.* Boulder, Colo.: Westview.

Kamarck, Andrew M. 1967. *The economics of African development.* New York: Praeger.

Kihwan, Kim, and Danny Leipziger. 1992. Korea: The case of effective government-led development. Washington, D.C.: World Bank. Mimeograph.

Kim, Jong-Il, and Lawrence Lau. 1993. The sources of economic growth of the East Asian newly industrialized countries. Washington, D.C.: International Monetary Fund.

Kim, Kwang Suk. 1985. Lessons from South Korea's experience with industrialization. In *Export-oriented development strategies,* ed. Vittorio Corbo, Anne Krueger, and Fernando Ossa. Boulder, Colo.: Westview.

King, Robert, and Ross Levine. 1993. Finance, entrepreneurship, and growth. *Journal of Monetary Economics* 32: 513–42.

Kremer, Michael. 1993. The O-ring theory of economic development. *Quarterly Journal of Economics* 108: 551–76.

Krueger, Anne. 1985. The experience and lessons of Asia's super exporters. In *Export-oriented development strategies,* ed. Vittorio Corbo, Anne Krueger, and Fernando Ossa. Boulder, Colo.: Westview Press.

———. 1990. Asian trade and growth lessons. *American Economic Review* 80: 108–12.

Krugman, Paul. 1991. *Geography and trade.* Cambridge: MIT Press.

Kuznets, Simon. 1966. *Modern economic growth: Rate, structure, and spread.* New Haven, Conn.: Yale University Press.

Lehmann, Jean-Pierre. 1992. *In support of Asian development.* Study commissioned by the Department for International Development Cooperation, Ministry for Foreign Affairs, Sweden.

Levine, Ross, and David Renelt. 1992. A sensitivity analysis of cross-country growth regressions. *American Economic Review* 82: 942–63.

Lipton, David, and Jeffrey Sachs. 1992. Prospects for Russia's economic reforms. *Brookings Papers on Economic Activity,* no. 2: 213–83.

Liu, Phillip. 1993. The rough road to privatization. *Free China Review,* July, 36–41.

Lucas, Robert E. 1993. Making a miracle. *Econometrica* 61: 251–72.

MacFarquhar, Roderick. 1980. The Post-Confucian challenge. *The Economist,* February 9, 67–72.

Maddison, Angus. 1989. *The world economy in the twentieth century.* Development Centre Studies. Paris: OECD.

Meier, G. M. 1964. *Leading issues in development economics.* New York: Oxford University Press.

Nam, Sang-Woo. 1988. Alternative growth and adjustment strategies of newly industrializing countries in Southeast Asia. In *Beyond adjustment: The Asian experiment,* ed. Paul Streeten. Washington, D.C.: International Monetary Fund.

Pack, Howard, and John M. Page. 1993. Accumulation, exports and growth in the high performing Asian economies. Washington, D.C.: World Bank. Mimeograph.

Pack, H., and L. E. Westphal. 1986. Industrial strategy and technological change: Theory vs. reality. *Journal of Development Economics* 22: 87–126.

Page, John M., and Peter A. Petri. 1993. Productivity change and strategic growth policy in the Asian miracle. Washington, D.C.: World Bank. Mimeograph.

Parry, Thomas. 1988. The role of foreign capital in East Asian industrialization, growth and development. In *Achieving industrialization in East Asia,* ed. Helen Hughes. New York: Cambridge University Press.

Rauch, James. 1993. Productivity gains from geographic concentration of human capital: Evidence from the cities. *Journal of Urban Economics,* forthcoming.

Romer, Paul. 1986. Increasing returns and long-run growth. *Journal of Political Economy* 94: 1002–37.

———. 1993. Ideas and objects in economic development. *Journal of Monetary Economics* 32: 543–74.

Sen, Amartya. 1993. Economic regress: Concepts and features. Paper presented at annual World Bank Conference on Development Economics. Washington, D.C.: World Bank. Processed.

Stiglitz, Joseph E. 1992. Some lessons from the Asia miracle. Department of Economics, Stanford University. Mimeograph.

Summers, Robert, and Alan Heston. 1988. A new set of international comparisons of real product and price levels: Estimates for 130 countries. *Review of Income and Wealth* 34: 1–25.

———. 1991. The Penn World Table (Mark 5): An expanded set of international comparisons, 1950–1988. *Quarterly Journal of Economics* 106: 327–68.

Thomas, Vinod, and Yan Wang. 1993. Government policies and productivity growth: Is East Asia an exemption? Washington, D.C.: World Bank. Mimeograph.

Wade, Robert. 1989. What can economies learn from East Asian success? *Annals of the American Academy of Political Science* 505: 68–79.

———. 1990. *Governing the market: Economic theory and the role of government in East Asian industrialization.* Princeton, N.J.: Princeton University Press.

Wang, Fang-Yi, and Ashoka Mody. 1993. Industrial growth in Coastal China: Economic reforms . . . and what else? Washington, D.C.: World Bank. Mimeograph.

World Bank. 1993a. *The East Asian miracle.* New York: Oxford University Press.

———. 1993b. *Sustaining rapid development in East Asia and the Pacific.* Washington, D.C.: World Bank.

Young, Alwyn. 1992. A tale of two cities: Productivity growth in Hong Kong and Singapore. *NBER Macroeconomics Annual 1992.* Cambridge, Mass.: National Bureau of Economic Research.

Comment Takatoshi Ito

Easterly has done a good job in drawing our attention to the remarkable Asian growth experiences in the large-scale, cross-country growth regressions. He handles data well and his presentation is clear, and we learn a lot from his paper. Although I will differ in my interpretation of the findings, Easterly's regressions provide us a good overview of East Asian experiences in the modern literature on growth. His regressions highlight how exceptional the Asian growth experiences have been compared to the world standard. Can they be explained by economic conditions and economic logic—maybe a fast catch up with a low starting point—or by random elements? This is the challenge presented to us by Easterly's findings.

My comments are directed both to the interpretation of Easterly's findings and to the promising literature of growth convergence in general.

How Do We Take Solow's Residual?

In the original growth accounting literature, Solow's residuals were an em barrassment, in that they represented portions of growth that the model could not explain. Models became sophisticated to account for technological changes embodied in capital or in labor, but still some residuals were present, which was taken to be a failure of modeling.

In the more recent interpretation of total factor productivity (TFP), what used to be Solow's residuals became something wonderful, in that they represent a country's "miracle," possibly due to increasing returns. When Alwyn Young concluded that Singapore overinvested in capital and switched technologies too quickly, one of his supporting pieces of evidence was a low TFP.

Now we have Easterly who tells us that it is all but natural for miracle countries to have large positive residuals in growth regressions. He argues that "observations at one extreme of the sample are the most likely to have large residuals." Winners should all have the lucky components.

I still think that residuals are residuals. Large residuals show a failure of the assumptions (such as constant returns) that underlie the regression. This may be "suggestive" of an alternative (such as increasing returns), but does not positively identify the reason.[1]

Takatoshi Ito is professor of economics at Hitotsubashi University, visiting professor at Harvard University, and a research associate at the National Bureau of Economic Research.

The author is indebted to Anne O. Krueger and David Weil for their helpful comments on an earlier version of these comments.

1. If the unit of man-hours for "labor input" produces large residuals, then an econometrician may want to improve the labor input variable by including "education," "years of experience," etc., to take into account the quality of labor. Large residuals should not stop one from thinking of alternatives.

What Is Convergence?

It is quite popular these days to run time-series and/or cross-country regressions attempting to prove that low-income countries grow faster than high-income countries. This is called a growth regression, or a regression to prove convergence.

Suppose that technological change is Harrod neutral, that is, technological progress is labor augmenting. It is well known (from the literature in the 1960s) that Harrod-neutral technological change produces a steady state where Y/L and K/L increase at the same rate, while Y/LH and K/LH stay constant (where Y denotes income, L natural units of labor, K capital, and H human capital). However, if initial conditions are not at the steady state, then the economy moves toward a steady state (given that a stability condition such as the Inada condition is met).

If capital is below its steady state level at the start (i.e., right after the revolution or war, or the first year of observation for an econometrician), then one might expect that the growth rate is higher when the country is underdeveloped, catching up to the world standard. For example, Japan grew at an average annual rate exceeding 10 percent from 1955 to 1973, while its average annual growth rate dropped below 5 percent after 1974. This can be interpreted as the result that Japan did "catch up."

Let me illustrate this point by some figures. Figure 11C.1, panel (a) is a standard growth figure showing the relationship between k $(=K/HL)$ and y $(=Y/HL)$, linearized at the steady state, (k^*, y^*). Various countries (or different years of the same country) are shown as dots on this line, with growth velocities corresponding to the lengths of arrows. Assume the same Harrod-neutral production function with the same steady saving rate (and thus the same steady state levels) and the precise measurement of K, L, H, and Y. The theory predicts that a state with low y is associated with a long arrow, a high growth rate (dy/y), and a state with high y is associated with a short arrow, a low growth rate (dy/y). This is shown in figure 11C.1, panel (b).

Now the same line is shown in figure 11C.2, where the vertical and horizontal axes have been switched.

If the theory is right and all assumptions are true, we will find countries on the solid line in figure 11C.1 (b), or figure 11C.2. Of course, there are shocks to the production function, and thus to the growth rates. Then we will have scatter dots around the line. Vertical deviations from the solid line are "residuals" in the growth regressions.

Now Easterly's argument, or the theory of lucky growth, is that, after ranking countries by "actual" growth (dy/y), we find that the top-growth countries are countries with large residuals (vertical deviations from the line). As shown in figure 11C.2, the states with the highest growth rates (circled dots) have large positive "residuals"; in fact, two of them have the largest residuals in the sample.

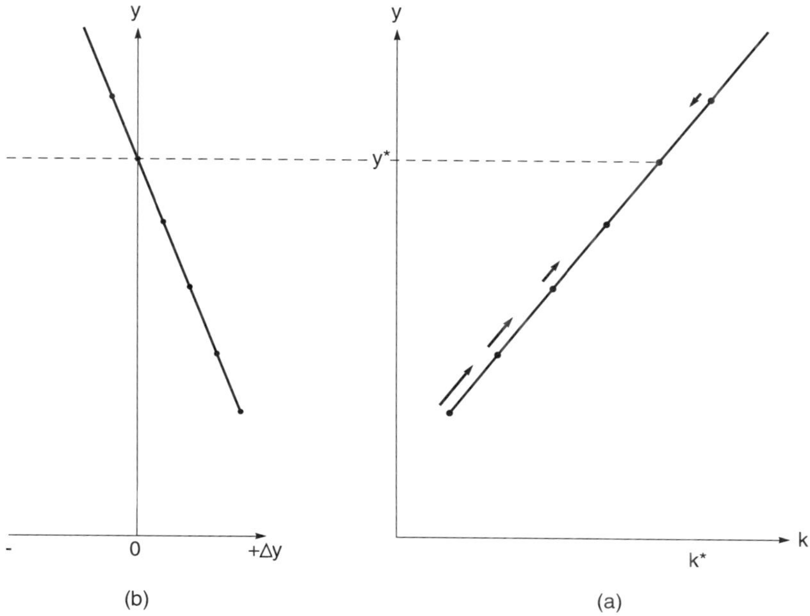

Fig. 11C.1 Relations between capital, income, and growth
Note: Δy = per capita growth rate; k^* = steady state capital per capita; y^* = steady state income per capita; k = capital per capita; y = income per capita.

But notice three factors, all now clear from figure 11C.2, that contribute to the "lucky growth theory." First, the order in growth rates would be exactly the order of residuals, if the solid line were flat. In general, the flatter the slope is, the more correlated are the rankings of growth rates and residuals, given the vertical scatters of dots (given *y*) around the line. Second, if dots are widely scattered given *y*, then the ranking correlation is more likely to hold. In other words, a high correlation of rankings is equivalent to low R^2, of course. Third, even in 1950s and 1960s, the Four Tigers were not among the least developed countries (LDCs), the left-most countries on the horizontal axis in figure 11C.2.

In sum, the theory of lucky growth, as argued by Easterly, is a confession of a (apparent) low correlation between *y* and *dy/y*, and low R^2. I do not consider it a "natural" outcome of regression analysis.

In the following, I will elaborate on these observations and present an alternative way of thinking about the growth experiences represented in Easterly's findings. In the next section, I will give a reason why the slope coefficient may have a downward bias. In the following section, I will argue that growth experience may be a "nonlinear" process, citing the traditional development literature.

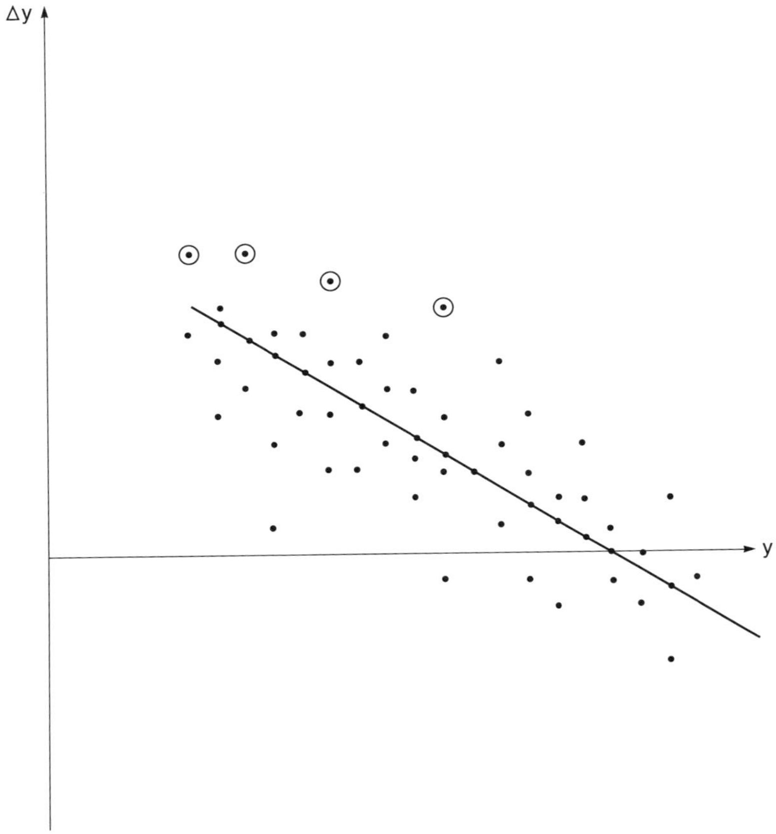

Fig. 11C.2 Growth versus level of income
Note: Each dot represents a hypothetical country's level of income and growth rate. Circled dots represent the Four Tigers

Permanent Growth Theory

The catch-up story of the preceding section is more likely to hold as a long-run relationship, while business cycles and other transitory disturbances affect both growth rates and the level of income in the short run. In other words, the true relationship between the level of income y and the growth rate g (= dy/y) is in their permanent components, y^p, and g^p:

$$y^p = b * g^p,$$

while what is observed is a combination of a permanent component and a transitory component:

$$y = y^p + e_y,$$

$$g = g^{p} + e_{g},$$

where e_y and e_g are "transitory" components and are assumed to be uncorrelated. Then a regression of g on y, such as

$$g = a + b^{*}y + e,$$

would produce a case of "errors in variables." The estimated coefficient of b would be biased downward. This is a straightforward application of the permanent income hypothesis of Milton Friedman.

Since the estimated b is biased downward, there would be apparently less correlation between y and g, leading to a case of "lucky growth" as explained in the preceding section.

One might rebut the above reason for caution, however. The income level used on the right-hand side of the regression is usually an average of several years, so that the "transitory" component of y is smoothed out. Moreover, the business cycle in one country (e_y) is relatively small compared to the cross-country differences in y^{p}.

Growth versus Development

We were taught in the 1960s that growth theory and development theory are to be distinguished. Growth theory is applicable to advanced countries where quantitative changes are the issue, while development theory is intended to describe or to explain the qualitative change from an underdeveloped state to an industrialized state. Development theory describes the change from an agrarian society to a modern economy through industrial revolution. Components of exports and imports change as industrialization proceeds. Fertility and mortality rates change dramatically. Savings rates also increase as growth rates accelerate. Education level will rise as less youth are needed in the production of subsistence food. In fact, there is some crucial point in the progress from a low-growth equilibrium (poverty cycle) to a speed-up in the growth rate. Concepts such as modern economic growth (MEG) proposed and studied by Kuznets and "big push" and "take off" by Rostow suggest a nonlinear relationship between y and g, where a crucial jump in g plays an important role in catching up. I will take these observations of the old development theory seriously.

The multiple equilibria case in growth theory can be depicted in figure 11C.3, where the production function does not satisfy a condition for uniqueness of equilibrium. In figure 11C.3, two economies, one high-saving and one low-saving, are depicted: k^{*} is the high-income equilibrium in the low-saving economy; k^{**} is the low-income equilibrium in the low-saving economy; k^{c} is a critical point for convergence, in the sense that any historical starting point below (above) k^{c} will eventually converge to k^{*} (k^{**}); k^{h} is the equilibrium for the high-saving economy. There are two locally stable equilibria, one with high income and one with low income, if the saving rate is relatively low. However, if the saving rate becomes higher, the low-income equilibrium disappears, and

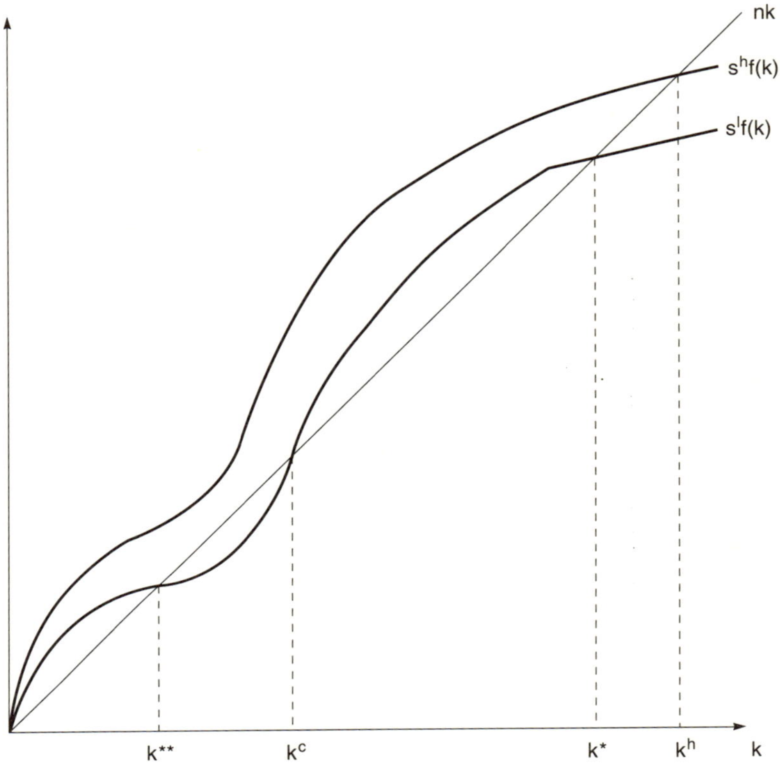

Fig. 11C.3 Multiple equilibria
Note: s^l = low saving rate case; s^h = high saving rate case; k^* = high equilibrium (steady state) with s^l; k^{**} = low equilibrium (steady state) with s^l; k^h = unique equilibrium with s^h.

the country will eventually converge to a high-income equilibrium. Suppose that some country, initially low income, succeeds in raising its saving rate, so that it leaves the low-income equilibrium state and "catches up" to the high-income state. Then we will observe three kinds of countries: high-income countries, low-income countries, and those in the process of catching up from a low equilibrium to a high equilibrium. Note that the small change in the saving rate can result in a large change in this framework.[2]

The economy breaks off from an old low equilibrium and moves to the re-

2. I am indebted to David Weil for the discussion in this section. Alternatively, I can illustrate the phenomenon of "a small change producing large results" with a uniform saving rate alone (without a high saving rate curve) in fig. 11C.3. Suppose that the capital-labor ratio (or income) level is subject to "disturbances" or "transitory shocks." Then some low-income countries may exit the boundary of the poverty cycle (the field of attraction to the low equilibrium) and start moving up to a high equilibrium.

gion of high equilibrium when some fortuitous shock arrives, such as political stability, an increase in domestic saving, or an increase in food production, and moves it out of the low-income equilibrium.

If some low-income countries "take off" from a low equilibrium, then they start to catch up with high-income countries by accelerating growth. Latecomers like Japan, Korea, Taiwan, Singapore, and Hong Kong move toward a high equilibrium, or toward joining an advanced nation club, such as the OECD. This is depicted in figure 11C.4. This observation is consistent with Easterly's claim that "rapid growth is surprisingly transitory."

Now suppose we run a growth regression (growth rate on the level of income) mixing countries near a high equilibrium, those near a low equilibrium, and those in the process of catching up. Although countries near an equilibrium will show convergence to that equilibrium, mixing countries near two different equilibria would make the point estimate biased toward zero and make the standard error of coefficient large. Countries in transition from a low equilibrium to a high equilibrium will have large residuals.

Summary

I first pointed out that Easterly's "theory of lucky growth" amounts to saying that the growth regressions have low R^2. Low R^2 values mean that the coeffi-

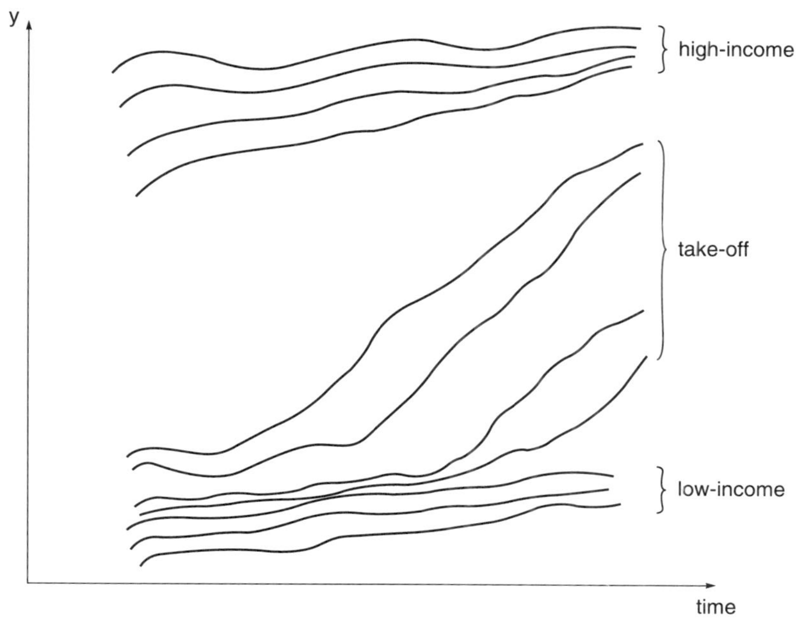

Fig. 11C.4 Model of nonlinear growth
Note: Figure shows conceptual paths of countries' income.

cient on the income level is close to zero, and the variance in growth rates is large.

I cited two different reasons why the coefficient on the income level may *apparently* be close to zero. Put differently, the coefficient is biased downward in the regression. First, downward bias will occur when there are measurement errors in income as well as in the growth rate. Second, if there are multiple equilibria and if there are some countries in transition from a low-income equilibrium to a high-income equilibrium, a regression with heterogeneous sample countries will result in the downward biased coefficient.

These comments are meant to be taken as constructive suggestions to improve the specification of growth regression in the future.

Comment T. N. Srinivasan

I enjoyed reading Easterly's paper, particularly his sarcasm about our profession's amazing ability to read confirmation of mutually contradictory explanations or hypotheses from the same data! He is right in saying that we tend to pay less attention to learning from development disasters (e.g., the Central African Republic) than from development miracles (e.g., Singapore). But, on the other hand, the former prime minister of Singapore, Lee Kuan Yew, is a far more interesting personality, with his economic philosophy and ideas on who should marry whom and how many children the couple should have, than the former emperor Bokassa of the Central African Republic ever was, with his penchant for an expensive coronation and gifts of diamonds to the French president, Giscard d'Estaing. No wonder that since 1969 there have been 717 articles in the economics journals on Singapore, compared to only one on the Central African Republic! Easterly is right that we should pay as much attention to the dogs that did not bark as to the tigers that roar.

Easterly asserts that because the Gang of Four were outliers (i.e., in the top 1 percent) of the *marginal distribution* of growth rates, they must also be outliers in the *distribution of residuals* from a regression explaining growth rates. Of course, if the regression has no explanatory power, this would be true. But, if it has significant power, it is possible that it explains very well the spectacular growth performance of the outliers so that their residuals are in no sense outliers and could even be zero. On the other hand, a country which is not an outlier in the marginal distribution of growth rates might still be an outlier in the distribution of residuals. That is, its growth rate might be too high (or too low for that matter) relative to that explained by the regression. However, one must also be very careful in using an appropriate statistical tool, such as tolerance (as contrasted with confidence) intervals, in detecting outliers in a distribution of residuals.

T. N. Srinivasan is professor of economics at Yale University.

Easterly is not quite correct in equating the performance of the explanatory variables in predicting the growth rates of the Gang of Four with the expectation that they must also be outliers in the *distribution* of each of the important explanatory variables. Since different explanatory variables could substitute for each other in explaining growth performance, a country need not be in the top 1 percent of the distribution of *any* of the explanatory variables for it to be in the top 1 percent of the distribution of *expected* growth rates from the regression or of the *marginal* distribution of *actual* growth rates.

Easterly sensibly raises the issue of persistence of growth performance over time. In analogy with biostatistics in which a common genetic component and an idiosyncratic component are attributed to siblings, one can write the observed growth rate g_{it} of country i in period t as the sum of a country-specific effect g_i, a time-specific effect g_t (possibly that of common external shocks, such as oil shocks affecting all countries), and a residual u_{it}. If g_i, g_t, and u_{it} are uncorrelated, then the variance σ^2 of g_{it} is the sum of the variances σ_1^2 of g_i, σ_2^2 of g_t, and σ_3^2 of u_{it}. Now, if the u_{it} are serially uncorrelated, then the correlation between g_{it} and g_{it-1} is easily seen to be the proportion $\sigma_1^2/(\sigma_1^2 + \sigma_2^2 + \sigma_3^2)$. This correlation, known as the intraclass correlation, measures the contribution of *persistence* in growth of countries over time. Thus, if the variance in g_t and u_{it} are small relative to that in g_i, then there will be strong persistence. Thus, in analogy with biostatistics, the *genetic* component explains most of the variation among the performance of the offspring of different families. I do not know whether Easterly is among those who attribute the stellar performance of the Gang of Four to their common "genetic" endowment, namely, their Confucian heritage. I am afraid, like the use of a "dummy" (or should I say "dumb") variable for the Gang of Four, Confucian heritage attribution is mere labeling (without even the saving grace of quantification in terms of the coefficient of a Gang of Four dummy!) without any policy or scientific significance.

Let me conclude by saying that Easterly is unduly harsh in holding the predictions of an earlier generation of economists to the piercing light of hindsight. After all, like all rational persons, they made their best predictions *given their models* (i.e., the economic theory then available) *and the information* available to them. Of course, if either the models were wrong in some respects or the information then available was incomplete and inaccurate, predictions would prove wrong as well. I am not entirely convinced that we now have a better theory of development, but we certainly have lots more data about the past, though not all of it is necessarily reliable. For example, if the early development economists had known that, contrary to the experience of the interwar period, world trade would grow at unprecedented rates, their enthusiasm for inward orientation and, hence, their confidence in the development prospects of economies with large internal markets and natural resources would have been muted. Put another way, one can and should criticize, as I am fond of doing, the present generation for ignoring the past, but not the past generation for ignoring the future!

Contributors

Geoffrey Carliner
National Bureau of Economic Research
1050 Massachusetts Avenue
Cambridge, MA 02138

CHIA Siow Yue
National University of Singapore
Department of Economics
10 Kent Ridge Crescent
Singapore 0511

Ji Chou
Chung-Hua Institution for Economic Research
75 Chang Hsing Street
Taipei, Taiwan 10671
Republic of China

William Easterly
The World Bank
1818 H Street
Washington, DC 20433

Shin-ichi Fukuda
Institute of Economic Research
Hitotsubashi University
Kunitachi Tokyo 186
Japan

Koichi Hamada
Department of Economics
Economic Growth Center
Yale University
27 Hillhouse Avenue
New Haven, CT 06520

Chen-Min Hsu
Department of Economics
College of Law
National Taiwan University
Hsu Chow Road, Taipei, Taiwan
Republic of China

Ponciano S. Intal, Jr.
Philippine Institute for Development Studies
NEDA sa Makati Bldg.
106 Amorsolo St., Legaspi Village
Makati, Metro Manila
The Philippines

Takatoshi Ito
Institute of Economic Research
Hitotsubashi University
Kunitachi, Tokyo 186
Japan

Joon Kyung Kim
Korea Development Institute
P.O. Box 113, Cheongnyang
Seoul 130–012
Korea

Jun Il Kim
Korea Development Institute
P.O. Box 113, Cheongnyang
Seoul 130–012
Korea

Hirohisa Kohama
Faculty of International Relations
University of Shizuoka
52–1, Yada, Shizuoka
Shizuoka, 422
Japan

Anne O. Krueger
Department of Economics
Stanford University
Stanford, CA 94305–6072

Chong-Hyun Nam
Department of Economics
Korea University
1, 5-Ga, Anam-dong, Sungbuk-ku
Seoul 136–701
Korea

John Page
The World Bank
Room H-7055
1818 H Street
Washington, DC 20433

Hak K. Pyo
Department of International Economics
Seoul National University
Seoul 151–742
Korea

Paul M. Romer
Department of Economics
787 Evans Hall
University of California
Berkeley, CA 94720

Sang Dal Shim
Korea Development Institute
P.O. Box 113, Cheongnyang
Seoul 130–012
Korea

T. N. Srinivasan
Department of Economics
Economic Growth Center
Yale University
Box 208269, Yale Station
New Haven, CT 06520–8269

Yun-Wing Sung
Department of Economics
The Chinese University of Hong Kong
Shatin NT
Hong Kong

Hideki Toya
Institute of Economic Research
Hitotsubashi University
Kunitachi, Tokyo 186
Japan

Shang-Jin Wei
Kennedy School of Government
Harvard University
79 JFK Street
Cambridge, MA 02138

Author Index

Subject Index